T0328579

The Economics of Globally Shared and Public Goods

The Economics of Globally Shared and Public Goods

S. Niggol Seo
Muaebak Institute of Global Warming Studies, Seoul, South Korea

ACADEMIC PRESS

An imprint of Elsevier

Academic Press is an imprint of Elsevier
125 London Wall, London EC2Y 5AS, United Kingdom
525 B Street, Suite 1650, San Diego, CA 92101, United States
50 Hampshire Street, 5th Floor, Cambridge, MA 02139, United States
The Boulevard, Langford Lane, Kidlington, Oxford OX5 1GB, United Kingdom

Notices
Knowledge and best practice in this field are constantly changing. As new research and experience broaden our understanding, changes in research methods, professional practices, or medical treatment may become necessary.

Practitioners and researchers must always rely on their own experience and knowledge in evaluating and using any information, methods, compounds, or experiments described herein. In using such information or methods they should be mindful of their own safety and the safety of others, including parties for whom they have a professional responsibility.

To the fullest extent of the law, neither the Publisher nor the authors, contributors, or editors, assume any liability for any injury and/or damage to persons or property as a matter of products liability, negligence or otherwise, or from any use or operation of any methods, products, instructions, or ideas contained in the material herein.

British Library Cataloguing-in-Publication Data
A catalogue record for this book is available from the British Library

Library of Congress Cataloging-in-Publication Data
A catalog record for this book is available from the Library of Congress

ISBN: 978-0-12-819658-8

For Information on all Academic Press publications
visit our website at https://www.elsevier.com/books-and-journals

Publisher: Brian Romer
Editorial Project Manager: Ruby Smith
Production Project Manager: Swapna Srinivasan
Cover Designer: Victoria Pearson

Typeset by MPS Limited, Chennai, India

Working together
to grow libraries in
developing countries

www.elsevier.com • www.bookaid.org

Dedication

This book is dedicated to Moonsoo.

Contents

About the author   xi
Preface   xiii

1. An introduction to the challenges of public and globally shared
    goods in economics and policy-making   1
    1.1   Introduction   1
    1.2   Public goods and globally shared goods examined   4
    1.3   The furor, dances, and charade over global public goods   9
    1.4   The economic theories of public goods   11
    1.5   Three critiques   16
    1.6   The economics of globally shared goods   20
    1.7   Structure of the book   25
    References   27
    Further reading   35

2. The economics of public goods and club goods   37
    2.1   The emergence of the term public goods   37
    2.2   Samuelson's pure theory   38
    2.3   Friedman's public sector versus private sector   40
    2.4   Club goods   43
    2.5   An efficient provision versus market provision of a public good   46
    2.6   Policy instruments for providing the public good optimally   51
    2.7   Morality, private provision, specialized markets   58
    2.8   Valuation methods   62
    2.9   Uncertainty and policy options   66
    2.10 Wealth redistributions and policy options   68
    2.11 Concluding remarks   72
    References   72

3. The economics of global-scale public goods: key challenges and
    theories   77
    3.1   Introduction   77
    3.2   Spatio-political scales of a public good   80
    3.3   Global public goods   84
    3.4   Production technologies   85
    3.5   A globally harmonized carbon price or tax   87

3.6   Economics of the value of time   94
3.7   Uncertainty, catastrophe, and precautionary principle   100
3.8   Optimal mutually beneficial monetary transfers   107
3.9   The public sector for global public goods   109
3.10 Conclusion   111
References   112

4.   **A critique of the economics of global public goods:
     a microbehavioral theory and model**   **121**
4.1   Introduction   121
4.2   A theory of the microbehavioral economics of globally shared
      goods   123
4.3   The microbehavioral economic model   126
4.4   Empirical analyses of the microbehavioral model   133
4.5   Adaptation behaviors and strategies in the microbehavioral
      model   139
      4.5.1   Adopting livestock species   139
      4.5.2   Switching agricultural systems   141
      4.5.3   Switching agricultural systems under increased climate risk
              scenarios   142
      4.5.4   Switching to natural resource intensive enterprises   144
      4.5.5   Public adaptations   146
4.6   Microbehavioral models in the economics of global
      public goods   148
4.7   Mitigation and sinks in the microbehavioral model   150
References   152

5.   **A critique of the economics of global public goods: economics of
     noncooperative games**   **161**
5.1   Introduction   161
5.2   The premise of cooperation in the theory of global
      public goods   163
5.3   The parameters of contention in the cooperative DICE model   167
5.4   An analysis of noncooperation: disparate incentives of parties
      under a business-as-usual scenario   173
5.5   An analysis of noncooperation: alterations of incentives
      under a globally optimal policy scenario   176
5.6   Optimal monetary transfers or a climate club   181
5.7   Concluding remarks   186
References   187

6.   **A critique of the economics of global public goods: the economics
     of a global public good fund**   **191**
6.1   Introduction   191
6.2   Global public good funds   193

6.2.1   Types of a public good fund   193
6.2.2   Green climate fund   195
6.2.3   Allocating the green climate fund: investment criteria   196
6.2.4   Funding models of the green climate fund   202
6.3   The economics behind the green climate fund as a policy alternative   203
6.3.1   Economics of public expenditure   203
6.3.2   Economics of efficient land and resource uses   204
6.3.3   Economics of public adaptation   206
6.4   Evaluation 1: A public adaptation theory test   209
6.5   Evaluation 2: a public expenditure theory test   212
6.6   Evaluation 3: a land/resource use efficiency theory test   218
6.7   International fairness in the theory of a global public good fund   228
References   232

7.   **The economics of globally shared goods**   **239**
7.1   Introduction   239
7.2   Globally shared goods   241
7.3   Microbehavioral decisions for a globally shared good   245
7.4   The economics of foresight for a globally shared good   253
7.5   The economics of greenhouse technologies   262
7.6   Additional clarifications   271
References   272

8.   **Extensions of the economic theory to a basket of globally
     shared goods**   **281**
8.1   Introduction   281
8.2   The basket of globally shared challenges examined   282
8.3   An economics of globally shared goods analysis of the
      protection against asteroids   287
8.4   An economics of globally shared goods analysis of nuclear
      nonproliferation and disarmaments   288
8.5   An economics of globally shared goods analysis of the
      strangelet and a runaway catastrophe   292
8.6   An economics of globally shared goods analysis of the artificial
      intelligence and superintelligent robots   295
8.7   Evaluating the four extensions of the theory   299
8.8   Final words on the economics of globally shared and public goods   301
References   302

**Appendix A: A succinct mathematical disproof of the dismal
              theorem of economics**   **307**
Index   **311**

About the author

S. Niggol Seo is a natural resource economist who has specialized in the study of global warming and globally shared goods. He received a PhD degree in Environmental and Natural Resource Economics from Yale University in May 2006 with a dissertation on microbehavioral models of global warming. While at Yale, he learned from Professor Robert Mendelsohn and Professor William Nordhaus (Nobel Prize in 2018) on the economics of global warming. Since 2003, he has worked on various World Bank projects on climate change in Africa, Latin America, and South Asia. He held professor positions in the UK, Spain, and Australia from 2006 to 2015.

Professor Seo has published over a hundred (peer reviewed) articles on global warming economics, which include seven books. He has been on the editorial boards of the three journals: Food Policy, Climatic Change, and Applied Economic Perspectives and Policy. He received an Outstanding Applied Economic Perspectives and Policy Article Award from the Agricultural and Applied Economics Association (AAEA) in Pittsburgh in June 2011 for developing a microbehavioral economic model of adaptations to climate change.

Preface

This book presents a novel theory of the economics of globally shared goods and public goods. This literature can be traced back to the early and mid-20th century economists including Hayek, Bowen, Samuelson, Musgrave, Friedman, and Buchanan and has surged to be a prominent economics field with the emergence of global-scale challenges at around the dawn of the 21st century.

This book offers the three critiques on the classical economics of global public goods from the vantage points of the microbehavioral economics, the concept of which will be made clear throughout this book. The book adopts the term "globally shared goods" over the conventional "global public goods" or "global commons." The three critiques are presented in Chapter 4, A Critique of the Economics of Global Public Goods: A Microbehavioral Theory and Model, with a perspective of microbehavioral models, in Chapter 5, A Critique of the Economics of Global Public Goods: Economics of Noncooperative Games, with a perspective of noncooperative games in a global optimal policy, and in Chapter 6, A Critique of the Economics of Global Public Goods: The Economics of a Global Public Good Fund, with a perspective of a global public good fund.

The novel economics of globally shared goods, advanced in this book, is composed of the three elements that are three facets of the microbehavioral economics: microbehavioral efficient decisions, foresight economics (forward-looking or prescient decisions), and greenhouse technologies. The economic theory is developed with examinations of the five globally shared goods and challenges: global warming, asteroid collisions, nuclear disarmaments, a strangelet catastrophe, and artificial intelligence.

The present author had the honor to learn global warming economics from Robert Mendelsohn at Yale University whose doctoral advisor during the 1970s was a young Professor William Nordhaus at the same institution. Nordhaus learned primarily from Paul Samuelson who laid the foundation for the economics of public goods. Reflecting on this, it is strongly felt that this book is no coincidence but rather inevitable.

With the transportation and communication revolutions since the commercialization of personal computers during the last decade of the 20th century, the globally shared challenges that were not perceived by the founders of the classical economics have become a critical economic question and a high-priority issue of the society. There is a big intellectual gap that economists must answer to fill, sooner than later, with regard to the challenges thereof. The challenges on both the theory side and the policy side are amply highlighted throughout this book.

This book offers a "grand" economic theory, in the sense that it is integrative and comprehensive, as per these challenges by reimagining the economics of the global-scale shared goods through the three foundations: microbehavioral decisions, a time horizon beyond one's lifetime, and Planet-altering "greenhouse" technologies.

That the economic theory of global-scale public goods should start from an individual's decisions, in other words, not from a global optimization decision model or a global fund, may surprise many who have long been a student or a practitioner of the field. This book demonstrates that a novel path is indeed an ancient road which turns out to lead us farther than anyone has expected. In retrospect of the past four decades, the present author feels that economists could have taken this alternative path right from the beginning of it all.

I am thankful from the heart to Paul Samuelson, James M. Buchanan, Ronald Coase, Thomas Schelling, Kenneth Arrow, William Baumol, and Martin Weitzman for their works' enduring contributions to this important literature which I am certain that will survive in the 21st century. I would also like to express my gratitude to the Academic Press (Elsevier) team, especially J. Scott Bentley, Ruby Smith and Swapna Srinivasan, who had the foresight and skillfulness to publish this book and for their outstanding editorial works in producing this book.

S. Niggol Seo
The Muaebak Institute Visiting Bangkok, Thailand

An introduction to the challenges of public and globally shared goods in economics and policy-making

1

1.1 Introduction

A public good, also referred to as a social good by some scholars and a public economy by others, has long been seen as a troubling spot for the economics profession and literature for nearly a century (Hayek, 1948; Bowen, 1943). The crux of the troublesomeness is that the efficient market cannot provide this type of good efficiently, that is, it will underprovide it or not provide it at all (Samuelson, 1954). As the age of a globalized Earth dawned somewhere around the beginning of the 21st century owing to the revolutions in internet and communication technologies and transportations, the troubling spot has become a one big ill of the Planet that economists cannot provide a lucid exposition, that is, an effective medicine (Nordhaus, 2008; Weitzman, 2009). This book is an ambitious endeavor to elucidate the economic problems, explain the contemporary economic theories, account for severe political ramifications, and, building upon these efforts, develop a novel economic theory for the provision of the public and globally shared goods.

A public good is a short form for a public consumption good, both of which were coined by Paul Samuelson, an iconic American economist of the 20th century. Samuelson initially called it a jointly consumed good and then a publicly consumed good, which conveys the meaning of the term unmistakably (Samuelson, 1955). It is a good, once provided at all, that must be consumed by a large group of people. It cannot be provided exclusively to a single individual.

The group of people in this context can be a local village, a municipality, a state, a country, or even a global community at large (Samuelson and Nordhaus, 2009). The term public goods, however, in most occasions, refer to the public goods consumed jointly at the national level, that is, national public goods (Mas-Colell et al., 1995). The economic theories on public goods were developed with a national public good in mind, which was in part because national policy-makers have keen interests in a national-scale public good for the reasons to be elaborated shortly.

A national public good is an indispensable part of everyday life for any private citizen of any country, the basket of which includes national defense, public education, public roads, police works, public works, and air pollution. Unlike a vast basket of private consumption goods which the market provides efficiently, a public good, both each and all of them, cannot be provided efficiently in the market.

The Economics of Globally Shared and Public Goods. DOI: https://doi.org/10.1016/B978-0-12-819658-8.00001-9

As such, without doubt, each of these subjects is one of the most important public policy issues of any nation.

It means that the market cannot provide these essential goods optimally to the society and also means that there is vast literature on each of these subjects with regard to how the society should attempt to provide each of them, including the literature of public finance, economic growth, environmental pollution, and resource uses (Musgrave, 1959; Nordhaus and Tobin, 1972; Baumol and Oates, 1975; Hartwick and Olewiler, 1997). This, however, does not mean that each of the literatures is unanimous on a remedy, governmental policy or not, for the problem. On the contrary the basket of policy solutions offered in each of the public good literatures has contained many different fruits and breads of dissimilar sizes.

The entire spectrum of rivaling views and theories on the provision of public goods includes, to name only the prominent ones, a governmental taxation (price), a quantity standard set by the government, a precautionary principle, a tradable permit system, a zero discounting-based policy, a voluntary bargaining, a progressive taxation, a private provision, and offset credits (Coase, 1960; Baumol and Oates, 1971; Montgomery, 1972; Weitzman, 1974; Stavins, 1998). Across the entire range of policy discussions on these policy instruments, there lies the hurricane's eye around which all things are whirling, that is, the question of how to put a monetary value on a public good (Mendelsohn, 1980; Hanemann, 1994; Mendelsohn and Olmstead, 2009; Freeman et al., 2014).

The rival theories and concepts have resulted in the establishment of institutions to tackle these issues and the host of laws and regulations that define national policies on various public good areas. For example, the Environmental Protection Agency (EPA) in the United States was established in 1970 through which a host of major environmental laws began to be administered including the Clean Air Act (CAA) and the Clean Water Act (CWA) (USEPA, 2010). Internationally the first conference on the human-caused environmental issues was held in 1972 in Stockholm, Sweden (UN, 1972).

The studies of public goods in economics and many related disciplines during the 20th century up to the beginning of the 1990s had set the ideal conditions for a perfect storm: the emergence of a truly global-scale public good. By the early 21st century, the economics and policy negotiations of public goods at a global scale surged to the forefront of economics, sciences, and policy discussions (Nobel Prize, 2007, 2018). Although the Treaty of Nonproliferation of Nuclear Weapons (NPT), one of the global public goods analyzed in this book, was signed and entered into force in 1970, negotiations and economic studies had remained focused primarily on the cold war competition between the US and the USSR, as well as nuclear containments of rogue regimes (UNODA, 2019). The academic field of global public goods came to be a salient research area with the emergence of the study of global warming and the establishments of international conferences and organizations such as the Villach Climate Change Conference in 1985, the Intergovernmental Panel on Climate Change (IPCC) in 1988, and the United Nations Framework Convention on Climate Change (UNFCCC) in 1992 (WMO, 1985; IPCC, 1990; UNFCCC, 1992).

The academic literature, especially that of economics, has flourished since around the entry into the 21st century. The economics of global warming was elegantly explained by William Nordhaus with a policy proposition of a globally harmonized price of carbon dioxide, which was recognized with a Nobel Prize in economics in 2018 (Nordhaus, 1991, 1992, 1994). Researchers had delved into developing an integrated assessment model for a global warming policy tool (Manne et al., 1995). The debate on how damaging climate change will be erupted and is still a central battleground in global warming economics (Adams et al., 1990; Mendelsohn et al., 1994; Tol, 2002; Schlenker and Roberts, 2009; Bakkensen and Mendelsohn, 2016). The study of how individuals can adapt to changes in the climate system has gradually moved from the periphery to the center of climate change economics (Seo, 2006, 2010a, 2016a,b, 2017a). The question of whether the benefit-cost analysis is an adequate policy analysis tool for the problem of global warming or not has raged among the economists (Weitzman, 2009; Nordhaus, 2011; Seo, 2018). Economists were divided on whether the discount rate for a global warming policy should be near zero or close to a market interest rate (Arrow et al., 1996a; Stern, 2007). The emerging battle ground of economists is whether a global public good fund such as the Green Climate Fund (GCF) can be an effective solution for the global public good problem (GCF, 2011; Seo, 2019a).

The richness and high quality of the global warming economics were triggered by the significant progress in climate science, both in quantity and quality. A simple carbon dioxide-global average temperature equation at the end of the 19th century by Svante Arrhenius has turned into a global scale machine of which each scientist group took on one aspect of climate science or another. The progresses of climate science have been well summarized and reported to the public through the IPCC reports (Arrhenius, 1889; Revelle and Suess, 1957; Hansen et al., 1981; IPCC, 1990, 2014). Once the greenhouse effect of carbon dioxide and other chemicals was established, the genie was truly out of the bottle to search for and inspect every parcel of the globe and leave not a stone unturned. It became a truly globalized endeavor (Le Treut et al., 2007).

The scientific frenzy has translated without interpretations into a massive global policy undertaking through the United Nations. Tens of thousands of politicians and scientists from about 200 countries convene annually during the 2 weeks before Christmas holidays. The meeting is called the Conference of the Parties (COP). Of the most successful COPs were the Kyoto Conference in 1997, the Copenhagen Conference in 2009, and the Paris Conference in 2015, which produced the Kyoto Protocol, Copenhagen Accord, and Paris Agreement, respectively (UNFCCC, 1997, 2009, 2015).

Despite the 25 COPs held since the establishment of the UNFCCC, it can be judged that there is still no global policy on global warming. The Kyoto Protocol was the only legally binding treaty, but the policy scale and effectiveness were severely constrained by the exclusion of China, India, the US, and other developing countries (Manne and Richels, 1999; Nordhaus and Boyer, 1999). The Copenhagen Accord was not able to negotiate an expanded Kyoto Protocol due to disagreements between developing countries and developed countries (Nordhaus, 2010). The Paris Agreement, while hailed as a turning point for our Planet by President Obama, was not a legally binding agreement (CBS, 2016; Seo, 2017a). With the withdrawal from the Trump Administration in June 2017, the Paris Agreement became even further toothless (White House, 2017; Seo, 2019b).

The globally shared goods, commonly referred to as global public goods by economists, include not only global warming but also other prominent international issues such as nuclear nonproliferation and disarmaments, asteroid collisions, scientific experiments with global scale risk, and artificial intelligence (Sandler, 1997; Posner, 2004). The global community has made extensive policy efforts in some of these challenges but nearly no efforts in others up until this moment.

What has become evident in global warming policy negotiations over the past three decades, also in nuclear disarmament talks, is the lack of a truly global treaty that is adopted by all the members and implemented across the Planet. On the contrary the history of negotiations is filled with repeated tales of failures on reaching such a forceful agreement, which is by now most clearly exhibited in the global climate change negotiations (Seo, 2017a,c).

With this background this book examines the intellectual traditions in economics concerning the public good problems and explains how they have been applied to interpret and provide policy recommendations on the aforementioned global public good challenges. Through a critical examination of the theoretical traditions, the present author will offer a novel theory on the provision of globally shared goods. The novel theory will be developed not only as a potpourri of incongruent ideas but also as a consistent and cohesive theoretical framework whose foundation is firmly established upon microbehavioral economics (Seo, 2006, 2016a).

In Chapter 2, The Economics of Public Goods, and Chapter 3, The Economics of Global-Scale Public Goods: Key Challenges and Theories, a comprehensive review of the economic theories on public goods and global public goods is offered. This is followed by the three chapters, each of which is devoted to a major critique of the classical theories from each unique perspective: Chapter 4, A Critique of the Economics of Global Public Goods: A Microbehavioral Theory and Model, on microbehavioral decisions, Chapter 5, A Critique of the Economics of Global Public Goods: Economics of Noncooperative Games, on noncooperative games, Chapter 6, A Critique of the Economics of Global Public Goods: The Economics of a Global Public Good Fund, on a global public good fund. Chapter 7, The Economics of Globally Shared Goods, provides a full description of the economics of globally shared goods that this book ultimately offers to the readers. In Chapter 8, Extensions of the Economic Theory to a Basket of Globally Shared Goods, the economic theory thus developed is extended to a basket of aforementioned globally shared goods and provides novel interpretations and remedies of these global-scale challenges.

1.2 Public goods and globally shared goods examined

The theory of public goods, emerged nearly nine decades ago, was formulated in the context of a national economy. When the concept of a public good as we know it now was first defined, it was not called a public good but a social good (Bowen, 1943). The term social goods may convey an impression that the basket of public goods in the national economy may be large, that is, there may be a large number of public goods in the nation's economy. However, as Buchanan clarified it, in between the spectrum of pure private goods and pure public goods, there is a list of goods, referred to as a club good that has the characteristics of both types of goods (Buchanan, 1965). The number of a pure public good, therefore, may be limited, so may be the number of a pure private good.

A taxonomy of public goods was provided in the economics textbook by Samuelson and Nordhaus (2009). By the political scale of a public good, the authors classify the host of public goods into a local public good, a municipal public good, a State public good, a national public good, and a global public good. The scale can be defined not only by a political dimension but also by a geographical dimension.

The textbook classifies a national defense system, a national public education system, a national public road, and a natural park system as a national public good; police works and environmental pollution problems as a State public good; public works and public libraries as a municipal public good; a local communal area and a lighthouse as a local public good. For a global public good, the authors refer to a global warming policy and a nuclear disarmament effort. Further there can be a multistate public good such as an interstate pollution problem, for example, acid rain and a multinational public good such as a crossboundary pollution problem, for example, a crossnational fine particulate matter pollution (Woodruff et al., 2006; Muller and Mendelsohn, 2009).

An important lesson we are taught from the history and the taxonomy of public goods is that the economics of public goods was not developed because of the environmental pollution problems. Samuelson, Buchanan, Bowen, Musgrave, and other economists at the dawn of the literature were concerned about the economic system, more specifically, how it would function in the free market economy when there are public consumption goods. It is when the problems of global public goods became prominent in the economics literature, the theory of public goods became entangled with the global environmental issues (Nordhaus, 1994; Kaul et al., 2003).

This book will follow this historical development. The present author will present the theories of public goods in the broader national economic context, that is, not limited to environmental issues. As the readers will be able to verify, however, when it comes to economic policy decisions on public goods, environmental pollution issues, including air pollution, water pollution, toxic chemicals, and endangered species, have turned out to be the most contentious as well as fascinating fields of the economics literature (Baumol and Oates, 1975; Mendelsohn and Olmstead, 2009).

Of the environmental issues, air pollution problems such as acid rain and smog are the most salient economic issues in relation to the national and subnational public goods (USEPA, 1990). For many countries on the globe, the acid rain phenomenon is a national public good while it is a multistate public good for a large-size country like the United States (Likens and Bormann, 1974). The smog event is most often a municipal public good, that is, a public good at the level of a city and metropolitan area.

The economics contribution to the environmental pollution issues is vast, to say modestly. Especially in the two fields, contributions are the most prominent. One is the field of how to measure the damage of environmental pollutants, and the other is the field of how to design an economic policy instrument to address the environmental pollution problems. For the former, economists have built an ever more refined integrated assessment models since the late 1970s (Mendelsohn, 1980; Smith and Huang, 1995; Muller and Mendelsohn, 2009; Muller et al., 2011; Freeman et al., 2014). Further, a range of valuation techniques were developed and applied to value the damages from numerous pollutants (Rosen, 1974; Viscusi, 1979; Hanemann, 1994; Greenstone and Gallagher, 2008). For the latter, economists have proposed a basket of policy instruments such as an efficient price and taxation, a tradable emissions allowance, and a bundle of standards (Montgomery, 1972; Baumol and Oates, 1975; Hahn and Dudley, 2007; Schmalensee and Stavins, 2013).

In tandem with the advances in the economics research, pollution control policies were introduced and have become amended multiple times since 1970 (USEPA, 2010). The most prominent environmental policy is perhaps the CAA of the United States. It defined six criteria pollutants, for each of which national ambient air quality standards were determined and updated. The CAA 1990 amendments also introduced the economic policy concepts through the sulfur dioxide allowance trading program (USEPA, 1990). Further, the CAA became the basis for the Obama Administration's Clean Power Plan for controlling carbon emissions from existing power plants (USEPA, 2014).

Of the range of possible global-scale public goods, this book focuses on the following five topics: global warming, asteroid collisions, nuclear nonproliferation and disarmaments, the high-risk Large Hadron Collider experiments, and artificial intelligence (Sandler, 1997; Kaul et al., 2003; Posner, 2004; Seo, 2018). In developing the economics of globally shared goods in Chapter 7, The Economics of Globally Shared Goods, the literature on global warming and climate with the big array of reported empirical studies in the literature, both sciences and economics, will provide essential materials for the foundation and justification of the novel theory. The economic theory will then be extended in Chapter 8, Extensions of the Economic Theory to a Basket of Globally Shared Goods, to address the aforementioned four global-scale challenges.

As noted previously the term "global public goods" was mentioned for the first time in the economics literature in an effort to explain the economic problems of global warming (Nordhaus and Yang 1996; Barrett, 1994). Nordhaus was the first one to coin the term "global commons" to indicate the globally shared resource (Nordhaus, 1982). It is therefore appropriate that this book takes the challenges of global warming as the primary global-scale public good in the elucidation of the novel economic theory. In addition, it is also a practical decision considering the vast corpus of the economics literature, especially empirical studies, that have been made available during the three preceding decades. Moreover, the explosions of climate change science reports and papers during the past three decades provide the present author with rich resources to resort to in establishing the economic concepts offered in this book (IPCC, 1990, 2014; Le Treut et al., 2007).

There is another well-perceived reason that the conundrum of global warming has been and is at the center of the economics of global public goods, that is, globally shared goods. Unlike the other global-scale problems, every person on this Earth contributes to the global warming phenomenon by emitting ineluctably Planet-heating gases including carbon dioxide. This means that a successful control of the global warming trend can only be resulted from the aggregate reduction of greenhouse gases (GHG) of all the nations, more extensively all the individuals, on Earth. To phrase it in economic terms, the production function of the global warming global public good exhibits a cumulative production technology (Hirshleifer, 1983). To put it dramatically, an exclusion of China from a globally agreed GHG mitigation program would not yield any discernible result on the changes in the global climate system if China's emissions were to rise steeply during the 21st century. This is in fact what happened to the Kyoto Protocol at the end of its demise in 2012, that is, the participation rate to the Protocol was too low to be anything effective (Nordhaus, 2008).

The second globally shared good examined in this book is a possible collision with a killer asteroid which has the potential to cause a global-scale disaster. An asteroid is a small-sized solar system body that orbits the Sun and, when deviated from its orbit, can collide against the Earth (NRC, 2010). The National Aeronautics and Space Administration (NASA) defines that an asteroid with its diameter greater than 1 km can cause a global scale destruction. Of the 18,000 Near-Earth Asteroids (NEA) discovered up to this point, about 1000 asteroids are such asteroids (CNEOS, 2019). For a meaningful reference, the asteroid that fell to the coasts of Yucatan Peninsula ended the era of dinosaurs on the Planet and kicked off the human-dominated era, whose diameter was estimated to be 10 km (Kaiho and Oshima, 2017).

The protection of Earth against such a large-size asteroid is a globally shared good. The benefit of the protection would accrue to all the sentient beings on the Planet, let alone all the humans. An individual cannot be excluded from the benefit of a successful defense against the asteroid. The benefit that an individual receives does not diminish the benefit of another individual. The two clear marks of a public good (Mas-Colell et al., 1995)!

To an individual member country of the Planet, there is a strong incentive to be a free-rider in the asteroid defense program (Buchanan, 1968). It is also supported by the empirical evidence that 95% of the discovered Near-Earth Objects (NEO) until now have been discovered by the NASA (CNEOS, 2019). There is also a strong economic justification for such a one-sided effort by the United States: given the most advanced space technology that the US commands, it would be unjustifiable for another country to attempt to defend against the killer asteroids, at a big cost to the country. The book will give an account of the international collaboration involving China and the European Space Agency.

The third global public good this book examines is nuclear nonproliferation and disarmament efforts. Scientists proposed more than one global catastrophe scenarios from nuclear conflicts or explosions, including a nuclear winter hypothesis and a massive ozone loss hypothesis (Turco et al., 1983; Mills et al., 2008; Toon et al. 2019). In both scenarios nuclear explosions would cause a global-scale destruction through a series of disruptions in the global atmosphere.

In contrast to the asteroid defense, artificial intelligence, and a strangelet runaway catastrophe analyzed in the book, nuclear negotiations among the world nations have a long history beginning from the 1960s. The international policy framework is encapsulated in the Treaty on NPT to which 195 countries are signatories, which entered into force in 1970 (UNODA, 2019).

In parallel with the policy efforts, theoreticians have come up with multiple solution mechanisms to the global challenge, including a Nash bargaining theory, a containment theory, a nuclear umbrella theory, and a zero nuclear arms theory (Selten, 1965; Schelling, 1966; Campbell et al., 2004). These theories will offer rich resources for the economic analysis to be conducted in this book with regard to the topic. On the other hand these theories will also highlight the complexity and difficulty of the nuclear disarmament negotiations that the general public come across nearly every day through the media, including the tensions concerning nuclear arms programs in Iran, North Korea, Pakistan, and India.

The fourth globally shared good examined in the book is a runaway catastrophe hypothesis of a strangelet which might be created, as argued by some scientists, from the experiments in Large Hadron Collider (LHC) in Europe and the Relativistic Heavy Ion Collider (RHIC) in the United States (CERN, 2017). Of the five global public goods analyzed in this book, the strangelet catastrophe is typical of a runaway catastrophe which can unfold even in a split second to end the human civilization and even the entire universe.

The LHC, built along the Switzerland—France border, is a particle accelerator through which scientists aim to examine the states of the universe right after the Big Bang. Critics argued that the particle accelerator may unintentionally produce a strangelet to form a stable black hole which can suck the entire universe in (Wagner, 1999). Multiple risk assessment groups concluded, however, that the LHC/RHIC experiments present no danger because, among other reasons, such collisions are naturally occurring frequently (Jaffe et al., 2000; Ellis et al., 2008).

The fifth globally shared good to be explained in this book is artificial intelligence (AI) and the threat of a singularity. The AI robots and machines are already quite widely used in businesses, offices, hospitals, and many other areas. The fear about the AI has also been surging, especially with regard to the possibility of a singularity (Hawking et al., 2014). The singularity is the moment when the brain capacity of the AI superintelligent robots equals that of the humans (Kurzweil, 2005). The moment may become the greatest moment of the human civilization but, as Hawking and others warned, the last moment.

Although both the LHC strangelet hypothesis and the AI singularity hypothesis are an expression of fear concerning the rapid progress in science and technological capabilities of the humanity, many experts express that the latter is far more plausible and may even become a reality in a few decades. The singularity point is certainly a globally shared good, or more pertinently, the avoidance of the singularity point. At the moment there is little policy effort at the global level on this critical topic.

Further many prominent experts and entrepreneurs view the AI as the next big frontier for humanity's progress and/or military dominance. To give you an adequate example, the first humanoid robot unveiled in 2014, the Pepper, can detect your emotions and talk back to you in 15 different languages. Pepper now works as a receptionist in tens of thousands of offices (SoftBank Robotics, 2019).

1.3 The furor, dances, and charade over global public goods

It should not be unexpected that individuals and nations attach strong emotions to a global public good, especially to an agreement reached on its provision by international negotiators. This is because some nations will inevitably feel that they did not get a fair deal from an international agreement or another. This discontent, in turn, arises more fundamentally from the fact that the globally shared good is also ineluctably under the sovereignty of an individual nation.

Even for the host of national public goods, a policy intervention by the government inevitably leads to the creation of a group of winners and another group of losers from the policy implementation. A supporter group and an opposition group may clash on a certain policy intervention regarding a public good. There is, however, no infringement of national sovereignty by one way or another of providing the public good. Further there is always the government that is ultimately responsible for providing the public good, and, in a democratic nation, the government has the mandate from the people and legal means to do so.

For a global public good provision, a possible infringement of national sovereignty attributable to a provision or no provision of the public good is one of the biggest obstacles that have to be overcome in any successful international agreement. Even if an agreement or a treaty would be signed, there is no global government that is responsible for a provision of a global public good with a global mandate and legal means, which inevitably further dims the prospect of a successful provision.

The two obstacles have been at the core of repeated failures in establishing a legally binding truly global climate change treaty. In global warming policy negotiations, the furor expressed by national negotiators with regard to a potential violation of sovereignty and governance issues has always been frequent and disruptive. The shambles in the UN-led global conferences attributable to the disagreements among the conference parities on these fundamental issues were evident to the observers and widely reported (Seo, 2017a,c).

Let me briefly describe a few of these chaotic and emotional scenes recurring quite often in the conferences. It is not hard to find a roundtable in which developed nations argue that a proposed agreement or treaty is of little meaning as a solution because of the exemption of certain developing nations from the responsibility of certain actions. The underdeveloped nations, for example, India or China, would counter that argument by saying that the global warming phenomenon that is unfolding at the present time should be attributed to the historical carbon emissions by the rich nations, and therefore the rich nations should take most of the burden of stopping the global warming (NYT, 2009).

Another frequent line of argument is the existential threat argument put forward by some group of nations. For example, the Alliance of Small Island States (AOSIS) members, for example, Palau, Vanuatu, or Seychelles, of the UN conferences would argue that the rapid rise observed in the sea level which is in most part attributable to the global warming phenomenon would sink their island nations below the sea level "sooner or later." Having caused the existential crisis to the islands, they would continue, the rich nations must funnel sufficient funds to these small island nations in order to save the islanders and protect the islands from the rising seas (Economic Times of India, 2015).

Another dramatic emotional story is told from a future generation's perspective: at a recent UN meeting on climate actions of world leaders in New York, a 16-year old climate activist passionately rebuked that the adults "stole my childhood with your empty words." She chided that "People are suffering, people are dying, entire ecosystems are collapsing. ... We are at the beginning of a mass extinction, and all you can talk about is money and fairy tales of eternal economic growth (DW, 2019)."

The strong sentiment expressed by a young girl echoes those expressed by the academics and politicians such as, to note some of them, "the end of human civilization as we know it," "a point of no return in the next 10 years," "an existential crisis," and "the greatest threat to humanity (Gore, 2006; Weitzman, 2009)." But certainly there is more to it. To put it coarsely, is the current generation destroying the lives of the future generations and will the latter come back in a certain way or another to ask for actions and compensations?

At the conclusion of any of these global negotiators' conferences which is held annually for about 2−3 weeks at the end of a year just before Christmas, concerned people and experts are very likely deeply divided on what they saw and what was accomplished on that conference. Many of them would hail an agreement with dances at the conference using flamboyant terms such as a "landmark" or "turning point" while the others would call the same conference and the outcome as a "sham" or "charade (CBS, 2016)."

The furor and the shambles observed in the UN-led global conferences are expressions of disparate national interests with regard to the provision of a global public good, in this case, a global climate system. Underneath the disarrays on the international stage lie the differing viewpoints that sway political power grabs at the national stage. In the US, a basket of climate regulations and policies by President Obama who called them as the greatest legacy of his presidency was quickly replaced by President Trump who defended American interests through the "America First" principle (White House, 2013, 2017). A similarly abrupt transition from one extreme position on global warming negotiations to the other occurred in Australia, Brazil, and other countries in 2017.

The political power battles at the national stages of these nations around a global warming treaty reflect the maturing public opinions on the globally shared good: an agreement in one form or another at the international stage is not simply a rose in the garden blossoming during the spring but rather will no doubt call for costly actions that can pain the country and individual voters. This means that the politicians must face double pressure in determining their actions: one from the voters in the nation and the other from the international negotiation parties.

Of the five global-scale public goods examined in this book, such emotional responses at the micro level, that is, at the individual voter level, may only occur at the global warming and climate change negotiations. This is due to the realization that a global warming treaty or agreement will force an individual voter to make sacrifices, monetary and nonmonetary. What this book will highlight, which has long been overlooked by the concerned people, is that the provision of a global public good may not mean a global action as a whole but rather actions at the micro voter level and sacrifices at the micro voter level, which is certainly the case for a global warming policy.

The emotionally charged atmosphere similar to the one depicted in the above also arises from another conspicuous characteristic of a certain type of global challenges: the fear of a truly catastrophic consequence even from a single defector or a single failure (Seo, 2018). Consider the nuclear nonproliferation and disarmaments and the consequences of an ultimate failure of the negotiations. Even though the NPT treaty is ratified by nearly all the countries in the world, that is to say, with the participation rate of 98%, only a few exceptions such as Iran and North Korea often seems to make the possibility of a nuclear war very high. For another example, consider the LHC strangelet catastrophe hypothesis. A single failure in preventing the creation of a stable black hole would mean, as proponents repeatedly argued, the end of humanity. In the artificial intelligence hypothesis the singularity point is predicted to be the last moment of the humanity. The singularity may arrive very soon and do so even without the humanity having the chance to stop it.

Taking into consideration the "catastrophe" characteristic of these global-scale challenges, it is not difficult to understand the popularity and contagiousness, among the academics and the public, of the terms and concepts that were originated from the catastrophe and chaos theories in mathematics (Lorenz, 1963; Thom, 1975). On the one side of the Planet, such an association would no doubt turn the citizens thereof extremely heated about such possibilities.

On the opposite side of the Planet, notwithstanding, the citizens thereof will give icy cold looks to these theorists and dismiss them as a doomsday forecaster. They may reason that the chance of realization of each of the aforementioned truly catastrophic events is extremely low, perhaps as low as the chance of the sky collapsing. Why worry about it, they will argue.

1.4 The economic theories of public goods

It is unmistakable that economists recognized the study of public goods as one of the most critical fields in the science of economics because the latter was built on the foundation of the market transactions among market participants (Smith, 1776; Ricardo, 1817; Hayek, 1948). There was certainly a need to explain the role of the government and governmental transactions in the economic system. The field of public finance, also called public economy, naturally emerged to fill this gap (Musgrave, 1939, 1959).

The theoretical challenge faced by economists was most elegantly posed by Samuelson when he put forth the pure theory of public expenditure and coined the term public consumption goods and later public goods (Samuelson, 1954, 1955). He concluded that a public good cannot be provided by the market alone efficiently. He then proposed an economic instrument that can fix the problem which is the creation of a price for the public good. The federal government should implement this price, which is in essence a tax for a public good.

A closer examination of the pure theory can be found in the theory of club goods by Buchanan and others (Buchanan, 1965; Brown, 1973). Buchanan advanced the theory by clarifying that there may be a club good which is a private good in one sense and a public good in another sense. Only in the extreme is a pure public good that fits the Samuelson's description.

Another critical literature on the pure theory by Samuelson is that of spillover effects or neighborhood effects by Milton Friedman and other economists from the Chicago School (Friedman, 1962). The upshot of their arguments is that a private good or activity may yield the effects that are beyond the private individual. The way to deal with the problem, however, of spillover effects that exist in a large number of goods and services in the market is not through a government intervention. The voluntary bargaining among the concerned parties in the problem of social cost is one exemplary research regarding this theory (Coase, 1960).

Whether one agreed or disagreed with one of the three theoretical viewpoints, that is, Samuelson's, Friedman/Coase's, and Buchanan's, a long list of other conceptual questions had surfaced and turned out to be unavoidable for any serious theorist who attempted to address the problems of a public good or another. The corpus of these questions and answers includes the following: what should be the price level for a public good (Baumol and Oates, 1975)?; how should the benefit of a public good policy be measured (Mendelsohn, 1980; Muller and Mendelsohn, 2009)?; in quantifying the benefits of a policy, what should be the value of a life saved (Viscusi and Aldy, 2003)? Is the price policy always preferable to the quantity (standard) policy (Weitzman, 1974)?; how should the government pick one project over the other possible projects for providing a public good (Hahn and Dudley, 2007)?; what should be the discount rate if the benefits and damages were to accrue over a long time horizon (Arrow et al., 1996a; Weitzman, 1998)?; is the benefit-cost analysis always meaningful (Arrow et al., 1996b)?; can a public good policy be designed despite the incomplete information as well as hidden information from the actors to be affected by the policy? (Clarke, 1971; Groves, 1973); can a blended policy of the price approach and the quantity approach be designed, such as the tradable emissions allowance system? (Montgomery, 1972; Stavins, 1998) This book will have the space to elaborate these questions in detail as well as other important questions regarding the theories of public goods.

Witnessing a gradual emergence of the global-scale challenges through the 1970s and 1980s such as a nuclear weapons race and a global warming prediction (Hansen et al., 1981; Turco et al., 1983), some economists might have come to the realization that the economics of public goods as set forth by the aforementioned pioneers in economics was in fact constrained to the realm of the national economy. They might have asked whether the economic theory of public goods would still be meaningful for an analysis of the global-scale challenges (Nordhaus, 1982).

After witnessing nearly two decades of the emergence of these global issues, the highly acclaimed pioneer of the economics of global public goods, William Nordhaus, in fact pointed to a novel way for the economists to proceed by developing an integrated assessment model (IAM) of global warming, which he named the DICE model short for the Dynamic Integrated model of Climate and the Economy (DICE) (Nordhaus, 1991, 1992, 1994; Nordhaus, 2006). What he accomplished is, with the fundamental theory of the economics of public goods intact, he came to the creation of a novel economic concept through the IAM framework: a globally harmonized price (tax) of carbon. After over another two decades of the DICE model, the carbon price came to be called, through the Obama Administration's inter-agency working group on social cost of carbon, the social cost of carbon (NRC, 2017; Nordhaus, 2017).

To arrive at the critical economic concept which was explained so elegantly for the past three decades to the academics and the public alike, he set out to and succeeded in integrating not only the national economies across the globe but also the atmospheric and ecological systems with the economic systems. This impressive work has since then set the benchmark for all global public good economists (Seo, 2017a).

With clarity and consistency, he provided an updated and consistent version of the DICE model for the past three decades (Nordhaus, 1994, 2008, 2013). This set of works can be compared to the Revelle and Suess's work on the carbon dioxide exchange model between ocean and atmosphere as well as the Keeling's work on the CO_2 measurement at the Mauna Loa Observatory since the 1970s, two monumental scientific works on climate change (Revelle and Suess, 1957; Keeling et al., 2005).

The biggest challenge faced by the DICE modeling that was recognized from the early days was the question of how the monetary damage or benefit from the global warming can be measured precisely. It did not take long for the field of the economic modeling of climate change impacts to surge to the fore of global warming economics. The early studies were concentrated on the economic sectors that had long been recognized to be sensitive to climate and weather conditions, the prime example of which was agriculture, especially in the low-latitude tropical underdeveloped countries such as Sub-Saharan Africa (Adams et al., 1990; Rosenzweig and Parry, 1994; Mendelsohn et al., 1994; Schlenker and Roberts, 2009; Seo, 2010a). Another major area of the economic impact modeling in the early years was the impact of sea level rise (IPCC, 1990; Yohe and Schlesinger, 1998). Recent impact studies have shifted their focus to the areas where a catastrophic consequence of climate change is the primary concern, for example, hurricanes/tropical cyclones/

typhoons (Bakkensen and Mendelsohn, 2016; Seo, 2015b, 2017b) and a monsoon climate system (Seo, 2016e, 2019c). The impact literature in the economics of public goods has become the most contentious and emotially charged area of all, beyond economists and scientists to the general public.

Another provocative economic theory was put forward by Martin Weitzman who challenged the widely recognized norm of the economics of global public goods, that is, the need for a benefit-cost analysis through the DICE and other models (Weitzman, 2009). In a dramatic and simplistic modeling, he introduced the "dismal theorem" which states that the cost-benefit analysis is of no meaning when the uncertainty is very large as is in the economic analysis of a global warming policy. Instead he argued that the world should put a strict limit on the emissions of carbon dioxide as soon as possible as a general precaution against the end of all civilizations on the Planet.

At the time the economist club of global warming seemed to get split into two clubs after the Weitzman's influential argument. In addition scientists who foresaw climate change doomsdays and climate activists who believed in such doomsdays have broadly embraced his argument. Nonetheless, many informed economists warned that his conclusion is only valid in a very limited situation and strong assumptions such as no adaptation and a fat-tail distribution (Nordhaus, 2011; Seo, 2018).

The points clarified thus far on the global warming economics are all highly pertinent to the analysis of global-scale challenges, that is, globally shared goods. Another salient economic theory that was developed in economics and applied to the global-scale problems, especially a nuclear arms race and disarmaments, is the game theory. As described earlier in this chapter, the problem of nuclear proliferation and the goal of nuclear disarmaments will remain unresolved as long as there is a defector or two from a global treaty of disarmaments. On the other side, the nuclear-weapons nations would not voluntarily discard all nuclear weapons, as many of them have not ratified the Comprehensive Nuclear Test Ban Treaty adopted in 1996 (UNODA, 1996). These situations have often been analyzed in a game-theoretic framework.

A nuclear conflict was put into a game played by the two parties, whether it is a game between nuclear-weapons nations and nonnuclear-weapons nations or a game between the United States and the Soviet Union. What is the subgame perfect Nash equilibrium in this game? Could the world achieve a zero nuclear arms state or should the world aim to deter nuclear conflicts and wars, rogue nations with nuclear weapons? Will the currently NPT party countries remain as a signatory to the Treaty under the "grand bargain" of a nuclear umbrella even if one of their hostile neighbors aggressively pursue nuclear arms (Nash, 1950; Selten, 1965; Schelling, 1966; Kissinger et al., 2011)?

The agreements inscribed in the NPT treaty provide a backbone to the continuing nuclear negotiations (Campbell et al., 2004). In the global warming economics, an adoption of an international agreement that is comparable to the NPT treaty has turned out to be elusive. The monumental efforts during the past three decades including Kyoto Conference in 1997, Copenhagen Conference in 2009,

Paris Conference in 2015 have failed to produce a legally binding global-scale treaty (Seo, 2017a,c).

Parallel to the UN-led international conferences, economists have endeavored to explicate and devise a way to achieve global cooperation (Barrett, 1994; Carraro et al., 2006; Seo, 2012a; Nordhaus, 2015). This literature has come up with the suggestions of the mechanisms for increasing participation from individual countries. The mechanisms included a climate club and tariffs for nonclub members, a compensation scheme to the victims, and benefit transfers.

From the international conferences led by the UN, a concrete policy instrument for enhancing international cooperation surfaced from the Copenhagen Accord, held in the first year of Obama Presidency, by the pledge from Mrs. Clinton as Secretary of State of the Obama Administration who announced US$ 100 billion contribution annually (UNFCCC, 2009). She announced that the fund will help low-latitude developing countries adapt to the challenges of climate change. This materialized as the GCF, which began disbursements of the funds to the selected projects in developing countries in December 2015 (GCF, 2011; Seo, 2019a).

It is fair to say that, given the absence of an international treaty, the GCF funding activities have become the centerpiece of the international efforts, so have the economics of the GCF funding moved to the center of the economics. Since the first batch of allocations of the GCF funds made in late 2015, 111 + project proposals submitted by the countries in Africa, Latin America, South Asia, Central Asia, and Eastern Europe have received a grant from the GCF. The total funding size is US$ 2.4 billion, as of July 2019, with the minimum grant of US$ 26 million and the maximum grant of US$ 1.4 billion (GCF, 2019c). The GCF activities have suffered from the lack of new contributions of member countries, with 80% of the total contribution made by the five countries. With the US withdrawal of the initial pledge to the GCF, the GCF has struggled to generate additional funds (Seo, 2019b; GCF, 2019b).

A succinct description of the economics of global-scale public goods up to this point certainly belies the complexity and depth of the literature as well as a great divergence of opinions among the researchers. The present author will give an in-depth explanation of the literature with a balanced presentation of opposing views throughout this book, especially in Chapters 2–6. Among the most prominent diverging points are whether a carbon price (tax) should be preferred over a quantitative threshold such as emissions limits or a temperature ceiling at 2°C; How can a cap-and-trade system such as the European Union Emissions Trading Scheme (ETS) be designed and made effective (Ellerman and Buchner, 2007; Stavins, 2007)?; Should the climate policy apply a zero discounting rate for the future damages or a market-based discounting rate including a hyperbolic discounting (Laibson, 1997; Stern, 2007)?; Will the damage on the world agriculture be severe or modest?; Will farmers be able to adapt to changes in the climate system and if so, how?; Will the increase in climate risk and variability be more harming than the increase in global average temperature?; Will catastrophic events become more frequent and intense, wreaking havoc on the vulnerable communities, for example, severe hurricanes and tropical cyclones, an intense monsoon system?

1.5   Three critiques

This book provides a consistent set of critiques on the economics literature of global warming and more broadly of global public goods. The three critiques presented in Chapters 4–6 have a common denominator which is microbehavioral incentives and choices faced with the changes in the global climate system as well as the changes in the global policy. Put slightly differently, the common idea penetrating across the three critiques is how the literature fails to clarify and integrate choices of individuals and communities faced with external changes into policy designs.

The present author begins with the presentation of the microbehavioral economics of global warming in Chapter 4, A Critique of the Economics of Global Public Goods: A Microbehavioral Theory and Model, where the major empirical results from the microbehavioral modeling studies will also be summarized. The idea of the microbehavioral economics of global public goods would be quite strange, I believe, to many readers and academics in the fields. This is attributable to the three decades of academic endeavors to frame the problem as a global level policy decision, as the present author has described in the above section. To note only several policy variables from such models: a globally harmonized carbon tax, a global treaty that limits carbon dioxide equivalent emissions, a global temperature ceiling, a global carbon budget, and a global policy discounting rate. The suggestion that the economics of global-scale public goods should start at an individual may surprise many who have acquainted themselves with these models.

To assure tentative readers, the rationale of the microbehavioral economics of global warming is more solid than that of the aforementioned global-level policy economic models if you consider that (1) the problem is a cumulative one, that is, any individual is an emitter as well as an absorber of GHG; (2) the changes in the global system, either climate or climate policy, will have locally different impacts; and (3) the changes in the global system will be anticipated and adapted by individual actors.

The first comprehensive presentation of the microbehavioral economics was done by the present author in 2006 by the dissertation entitled "Modeling Farmer Responses to Climate Change" at Yale University and a complete presentation was offered in the two books "Microbehavioral Econometric Methods" published in 2016 and "The Behavioral Economics of Climate Change" published in 2017 (Seo, 2006, 2016a, 2017a). The two books were based on the analyses of the household survey of farm decisions in 11 African countries and that of 7 Latin American countries, both of which were financially supported by the World Bank.

The large array of adaptation decisions that the farmers in the countries in the two continents have made in response to and anticipation of the changes in the climate system, to be described in this book rather thoroughly, will fascinate many readers of this book. But, more importantly, it will cast doubt on the minds of many readers, for more than one reasons, about a heavy emphasis by the economists on the global-level policy decision-making. The global-level policy decision models will not be able to describe these micro level decisions, let alone formulate them as a critical policy decision variable. Further the outcomes from the global-level policy models will be swung widely by the assumptions on microbehavioral adaptation decisions.

The second critique to be presented in Chapter 5, A Critique of the Economics of Global Public Goods: Economics of Noncooperative Games, will go a step further, in the spirit of the contrast between the global modeling and the microbehavioral modeling, to provide an empirical analysis of the regional effects of a global-level policy decision-making. The highlight of the analytical outcomes in the chapter is an elucidation of how individual countries in front of a possible global-level policy measure have disparate incentives about it and consequently will decide not to cooperate on it (Seo, 2012a).

The analysis will reveal that a global-level optimization policy framework is assuming implicitly that more than 200 member nations of the United Nations will cooperate on a global treaty or, put slightly differently, be able to reach an agreement on a global policy measure. The history of the UN-led negotiations during the past three decades has proved pretty unequivocally that the assumption is not valid, at least up to this point. To state it more subtly, the global policy models may have greatly overlooked the problem of nonexistence of the government in global affairs and the issue of sovereignty of individual member nations under a global-scale policy intervention.

The analytical framework in Chapter 5, A Critique of the Economics of Global Public Goods: Economics of Noncooperative Games, is straightforward. We will explain an integrated assessment model of climate change policy-making in which a dynamic optimization of the world's welfare is achieved. From the optimization model, we will find an efficient price of carbon dioxide (equivalent emissions) at the present period which is then updated every decade in the future periods. Applying the efficient prices of carbon dioxide thus determined to all countries/regions in the model, we will measure the total cost of implementing the carbon prices for each of the countries for each time period.

The analysis will reveal the winners and losers from a globally optimal carbon policy. Further it will reveal the winner countries and loser countries in an alternative global policy, that is, the scenario of a business-as-usual. Moreover, the analysis will measure the additional costs of the winner countries and the loser countries when the world community decides to move from a business-as-usual state to a globally optimal policy state. The considerations of the outcomes from the three scenarios will point that there will be no agreement among the UN member nations on any of the climate change policy scenarios owing to largely disparate impacts of it across member nations.

The conclusion derived from the analysis in Chapter 5, A Critique of the Economics of Global Public Goods: Economics of Noncooperative Games, will offer one interpretation of the repeated failures in the global warming negotiations since the UNFCCC was signed in 1992 (UNFCCC, 1992). In each of the major conferences led by the UNFCCC such as the Kyoto Conference in 1997, Bonn Conference in 2001, Copenhagen Conference in 2009, Durban Conference in 2011,

Paris Conference in 2015, Katowice Conference in 2018, and Madrid Conference in 2019, disagreements and divisions between the potential winner countries and the potential loser countries, similar to those depicted in Chapter 5, A Critique of the Economics of Global Public Goods: Economics of Noncooperative Games, derailed an agreement on a legally forceful policy framework (UNFCCC, 1997, 2009, 2015; Nordhaus, 2010; Seo, 2017c).

The third critique, to be presented in Chapter 6, A Critique of the Economics of Global Public Goods: The Economics of a Global Public Good Fund, is a critical examination of a global public good fund as an alternative solution, in particular, the GCF as an alternative policy solution to the global warming challenge. The GCF is an ambitious international project, whose fund size is about 10 times larger than the United Nations regular budget and many other well-established international funds. Even with that size, some groups are pushing for a further 10-fold increase in the fund size. Considering the ambition of the international negotiators and the pledges already made contrasted with the repeated failures in the other policy negotiations, the GCF may be the only visible instrument of the global policy efforts as of the end of 2019.

With its stated ambition declared a decade ago in Copenhagen, the COPs since then moved speedily to mobilize the Fund with enthusiastic supports from the UN Secretary General Ban Ki-moon and the US President Barak Obama, formulating the governing instrument in 2011, establishing the GCF Secretariat in Songdo city in South Korea in 2012, and beginning an initial allocation of the funds to a batch of five projects in November 2015. As of the time of this writing, 111 projects proposed by a developing country application have received a GCF grant, whose total size of disbursements is US$ 2.4 billion (GCF, 2011, 2019c).

The expressed size and ambition about the GCF mechanism raise a serious economic and policy question, which has been largely unattended to by the economists and analysts up to this point (See Seo, 2019a for a comprehensive account): will it be an effective policy instrument to achieve a global community's goal on climate change? Will the international fund allocations to the development country projects have unintended consequences of increasing the climate risk? Will the GCF funding activities help international negotiations or interfere to make them even more contentious? It needs no mentioning that there are many other important questions to be asked and answered despite the large-scale allocation operations already set in motion.

It should be also emphasized that the GCF is only one of the many global funds that are created and implemented to address a global-scale shared problem or another, even if not stated publicly as such by each of such funds. Consider, for example, the World Food Programme or the Medicins Sans Frontieres (Doctors without Borders). The array of international funds that are operating today, in addition to the GCF, will make the analysis in Chapter 6, A Critique of the Economics of Global Public Goods: The Economics of a Global Public Good Fund, particularly pertinent to an economic analysis of global-scale public goods (Seo, 2019a).

The creation of the GCF mechanism may have had a deep root in the economics, although not apparent to the observers. Concerned economists have proposed a compensation scheme as a global warming policy solution in one form or another: a compensation by the developed country party to the developing country party as a replacement for a global mitigation policy, a compensation scheme from the winner countries to the loser countries, a compensation package to the victims of a particular climate change-linked disaster, or a compensation scheme for the purpose of increasing the participation of the poor countries and victims in a global treaty (Schelling, 1991; Carraro et al., 2006; Barrett, 2003).

More broadly, beyond the global warming economics, international funds in the form of a foreign development aid or a sustainable development aid are widely appreciated, especially in the development economics and policy circles, and practiced as a major tool to address a global challenge of hunger and poverty (Sachs, 2005; Banerjee and Duflo, 2019).

From the vantage point of the microbehavioral economics, the GCF's governing instrument and its funding activities, well made public by the organization, provide a trove of valuable resources against which the microbehavioral economic models and studies can be recalled to provide an incisive insight into each of the more than 100 GCF projects to which grants were already disbursed. Let me rephrase it more concretely. The GCF has already offered many grants to many projects submitted from Sub-Saharan African countries on the grounds of agricultural and/or farm vulnerabilities to climatic changes. At the same time the empirical economic studies of African agriculture and farm households go way back to the late 1970s and the microbehavioral economic studies of African agriculture go way back nearly two decades. Chapter 6, A Critique of the Economics of Global Public Goods: The Economics of a Global Public Good Fund, will ask whether or not the results and conclusions from the past economic studies of African agriculture and farms faced with the constraints of climate change are supportive of the GCF's grant allocations to specific activities proposed by the selected projects on the basis of changes of farmers' behaviors and economic outcomes of chosen activities predicted by the economic models.

The GCF funds are allocated to the projects submitted by the accredited entities from Africa, Latin America and the Caribbean, South Asia, Eastern Europe, Central Asia, and the Asia-Pacific island nations based on the projects' merits defined by the GCF. The critique in Chapter 6, A Critique of the Economics of Global Public Goods: The Economics of a Global Public Good Fund, will therefore provide a fascinating look at the different regions of the world and their diverse economic activities as well as their challenges, both of which are, as the readers will come to learn in this book, climate and weather dependent.

This book goes several steps deeper to an analysis of the soundness of the set of GCF fund allocation criteria, called the investment framework. The investment criteria determine whether or not a project proposal should receive a grant. The scores received by each proposal on the criteria give the GCF Board essential information for its final decision which is made by a unanimous decision rule by the 24 board members (GCF, 2019a). The six criteria determined by the GCF are impact potential (mitigation and adaptation), paradigm shift potential, sustainable development potential, needs of the recipient, country ownership, and lastly efficiency and effectiveness. Chapter 6, A Critique of the Economics of Global Public Goods: The Economics of a Global Public Good Fund, will reveal what values each of the GCF-funded projects received on each of the decision criteria. The ensemble of GCF funding criteria is then compared and contrasted with the basket of the microbehavioral decision variables such as optimality, profits, values, and incomes that can be defined at the level of each project.

1.6 The economics of globally shared goods

The three critiques on the economics corpus of global public goods, provided in Chapters 4–6, will convince the readers of this book that the traditional economics of public goods as well as global public goods is founded on a fragile land of a global-level decision framework, more generally speaking, an aggregated decision framework, which has turned out repeatedly to be ineffective as a solution for a global-scale public good challenge. Further the readers will be convinced that the failures can be attributed to the inadequacy and inability of the global-level conceptualizations and models to account for and utilize microbehavioral decisions as a key policy variable.

After arriving at this critical evaluation of the literature, the present author has endeavored to reformulate the economics of public goods and global public goods in a novel way founded on microbehavioral decisions and consequences (Seo, 2015a, 2016c, 2017a). This book presents the new theory in Chapter 7, The Economics of Globally Shared Goods, in a complete form. The applications of the new theory to a host of global public good problems are presented in Chapter 8, Extensions of the Economic Theory to a Basket of Globally Shared Goods.

The present author chooses the term "globally shared goods" over the more commonly and pervasively used terminologies in the literature such as global public goods, global commons, and social goods (Bowen, 1943; Nordhaus, 1982; Barrett, 1994). This choice is motivated by the recognition that a distinction of the public sector and the private sector is adequate for a national economy but there is no such government or public sector that has the authority and power to address the global-scale public good problems.

The economics of globally shared goods (EGSG) is presented with the three decisions that are not mutually exclusive: microbehavioral decisions, foresighted decisions, and greenhouse economics. All three decisions are profit-maximizing decisions of individual economic actors but tackle three different aspects of the global warming problem. To elaborate further the greenhouse economics is concerned with the incentives of individual inventors to develop breakthrough technologies, called in the book silver-bullet technologies or backstop technologies (Romer, 1990; NRC, 2015a,b). The foresight economics is concerned with the microbehavioral efficient decisions that take into account a long-term time horizon beyond one's lifetime, that is, half a century or a century (Fisher, 1930; Arrow et al., 1996a).

Let me explain the three elements of the EGSG one by one. The first, which lays the foundation for the economics of globally shared goods, is the microbehavioral efficient decisions. The microbehaviors refer to changes in choices by an individual decision-maker, of which efficient decisions are microbehavioral efficient decisions. The efficiency refers to the choice that maximizes the profit earned from the whole portfolio of options that is available to the decision-maker (Seo, 2006, 2016a).

A microbehavioral efficient decision is well clarified in the economics literature and in fact has a long historical root going back to the Ricardo's rent theory and the von Thunen's spatial land use theory (Ricardo, 1817; von Thunen, 1826). This is also the foundational concept of the modern economics in explaining firm/consumer decisions and natural resource use decisions (von Neumann and Morgenstern, 1947; Hartwick and Olewiler, 1997).

In the literature of climate change and global warming, these decisions are studied under the banner of the economics of adaptation to climate change (Mendelsohn, 2000; Seo, 2006). Of the most well-established adaptation decisions that are routinely employed by natural resource managers to cope with different climatic conditions are a natural resource enterprise choice, an agricultural system choice, and a farm animal choice. Let me state several concrete examples of the adaptation decisions. In a hotter and more arid (more humid) climate zone, African farmers got adapted by switching to sheep (goats) (Seo and Mendelsohn, 2008). When the regional climate system becomes riskier via an increased variability of precipitation across the years and months, Sub-Saharan African farmers have coped by adopting more frequently the diversified crop-livestock system of agriculture which outperforms specialized systems such as a crops-only system or a livestock-only system (Seo, 2012b). If the regional climate system were to become hotter and have larger rainfall, Latin American managers would shift from crop farming or livestock management to forest-based enterprises, for example, a crops-forests enterprise, a forests-only enterprise (Seo, 2010b, 2012c, 2016d).

The implication of these and other adaptation decisions is massive in the economics and policy literature of global climate change, many of which will be elucidated in Chapter 7, The Economics of Globally Shared Goods, and more broadly of global-scale shared goods (Seo, 2015c, 2019a). The microbehavioral adaptation studies also point to the decisions and support programs that have been popular among the economists but are not efficient when it comes to a changing climate system and therefore have failed to accomplish intended outcomes (Byerlee and Eicher, 1997; World Bank, 2009).

The second component of the economics of globally shared goods is what I call foresighted decisions or economics of foresight. A foresighted decision is a decision made in consideration of an extraordinarily long time-horizon such as a century or half a century, more meaningfully, a time-horizon beyond one's lifetime. In this book the foresighted decisions are further refined to forward-looking decisions and prescient decisions. The two types of decisions are again microbehaviorally efficient.

Of the microbehaviorally efficient adaptation decisions described above, consider the crops-forest enterprise or the forest-only enterprise. If an individual resource manager plans his activities for a long time-horizon, she will see that the forest-based enterprises are welfare maximizing choices because of increasing carbon concentration in the atmosphere as well as higher rainfall from a changing climate system, both of which help growth of forests and nontimber forest products (Seo, 2010b, 2015a). Further the forests sink carbon dioxide from the atmosphere for photosynthesis (Ainsworth and Long, 2005). The forest carbon dioxide sink not only helps the manager to receive carbon dioxide offset credits but also aids the international climate change mitigation efforts (EC, 2018; CARB, 2019). Therefore it is a forward-looking decision for the manager.

On the contrary, again of the adaptation decisions described above, consider the mixed crops-livestock system of agriculture (Seo, 2010a, 2014). It is not a foresighted decision as long as it is a high methane-emitting system, another potent Earth-heating greenhouse gas (Schaefer et al., 2016). The methane emission will become costly in the future. Consider instead the mixed crops-livestock system with the methane capture technologies embedded (Hristov et al., 2015). An adoption of this low-methane system is a prescient decision because a needed technology installation for this system of agriculture is costly to the manager today. In other words, to take such a costly action today, s/he should be not only forward-looking but also prescient about the future climate change if she hopes to be rewarded sufficiently for such a costly action at some point in the future, put differently, if she hopes to justify the costly investment today from an efficiency standpoint.

The economics of foresight, thus described by forward-looking and prescient decisions, offers the possibility of absorptions (sinks) of GHG through economic activities by individuals and reductions in the releases of GHG by individual economic actors. This is a key link from the microbehavioral economics, presented by this book, to the traditional mitigation literature, both science and economics. The present author will explain in Chapter 7, The Economics of Globally Shared Goods, how large and meaningful quantitatively aforementioned foresighted decisions will be with reference to the emissions mitigation targets often cited in the policy literature such as the Intended Nationally Determined Contributions (INDC) and the emissions gap (UNFCCC, 2015; UNEP, 2017).

The third component of the novel economics of globally shared goods in greenhouse economics, which is a drastically different term, newly coined for this book, from the economics of GHG which is often used equivalently to the economics of global warming. The greenhouse economics rather refers to the incentives and developments by an individual actor of a technology that controls the climate system for the financial benefit of the individual inventor. The term was coined by the present author reflecting on the fact that a greenhouse is one of the primitive climate control technologies developed by humanity for the economic benefits, whose origin may go back to the 15th century in East Asia and further to the Roman empire (GLASE, 2019). During the latter half of the 20th century, a greenhouse with the capacity of carbon dioxide enrichment for plant growth was built (Wittwer and Robb, 1964).

In the literature of the global climate system some of the greenhouse technologies are referred to as a backstop technology and sometimes a silver-bullet technology. Widely discussed as a backstop technology are a direct air carbon capture and sequestration, a nuclear fusion energy technology, and reflecting Sunlight to cool Earth (NRC, 2015a,b). The last of these technologies is more formally referred to as an Albedo Modification (AM) technology. The AM may be accomplished either through the creation of a stratospheric aerosol layer or marine cloud brightening (Budyko, 1974; Twomey, 1974). The former is achieved through tens of millions of aerosol-forming gases introduced into the stratosphere to form a layer which reflects Sunlight. The latter is achieved through adding additional aerosols into the marine clouds to act as cloud condensation nuclei which then reflect Sunlight. You can imagine the two techniques as a mirror that reflects the Sunlight.

Some technologies, although perhaps as powerful as the above technologies, are less frequently discussed by the experts, for example, an ocean iron fertilization technique, owing to higher risks than other technologies (Martin et al., 1994). Other technologies provide a powerful remedy but only a partial solution to the problem of global warming, for example, solar energy, new lighting methods.

These silver-bullet technologies are already an effective technology and deployed at a local level, with an exception of a nuclear fusion technology which is still at an experimental stage (ITER, 2015). However, even for the nuclear energy, a nuclear fission is a proven technology which has been increasingly adopted across the globe, with novel solutions to a nuclear waste storage issue employed. Considering the feasibilities, the key variable that determines actual deployments of these technologies, either at a local scale or at a global scale, is the relative costs of deploying these technologies (Nordhaus, 2008).

The costs of the above-described technologies are varied, which means that some of them will be adopted earlier than the others. One way to compare the costs of deploying these technologies is the Levelized Cost of Electricity (LCOE). The LCOE is the lifetime cost divided by total energy production of a power plant. According to the US Energy Information Agency (EIA), the LCOE for an advanced nuclear power plant is estimated to be US\$ 95.2/Mwh of electricity generated which is higher than the LCOE from a conventional coal-fired power plant (95.1 US\$/Mwh) or the LCOE from a conventional natural gas-fired power plant (75.2 US\$/Mwh). The LCOE of nuclear energy is, however, far lower than the LCOEs from a host of renewable energy generation technologies: for example, solar PV (125 US\$/Mwh), offshore wind (196 US\$/Mwh). An exception is a hydroelectric power plant (84 US\$/Mwh) (USEIA, 2015). The LCOE estimates offer a guidance on which technology should be adopted earlier than others.

The LCOEs of these technologies can be also compared with those from advanced fossil fuel-fired power plants with the carbon capture and storage (CCS) capacity. The coal-fired power plant with an advanced and CCS technology has the LCOE of 144 US\$/Mwh while the natural gas-fired power plant with an advanced and CCS technology has the LCOE of 100 US\$/Mwh (USEIA, 2015).

In the greenhouse economics, the society will adopt one technology and then another considering the relative costs of adopting these technologies, such as the

LCOEs, against the costs of producing electricity from fossil fuels and the costs of abating carbon dioxide at the present time. Gauging the above cost estimates and others in the literature, the nuclear fission energy may first be adopted, then one of the sunlight reflection technologies, then fossil fuel-fired power generations with a CCS facility installed (Al-Juaied and Whitmore, 2009). If the risk of the sunlight reflection technology is deemed too high for the global community, the third option may precede the second option. The direct air capture and sequester technology may come next in greenhouse technology adoptions, the cost of which is estimated to be in the range of US$380–600 per ton of carbon dioxide removal according to multiple optimization model assessments (APS, 2011; Mazzotti et al., 2013). The last option may be a nuclear fusion energy technology if the ongoing experiments such as the ITER project should turn out to be successful.

It can be said that the adoptions and transitions to these technological remedies are all incorporated in the current economics of global warming, albeit implicitly (Nordhaus, 2013). In the global warming economic optimization models, technological changes are accounted for by changes in carbon intensity of the economy and changes in the total factor productivity (TFP). What distinguishes the greenhouse economics expounded in this book from the current economics and models is its revelation of the incentives of an individual manger/inventor to develop and adopt a "greenhouse" technology for its economic benefits, that is, the climate-control or carbon-capture technologies.

The carbon capture for the purpose of enhancing growth of plants may be already in wide use across the world (Wittwer and Robb, 1964; GLASE, 2019). In addition, many countries may already be employing different climate control technologies to combat weather-climate-related disasters, for example, a technology for mitigating heat stress, a technology for increasing local rainfall for economic purposes, a technology for cleaning up the air temporarily. A deployment of these technologies is certainly in the country' interests (SCMP, 2018). For these technologies, the aforementioned silver-bullet technologies, that is, a stratospheric aerosol layer and a marine cloud brightening, are a basis technique. It is not difficult to imagine that the direct air capture and sequester technology would be a big interest to an investor or a country's policy-makers, so would be the nuclear fusion technology.

The economic theory of globally shared goods is extended in Chapter 8, Extensions of the Economic Theory to a Basket of Globally Shared Goods, to provide a fresh explanation of the four global-scale challenges: a global defense against an asteroid collision, nuclear nonproliferation and disarmaments, a strangelet catastrophe from the Large Hadron Collider (LHC) experiments, and artificial intelligence (AI). Specifically, each of these globally shared challenges is reanalyzed by the present author from the three elements of the EGSG: microbehaviorally efficient decisions, economics of foresight, and greenhouse economics.

The analyses in Chapter 8, Extensions of the Economic Theory to a Basket of Globally Shared Goods, will reveal that the four problems are different from each other in their characteristics as a globally shared problem. To mention a few, a solution to an asteroid collision calls for a single effective "shot" while a solution to global warming calls for a large portfolio of strategies and cumulative actions (Chapman and Morrison, 1994). By contrast, a successful nuclear nonproliferation and disarmaments may hinge on a few notable defectors in the negotiations (Campbell et al., 2004). The strangelet hypothesis from the high risk scientific experiment is given an extremely low probability by the scientific community while the artificial intelligence singularity is given a high chance of realization in the "near" future, both of which nonetheless will fundamentally change the ways of human life, perhaps catastrophically (Ellis et al., 2008; Hawking et al., 2014).

Readers will find that one of the three elements of the EGSG turns out to be a pivotal idea than the other elements in addressing each of these challenges. A forward-looking decision, for instance, is critical in nuclear disarmaments while a scientific/technological assessment is critical in the solution to the hypothesized strangelet catastrophe. The chapter will highlight that the EGSG offers a unique, although not completely different, perspective on addressing these global-scale challenges different from the existing basket of policy approaches and solutions. To note one of such, a microbehavioral incentive for nuclear energy, although by and large set aside in nuclear disarmament negotiations, is emphasized in the EGSG framework.

1.7 Structure of the book

The book is structured into four parts. Chapter 1, An Introduction to the Challenges of Public and Globally Shared Goods in Economics and Policy-Making, gives an introduction to the book, which forms Part I of the book (Table 1.1). Part II is the presentation of the theories of the economics of public goods and of global public goods. Part II covers Chapter 2, The Economics of Public Goods and Club Goods, and Chapter 3, The Economics of Global-Scale Public Goods: Key Challenges and Theories. Chapter 2, The Economics of Public Goods and Club Goods, provides an in-depth explanation of the economics of public goods while Chapter 3, The Economics of Global-Scale Public Goods: Key Challenges and Theories, provides a review of the economic issues in the global public good problems.

Part III of the book covers Chapters 4–6, whose goal is to provide a critique of the economic theories of public goods and global public goods reviewed in Part II. Chapter 4, A Critique of the Economics of Global Public Goods: A Microbehavioral Theory and Model, gives an in-depth explanation of the theory of microbehavioral economics and its relevance to the economics of global public goods is demonstrated through empirical results from the microbehavioral modeling studies.

Chapter 5, A Critique of the Economics of Global Public Goods: Economics of Noncooperative Games, offers a critique from the perspective of a noncooperation incentive among the countries in negotiating a global public good policy. The assumption of a global deal on global warming policy would make it possible to adopt a globally harmonized carbon tax as a policy instrument. The chapter

Table 1.1 Structure of the book.

Parts	Part contents	Chapters	Chapter titles
I	Introduction	1	An Introduction to the Challenges of Public and Globally Shared Goods in Economics and Policy-Making
II	Current economics of public goods and global public goods	2	The Economics of Public Goods and Club Goods
		3	The Economics of Global-Scale Public Goods: Key Challenges and Theories
III	Critiques of the current economics	4	A Critique of the Economics of Global Public Goods: A Microbehavioral Theory and Model
		5	A critique of the economics of global public goods: economics of noncooperative games
		6	A Critique of the Economics of Global Public Goods: The Economics of a Global Public Good Fund
IV	A novel economics of globally shared goods	7	The Economics of Globally Shared Goods
		8	Extensions of the Economic Theory to a Basket of Globally Shared Goods

examines the disparate impacts of a global carbon tax on the countries and shows that a global deal may not be accomplished.

Chapter 6, A Critique of the Economics of Global Public Goods: The Economics of a Global Public Good Fund, provides a critique of a global public good fund through an analysis of the GCF set up by the United Nations. The chapter examines the investment decisions by the GCF Board with regard to 111 funded projects as well as the potential impacts of the GCF funding on the provision of a global public good.

Part IV of the book, comprising Chapter 7, The Economics of Globally Shared Goods, and Chapter 8, Extensions of the Economic Theory to a Basket of Globally Shared Goods, elucidates the economics of globally shared goods advanced in this book by the present author. Chapter 7, The Economics of Globally Shared Goods, describes the fundamental economic theory and Chapter 8, Extensions of the Economic Theory to a Basket of Globally Shared Goods, provides an extension of the theory to a family of globally shared challenges as described above.

With this, I feel this has been a sufficient introduction to the book and you are well prepared for a fascinating journey. Bon Voyage!

References

Adams, R., Rosenzweig, C., Peart, R.M., Ritchie, J.T., McCarl, B.A., Glyer, J.D., et al., 1990. Global climate change and US agriculture. Nature 345, 219−224.

Ainsworth, E.A., Long, S.P., 2005. What have we learned from 15 years of free-air CO_2 enrichment (FACE)? A meta analysis of the responses of photosynthesis, canopy properties and plant production to rising CO_2. N. Phytologist 165, 351−372.

Al-Juaied, M., Whitmore, A., 2009. Realistic Costs of Carbon Capture. Discussion Paper 2008-09. Energy Technology Innovation Research Group, Belfer Center for Science and International Affairs. Harvard Kennedy School, Cambridge, MA.

American Physical Society (APS), 2011. Direct Air Capture of CO_2 with Chemicals: A Technology Assessment for the APS Panel on Public Affairs. APS, College Park, MD.

Arrhenius, S.A., 1889. Über die Dissociationswärme und den Einfluß der Temperatur auf den Dissociationsgrad der Elektrolyte. Z. Phys. Chem. 4, 96−116.

Arrow, K.J., Cline, W., Maler, K.G., Munasinghe, M., Squitieri, R., Stiglitz, J., 1996a. Intertemporal equity, discounting, and economic efficiency. In: Bruce, J.P., Lee, H., Haites, E.F. (Eds.), Climate Change 1995: Economic and Social Dimensions of Climate Change, Intergovernmental Panel on Climate Change. Cambridge University Press, New York.

Arrow, K.J., Cropper, M.L., Eads, G.C., Hahn, R.W., Lave, L.B., Noll, R.G., et al., 1996b. Is there a role for benefit-cost analysis in environmental, health, and safety regulation? Science 272, 221−222.

Bakkensen, L.A., Mendelsohn, R., 2016. Risk and adaptation: evidence from global hurricane damages and fatalities. J. Assoc. Environ. Resour. Econ. 3, 555−587.

Banerjee, A.V., Duflo, E., 2019. Good Economics for Hard Times: Better Answers to Our Biggest Problems. PublicAffairs Books, New York.

Barrett, S., 1994. Self-enforcing international environmental agreements. Oxf. Economic Pap. 46, 878−894.

Barrett, S., 2003. Environment and Statecraft: The Strategy of Environmental Treaty. Oxford University Press, Oxford.

Baumol, W.J., Oates, W.E., 1971. The use of standards and prices for protection of the environment. Swed. J. Econ. 73, 42−54.

Baumol, W.J., Oates, O.A., 1975. The Theory of Environmental Policy. Prentice Hall, Upper Saddle River, NJ.

Bowen, H.R., 1943. The interpretation of voting in the allocation of economic resources. Q. J. Econ. 58 (1), 27−48.

Brown, K.M., 1973. Welfare implications of congestion in public goods. Rev. Soc. Economy 31, 89−92.

Buchanan, J.M., 1965. An economy theory of clubs. Economica 32, 1−24.

Buchanan, J.M., 1968. The Demand and Supply of Public Goods. Rand McNally & Co., Chicago, IL.

Budyko, M.I., 1974. Climate and Life. Academic Press, New York.

Byerlee, D., Eicher, C.K., 1997. Africa's Emerging Maize Revolution. Lynne Rienner Publishers Inc., Boulder, CO.

California Air Resources Board (CARB), 2019. Assembly Bill (AB) Compliance Offset Program. ARB, Sacramento, CA. Available from: https://ww3.arb.ca.gov/cc/capand-trade/offsets/offsets.htm.

Campbell, K.M., Einhorn, R.J., Reiss, M.B. (Eds.), 2004. The Nuclear Tipping Point: Why States Reconsider their Nuclear Choices. Brookings Institution Press, Washington, DC.

Carraro, C., Eyckmans, J., Finus, N., 2006. Optimal transfers and participation decisions in international environmental agreements. Rev. Int. Organ. 1, 379–396.

Center for Near Earth Object Studies (CNEOS), 2019. Discovery Statistics. CNEOS, NASA, Washington, DC.

CERN (European Organization for Nuclear Research), 2017. The Accelerator Complex. CERN, Geneva, Switzerland, Accessed from: < https://home.cern/about/accelerators > .

Chapman, C.R., Morrison, D., 1994. Impacts on the Earth by asteroids and comets: assessing the hazard. Nature 367, 33–40.

Clarke, E., 1971. Multipart pricing of public goods. Public. Choice 11 (1), 17–33.

Coase, R., 1960. The problem of social costs. J. Law Econ. 3, 1–44.

Columbia Broadcasting System (CBS), 2016. Obama calls Paris agreement "a turning point for our planet". Published on October 15, 2016. Accessed from: <https://www.cbsnews.com/news/obamacalls-paris-agreement-a-turning-point-for-our-planet/>.

DW, 2019. Greta Thunberg to UN: 'You've Stolen my Childhood with Your Empty Words'. DW, published on September 23, 2019. Accessed from: <https://www.dw.com/en/greta-thunberg-to-un-youve-stolen-my-childhood-with-your-empty-words/a-50550787>.

Economic Times of India, 2015. Green Climate Fund of $100 Billion/Year not Enough to Tackle Climate Change: India. Published on July 14, 2015. Accessed from: <https://economictimes.indiatimes.com/news/politics-and-nation/green-climate-fund-of-100-billion/year-not-enoughto-tackle-climate-change-india/articleshow/48070235.cms>.

Ellerman, A.D., Buchner, B.K., 2007. The European Union Emissions Trading Scheme: origins, allocations, and early results. Rev. Environ. Econ. Policy 1, 66–87.

Ellis, J., Giudice, G., Mangano, M., Tkachev, I., Wiedemann, U., 2008. Review of the safety of LHC collisions. J. Phys. G: Nucl. Part. Phys. 35 (11). Available from: https://doi.org/10.1088/0954-3899/35/11/115004.

European Commission (EC), 2018. EU ETS Handbook. European Commission, Brussels.

Fisher, I., 1930. The Theory of Interest. Macmillan, New York.

Freeman III, A.M., Herriges, J.A., Cling, C.L., 2014. The Measurements of Environmental and Resource Values: Theory and Practice. RFF Press, New York.

Friedman, M., 1962. Capitalism and Freedom. The University of Chicago Press, Chicago, IL.

Gore, A., 2006. An Inconvenient Truth: The Planetary Emergency of Global Warming and What We Can Do About It. Rodale Books, Emmaus, PA.

Green Climate Fund (GCF), 2011. Governing Instrument for the Green Climate Fund. GCF, Songdo City, South Korea.

Green Climate Fund (GCF), 2019a. Annex III: Investment Framework. GCF, Songdo City, South Korea.

Green Climate Fund (GCF), 2019c. Projects + Programmes. GCF, Songdo City, South Korea, Accessed from: <https://www.greenclimate.fund/what-we-do/projects-programmes>.

Greenhouse Lighting & Systems Engineering (GLASE), 2019. Growing the World's Food in Greenhouses. The GLASE, Cornell University, Ithaca, NY.

Greenstone, M., Gallagher, J., 2008. Does hazardous waste matter? Evidence from the housing market and the Superfund program. Q. J. Econ. 123, 951–1003.

Groves, T., 1973. Incentives in teams. Econometrica 41 (4), 617–631.

Hahn, R.W., Dudley, P.M., 2007. How well does the U.S. government do benefit-cost analysis? Rev. Environ. Econ. Policy 1, 192–211.

Hanemann, W.M., 1994. Valuing the environment through contingent valuation. J. Economic Perspect. 8, 19−43.

Hansen, J., Johnson, D., Lacis, A., Lebedeff, S., Lee, P., Rind, D., et al., 1981. Climate impact of increasing atmospheric carbon dioxide, Science, 213. pp. 957−966.

Hartwick, J.M., Olewiler, N.D., 1997. The Economics of Natural Resource Use, second ed. Pearson, New York.

Hayek, F.A., 1948. Individualism and Economic Order. The University of Chicago Press, Chicago, IL.

Hawking, S., Tegmark, M., Russell, S., Wilczek, F., 2014. Transcending Complacency on Superintelligent Machines. Huffington Post. Accessed from https://www.huffingtonpost. com/stephen-hawking/artificial-intelligence_b_5174265.html.

Hirshleifer, J., 1983. From weakest-link to best-shot: the voluntary provision of public goods. Public. Choice 41, 371−386.

Hristov, A.N., Joonpyo, O.H., Fabio Giallongo, F., Tyler, W., Frederick, T.W., Michael, T., et al., 2015. An inhibitor persistently decreased enteric methane emission from dairy cows with no negative effect on milk production. Proc. Natl Acad. Sci. U S Am. 112 (34), 10663−10668.

Intergovernmental Panel on Climate Change (IPCC), 1990. Climate Change: The IPCC Scientific Assessment. Cambridge University Press, Cambridge.

Intergovernmental Panel on Climate Change (IPCC), 2014. Climate Change 2014: The Physical Science Basis, The Fifth Assessment Report of the IPCC. Cambridge University Press, Cambridge.

International Thermonuclear Experimental Reactor (ITER), 2015. ITER: The World's Largest Tokamak. Available at: <https://www.iter.org/mach>.

Jaffe, R.L., Buszaa, W., Sandweiss, J., Wilczek, F., 2000. Review of speculative disaster scenarios at RHIC. Rev. Mod. Phys. 72, 1125−1140.

Kaiho, K., Oshima, N., 2017. Site of asteroid impact changed the history of life on earth: the low probability of mass extinction. Sci. Rep. 7, 14855. Available from: https://doi.org/ 10.1038/s41598-017.

Kaul, I., Conceicao, P., Goulven, K.L., Mendoza, R.U. (Eds.), 2003. Providing Global Public Goods: Managing Globalization. Oxford University Press, Oxford.

Keeling, C.D., Piper, S.C., Bacastow, R.B., Wahlen, M., Whorf, T.P., Heimann, M., et al., 2005. Atmospheric CO_2 and $^{13}CO_2$ exchange with the terrestrial biosphere and oceans from 1978 to 2000: observations and carbon cycle implications. In: Ehleringer, J.R., Cerling, T.E., Dearing, M.D. (Eds.), A History of Atmospheric CO_2 and Its Effects on Plants, Animals, and Ecosystems. SpringerVerlag, New York, pp. 83−113.

Kissinger, H., Perry, B., Shultz, G., Nunn, S., 2011. Nuclear Endgame: The Growing Appeal of Zero. Economist, London.

Kurzweil, R., 2005. The singularity is near. Penguin, New York.

Laibson, D., 1997. Golden eggs and hyperbolic discounting. Q. J. Econ. 112 (2), 443−477.

Le Treut, H., Somerville, R., Cubasch, U., Ding, Y., Mauritzen, C., Mokssit, A., et al., 2007. Historical overview of climate change. In: Solomon, S., Qin, D., Manning, M., Chen, Z., Marquis, M., Averyt, K.B., Tignor, M., Miller, H.L. (Eds.), Climate Change 2007: The Physical Science Basis. Contribution of Working Group I to the Fourth Assessment Report of the Intergovernmental Panel on Climate Change. Cambridge University Press, Cambridge.

Likens, G.E., Bormann, F.H., 1974. Acid rain: a serious regional environmental problem. Science 184, 1176−1179.

Lorenz, E.N., 1963. Deterministic nonperiodic flow. J. Atmos. Sci. 20, 130–141.

Manne, A.S., Richels, R.G., 1999. The Kyoto Protocol: a cost-effective strategy for meeting environmental objectives? Energy J. 20 (Special Issue), 1–23.

Manne, A.S., Mendelsohn, R., Richels, R.G., 1995. MERGE: a model for evaluating regional and global effects of GHG reduction policies. Energy Policy 23, 17–34.

Martin, J.H., Coale, K.H., Johnson, K.S., Fitzwater, S.E., et al., 1994. Testing the iron hypothesis in ecosystems of the equatorial Pacific Ocean. Nature 371, 123–129.

Mas-Colell, A., Whinston, M.D., Green, J.R., 1995. Microeconomic Theory. Oxford University Press, Oxford.

Mazzotti, M., Baciocchi, R., Desmond, M.J., Socolow, R.H., 2013. Direct air capture of CO_2 with chemicals: optimization of a two-loop hydroxide carbonate system using a counter-current air-liquid contactor. Climatic Change 118 (1), 119–135.

Mendelsohn, R., 1980. An economic analysis of air pollution from coal-fired power plants. J. Environ. Econ. Manag. 7, 30–43.

Mendelsohn, R., 2000. Efficient adaptation to climate change. Clim. Change 45:583–600.

Mendelsohn, R., Nordhaus, W., Shaw, D., 1994. The impact of global warming on agriculture: a Ricardian analysis. Am. Economic Rev. 84, 753–771.

Mendelsohn, R., Olmstead, S., 2009. The economic valuation of environmental amenities and disamenities: methods and applications. Annu. Rev. Resour. 34, 325–347.

Mills, M.J., Toon, O.B., Turco, R.P., Kinnison, D.E., Garcia, R.R., 2008. Massive global ozone loss predicted following regional nuclear conflict. Proceedings of the National Academy of Sciences of the United States of America 105, 5307–5312.

Montgomery, W.D., 1972. Markets in licenses and efficient pollution control programs. J. Economic Theory 5, 395–418.

Muller, N.Z., Mendelsohn, R., 2009. Efficient pollution regulation: getting the prices right. Am. Economic Rev. 99, 1714–1739.

Muller, N.Z., Mendelsohn, R., Nordhaus, W., 2011. Environmental accounting for pollution in the United States economy. Am. Economic Rev. 101, 1649–1675.

Musgrave, R., 1939. The voluntary exchange theory of public economy. Q. J. Econ. 53, 213–237.

Musgrave, R., 1959. The Theory of Public Finance. McGraw-Hill, New York.

Nash, J., 1950. Equilibrium points in n-person games. Proc. Natl Acad. Sci. 36 (1), 48–49.

National Research Council, 2010. Defending Planet Earth: Near-Earth-object Surveys and Hazard Mitigation Strategies. National Academies Press, Washington, DC.

National Research Council (NRC), 2015a. Climate Intervention: Reflecting Sunlight to Cool Earth. Committee on Geoengineering Climate: Technical Evaluation and Discussion of Impacts. The National Academies Press, Washington, DC.

National Research Council (NRC), 2015b. Climate Intervention: Carbon Dioxide Removal and Reliable Sequestration. The National Academies Press, Washington, DC.

National Research Council (NRC), 2017. Valuing Climate Damages: Updating Estimation of the Social Cost Of Carbon Dioxide. The National Academies Press, Washington, DC.

New York Times (NYT), 2009. An Air of Frustration for Europe at Climate Talks. Published on December 21, 2009. NYT, New York.

Nobel Prize, 2007. The Nobel Peace Prize for 2007: The Intergovernmental Panel on Climate Change (IPCC) & Albert (Al) Arnold Gore Jr. Accessed from <NobelPrize.org>.

Nobel Prize, 2018. The Prize in Economic Sciences 2018: William D. Nordhaus & Paul M. Romer. Accessed from: <NobelPrize.org>.

Nordhaus, W., 1982. How fast should we graze the global commons? Am. Economic Rev. 72, 242–246.

Nordhaus, W., 1991. To slow or not to slow: the economics of the greenhouse effects. Economic J. 101, 920–937.

Nordhaus, W., 1992. An optimal transition path for controlling greenhouse gases. Science 258, 1315–1319.

Nordhaus, W., 1994. Managing the Global Commons. MIT Press, Massachusetts.

Nordhaus, W.D., 2006. Paul Samuelson and global public goods. In: Szenberg, M., Ramrattan. L., Gottesman. A.A. (Eds.), Samuelsonian Economics and the Twenty-First Century. Oxford Scholarship Online.

Nordhaus, W.D., 2008. A Question Of Balance-Weighing The Options On Global Warming Policies. Yale University Press, New Haven, CT.

Nordhaus, W., 2010. Economic aspects of global warming in a post-Copenhagen environment. Proc. Natl Acad. Sci. U. S. A. 107 (26), 11721–11726.

Nordhaus, W., 2011. The economics of tail events with an application to climate change. Rev. Environ. Econ. Policy 5, 240–257.

Nordhaus, W., 2013. The Climate Casino: Risk, Uncertainty, and Economics for a Warming World. Yale University Press, New Haven, CT.

Nordhaus, W., 2015. Climate clubs: overcoming free-riding in international climate policy. Am. Econ. Rev. 105 (4), 1339–1370.

Nordhaus, W.D., 2017. Revisiting the social cost of carbon. Proc. Natl Acad. Sci. U. S. A. 114, 1518–1523.

Nordhaus, W.D., Tobin, J., 1972. Is Growth Obsolete? National Bureau of Economic Research, Cambrdige, MA.

Nordhaus, W.D., Boyer, J.G., 1999. Requiem for Kyoto: an economic analysis of the Kyoto Protocol. Energy J. 20 (Special Issue), 93–130.

Nordhaus, W., Yang, Z., 1996. A regional dynamic general-equilibrium model of alternative climate change strategies. Am. Economic Rev. 86, 741–765.

Posner, R.A., 2004. Catastrophe: Risk and Response. Oxford University Press, New York.

Revelle, R., Suess, H.E., 1957. Carbon dioxide exchange between atmosphere and ocean and the question of an increase of atmospheric CO_2 during the past decades. Tellus 9, 18–27.

Ricardo, D., 1817. On the Principles Of Political Economy and Taxation. John Murray, London.

Romer, P., 1990. Endogenous technical change. J. Political Economy 98, S71–S102.

Rosen, S., 1974. Hedonic prices and implicit markets: product differentiation in pure competition. J. Political Economy 82, 34–55.

Rosenzweig, C., Parry, M., 1994. Potential impact of climate change on world food supply. Nature 367, 133–138.

Sachs, J., 2005. The End of Poverty: Economic Possibilities of Our Time. Penguin Press, London.

Samuelson, P., 1954. The pure theory of public expenditure. Rev. Econ. Stat. 36, 387–389.

Samuelson, P., 1955. Diagrammatic exposition of a theory of public expenditure. Rev. Econ. Stat. 37, 350–356.

Samuelson, P., Nordhaus, W., 2009. Economics, nineteenth ed. McGraw-Hill Education, New York.

Sandler, T., 1997. Global Challenges: An Approach to Environmental, Political, and Economic Problems. Cambridge University Press, Cambridge.

Schaefer, H., Fletcher, S.E.M., Veidt, C., et al., 2016. A 21st century shift from fossil-fuel to biogenic methane emissions indicated by $^{13}CH_4$. Science 352, 80–84.

Schelling, T.C., 1966. Arms and Influence. Yale University Press, New Haven, CT.

Schelling, T.C., 1991. Greenhouse Effect, Presidential Address at 103 Annual Meeting. American Economic Association, Washington, DC.

Schlenker, W., Roberts, M., 2009. Nonlinear temperature effects indicate severe damages to crop yields under climate change. Proc. Natl Acad. Sci. U. S. A. 106 (37), 15594–15598.

Schmalensee, R., Stavins, R.N., 2013. The SO_2 allowance trading system: the ironic history of a grand policy experiment. J. Econ. Perspect. 27, 103–122.

Selten, R., 1965. Spieltheoretische Behandlung eines Oligopolmodells mit Nachfragetragheit. Z. für Gesamte Staatsivissenschaft 121, 301–324.

Seo, S.N., 2006. Modeling Farmer Responses to Climate Change: Climate Change Impacts and Adaptations in Livestock Management in Africa (Ph.D. dissertation). Yale University, New Haven, CT.

Seo, S.N., 2010a. A microeconometric analysis of adapting portfolios to climate change: adoption of agricultural systems in Latin America. Appl. Economic Perspect. Policy 32, 489–514.

Seo, S.N., 2010b. Managing forests, livestock, and crops under global warming: a microeconometric analysis of land use changes in Africa. Australian J. Agric. Resour. Econ. 54 (2), 239–258.

Seo, S.N., 2012a. What eludes global agreements on climate change? Economic Aff. 32, 73–79.

Seo, S.N., 2012b. Decision making under climate risks: an analysis of sub-Saharan farmers' adaptation behaviors. Weather, Clim. Soc. 4, 285–299.

Seo, S.N., 2012c. Adapting natural resource enterprises under global warming in South America: a mixed logit analysis. Economia: J. Lat. Am. Caribb. Economic Assoc. 12, 111–135.

Seo, S.N., 2014. Evaluation of agro-ecological zone methods for the study of climate change with micro farming decisions in sub-Saharan Africa. Eur. J. Agron. 52, 157–165.

Seo, S.N., 2015a. Adaptation to global warming as an optimal transition process to a greenhouse world. Economic Aff. 35, 272–284.

Seo, S.N., 2015b. Fatalities of neglect: adapt to more intense hurricanes? Int. J. Climatol. 35, 3505–3514.

Seo, S.N., 2015c. Helping low-latitude, poor countries with climate change. Regulation. Winter 2015–2016: 6–8.

Seo, S.N., 2016a. Microbehavioral Econometric Methods: Theories, Models, and Applications for the Study of Environmental and Natural Resources. Academic Press, Amsterdam.

Seo, S.N., 2016b. Modeling farmer adaptations to climate change in South America: a microbehavioral economic perspective. Environ. Ecol. Stat. 23, 1–21.

Seo, S.N., 2016c. A theory of global public goods and their provisions. J. Public. Aff. 16, 394–405.

Seo, S.N., 2016d. The micro-behavioral framework for estimating total damage of global warming on natural resource enterprises with full adaptations. J. Agr. Biol. Environ. Stat. 21, 328–347.

Seo, S.N., 2016e. Untold tales of goats in deadly Indian monsoons: adapt or rain-retreat under global warming? J. Extreme Events. Available from: https://doi.org/10.1142/S2345737616500019.

Seo, S.N., 2017a. The Behavioral Economics of Climate Change: Adaptation Behaviors, Global Public Goods, Breakthrough Technologies, and Policy-making. Academic Press (Elsevier), Amsterdam, The Netherlands.

Seo, S.N., 2017b. Measuring policy benefits of the cyclone shelter program in the North Indian Ocean: protection from intense winds or high storm surges? Clim. Change Econ. 8 (4), 1−18.

Seo, S.N., 2017c. Beyond the Paris Agreement: climate change policy negotiations and future directions. Regional Sci. Policy Pract. 9, 121−140.

Seo, S.N., 2018. Natural and Man-Made Catastrophes: Theories, Economics, and Policy Designs. Wiley-Blackwell, London.

Seo, S.N., 2019a. The Economics of Global Allocations of the Green Climate Fund: An Assessment From Four Scientific Traditions of Modeling Adaptation Strategies. Springer Nature, Switzerland.

Seo, S.N., 2019b. Economic questions on global warming during the Trump years. J. Public. Aff. 19, e1914. Available from: http://doi.org/10.1002/pa.1914.

Seo, S.N., 2019c. Will farmers fully adapt to monsoonal climate changes through technological developments? An analysis of rice and livestock production in Thailand. J. Agric. Sci. 157, 97−108.

Seo, S.N., Mendelsohn, R., 2008. Measuring impacts and adaptations to climate change: a structural Ricardian model of African livestock management. Agric. Econ. 38, 151−165.

Smith, A., 1776. In: Cannan, Edwin (Ed.), An Inquiry Into the Nature and Causes of the Wealth of Nations. University of Chicago Press, Chicago, IL.

Smith, V.K., Huang, J.-C., 1995. Can markets value air quality? A meta-analysis of hedonic property value models. J. Political Economy 103, 209−227.

Soft Bank Robotics, 2019. Pepper. Soft Bank, Tokyo, Accessed from https://www.softbank-robotics.com/emea/en/pepper.

South China Morning Post (SCMP), 2018. China Needs More Water. So It's Building a Rain-Making Network Three Times the Size of Spain. SCMP, Published on March 26, 2018.

Stavins, R., 1998. What can we learn from the grand policy experiment? Lessons from SO_2 allowance trading. J. Economic Perspect. 12, 69−88.

Stavins, R., 2007. A US Cap-and-Trade System to Address Global Climate Change. Hamilton Project Discussion Paper 2007−13. The Brookings Institution, Washington, DC.

Stern, N., 2007. The Economics of Climate Ehange: The Stern Review. Cambridge University Press, New York.

Thom, R., 1975. Structural Stability and Morphogenesis. Benjamin-Addison-Wesley, New York.

Tol, R.S.J., 2002. Estimates of the damage costs of climate change—part 1: benchmark estimates. Environ. Resour. Econ. 21, 47−73.

Toon, O.B., Bardeen, C.G., Robock, A., Xia, L., Kristensen, H., McKinzie, M., et al., 2019. Rapidly expanding nuclear arsenals in Pakistan and India portend regional and global catastrophe. Sci. Adv. 5 (10). Available from: https://doi.org/10.1126/sciadv.aay5478.

Turco, R.P., Toon, O.B., Ackerman, T.P., Pollack, J.B., Sagan, C., 1983. Nuclear winter: global consequences of multiple nuclear explosions. Science 222, 1283−1292.

Twomey, S., 1974. Pollution and the planetary albedo. Atmos. Environ. 8 (12), 1251−1256.

United Nations, 1972. Report of the United Nations Conference on Human Environment. Stockholm, Sweden.

United Nations Environment Programme, 2017. The Emissions Gap Report 2017: A UN Environment Synthesis Report. UNEP, Nairobi.

United Nations Framework Convention on Climate Change (UNFCCC), 1992. United Nations Framework Convention on Climate Change. New York.

United Nations Framework Convention on Climate Change (UNFCCC), 1997. Kyoto Protocol to the United Nations Framework Convention on Climate Change. UNFCCC, New York.

United Nations Framework Convention on Climate Change (UNFCCC), 2009. Copenhagen Accord. UNFCCC, New York.

United Nations Framework Convention on Climate Change (UNFCCC), 2015. The Paris Agreement. Conference Of the Parties (COP) 21. UNFCCC, New York.

United Nations Office for Disarmament Affairs (UNODA), 1996. The Comprehensive Nuclear-Test-Ban Treaty (CTBT). United Nations, New York.

United Nations Office for Disarmament Affairs (UNODA), 2019. Treaty on the Non-Proliferation of Nuclear Weapons. Available at: <http://www.un.org/disarmament/WMD/Nuclear/NPT.shtml>.

United States Energy Information Administration (US EIA), 2015. Annual Energy Outlook 2015. US EIA, Department of Energy, Washington, DC.

United States Environmental Protection Agency (US EPA), 1990. The Clean Air Act Amendments. US EPA, Washington, DC.

United States Environmental Protection Agency (US EPA), 2010. The 40th Anniversary of the Clean Air Act. US EPA, Washington, DC. Available at: <http://www.epa.gov/air-progm/oar/caa/40th.html>.

United States Environmental Protection Agency (US EPA), 2014. Carbon Pollution Emission Guidelines for Existing Stationary Sources: Electric Utility Generating Units. US EPA, Washington, DC.

Viscusi, W.K., 1979. Employment Hazards: An Investigation of Market Performance. Harvard University Press, Cambridge, MA.

Viscusi, W.K., Aldy, J.E., 2003. The value of a statistical life: a critical review of market estimates throughout the world. J. Risk Uncertain. 5, 5−76.

von Neumann, J., Morgenstern, O., 1947. Theory of Games and Economic Behavior, 2nd ed. Princeton University Press, Princeton, NJ.

von Thunen, J.H., 1826. Der Isolierte Staat in Beziehung auf Landwirtschaft und Nationalökonomie, Hamburg, Perthes. (English trans. by Wartenberg CM (1996) The Isolated State. Pergamon Press, Oxford).

Wagner, W., 1999. Black holes at Brookhaven? Letters to the Editors. Sci. Am. 281 (1), 8.

Weitzman, M.L., 1974. Prices versus quantities. Rev. Economic Stud. 41, 477−491.

Weitzman, M.L., 1998. Why the far-distant future should be discounted at its lowest possible rate. J. Environ. Econ. Manag. 36, 201−208.

Weitzman, M.L., 2009. On modeling and interpreting the economics of catastrophic climate change. Rev. Econ. Stat. 91, 1−19.

White House, 2013. The President's Climate Action Plan. Executive Office of the President. The White House, Washington, DC.

White House, 2017. Statement by President Trump on the Paris Climate Accord. White House, Washington, DC.

Wittwer, S.H., Robb, W.M., 1964. Carbon dioxide enrichment of greenhouse atmospheres for food crop production. Econ. Bot. 18, 34−56.

Woodruff, T.J., Parker, J.D., Schoendorf, K.C., 2006. Fine Particulate Matter (PM2.5) air pollution and selected causes of postneonatal infant mortality in California. Environ. Health Perspect. 114, 786–790.

World Bank, 2009. Awakening Africa's Sleeping Giant: Prospects for Commercial Agriculture in the Guinea Savannah Zone and Beyond. World Bank and FAO, Washington, DC.

World Meteorological Organization (WMO), 1985. Report of the International Conference on the Assessment of the Role of Carbon dioxide and of Other Greenhouse Gases in Climate Variations and Associated Impacts. Villach, Austria.

Yohe, G.W., Schlesinger, M.E., 1998. Sea level change: the expected economic cost of protection or abandonment in the United States. Climatic Change 38, 337–342.

Further reading

Green Climate Fund (GCF), 2019b. Status of Pledges and Contributions Made to the Green Climate Fund. GCF, Songdo City, South Korea.

The economics of public goods and club goods

2

2.1 The emergence of the term public goods

The term, a public good, had become a standard terminology in economics through the 1950s and 1960s. Nearly all modern economics textbooks adopt the term and devote at least a single chapter to explain the economics of public goods (Mas-Colell et al., 1995; Mankiw, 2014). The essential concepts of the economics of public goods are also pervasive in the chapters that are concerned with the roles of the public sector or the government.

The conceptualization of the concept of the public good as we know the term today first appeared in the Bowen's interpretation of voting (Bowen, 1943), Bowen referred to it as "social goods" but did not go further to derive the most critical economic implication of the public goods in the competitive market economy.

Contrasting social goods against individual goods, Bowen described the former as follows (Bowen, 1943):

> Social goods, on the other hand, are not divisible into units that can be the unique possession of individuals. Rather, they tend to become part of the general environment - available to all persons within that environment (e.g. education, protection against foreign enemies, beautification of the landscape, flood control). Consequently, these goods cannot easily be sold to individual consumers and the quantities available to different individuals cannot be adjusted according to their respective tastes. The amount of the good must be set by a single decision applicable jointly to all persons. Social goods, therefore, are subject to collective or political rather than individual demand.

Before Bowen, the concept of a public good was only implicit in the economic analysis. In the Musgrave's article entitled "The Voluntary Exchange Theory of Public Economy," neither a public good nor a social good appeared (Musgrave, 1939). His primary concern was a revenue-expenditure process of the public taxation (Musgrave, 1959).

Paul Samuelson's "The Pure Theory of Public Expenditures" was published in 1954 and can be credited to be the definitive work on the economics of public goods. In this article he relied on the term collective consumption goods and jointly consumed goods. The article was written in a Samuelson style, mathematical and only three pages long (Samuelson, 1954).

In the article published the following year in 1955 which was meant to be a heuristic explanation of the above pure theory article, he adds additional explanations,

The Economics of Globally Shared and Public Goods. DOI: https://doi.org/10.1016/B978-0-12-819658-8.00002-0

clarifications, and diagrams to explain the essential concepts and conclusions of the Pure Theory (Samuelson, 1955). The term "public goods" first appeared in this article. He distinguished two types of goods: private consumption goods and public consumption goods. He used the term public goods multiple times in the article against the term private goods.

A decade later, when James Buchanan wrote on the theory of clubs, he referred to the Samuelson's theory as "the theory of public goods," that is, instead of the theory of public expenditure, while crediting the Samuelson's papers to be fundamental (Buchanan, 1965).

Outside the economics profession, alternative terms are often more widely accepted. For example, sociologists and political scientists seem to prefer social goods to public goods. Among the socialists and Marxists, social capital is a standard terminology. It should be noted that neither the social good nor the social capital is the same concept as the public good as defined in this chapter.

2.2   Samuelson's pure theory

The mathematical model Samuelson put forward in 1954 still remains the fundamental economic model of public goods (Samuelson, 1954). Samuelson differentiated two types of goods in the economy (Samuelson, 1954): (1) n private consumption goods denoted by $(X_1, \ldots, X_n)$; (2) m public consumption goods denoted by $(X_{n+1}, \ldots, X_{n+m})$. For the private good denoted by X_j, the following condition holds in a competitive market economy, with i denoting an individual consumer:

$$X_j = \sum_{i=1}^{s} X_j^i. \tag{2.1}$$

Samuelson defined the public consumption good as the good that *all enjoy in common in the sense that each individual's consumption of such a good leads to no subtraction from any other individual's consumption of that good, so that simultaneously for each and every individual and each collective consumption good.* For such a good, an individual's consumption is the same as the market consumption:

$$X_{n+j} = X_{n+j}^i. \tag{2.2}$$

Samuelson assumes that an individual has a consistent set of ordinal preferences over his consumption of all goods which can be summarized by a regularly smooth and convex utility function $\mu^i = \mu^i(X_1^i, \ldots, X_{n+m}^i)$. A social welfare function is simply $U = U(\mu^1, \ldots, \mu^s)$ with $U_j > 0$.

The production side of the economy is expressed by a production-possibility schedule F:

$F(X_1,\ldots,X_{n+m})$ with $F_j > 0$. The marginal rate of transformation is F_j/F_n.

Using these assumptions, a "best state of the world" is described. The optimality conditions are expressed using the marginal rate of substitution and the marginal rate of transformation in the production

$$\frac{u_j^i}{u_r^i} = \frac{F_j}{F_r}, \quad \text{for } r, \ j = 1,\ldots,n. \tag{2.3}$$

$$\sum_{i=1}^{s} \frac{u_{n+j}^i}{u_r^i} = \frac{F_{n+j}}{F_r}, \quad \text{for } j = 1,\ldots,m; r = 1,\ldots,n. \tag{2.4}$$

$$\frac{U_i u_k^i}{U_q u_k^q} = 1, \quad \text{for } i,q = 1,\ldots,s; \ k = 1,\ldots,n. \tag{2.5}$$

Eqs. (2.3) and (2.5) are the equations of private consumption goods, for which competitive market prices exists, so the Eq. (2.3) can be rewritten with them:

$$\frac{u_j^i}{u_r^i} = \frac{P_j}{P_r} = \frac{F_j}{F_r}, \quad \text{for } r, \ j = 1,\ldots,n. \tag{2.3$'$}$$

The budget equation for each individual is as follows:

$$P_1 X_1^i + P_2 X_2^i + \ldots + P_n X_n^i = L^i \quad \forall \ i. \tag{2.3$''$}$$

Samuelson called Eq. (2.4) the pure theory of collective consumption goods, that is, public goods. He argued that no decentralized pricing system can determine optimal levels of the public goods in Eq. (2.4). This is because there is no market mechanism that guarantees the equality of the two sides in Eq. (2.4). In particular the equation involves the sum of marginal rate of substitution across all the individuals in the economy, that is, $\{i = 1, 2, \ldots, s\}$.

Samuelson, on the other hand, suggested that the solution to the set of equations in Eqs. (2.3)–(2.5) exists, and the only problem is how to find it. He put forward a "parametric decentralized bureaucrat" who reveals his preferences "by signaling" in response to price parameters, to questionnaires, or to other devices, whose preferences in turn can be used to infer the quantitative terms on the left-hand side of Eq. (2.4).

Notwithstanding, Samuelson concluded his seminal paper by emphasizing the "fundamental technical difference going to the heart of the whole problem of social economy" which has two aspects (Samuelson, 1954):

1. *By departing from his indoctrinated rules, any one person can hope to snatch some selfish benefit in a way not possible under the self-policing competitive pricing of private goods;*

2. *The "external economies" or "jointness of demand" intrinsic to the very concepts of collective goods and governmental activities make it impossible for the grand ensemble of optimizing equations to have that special pattern of zeros which makes laissez-faire competition even theoretically possible as an analogue computer.*

The first of the above statements points to an incentive for an individual to free ride when it comes to public goods. The second statement seems to be suggesting an impossibility of a laissez-faire solution to the public goods' economy owing to the intrinsic "external economies" or "jointness of demand." The external economies here seem to refer to the externalities of some economic activities (Pigou, 1920).

The free rider problem is at the essence of the societal problem of public goods: owing to the nonexcludability of individual consumptions, people will free ride and expect to enjoy the benefits of a public good once others pay the cost and provide the public good. If all individuals expect the same way, the consequence will be no provision of the public good in the free market economy. The free rider problem has emerged prominently in the past two decades in the global negotiations of a global climate change policy, becoming the primary obstacle for a global climate deal (Nordhaus, 2015; Seo, 2017a,b).

The term "free rider" did not appear in the Samuelson's two seminal papers, nor in the Friedman's book in 1962, to be discussed shortly (Friedman, 1962). The term was not used either in the Musgrave book in 1959 entitled *The Theory of Public Finance* (Musgrave, 1959). Buchanan described the free rider problem first in 1965 as follows in his theory of clubs (Buchanan, 1965), which became a prominent concept in his succeeding book on public goods (Buchanan, 1968):

> *This is not, of course, to suggest that property rights will, in practice, always be adjusted to allow for optimal exclusion. If they are not, the "free rider" problem arises. . . . If individuals think that exclusion will not be fully possible, that they can expect to secure benefits as free riders without really becoming full-fledged contributing members of the club, they may be reluctant to enter voluntarily into cost-sharing arrangements.*

2.3   Friedman's public sector versus private sector

The pure theory by Samuelson provides a justification of the role of the government to intervene in the provision of a public good or another. Milton Friedman, arguably the most influential economist of the 20th century who ardently espoused a free private enterprise exchange economy or competitive capitalism, offered a different analysis on the issue of the public goods by way of the comparisons between the private sector and the public sector.

According to the *New York Times* obituary of Paul Samuelson in December 2009, the two men met in 1933 at the University of Chicago when they were both students thereof. After both men winning the Nobel Prize in 1970 and 1976, respectively, they debated often in public forums, in testimony before Congressional Committees, and in columns and op-eds. The NYT article quoted the Samuelson's assessment about debating Friedman publicly (NYT, 2009):

> *If you looked at a transcript afterward, it might seem clear that you had won the debate on points. But somehow, with members of the audience, you always seemed to come off as elite, and Milton seemed to have won the day.*

The analysis by Friedman on the public versus private sector is well articulated in, for example, his widely popular book entitled *Capitalism and Freedom* first published in 1962, from which the present author will review shortly in this section the Friedman's views on the role of government in the capitalist economy (Friedman, 1962).

His influences on the academic and public debates on the topic of the public sector were not limited to his writings and speeches. Through the Chicago School of Economics, many influential thinkers were raised and brought in, who in turn produced not-a-few landmark researches on the issues related to the public sector. To name just one, it is often recounted how Chicago economists invited Ronald H. Coase to a dinner in Chicago whose attendees included Friedman. After the exhilarating debate that lasted 2 hours, *The Problem of Social Cost* was conceived and eventually published at the *Journal of Law & Economics* (NYT, 2013). In the article Coase laid out the so-called Coase Theorem which explains a mutually agreeable bargaining solution to the problems of external costs especially when the transaction cost among the parties is modest (Coase, 1960).

To Friedman, a free private enterprise exchange economy or competitive capitalism is the ultimate goal of the economic system, and the government role should be limited to the minimum actions possible. In his book, he also credited Friedrich A. Hayek and Ludwig von Mises for defending such an economic system (Hayek, 1948; Mises, 1949).

Friedman envisioned the three roles of the government in the capitalist economy. The first is the role of government as a rule-maker and umpire. The second is the government interventions on the grounds of technical monopoly and neighborhood effects. The third is the government interventions on the paternalist grounds.

Of the three grounds, the neighborhood effect is what is directly pertinent to the theory of public goods explicated by Samuelson. Friedman defines the problem of neighborhood effects as the "cases when actions of individuals have effects on other individuals for which it is not possible to charge or recompense them (Friedman, 1962)." This definition is not analogous to that of the public good by Bowen and Samuelson. What Friedman defines is the concept of externalities accepted commonly in the environmental economics literature attributed to Pigou (Pigou, 1920).

Along with highways and parks, Friedman offered in the book the following example of the neighborhood effects, an upstream polluter (Friedman, 1962):

An obvious example is the pollution of a stream. The man who pollutes a stream is
in effect forcing others to exchange good water for bad. These others might be
willing to make the exchange at a price. But it is not feasible for them, acting
individually, to avoid the exchange or to enforce appropriate compensation.

An upstream polluter is one of the typical cases of external costs explained by
Ronald H. Coase in the problem of social cost (Coase, 1960). Like Coase,
Friedman points to the possibility of a voluntary negotiation between the polluter
and downstream victims and also the difficulties of such negotiations and an eventual deal owing to the transaction cost, more specifically, the cost of coordination
of the victims.

However, Friedman argues that the existence of the neighborhood effects does
not automatically justify governmental interventions and, on the contrary, can be
the grounds for limiting government interventions. The following arguments by
Friedman will be a recurring point of contention throughout this book (Friedman,
1962):

Neighborhood effects cut both ways. They can be a reason for limiting the
activities of government as well as for expanding them. . . . . .It is hard to know
when neighborhood effects are sufficiently large to justify particular costs in
overcoming them and even harder to distribute the costs in an appropriate fashion.
Consequently when government engages in activities to overcome neighborhood
effects, it will in part introduce an additional set of neighborhood effects by failing
to charge or to compensate individuals properly. Whether the original or the new
neighbourhood effects are the more serious can only be judged by the facts of the
individual case, and even then, only very approximately.

Furthermore, the use of government to overcome neighborhood effects itself has an
extremely important neighborhood effect which is unrelated to the particular
occasion for government action. Every act of government intervention limits the
area of individual freedom directly and threatens the preservation of freedom
indirectly for reasons elaborated in the first chapter.

The Friedman's definition of the neighborhood effects is quite encompassing
although it is not exactly the same as the concept of the public good. Further his
two points in the above cited paragraphs are on point. First, he points out that not
all the cases of neighborhood effects call for a governmental intervention. Restated
in the modern environmental/public economics language, a governmental action
may fail to pass the test of a benefit—cost ratio. In particular, a governmental action
intended to correct a problem of neighborhood effects may result in an even bigger
problem of neighborhood effects. The second point raises the possibility of a governmental intervention for overcoming neighborhood effects to have unintended
consequences of limiting the area of individual freedom. This is a very broad statement by Milton Friedman. Broadly speaking environmental/public economists do
not accept this proposition. More specifically, for example, when environmental
economists calculate the cost of a governmental intervention program, they do not

quantitatively take into account the effect of the program on individual freedom (Mendelsohn and Olmstead, 2009; Freeman et al., 2014).

Notwithstanding, it is widely accepted by environmental/public economists that when there are more than one policy options, a more flexible policy option that affords more freedom of choices to the policy-affected individuals should be preferred because such a policy tends to reduce the cost of implementing the governmental program. For this reason, to note just one example, economists have preferred a price-based approach to a command-and-control approach in the pollution control programs (Baumol and Oates, 1988; Tietenberg and Lewis, 2014).

2.4 Club goods

Since the publication of the theory of public expenditures by Samuelson, economists gradually came to notice that there is a category of goods that are neither purely private goods nor purely public goods. Put differently a large family of goods fall upon the range between an extreme of purely private goods and the other extreme of purely public goods. Such goods were called club goods (Buchanan, 1965).

A private consumption good is rivalrous in consumption, that is, the consumption of one unit of the private good by an individual reduces the consumption of the private good by other individuals by one unit. For the purely public good, on the other hand, its consumption is nonrivalrous. More formally, let X be the amount of the public good supplied in the market and x_i be the amount of consumption by individual i. Then, nonrivalry in the consumption of the purely public good can be expressed as follows (Brown, 1973):

$$x_1 = x_2 = \cdots = x_n = X. \tag{2.6}$$

For the goods that do not fall into the extremes of either purely private goods or purely public goods, a partial rivalry, also a partial nonrivalry, exists in their consumptions. Let us consider a country club membership. The members of the club will enjoy all the benefits that the club offers. The consumption is nonrivalrous in the club to some degree. However, as the number of its members becomes larger beyond a certain size, the members will start to enjoy less than the full benefits that the club offers because of crowding by its members. In the club membership, the consumption becomes rivalrous as the club membership increases. The goods of this sort are called club goods (Buchanan, 1965).

In the club goods, the consumption of one unit of a club good by an individual member diminishes the consumption of the good by the other members of the club to some degree, although not exactly by one unit. With the same notations used in Eq. (2.6) and k being the crowding or congestion effect parameter which is assumed to be ≤ 1, the crowding or congestion effect of a club good is expressed as follows (Brown, 1973):

$$x_1 = x_2 = \cdots = x_n = k \cdot X. \tag{2.7}$$

The larger the number of the club members, the larger the congestion/crowding effects and the smaller the k. The smaller the number of the club members, the smaller the congestion/crowding effects and the larger the k, that is, the closer the k is to 1.

When k equals 1, in which case Eq. (2.7) reverts to Eq. (2.6), the good is a purely public good. When $k = \frac{1}{n}$, it is a purely private good which is equally shared among the members. The club goods, as per Buchanan, exist in the *Samuelson gap between the purely private good and the purely public good* (Buchanan, 1965).

The congestion effect can be understood from another classical example of a club good, that is, a public highway (Brown, 1973). The benefits of the public highway get diminished as the number of users of the highway at a point in time increases. A congestion in the road makes the public highway less effective and less enjoyable to the users of the highway. The larger the congestion in the highway, the lower the k in Eq. (2.7).

James M. Buchanan went further to develop a general theory of the goods on the entire private–public spectrum, which he referred to as the theory of clubs (Buchanan, 1965). The theory of clubs is the theory of consumption ownership-membership arrangements in which an optimal size of the club for a good and an optimal level of consumption are determined simultaneously.

Buchanan defined, for the utility function of an individual i, N_j to be the optimal size of the club for good j and X_j the amount of the good available to the club of which the individual is a member. Then the individual's utility function as follows:

$$U^i = U^i \left[\left(X_1^i, N_1^i \right), \left(X_2^i, N_2^i \right), \ldots, \left(X_{n+m}^i, X_{n+m}^i \right) \right]. \tag{2.8}$$

Of the $n + m$ goods, one is designated as a numeraire, X_r, which is simply money or the unit of exchange. Using the lower case u as partial derivatives, Buchanan defined the following quantities:

$$\frac{u_j^i}{u_r^i} \tag{2.9a}$$

$$\frac{u_{N_j}^i}{u_r^i} \tag{2.9b}$$

Eq. (2.9a) is the marginal rate of substitution in consumption of the two goods for the individual. Eq. (2.9b) is the marginal rate of substitution in consumption between the size of the sharing group and the numeraire. More specifically, this ratio represents the rate at which the individual is willing to give up or accept money in exchange for additional member of the club.

The cost of production that is faced by the individual is defined as follows:

$$F = F^i \left[\left(X_1^i, N_1^i \right), \left(X_2^i, N_2^i \right), \ldots, \left(X_{n+m}^i, X_{n+m}^i \right) \right]. \tag{2.10}$$

Buchanan derives the necessary conditions for Pareto optimality:

$$\frac{u_j^i}{u_r^i} = \frac{f_j^i}{f_r^i} \tag{2.11}$$

$$\frac{u_{N_j}^i}{u_r^i} = \frac{f_{N_j}^i}{f_r^i} \tag{2.12}$$

Eq. (2.11) states that the marginal rate of substitution in consumption between the two goods should be equal to the marginal rate of substitution in production or exchange between the same two goods. Eq. (2.12) states that the marginal rate of substitution in consumption between the size of group sharing in the use of X_j and the numeraire good must be equal to the marginal rate of substitution in production. To put differently Eq. (2.12) states that in the equilibrium, the club size is such that the marginal benefits that the individual receives from having an additional member is equal to the marginal costs that s/he incurs from adding a member.

Combining Eqs. (2.11) and (2.12), we get the following necessary conditions for optimality:

$$\frac{u_j^i}{f_j^i} = \frac{u_r^i}{f_r^i} = \frac{u_{N_j}^i}{f_{N_j}^i} \tag{2.13}$$

In the optimal solution, the individual will have available to the club the optimal quantity of X_j, and at the same time she will be sharing this quantity over the club whose size, N_j, is determined.

Buchanan went on to state that when Eq. (2.13) is satisfied, Samuelson's Eq. (2.4) for the purely public goods is necessarily satisfied, provided only that the collectivity, that is, jointness, is making neither profit nor loss on providing the marginal unit of the public good. That is,

$$\frac{f_{n+j}}{f_r} = \sum_{i=1}^{S} \frac{f_{n+j}^i}{f_r^i} \tag{2.14}$$

The theory of club goods by Buchanan is a generalized theory that encompasses the entire range of goods on the private–public ownership plane. This is accomplished by the introduction of the club size attached to each product, N_j. In the national public good, the optimal club size is the entire national population. In the purely private goods, the optimal club size is 1.

What Buchanan did is to generalize the Samuelson's theory of the public goods by integrating the theory of private goods and the theory of public goods. What Buchanan did not do, put differently, what the theory of club goods did not inform is how the society can provide the public goods, which was clarified neither by Paul Samuelson beyond the fundamental market failure in the provision of the public goods.

2.5 An efficient provision versus market provision of a public good

From this point on, the present author will delineate the historical developments of the theories on the provision of a public good, which was set forth by the seminal works of Samuelson, Buchanan, and others as explained in the previous sections. A particular attention shall be paid to the basket of policy options as well as past policy experiences.

Let us first begin by the description of an optimal provision of a public good to the society. For this, we need first to define the concept of optimality, for which there are more than one ways to do. The Pareto optimality or efficiency, developed by the 19th century Italian economist Vilfred Pareto, provides the most widely adopted and encompassing definition of optimality in resource allocations in the economy (Pareto, 1906). Another crucial concept is Nash equilibrium developed in the context of a game played among multiple agents (Nash, 1950, 1951).

At the scale of a national economy, or equivalently, a macro economy, the Pareto optimality is defined as a state in the allocations of resources in the economy in which it is impossible to make one member of the economy better off without making another member worse off. From an initial state of allocations of resources across the members of the economy, a reallocation which makes at least one member better off without making any other member worse off is called a Pareto improvement. A state of resource allocations is defined to be Pareto optimal or Pareto efficient if no further Pareto improvement can be made from the state (Mas-Colell et al., 1995).

Let us consider the following macro economy composed of one public good, L traded private goods, and I consumers. Let x denotes the quantity of the public good, and $\mu_i(x)$ denotes the utility of individual i from the consumption of the public good. The cost of supplying q units of the public good is denoted by $c(q)$.

A Pareto optimal allocation must maximize the aggregate welfare, as will be clarified shortly, which occurs at the level of the public good which solves the following optimization problem:

$$\underset{q}{Max} \sum_{i=1}^{I} \mu_i(x) - c(q). \tag{2.15}$$

Several aspects of Eq. (2.15) must be discerned before we proceed further. First, there are no subscripts for x and q because there is only one public good in the model which is also a purely public good (Buchanan, 1965). Second, the model takes a partial equilibrium form in that the quantity of the public good has no effects on the prices of the private goods. Third, each consumer's utility function is quasilinear with respect to the traded private goods, set as the numeraire in the model.

The functional forms of the utility function and the cost function in Eq. (2.15) must be determined to solve the problem in the equation but they can be reasonably bounded by a set of standard assumptions on preferences and production costs (Mas-Colell et al., 1995). More specifically, first, the utility function is assumed to be twice differentiable, with $\mu_i''(x) < 0$ at all $x \geq 0$, that is, a diminishing marginal utility from consumption. Second, the cost function is also assumed to be twice differentiable, with $c''(q) > 0$ at all $q \geq 0$, that is, an increasing marginal cost of production. Third, for a desirable public good whose production is costly, we take $\mu_i'(x) > 0$ at all $i \geq 0$ and $c'(q) > 0$.

This formulation can be modified to be applied to the case of a public bad whose reduction is costly with $\mu_i'(x) < 0$ at all $i \geq 0$ and $c'(q) < 0$. This can be easily grasped by the correspondence that if x (or q) is a public bad, then $-x$ (or $-q$) should be a public good. More concretely, if a ton of sulfur dioxide emissions is a public bad, then the abatement of a ton of sulfur dioxide emissions is a public good.

Under this standard setting, which can be of course relaxed in applied analyses, the necessary and sufficient first-order condition (FOC) for a Pareto optimal solution for Eq. (2.15) is as follows, which is the essential point made by Samuelson and also Buchanan (Samuelson, 1954; Buchanan, 1965):

$$\sum_{i=1}^{I} \mu_i'(q^*) \leq c'(q^*), \text{ with equality if } q^* > 0. \tag{2.16}$$

At an interior solution, that is, $q^* > 0$, the equality in the above equation should hold. The interior solution is interpreted as follows: at the optimal level of the public good, the sum of the individuals' marginal benefits from consumption of the publicly consumed good is equal to the marginal cost of providing the public good to the consumers.

This optimality FOC for the public good is contrasted with the Pareto optimality FOC for the private good. In the purely private good whose characteristics are rivalrous and excludable in consumption, the FOC for optimality is such that "each" individual's marginal benefit from consumption of the privately consumed good be equal to the marginal cost of providing the private good.

The Pareto optimality condition described succinctly by Eq. (2.16) is guaranteed only if there are no other externalities or public goods in the economy than the public good concerned in Eq. (2.15) (Goulder et al., 1997). In the presence of other externalities or public goods, the solution is considered the second-best policy. However, it is possible for a policy modeler to restore the first-best policy by constructing a policy framework that addresses provisions of multiple public goods.

As Samuelson and Buchanan proposed, the market fails to deliver the optimal level of the public good, q^*. What is then the market solution to the problem in Eq. (2.15)? To describe it, let us imagine that there is a market for the public good and each participant in the market decides how much of the public good ($x_i \geq 0$) s/he buys, taking the market price of the public good (p^M) for granted. The superscript M signifies a market solution or mechanism. On the supply side, let us imagine that there is a single profit-maximizing firm with the cost function $c(\cdot)$ taking the market price as given.

At a competitive equilibrium with the price of the public good p^M, an individual consumer purchases x_i^M unit of the public good, which maximizes her utility by solving the following optimization problem:

$$\underset{x_i \geq 0}{Max}\, \mu_i \left(x_i + \sum_{k \neq i} x_k^M \right) - p^M x_i. \tag{2.17}$$

What is behind the optimization formulation of Eq. (2.17) is that, in determining her optimal purchase, the individual is assumed to take as given the amount of the public good purchased by other individuals in the market, that is, $\sum_{k \neq i} x_k^M$. The necessary and sufficient FOC for Pareto optimality for the purchase of the public good by the individual is then (Dixit, 1990):

$$\mu'_i \left(x_i^M + \sum_{k \neq i} x_k^M \right) \leq p^M, \text{ with equality if } x_i^M > 0. \tag{2.18}$$

Notice that $x_i^M + \sum_{k \neq i} x_k^M = x^M$, which is the equilibrium level of the public good in the market. Substituting this equality into Eq. (2.18) yields, for each individual,

$$\mu'_i \left(x^M \right) \leq p^M, \text{ with equality if } x_i^M > 0. \tag{2.19}$$

On the other side, the firm's problem is to supply q^M that solves the following optimization problem:

$$\underset{q \geq 0}{Max}\, (p^M q - c(q)). \tag{2.20}$$

The necessary and sufficient FOC for an optimal solution for the firm is

$$p^M \leq c' \left(q^M \right), \text{ with equality if } q^M > 0. \tag{2.21}$$

At a competitive equilibrium in the market, the following should hold: $q^M = x^M$. The FOCs in Eqs. (2.19) and (2.21) can be combined to form a single optimality condition using an indicator function Λ_i:

$$\sum_i \Lambda_i [\mu'_i(q^M) - c'(q^M)] = 0,$$

where

$$\Lambda_i = 1 \text{ if } x_i > 0 \text{ and } \Lambda_i = 0 \text{ if } x_i = 0 \tag{2.22}$$

Recalling the standard economic assumptions that the marginal utility of consumption of the good is positive $[\mu'_i(\cdot) > 0]$, and the marginal cost of production of the good is positive $[c'(\cdot) > 0]$, the optimality condition in Eq. (2.22) states that as long as there is more than one consumer of the public good in the market and the Pareto optimal level of the public good is greater than no provision, the following should hold:

$$\sum_{i=1}^{I} \mu'_i(q^M) > c'(q^M). \tag{2.23}$$

Note the difference between Eq. (2.23) and the term inside the bracket in Eq. (2.22): the aggregate marginal utility in the former and the individual marginal utility in the latter. Upon comparing Eq. (2.16) for the Pareto optimal solution with Eq. (2.23) for the market solution, it can be concluded that as long as $q^* > 0$ and $I > 1$, the level of the public good provided in the market is too low. More specifically $q^M < q^*$. To refresh you, this conclusion follows from the shapes of the utility function and the cost function assumed in the beginning of this section, that is, the decreasing marginal utility of consumption and the increasing marginal cost of production.

This conclusion can be explained graphically. An optimal provision of the public good is depicted in Fig. 2.1 along with a market provision of the public good. A Pareto optimal provision of the public good is determined by the intersection of the marginal cost curve and the aggregate marginal utility (benefit) curve at q^*. The aggregate marginal benefit curve is constructed by adding up the individual marginal benefit curves vertically given each level of the public good (Bowen, 1943). A market provision of the public good is determined by the intersection of the marginal cost curve and an individual marginal utility (benefit) curve at q^M. It might be assumed, without loss of generality, in Fig. 2.1 that all individual marginal benefit curves are exactly the same. The q^M is smaller than q^*, thus the market underprovides the public good.

The optimal price of the public good can be explained graphically concretely in Fig. 2.1 as the corresponding aggregate marginal benefit at the level of q^*, or equivalently, as the corresponding marginal cost at the level of q^*. In other words the optimal price of the public good equals the aggregate of marginal benefits of the society at the optimal level of the public good. At the same time, the optimal price equals the marginal cost of provision of the public good at the Pareto optimal level.

One of the salient differences of the public good economics from that of private goods is the aggregate or social marginal benefit of the public good is constructed by a vertical summation of the individual marginal benefits at each level of the

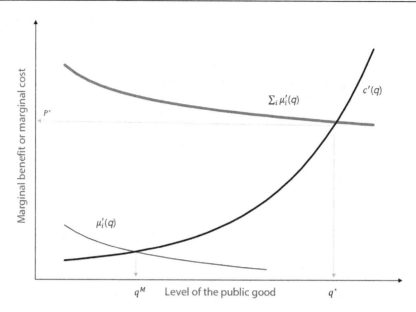

Figure 2.1 A market versus efficient provision of a public good.

public good, that is, $\sum_{i=1}^{I} \mu_i'(q)$, which has been highlighted by the theorists from the very beginning (Lindahl, 1919; Bowen, 1943). This feature can be contrasted with the aggregate demand curve of a private good which is constructed by summing "horizontally" the individual demand curves at each level of price of the private good.

Note also from Fig. 2.1 that the social marginal benefit is larger than the marginal cost of provision of the public good at the market provision of the public good. That is, $\sum_{i=1}^{I} \mu_i'(q^*) > c'(q^*)$. This means that the society will benefit from increasing the level of the public good marginally from the market level of provision. In other words, at the market equilibrium, there is still room for Pareto improvements by reallocating the society's resources. Alternatively there is social loss of welfare from the market provision of the public good.

The inefficiency of the market provision of the public good can be explained from the viewpoint of a free rider problem. Once the public good is provided by an individual provider, it benefits all the individuals in the economy. As such, an individual member has an incentive to wait for others to provide the public good and, once provided, enjoy the public good without paying for the cost of production. Buchanan puts the free rider problem this way: for the individual, *optimal results can be attained by allowing others to supply the public good to the maximum extent while he enjoys a "free ride"; that is, secures the benefits without contributing to the costs. Even if an individual should enter into such a cost-sharing agreement, he will have a strong incentive to break his own contract, to chisel on the agreed terms* (Buchanan, 1968).

A dramatic free rider situation can be presented as follows. Relaxing our assumption about the individual marginal benefit curves in the above, the free rider problem would take a specific form if individual marginal benefit curves should be arranged in a certain way. Let us suppose that individual members have varied preferences for the public good and their preferences can be ordered by the magnitudes of their marginal benefits from the provision of the public good as follows: $\mu_1'(x) < \mu_2'(x) < \cdots < \mu_I'(x)$ for all $x \geq 0$. Under this assumption, it would be individual I who might provide the public good, if it were to be provided at all. The marginal utilities of the other individuals are smaller than that of individual I. If individual I would not provide the good, the other members would certainly not do so. If individual I would provide the good, then there would be no reason for the other members to contribute. They are better off by free riding. In this case, the private provision of q^M in Fig. 2.1 will be determined by the marginal benefit function of individual I, that is, $\mu_I'(q)$.

2.6 Policy instruments for providing the public good optimally

If the market does not supply the public good to the society in a Pareto optimal manner, how should the society proceed to have the public good provided to its members? A wide spectrum of economists has justified a governmental intervention for the purpose of the provision of the public goods (Samuelson and Nordhaus, 2009; Baumol and Oates, 1988; Hartwick and Olewiler, 1997; Mankiw, 2014). Nonetheless it is noteworthy that even in the case of the public goods, there have been economists who argued for a limited role of the government (Hayek, 1948; Friedman, 1962). Refer to the quotation from the Friedman's book in the previous section that points to the possibility of the government interventions resulting in an even bigger loss of social welfare or the public good.

Taking for granted, in the meantime, the government's justifiable role to provide the public good, a central economic question is what policy instruments are available and which of the range of options should be preferred. Of the basket of policy options, two types of options are differentiated most saliently: a quantity-based instrument and a price-based instrument (Baumol and Oates, 1971, 1988; Hartwick and Olewiler, 1997).

In the quantity-based policy instrument, the Federal government determines the quantity of the public good at the socially optimal level, such as q^* in Fig. 2.1, or it can determine the quantity at any other level which may be deemed reasonable by the government sector. The government-determined quantity is then enforced through various means.

In the price-based instrument, the Federal government determines the equilibrium price at the socially optimal level of the public good, such as P^* in Fig. 2.1. By imposing the price on the economy through various means such as taxes or subsidies, the governmental sector alters consumption and production behaviors in the market economy to induce the optimal level of the public good.

In addition to these two options, a third policy option may be identified: a blended policy in which a price-based policy approach is complemented by a quantity-based policy approach, or *vice versa*. This option is often referred to as a cap-and-trade policy.

In the price-based policy approach, an economy-wide price is imposed in the form of a tax, a subsidy, or a penalty for each unit of the public good, which changes the prices of the marketed goods whose productions increase or decrease the public good (Nordhaus, 1991, 2007). In the following, the present author relies on the notations primarily from Baumol and Oates (1988) and Mas-Colell et al. (1995) to explain the price-based policy instruments and other policy instruments.

Let us suppose that there is one public good, x, and two consumers in the economy whose utility functions are $\mu_1(x_1 + x_2)$ and $\mu_2(x_1 + x_2)$, where x_i is the quantity of the public good purchased by consumer i, and $q^* > 0$, as before, is the optimal quantity of the public good. Let us suppose that a subsidy to each consumer for each unit of the public good purchased is imposed by $s_i = \mu'_{-i}(q^*)$. Equivalently, the government may impose a tax for each unit that the consumer's purchase of the public good falls below the optimal level of the public good by as much as $t_i = -\mu'_{-i}(q^*)$.

If $(\tilde{x}_1, \tilde{x}_2)$ are the competitive equilibrium levels of the public good purchased by the two consumers given the above-determined subsidy, and if $\tilde{p}$ is the market equilibrium price of the public good, then the consumer $i's$ purchase of the public good, $\tilde{x}_i$, in the competitive market must solve the following optimization problem:

$$\underset{x_1 \geq 0}{Max} \ \ \mu_1(x_1 + \tilde{x}_2) + s_1 x_1 - \tilde{p} x_1. \tag{2.24}$$

The necessary and sufficient FOC for the solution of the above optimization problem is:

$$\mu'_1(\tilde{x}_1 + \tilde{x}_2) + s_1 \leq \tilde{p}, \text{ with equality if } \tilde{x}_1 > 0. \tag{2.25}$$

Substituting for s_1 and using Eq. (2.21) and the market clearing condition that $\tilde{x}_1 + \tilde{x}_2 = \tilde{q}$, we conclude that $\tilde{q}$ is the total amount of the public good in the competitive equilibrium given the subsidy if and only if:

$$\mu'_1(\tilde{q}) + \mu'_{-1}(q^*) \leq c'(\tilde{q}), \text{ with equality for some } i \text{ if } \tilde{q} > 0. \tag{2.26}$$

Some clarifications are needed on the above notations for the tax and the subsidy. The subsidy, $s_i = \mu'_{-i}(q^*)$, is written this way to indicate that it is set at the positive externality—positive neighborhood effects according to Milton Friedman—of the consumer $i's$ action on the rest of the economy $(-i)$. Similarly the tax, $t_i = -\mu'_{-i}(q^*)$, is written this way to indicate that it is set at the negative externality—negative neighborhood effects—of the consumer $i's$ action on the rest of the economy $(-i)$. In both cases, the size of the tax or the subsidy is measured at the optimal level of the public good provision, that is, q^*.

The level of the tax or the subsidy determined in this way and implemented across the economy ensures that the solution to Eq. (2.26), $\tilde{q}$, is equal to the solution to Eq. (2.16), q^* (Baumol and Oates, 1988). This conclusion is of course dependent on the assumption that there should be no other public goods or external effects in the market economy, but the above model can also be extended to accommodate more than one public goods.

The second policy instrument for providing the public good is a quantity-based instrument or a policy of a set of standards, in which the Federal government enforces a limit (standard) on the amount of the public good which can be q^* or any other level that is chosen by the government. In the simplest form of this policy approach, the government would determine the economy-wide quantity of the public good and forces individual firms to provide a fraction of the total determined through a certain formula. This policy approach is often referred to as a command-and-control approach in the environmental economics literature (Field and Field, 2016).

The command-and-control approach was in fact the foundation of the first-generation environmental regulations introduced in the United States and other developed economies. To be more specific, the Clean Air Act (CAA) of 1970 and its subsequent amendments determined six "criteria pollutants" and set national ambient air quality standards for each of these pollutants (USEPA, 1990; Tietenberg and Lewis, 2014). In the 1970 CAA, the six criteria pollutants chosen by the Federal government were ground-level ozone (O_3), particulate matter (PM_x), carbon monoxide (CO), lead (Pb), sulfur dioxide (SO_2), and nitrogen dioxide (NO_x).

Notably, greenhouse gases including carbon dioxide (CO_2) were not included in the six criteria pollutants at the time, which four decades later became a central ground for fierce legal battles during the introduction of the greenhouse gas regulation by the Obama Administration called the Clean Power Plan on the legal basis of the CAA (SCOTUS, 2007; USEPA, 2009, 2014; Seo, 2019).

Another frequently analyzed example of the command-and-control type policy instrument for the provision of a public good is the Kyoto Protocol on the Earth's climate system (UNFCCC, 1997). The Kyoto Protocol, the first and the only international treaty on the global climate change problem, set the strict target, as the primary policy goal of the treaty, on the global carbon dioxide emissions at 5% below the 1990 level of global emissions. The target had to be achieved with legal liabilities by the members of the United Nations treaty by the first implementation phase of the Protocol (Manne and Richels, 1999; Nordhaus and Boyer, 1999; Seo, 2017a).

In the command-and-control policy approach, quantity standards or thresholds are, more often than not, set at an arbitrary level, more accurately, at a socially non-optimal level, because command-and-control policy designers do not find strong reasons to base such a threshold on an economically defined optimal level. The CAA's national ambient air quality standards effective since 1970 were determined without any rigorous benefit−cost analysis for each of the standards (Hahn and Dudley, 2007; USEPA, 1999). The standards were set, by and large, by the

Environmental Protection Agency at the threshold values beyond which harmful effects of the criteria pollutants were estimated to start accelerating sharply, based on a limited set of toxicological experiments.

Another big hurdle in the implementation of a standards regulation is that there is no consensus rule on how to divide and assign the economy-wide quantity target to individual firms and agents in the economy. An obvious choice might be to divide the policy target equally across the individual firms. This choice, however, fails to guarantee the cost-effectiveness of the policy intervention. That is, with this rule of burden sharing, the policy instrument is certain to fail to achieve the policy goal at the least cost. Another rule may be agreed upon by policy-makers. However, it is more or less certain that the alternative rule, without anchoring on the Pareto optimal price of the public good and different production costs across individual firms, also fails to force the cost-effectiveness of the policy (Hartwick and Olewiler, 1997).

The third type policy instrument is a hybrid system which blends a price-based approach with a quantity-based approach. As a matter of fact, a hybrid system is found in not-a-few environmental regulations and programs implemented in the United States and other developed economies. Most notable ones are the SO_2 and NO_x allowance trading in the US, the Emissions Trading Scheme (ETS) in the EU, and a cap-and-trade system proposed for carbon dioxide emissions in the US (Montgomery, 1972; Tietenberg, 1980; McKibbin and Wilcoxen, 2002; Ellerman and Buchner, 2007; Burtraw and Szambelan, 2009; Schmalensee and Stavins, 2013).

That the major environmental policies during the past two decades were designed after a hybrid system, albeit on a limited scale, tells much about the appeal of the hybrid approach, calling for a lucid analysis of the policy framework. Let the optimal level of the public good be q^*. Let us assume that the government has the capacity to calculate the optimal level. In the hybrid approach, the government first places a limit on the economy-wide amount of the public good to be provided at q^*. The limit is often called a cap. To enforce the cap, the government can issue a permit which allows the holder of the permit the right to claim one unit of the public good or the right to release one unit of the public bad. The government would issue as many permits as the total quantity of the public good that is enforced. For example, a permit may be traded for one ton of carbon dioxide or one ton of sulfur dioxide.

The total number of the permit issued by the government is then allocated to individual members of the economy according to a predetermined rule. Up to this point, this design is no different from that of the above-described command-and-control policy. A hybrid design emerges when the government allows individual holders of the permits to trade them among each other at a mutually negotiated price.

With the possibility of trading permits, a firm which is capable of abating the emissions of carbon dioxide, for example, at a lower cost would sell the CO_2 permits to another firm which is only capable of abating it at a higher cost. It is profitable for the low-cost firm (the former) to sell the permit to the high-cost firm (the latter) at a negotiated price which lies somewhere between the abatement cost of the low-cost firm and that of the high-cost firm. This transaction is mutually beneficial. In other words this transaction is Pareto improving, that is, benefits both parties of trade (Montgomery, 1972; Stavins, 2007).

At this point it is transparent that the hybrid system is a mixture of a quantitative cap set by the government and a mutually agreed price among the market participants. The critical question in this permit market is whether the mutually negotiated prices will settle at some level. That is, will there be an equilibrium price of the permit for, say, one ton of carbon dioxide emissions? The answer is yes. For a further analysis, let p_p be the price of one unit of the permit mutually agreed between the parties of a transaction. Given the total quantity of the permit, q^*, the equilibrium price per unit of the public good (bad) is p^* as before, with the same aggregate benefit function and the total number of the permits issued to the economy. Refer to Fig. 2.1 above if you need a clarification on this point. Let us suppose that there are two types of firms in the market: one is a low marginal cost firm with $c_l{}'$ and another is a high marginal cost firm with $c_h{}'$.

A high marginal cost firm is willing to purchase a permit as long as the permit price is below the marginal abatement cost of the firm. At the same time, a low marginal cost firm is willing to sell a permit as long as the permit price is above the marginal abatement cost of the firm. A transaction between the two parties will continue as long as

$$c_l{}' < p_p < c_h{}'. \tag{2.27}$$

The transactions will cease at the equilibrium price of the permit, $p_p{}^*$, in which the marginal abatement costs of the two firms are equal to the permit price. In other words, the no-arbitrage condition is:

$$c_l{}' = p_p{}^* = c_h{}'. \tag{2.28}$$

The equality in Eq. (2.28), along with the fact that the total number of the permits issued by the government is q^*, guarantees that the equilibrium permit price equals the optimal price of the public good (bad):

$$p_p{}^* = p^*. \tag{2.29}$$

The mathematical proof of the optimality condition for the permit trading market in Eqs. (2.28) and (2.29) can be given by a no-arbitrage condition. More specifically, at any price point that deviates from Eqs. (2.28) and (2.29), two firms will still have an incentive to make transactions that are mutual beneficial. The transactions will not stop as long as there is the possibility of an arbitrage among market participants.

The nuts and bolts of the cap-and-trade system thus explained, which is also called the emissions trading system (ETS) in the European Union, are depicted in Fig. 2.2. There are four functional relationships in the figure: the aggregate

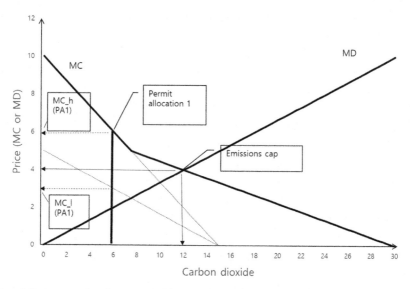

Figure 2.2 A cap-and-trade system with an equal allocation of permits.

marginal damage (*MD*) function, the marginal abatement cost for a low-cost firm (*MC_l*), the marginal abatement cost for a high-cost firm (*MC_h*), and the marginal abatement cost for the economy (*MC*).

At the intersection of the *MD* and the *MC*, the optimal quantity and the optimal price of the public good are determined, that is, $(q^*, p^*) = (12, 4)$. Let us assume that the policy-maker cap be the emission of carbon dioxide at 12 units. The figure marks the emissions cap and the price of the public good (bad) at that level.

More formally, the MD function and the two marginal abatement cost functions are assumed to have the following forms:

$$P_{MD} = \frac{1}{3}Q \tag{2.30a}$$

$$P_{MC\_l} = \frac{1}{3}(15 - Q) \tag{2.30b}$$

$$P_{MC\_h} = \frac{2}{3}(15 - Q) \tag{2.30c}$$

Note that it is twice more costly for the high-cost firm to abate one unit of emissions than it is for the low-cost firm. The social marginal abatement cost function is derived from Eqs. (2.30b) and (2.30c) by summing "horizontally" for each cost level:

$$P_{MC} = \frac{2}{9}(30 - Q) \tag{2.31}$$

Solving the four equations for $P_{MD} = P_{MC}$, we get $(q^*, p^*) = (12, 4)$. With the emissions cap at 12 units of carbon dioxide, the government agency should determine how the total number of emissions should be distributed across the firms. The figure assumes the equal distribution of the total number of permits as the initial allocation of the government. That is, the figure marks the permit allocation 1, which allocates 6 units to a high-cost firm and 6 units to a low-cost firm equally.

At the initial allocation of the permits, the figure shows that there is the difference in the cost of abatement between the two firms, that is, $MC\_h(PA_1) > MC\_l(PA_1)$. The difference motivates the high-cost firm to purchase a permit from the low-cost firm rather than to abate the emissions unit by itself. On the other hand, the low-cost firm has an incentive to abate the unit of emissions, given its low-cost abatement technology, and get paid from the high-cost firm in exchange for the permit. There is a possibility of arbitrage and the trades of permits will continue up to the no-arbitrage situation.

Note that the price of the permit traded between the two firms can lie anywhere between MC_h and MC_l. This is because any price agreed in the range between the two marginal costs is beneficial to both players.

The no-arbitrage equilibrium in the cap-and-trade market is drawn in Fig. 2.3. The equilibrium is marked by the equilibrium permit price which is 4. It is important to be aware that the permit market equilibrium price must equal the optimal price of the public good marked in Fig. 2.2. That is, the market settles at Eq. (2.29).

At the cap-and-trade market equilibrium, the equilibrium permit price determines the levels of abatement of the two individual firms. Plugging $P_p^* = 4$ into

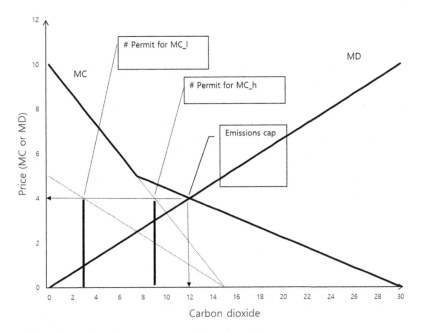

Figure 2.3 A cap-and-trade system at no-arbitrage equilibrium.

Eqs. (2.30b) and (2.30c), we obtain $Q_h^* = 9$ and $Q_l^* = 3$. This means the level of abatement for the high-cost firm is $A_h^* = 12 - 9 = 3$ and that for the low-cost firm is $A_l^* = 12 - 3 = 9$.

From the initial allocation of the permits at 6 units each, it is in the interest of the low-cost firm to cut the emissions by 3 more units, that is, 9 units because of its low-cost technology to do so. Again, from the initial allocation of the permits, it is in the interest of the high-cost firm to cut the emissions by 3 fewer units, that is, 3 units because of its high-cost technology to do so.

2.7   Morality, private provision, specialized markets

Other than the theoretically based policy instruments described thus far, there have been alternative policy recommendations on the provision of public goods that are less theoretical but nonetheless have garnered significant supports from both policy circles and academics. These alternative options put an emphasis on personal responsibility or moral sense. We will examine the following three: moral suasion, a private voluntary provision, and Lindahl equilibrium.

The moral suasion approach is not a formal policy in the sense that it is not written into a law or regulation. Rather it is a public or political response to a widely-perceived problem by the general public regarding a certain public good. The approach most certainly calls for voluntary actions by the public in addressing the perceived problem.

With the moral suasion, there is no contribution that is required of the individuals on a legal basis, either financial or material. Nor is there a penalty imposed on the individuals for not contributing voluntarily. Notwithstanding, the moral suasion has on occasions turned out to be a powerful policy option especially during the times of "a crisis" that was broadly recognized by the public.

During the energy crisis of the 1970s which saw oil prices to jump by as much as 400% in the United States, to give an example, politicians appealed to the public to reduce the uses of oil, drive their cars less, and take public transportations. The citizens complied voluntarily with the government advice for the sake of steering through the national crisis (Oates and Baumol, 1975).

In the global climate change policy debates, a morality-based proposal in one form or another has been prominent, especially in the noneconomics circles (Nordhaus, 2008). For example, it was pointed out by many that people are purchasing a hybrid vehicle such as Toyota Prius or an electric vehicle such as Tesla Model S because automobile buyers feel moral responsibility in averting global warming catastrophes. For another, people in the cold climate zones such as Canada are observed to be pushing for a costly global warming regulation even though they are expected to benefit from a warmer world. This irrational behavior on monetary terms is justified by their moral expressed concerns on polar bears.

To mention another case of a morality-driven legislative effort, the morality criterion is in fact at the heart of the recently proposed Green New Deal in 2019, which failed to advance in a vote of 0−57 in the US House of Representatives (US House of Representatives, 2019). In the House resolution, morality is imagined as the moral responsibility of the present generation to the future generations of humanity.

Researchers, including economists, doubt the efficacy of a long-term environmental or public good program that appeals solely to an individual's conscience and moral judgements because it ends up asking individuals to take costly actions over many years even decades but does neither offer any compensation in return nor guarantee satisfaction from a successful resolution of the concerned problem.

The moral suasion and voluntary action approach should therefore be understood in the context of an unexpected emergency or crisis in which there is a broad consensus across the society to make sacrifices at the individual level for the sake of a national recovery from or prevention of such drastic events.

Like the moral suasion approach, a private provision approach of a public good is rooted on voluntary actions of individuals. Unlike the former, however, this approach tends to embrace multiple factors other than the moral calling as a motivation for voluntary behaviors of individuals that lead to a provision of a public good. In addition, such factors are empirically examined through a statistical analysis of a market and behavioral data.

An illustrative example of a research on voluntary actions for providing a public good is found in an analysis of a specific environmental market such as a green electricity market in the US or a voluntary purchase market of hybrid or electric vehicles (Kotchen and Moore, 2007). In the most explicit case of the private provision, a voluntary action would take the form of a donation to a particular public good cause and the sum of individual donations is directed to a public good project.

The green electricity refers to the electricity produced from renewable energy sources such as solar radiation, wind, and geothermal heat. Compared with the electricity generations from fossil fuels, the green electricity generations tend to release a smaller amount of carbon dioxide into the atmosphere, thereby potentially providing a public good. Hybrid and electric vehicles burn less gasoline for each mile of driving, potentially providing similarly a public good of reducing the release of carbon dioxide.

Statistically examining the US households' participations in the country's green electricity programs relying on the household survey data, researchers reported that a household's participation into the voluntary programs increases with a higher household income, higher environmental concern, and a more altruistic attitude while it decreases with a larger number of people living in the household or a male name on the monthly energy bill. Note that, besides moral attitudes such as altruism, many economic variables affect individuals' choices, that is, voluntary private actions.

How effective would a private provision approach be in addressing the problem of a public good? Could it be effective over the long-term horizon during which the public good should be provided? Like the moral suasion approach, the answers to both questions are more likely to be negative. The primary reason is again the lack of compensation or satisfaction to the individuals over the long-term in return for the costly actions and measures that have to be employed by individuals. The instrument of offsets, a type of reward for a voluntary action, is one way to address the problem, which however can incur other similarly serious issues of inefficiency (Conte and Kotchen, 2010).

In addition, the stability of a voluntary provision mechanism such as the afore-mentioned green electricity market in the US cannot be guaranteed. This is because such factors as environmental concerns and altruistic attitudes can change quickly in tandem with the households' economies which are fluctuated by numerous personal and national variables.

Moving on from the private provision proposals, the present author would like to place the description of the proposal by Erik Lindahl at this point which offers an additional insight into the issue of the provision of a public good. Similar to the previous two approaches, the Lindahl mechanism emphasizes personal private markets. Even before Bowen and Samuelson, Lindahl proposed that there is a market institution that can achieve the Pareto optimality in the provision of a public good; therefore there is no need for a government intervention (Lindahl, 1919). To come to grips with the Lindahl equilibrium, as it is referred to as in the literature, based on the concept of personalized markets, we again adopt the notations from Mas-Colell et al. (1995).

Let us suppose that there is a public good with which the public is concerned, and that, for each consumer i, there is a market for the public good as experienced by consumer i. Put differently, Lindahl proposes that we should think of each consumer's consumption of the public good as a distinct commodity with its own market. Let the price of this personalized good be p_i. The p_i may differ across consumers. Suppose also that, given the equilibrium price p_i^{**}, each consumer decides on the amount of the public good she will consume, x_i, so as to solve the following optimization problem:

$$\underset{x_i \geq 0}{Max} \ \mu_i(x_i) - p_i^{**} x_i. \tag{2.32}$$

As usual, the necessary and sufficient FOC for the consumption level that solves the problem is then:

$$\mu_i'(x_i^{**}) \leq p_i^{**}, \text{with equality if } x_i^{**} > 0. \tag{2.33}$$

Let us assume that there is a firm that produces the public good. In the personalized markets, the firm is now viewed as producing a bundle of I goods with a fixed-proportions (Leontief production) technology, that is, the amount of production of each personalized good is necessarily the same. With $x_1^{**} = x_2^{**} = \ldots = x_I^{**} = q^{**}$, the firm solves the following:

$$\underset{q \geq 0}{Max} \ \left(\sum_{i=1}^{I} p_i^{**} q \right) - c(q). \tag{2.34}$$

The firm's equilibrium level of output q^{**} therefore satisfies the necessary and sufficient FOC:

$$\sum\nolimits_{i=1}^{I} p_i^{**} \leq c'(q^{**}), \text{ with equality if } q^{**} > 0. \tag{2.35}$$

In addition to Eqs. (2.33) and (2.35), the market clearing condition for the public good that $x_i^{**} = q^{**}$ for all i imply that:

$$\sum\nolimits_{i=1}^{I} \mu_i'(q^{**}) \leq c'(q^{**}), \text{ with equality if } q^{**} > 0. \tag{2.36}$$

Comparing Eq. (2.36) with Eq. (2.16), we arrive at the conclusion that the equilibrium level of the public good consumed by each consumer is exactly the efficient level: $q^{**} = q^*$.

This solution is known in the literature as a Lindahl equilibrium after Erik Lindahl who first developed the concept through personalized markets for a public good (Lindahl, 1919). In the Lindahl's personalized markets, each consumer accepts the market price as given and fully determines her own quantity of consumption of the public good. The producer then determines the supply quantity of the public good, assuming that the consumer will pay the market price for each unit of the public good.

In the Lindahl's framework, each consumer is willing to pay the full cost of the public good commensurate with her level of consumption, $p_i^{**} x_i$ in Eq. (2.32), taking the market price as it is. In other words, the consumer is not concerned at all about the free riders, nonexcludability, and nonrivalrous characteristics (Buchanan, 1968) of the public good. So the Lindahl's framework does not fully incorporate the unique characteristics of the public goods.

The realism of the Lindahl solution for the public goods is questionable, which can be discussed via the assumptions of the model (Mas-Colell et al., 1995). First, for the Lindahl equilibrium to make sense, it should be possible for a provider to exclude a nonpaying consumer from the appropriations of the public good. If it is not possible, there would be no reason for the consumer to believe that she would end up consuming none of the public good if she would not pay for any of it.

Second, in the personalized markets of the public good, there is only one consumer on the demand side for the personalized good assumed to be provided in the market. It is not rational, however, to assume that the consumer will behave as a price-taker in the personal market.

The Lindahl equilibrium can be further reinterpreted as an optimal supply mechanism of the public good in personalized markets via the diagrammatic example in Fig. 2.2. Let us go back to the Marginal Damage (MD) curve in Fig. 2.2. In the personalized markets, each individual is willing to pay for the damage equivalent to her MD function, that is, $MD_i(q^*)$. The aggregated MD curve is the sum of individual MD curves at each level of the public good:

$$MD(q) = \sum\nolimits_{i}^{I} MD_i(q). \tag{2.37}$$

The supplier has the marginal cost function which is equal to the aggregate marginal cost function in Fig. 2.2. The aggregate MD function and the aggregate marginal cost function then determines the optimal level of the public good and the optimal price, (q^*, p^*) as depicted in Fig. 2.2.

At the equilibrium the supplier receives the optimal price for each unit of the public good it provides to the individuals. Then for each unit of the public good, each individual pays according to the individual's marginal damage, $MD_i(q^*)$, which adds up to $MD(q^*)$ which is what is paid to the supplier, that is, $p(q^*)$.

In the Lindahl's personalized markets, each individual pays according to her marginal damage, say, marginal willingness to pay. In the nonpersonalized market, however, the individual's marginal willingness to pay function will depend on whether she can free ride on the public good provision by others, making her not a price-taker. When it is possible to free ride, it is expected that $MD_i(q^*) = 0$.

2.8   Valuation methods

Of the six of policy approaches suggested historically for solving an inefficient provision of a public good that the present author explained thus far, the first three approaches are by far more seriously considered by policy-makers than the latter three: a price-based approach, a command-and-control approach, and a hybrid approach.

In implementing one of these policies, policy-makers should know accurately the aggregate marginal benefit function (or the aggregate MD function) drawn in Figs. 2.1 and 2.2 before they can determine the optimal price or the optimal quantity of the public good (or the public bad). The former is necessary for a price-based approach, and the latter is necessary for a standards-based approach or a cap-and-trade system.

In reality, the governmental policy body does not have the a priori knowledge on the marginal benefit function for a public good. This absence of knowledge necessitates the research efforts of estimating the marginal benefit function of a concerned public good (Mendelsohn and Olmstead, 2009). Straightforwardly speaking, in the literature of environmental public goods, the valuation theories and methods for numerous environmental amenities and disamenities, for example, clean air, clean water, endangered species, and climate change, have gradually taken a central stage of both environmental economics and policy designs (Mendelsohn, 1980; Cropper and Oates, 1992; Hanemann, 1994; Weitzman, 1998; Viscusi and Aldy, 2003; Maler and Vincent, 2005; Greenstone and Gallagher, 2008; Smith, 2008).

Economists and policy scientists have endeavored to develop ever accurate and reliable methods for placing a dollar value on each of the host of environmental public goods (Freeman et al., 2014). Broadly speaking, there are two families of economic valuation methods: a stated preference method on the one hand and a revealed preference method on the other (Cropper and Oates, 1992; Mendelsohn and Olmstead, 2009). The two categories of valuation methods are depicted in Fig. 2.4, and each method included in the figure is explained presently one by one briefly.

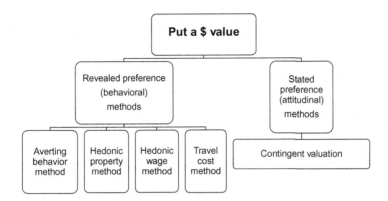

Figure 2.4 Methods for valuation.

For some, but not all, of the valuation methods and many of the revealed prefer-ence methods, valuation is conducted explicitly through an integrated assessment model which tracks the consequences of emissions from the smokestacks and tail-pipes to dollar changes through air quality changes, exposure, dose-response, and dollar values (Muller and Mendelsohn, 2009; USEPA, 1999).

A revealed preference method examines revealed and observed behaviors of individuals in the concerned markets, from which researchers derive the marginal willingness to pay of individuals for an improvement in a specific environmental quality indicator. Widely applied to environmental policy issues in this family of the economic valuation methods are an averting behavior method, a hedonic prop-erty method, a hedonic wage method, and a travel cost method.

When the averting behavior method is applied, a researcher examines changes of behaviors by individuals that are made in their attempts to mitigate the impacts of an environmental disamenity under consideration (Smith and Desvousges, 1986). To give an example, individuals in water polluted areas with low-quality tap water may increase purchases of a bottled water or a water purifier in order to avert harm-ful effects of water pollution. For another example, individuals who reside in the areas with a high level of air pollution such as ozone may reduce outdoor activities and increase indoor air-conditioning (Dickie and Gerking, 1991). The researcher can establish the relationship between the water/air pollution levels and the costs for taking these averting behaviors, from which the marginal willingness to pay for a water/air quality improvement is derived statistically.

The second of the set of the revealed preference methods is the hedonic property method (Ridker and Henning, 1967; Greenstone and Gallagher, 2008). A researcher who applies this method examines the variation of residential property values across the range of locations with varied environmental qualities. An environmental qual-ity indicator such as the level of smog in the study locations is interpreted to be one of the many characteristics of the property. Further, the owner of the property is assumed to have paid for the specific characteristic as one component of the prop-erty value at the time of purchase (Rosen, 1974; Freeman, 1974). Hence, the willingness to pay for a higher environmental quality is derived from the value placed on the environmental quality component of the property value.

The hedonic wage method, applying the same theory as the hedonic property method, examines the differentials in the wages that individuals receive given varied environmental characteristics of the jobs offered to the workers (Thaler and Rosen, 1976; Viscusi, 1979). A worker faces a tradeoff in a wage negotiation between a higher wage and a lower environmental risk. The higher the risk of the job, the higher the wage offered to the worker. The lower the risk of the job, the lower the wage offered to the worker. A certain environmental risk that the job entails, for example, risk of death while performing the job, is interpreted to be one of the many characteristics of the job and the worker gets paid for taking on the characteristic as one component of the wage offered to him.

An application of the hedonic wage method results in one of the most critical, also contested, concepts in the valuation theory and methods, that is, the value of statistical life (VSL). The value of risk is expressed as the willingness to accept of an individual in order to undertake the task which involves a certain probability of death while conducting the job. The value of risk eventually culminates in the critical concept of the VSL. A meta-analysis of the hedonic wage studies shows that the median VSL of the US workers is $7 million, and the income elasticity of the VSL is in the range of 0.5−0.6, which means that a lower-income country has a lower VSL (Viscusi and Aldy, 2003). This also means that a lower-income worker has a lower value of statistical life.

The quantitative estimates of the VSL derived from the hedonic method play a critical and also pivotal role in many policy areas, including an assessment of environmental benefits and damage, environmental accounting such as the Green GDP, and environmental policy decisions (Weitzman, 2009; Muller et al., 2011). This is primarily because mortality is the costly aspect of various environmental pollution problems (Likens and Bormann, 1974; Pope et al., 2002; Bell et al., 2004; Woodruff et al., 2006; Mauzerall et al., 2005). It should be reminded and emphasized that the VSL is not the same as the value of life itself. The measure is the willingness to pay of an individual for a marginal reduction in the risk of death which can be obtained from a large data set of wage settlements. The VSL is a meaningful measure of "life" because a host of environmental regulations purport to achieve exactly that, that is, a marginal reduction in the risk of death or a marginal improvement in the quality of environment.

The travel cost method, the fourth revealed preference method, exploits the cost that an individual incurs for a travel to a popular nature area such as the Yellowstone National Park (Clawson, 1959; Knetsch, 1963). A traveler pays for many items and amenities needed for a journey, including transportation fees, entrance fees, accommodation expenditures, and meal expenditures, to enjoy the national park. The travel cost method associates the travel costs with the demands for the park from which the willingness to pay of an individual to the park is derived.

More specifically, a researcher examines the variation in the travel cost to a site across the individuals, that is, the implicit price that an individual traveler pays for a visit to the site. The variation exists because individual visitors travel from different origins to the site. The researcher establishes an empirical relationship between the travel cost and the visitation rate, based upon which a demand function for the site is estimated.

Another family of the valuation methods is referred to as a stated preference method or an attitudinal method, which includes a contingent valuation (CV) method (Hanemann, 1994). Stated preference methods seek to obtain an individual's willingness to pay by directly asking her/him, through carefully designed surveys, how much s/he values a certain environmental good or service. The surveys are designed to create a hypothetical market in which respondents are asked to make a series of decisions on the concerned environmental good or service. These decisions are then evaluated by the CV researcher as if they were actual decisions that were taken places in the market.

The stated preference methods are susceptible to not-a-few well-defined biases. In responding to the survey, a respondent does not face real tradeoffs in the market when s/he decides to pick an answer to a specific question. Therefore the answer given in a hypothetical situation (market) may not reflect the true willingness to pay of her/him for the environmental amenity. Put differently, the answers given in a hypothetical market may not be the same as the choices made in the real marketplaces. Second, what answers a respondent gives to the questions in the survey depend on how the questions are framed in the questionnaire. Third, the answers given by the respondent can be swayed by various strategic reasons (Diamond and Hausman, 1994; Cropper and Oates, 1992).

Notwithstanding the severe critiques, many researchers also acknowledge that some types of values of natural assets or environmental amenities may not be measured by one of the revealed preference methods, that is, by reliance solely upon the behaviors observed in the marketplaces. They argue that for such values, there are no market behaviors that can be observed that contain information on such values. A primary example is existence value of, say, an animal species. An individual may be fully aware that s/he will never make use of a particular natural service during her/his lifetime, for example, polar bears in the Arctic, but nevertheless s/he may express high value for the preservation of the natural service. It is interpreted that the individual in this case simply puts a value on the existence of such a being or a place.

The existence value belongs to a broader category of nonuse value. The nonuse value can sometimes account for a large fraction of the total value attached to a certain policy issue such as a policy for protection of an endangered species or a policy for wilderness preservation. To the extent that there are no observed market (transaction) behaviors that help researchers to obtain the nonuse value or existence value, many researchers have continued to resort to attitudinal methods, despite the well-defined biases pointed out above. Economists have debated whether such values should be included in an economic analysis of a policy and attitudinal methods should be relied upon for policy decisions (Diamond and Hausman, 1994; Hanemann, 1994). For the same environmental regulation under consideration, the estimate of policy benefits measured through the attitudinal methods is often many times larger than the estimate of policy benefits measured by one of the revealed preference methods (Cropper and Oates, 1992; Mendelsohn and Olmstead, 2009).

It goes without saying that the descriptions of the valuation methods in this section are much limited, more specifically, do not sufficiently describe the merits and drawbacks of each of these methods, representative empirical studies, and applications to policy legislations. A full description of this literature would call for a separate book-length analysis (Mendelsohn and Neumann, 1999; Maler and Vincent, 2005; Freeman et al., 2014).

Besides the critiques leveled against each valuation method explained above briefly, there are critics who do not accept any validity of the valuation theory itself (Sandel, 2013). One of their points is that the host of valuation methods does not yield an about-the-same value for a particular environmental amenity or a natural asset. In fact, the value estimates may vary by an order of magnitude from one method to another. Moreover, some values may not be measured credibly. The critics go on to argue that a huge variation in the value estimate across the variety of the valuation methods renders a benefit−cost analytical framework less meaningful and even not pertinent (Broome, 1992).

The benefit−cost analysis has, however, increasingly been recognized as an essential tool, perhaps inevitable, for any assessments of many important public policy decisions, by both researchers and policy-makers (Arrow et al., 1996a,b). Even though the basket of valuation methods gives out a wide range of value estimates, they provide an important input into policy decision models (Hahn and Dudley, 2007; Muller et al., 2011). Further, a series of valuation studies have often complemented each other through the course of debates on a particular environmental regulation, from which the range of value estimates has often been narrowed over the course. In the United States, it is legally required that any environmental policy proposal should be accompanied by a benefit−cost analysis (USEPA, 1999; Mendelsohn and Olmstead, 2009).

2.9   Uncertainty and policy options

The variation in the value estimates of a particular environmental or natural asset is one component of the uncertainty in designing a public policy. Another component is the variation in the marginal cost of abatement across the firms in the economy. The policy-makers do not know the two components with certainty. Given the uncertainty on both sides, should we still prefer one policy instrument over another, for example, a price-based policy over a standards policy (Weitzman, 1974)?

Policy-makers only know the marginal benefit functions of individuals and the marginal abatement cost functions with a range of uncertainty, which is because there is hidden, privately held information on the parts of consumers and producers of the public good. Let us say that there is privately held, that is, hidden to others, information in each consumer of the public good and there is privately held, that is, hidden to others, information in each producer of the environmental public good.

Either of the hidden information leads to the uncertainty in either the marginal benefit functions or the marginal cost functions. To incorporate the uncertainty, we can write the consumer's utility function as $\mu(\bullet, \eta)$ with η denoting the type of the consumer where the type is determined by how much value s/he places on the concerned good. For example, s/he can be treated as either a high-value consumer or a low-value consumer. In the same manner, the firm's profit function can be written as $\pi(\bullet, \theta)$ with θ denoting the type of the firm where the type is determined by how much cost the firm incurs in producing a concerned good. For example, the firm can be treated as either a high-cost firm or a low-cost firm (Mas-Colell et al., 1995).

In the presence of the privately held information, which is hidden and also asymmetrically held by both consumers and producers of the public good, a voluntary bargaining solution between the party of firms and the party of consumers, such as the one proposed by Ronald Coase, is even more difficult to be realized than it is in the absence of such privately held hidden information (Coase, 1960). However, in a localized problem of external effects which involves a small number of victims and a small number of polluters, the Coase bargaining could provide a more efficient policy solution because the two parties will engage in the activities of revealing the true information held by their negotiating counterparts (Clarke, 1971; Groves, 1973; Milgrom, 2004). In a problem of a large-scale external effects, say, a national scale or a city scale, a large number of victims, and a large number of polluters have stakes in a possible policy intervention or a negotiated solution, which renders again the Coase bargaining solution practically ineffective when the uncertainties about involved agents are large.

Getting back to the first question posed in this section, there is a pertinent theoretical outcome from the literature: when there is privately held information that the policy-maker does not have the full knowledge, a quantity-based policy instrument and a price-based policy instrument are not perfect substitutes of each other anymore. Put differently, it is no longer possible to achieve the Pareto optimal solution for the public good provision, as depicted in Fig. 2.1 through one policy approach or the other. Which of the two instruments is superior in terms of welfare loss depends on the shape of the marginal utility function of consumers and that of the marginal profit function of firms (Weitzman, 1974).

Let us suppose that the policy-maker does not have the full knowledge on the shapes of the marginal abatement cost functions of individual firms. If the MD function is such that the optimal amount of the public good (bad) does not vary much with the type of the firm (θ), then the quantity-based approach is superior because the policy-maker can set the strict limit on the quantity of the good.

First, take the following situation for consideration: the MD function in Fig. 2.1 is so steep that it increases abruptly at a threshold level with an increase of the public bad and becomes nearly infinite beyond the threshold level of the public bad. In this situation, regardless of the shape of the marginal abatement cost function, the situation dictates that a quantity-based threshold policy should be preferred to a price-based policy.

Alternatively, let us suppose again that the policy-maker does not know the shapes of the marginal abatement cost functions of individual firms. At the same time, suppose that the MD function in Fig. 2.1 is independent of the level of the public bad. In this alternative situation, a price-based instrument is superior to a quantity-based standard policy. In this situation, regardless of the shape of the marginal abatement cost function, a price-based instrument can achieve the optimal level of the public bad by setting the price of the public bad at the fixed marginal damage. With the price set thus, individual firms will make optimizing decisions on the units of abatement of the public bad. There is no need for the government policy body to know with certainty the individual marginal abatement cost functions.

Once the two extreme cases are explained, it is far easier to draw a conclusion on a range of intermediate cases. In the intermediate cases, an advantage of one approach over the other will be determined by the elasticity of the MD function relative to the elasticity of the marginal abatement cost function (Weitzman, 1974; Pizer, 1997). If the elasticity of the MD function is larger than the elasticity of the marginal abatement cost function at around the optimal level of the public bad, a quantity-based standards policy is superior to a price-based approach as far as the expected social welfare from a chosen policy is concerned.

If, on the other hand, the elasticity of the MD function is smaller than the elasticity of the marginal abatement cost function at around the optimal level of the public bad, a price-based approach outperforms a quantity-based standards policy in terms of the expected social welfare from a chosen policy. The reason is not hard to grasp: in this situation, a misjudgment on the marginal abatement cost function by the policy board leads to a smaller welfare loss under a price-based approach than that under a quantity-based approach.

The analysis of uncertainty provided in this section is pertinent to an analysis of global warming policies which deal with a stock pollutant (Newell and Pizer, 2003). A stock pollutant is the pollutant which, once released, remains in the atmosphere for a long time, that is, as long as a century and more, and is accumulated in the atmosphere (Le Treut et al., 2007). An analyst must measure the societal damage of one ton of carbon dioxide emissions today that would unfold over the 100 years, which makes the impact estimates of global warming uncertain (Tol, 2002; Seo, 2016a,b).

2.10   Wealth redistributions and policy options

Section 2.7 arrived at the conclusion that both a price policy and a cap-and-trade system would achieve the Pareto optimal solution if the price is set optimally for the former and the total number of permits is issued at the optimal level of emissions for the latter. Are the two policies equivalent? The answer is no. In fact, the two policy instruments cause very different wealth redistributions among the parties affected by the policy. The choice of one policy instrument over the other determines the distribution of wealth from one group of stakeholders to another. Therefore it has important environmental justice as well as political implications.

Let me clarify this point with a notable policy experience in the United States. The American Clean Energy and Security Act of 2009, known more popularly as the Waxman-Markey Bill, attempted, although without success, to introduce a cap-and-trade system to control carbon dioxide emissions in the country (US House of Representatives, 2009). A major criticism leveled against the Bill was that a cap-and-trade system would reallocate the wealth from the public sector to carbon emitting businesses. By contrast, a carbon price approach would reallocate the wealth from carbon emitting businesses to the government and public sector, which would be eventually reallocated to the citizens (Stavins, 2007).

In the price scheme, carbon penalty (tax) is collected by the government from the polluting firms for each ton of unabated emissions which is charged at the level of the Pareto efficient price. As such, the wealth moves from the polluting businesses to the public sector. The tax revenue by the government in turn can be spent by the government for supporting various public welfare improvement projects. It may be used to support low-income families in an effort to alleviate income inequality in the country, for example (Metcalf, 2009).

The wealth redistribution effects of the two policy instruments considered for the Waxman-Markey Bill can be analyzed graphically through Fig. 2.5 which adds additional information on the expected wealth transfers to Figs. 2.2 and 2.3. For the price scheme, the Pareto efficient price is set at P^*. The economy-wide amount of emissions is then determined by the aggregate marginal cost curve to be Q^*. The social level of emissions is determined by the individual firms' decisions upon seeing the economy-wide carbon price (tax), that is, P^*. That is, the low-cost firm chooses the emissions level of 0D, and the high-cost firm chooses the emissions level of 0E, which add up to $0Q^*$.

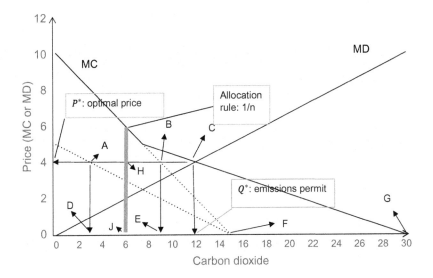

Figure 2.5 Wealth transfer under a price system versus a cap-and-trade system.

The total cost for each firm to comply with the carbon price policy is also depicted in the figure and summarized in Table 2.1. One component of the cost is abatement cost. The low-cost firm pays the cost of abatement equivalent to the triangle of FAE. The high-cost firm pays the cost of abatement equivalent to the triangle of FBE. Adding up, the society's cost of abatement equals the triangle of GCQ*.

The other component of the cost is carbon tax to be paid to the government. At the socially efficient price indicated in the figure, the low-cost firm pays the tax the amount equivalent to the rectangle of 0P*AD while the high-cost firm pays the amount equivalent to the rectangle of 0P*BE. The two firms' tax payments add up to the amount equivalent to the rectangle of 0P*CQ*.

The government receives the tax revenue equal to the rectangle 0P*CQ*. Under the price scheme, the wealth moves from the business sector to the public sector. The public sector may hold the tax revenue for fiscal stability of the country (Nordhaus, 2010). Alternatively the government can redistribute the tax revenue to the consumers through, for example, income-tax cuts to the low-income families (Metcalf, 2009). In the latter case, the government is at a zero sum and the policy is said to be revenue neutral.

The consumers are the beneficiary of the revenue neutral carbon tax policy. The benefit is equivalent to the tax revenue rectangle 0P*CQ*. Therefore the revenue neutral price policy ultimately redistributes the wealth from the business sector to the consumers via the public sector. This numerical analysis of the price scheme is summarized in Table 2.1.

The same analysis can be performed via Fig. 2.5 on the cap-and-trade system. We start with a permit allocation rule: a 1/n allocation across the firms. The figure marks the emissions cap as well as the number of permits received by each firm. With the initial allocation, firms will trade the permits for their own sake and, as analyzed in Section 2.7, will settle at the no-arbitrage situation.

At the no-arbitrage equilibrium of the cap-and-trade system, the abatement cost for the low-cost firm and that for the high-cost firm remain the same as those in the price system, which is expressed in Table 2.1 as the same triangles.

Under the cap-and-trade system, there is no tax payment required of the firms. Instead firms will trade the permits they were given by the government. The low-cost firm sells the permits and earns the profit from the sale, whose size is equal to the rectangle DAHJ. The high-cost firm purchases the permits from the low-cost firm. The expense for the high-cost firm is equivalent to the rectangle JHBE. For the economy as a whole, the trades end up with a zero sum.

For the cap-and-trade system, there is no revenue for the public sector. Hence there is no benefit that accrues to the consumers. They are no winners in the cap-and-trade policy as they are in the price policy. Who are then the winners of the cap-and-trade system? The winners are the business sector because the government allocates the permits for releasing carbon dioxide to the firms for free. A dominantly large number of permits in all existing cap-and-trade programs is distributed freely (EC, 2016; Korea Exchange, 2016).

Table 2.1 Components of wealth transfers under a price versus a cap-and-trade system.

Stakeholders		A price scheme: revenue neutral	A cap-and-trade system: allocation rule = 1/n
Businesses: abatement cost	Low-cost firm	− FAD	+ FAD
	High-cost firm	− FBE	− FBE
	Total	− GCQ* = −(FAD + FBE)	− GCQ* = −(FAD + FBE)
Businesses: tax payment or permit purchase	Low-cost firm	− 0P*AD	+ DAHJ
	High-cost firm	− 0P*BE	− JHBE
	Total	− 0P*CQ* = −(0P*AD + 0P*BE)	None = + DAHJ − JHBE
Government		+ 0P*CQ* −0P*CQ*	None
Consumers		+ 0P*CQ*	None

Of the two firms, the low-cost firm is the bigger winner because it can sell the extra permits to the high-cost firm, which is again attributable to the capability of the firm to abate the emissions at a lower cost. The cap-and-trade policy therefore can induce technological innovations of the business sector in that sense that the policy motivates the firms to develop techniques to cut emissions at a lower cost (Hartwick and Olewiler, 1997; Stavins, 2007).

2.11 Concluding remarks

This concludes the presentation of the economics of public goods. This chapter presented the essential concepts and theories as well as the fundamental analyses that pertain to the economics of public goods. The ensuing chapter will elaborate the complications that arise from real-world public good problems, especially those of global-scale public goods, and explicate how economists as well as policy negotiators have strived to address these complications.

References

Arrow, K.J., Cropper, M.L., Eads, G.C., Hahn, R.W., Lave, L.B., Noll, R.G., et al., 1996a. Is there a role for benefit-cost analysis in environmental, health, and safety regulation? Science 272, 221−222.

Arrow, K.J., Cline, W., Maler, K.G., Munasinghe, M., Squitieri, R., Stiglitz, J., 1996b. Intertemporal equity, discounting, and economic efficiency. In: Bruce, J.P., Lee, H., Haites, E.F. (Eds.), Climate Change 1995: Economic and Social Dimensions of Climate Change, Intergovernmental Panel on Climate Change. Cambridge University Press, New York.

Baumol, W.J., Oates, W.E., 1971. The use of standards and prices for protection of the environment. Swed. J. Econ. 73, 42−54.

Baumol, W.J., Oates, O.A., 1988. The Theory of Environmental Policy, 2nd edition Cambridge University Press, Cambridge.

Bell, M.L., McDermott, A., Zeger, S.L., Samet, J.M., Domenici, F., 2004. Ozone and short-term mortality in 95 US urban communities, 1987−2000. J. Am. Med. Assoc. 292, 2372−2378.

Bowen, H.R., 1943. The interpretation of voting in the allocation of economic resources. Q. J. Econ. 58 (1), 27−48.

Broome, J., 1992. Counting the Cost of Global Warming. The White Horse Press, Cambridge.

Brown, K.M., 1973. Welfare implications of congestion in public goods. Rev. Soc. Economy 31, 89−92.

Buchanan, J.M., 1965. An economy theory of clubs. Economica 32, 1−24.

Buchanan, J.M., 1968. The Demand and Supply of Public Goods. Rand McNally & Co., Chicago.

Burtraw, D., Szambelan, S.J., 2009. U.S. Emissions Trading Markets for SO_2 and NO_x. Resources for the Future Discussion Paper 09—40. Resources for the Future, Washington, DC.

Clarke, E., 1971. Multipart pricing of public goods. Public. Choice 11 (1), 17—33.

Clawson, M., 1959. Methods of measuring the demand and value of outdoor recreation. Resources For the Future, Washington, DC, Reprint.

Coase, R., 1960. The problem of social costs. J. Law Econ. 3, 1—44.

Conte, M.N., Kotchen, M.J., 2010. Explaining the price of voluntary carbon offsets. Clim. Change Econ. 1, 93—111.

Cropper, M.L., Oates, W.E., 1992. Environmental economics: a survey. J. Econ. Lit. 30, 675—740.

Diamond, P.A., Hausman, J.A., 1994. Contingent valuation: is some number better than no number? J. Econ. Perspect. 8, 45—64.

Dickie, M., Gerking, S., 1991. Willingness to pay for ozone control: inferences from the demand for medical care. J. Environ. Econ. Manag. 21, 1—16.

Dixit, A.K., 1990. Optimization in Economic Theory, 2nd edition Oxford University Press, Oxford.

Ellerman, A.D., Buchner, B.K., 2007. The European Union Emissions Trading Scheme: origins, allocations, and early results. Rev. Environ. Econ. Policy 1, 66—87.

European Commission (EC), 2016. EU ETS Handbook. European Commission, Brussels.

Field, B.C., Field, M.K., 2016. Environmental Economics: an Introduction, 6th edition The McGraw-Hill, New York.

Freeman III, A.M., 1974. On estimating air pollution control benefits from land value studies. J. Environ. Econ. Manag. 1, 74—83.

Freeman III, A.M., Herriges, J.A., Cling, C.L., 2014. The Measurements of Environmental and Resource Values: Theory and Practice. RFF Press, New York.

Friedman, M., 1962. Capitalism and Freedom. The University of Chicago Press, Chicago, IL.

Goulder, L.H., Parry, I.W.H., Burtraw, D., 1997. Revenue raising versus other approaches to environmental protection: the critical significance of pre-existing tax distortion. Rand J. Econ. 28, 708—731.

Greenstone, M., Gallagher, J., 2008. Does hazardous waste matter? Evidence from the housing market and the superfund program. Q. J. Econ. 123, 951—1003.

Groves, T., 1973. Incentives in teams. Econometrica 41 (4), 617—631.

Hahn, R.W., Dudley, P.M., 2007. How well does the U.S. government do benefit-cost analysis? Rev. Environ. Econ. Policy 1, 192—211.

Hanemann, W.M., 1994. Valuing the environment through contingent valuation. J. Economic Perspect. 8, 19—43.

Hartwick, J.M., Olewiler, N.D., 1997. The Economics of Natural Resource Use, 2nd edition Pearson, New York.

Hayek, F.A., 1948. Individualism and Economic Order. The University of Chicago Press, Chicago, IL.

Knetsch, J.L., 1963. Outdoor recreation demands and benefits. Land. Econ. 39, 387—396.

Korea Exchange (2016) Introduction to emissions trading scheme. Accessed from: <http://open.krx.co.kr/contents/OPN/01/01050401/OPN01050401.jsp>.

Kotchen, M., Moore, M.R., 2007. Private provision of environmental public goods: household participation in green-electricity programs. J. Environ. Econ. Manag. 53, 1—16.

Le Treut, H., Somerville, R., Cubasch, U., Ding, Y., Mauritzen, C., Mokssit, A., et al., 2007. Historical overview of climate change. In: Solomon, S., Qin, D., Manning, M., Chen, Z., Marquis, M., Averyt, K.B., Tignor, M., Miller, H.L. (Eds.), Climate Change 2007:

The Physical Science Basis. Contribution of Working Group I to the Fourth Assessment Report of the Intergovernmental Panel on Climate Change. Cambridge University Press, Cambridge.

Likens, G.E., Bormann, F.H., 1974. Acid rain: a serious regional environmental problem. Science 184, 1176–1179.

Lindahl, E., 1919. Just taxation—A positive solution. (Translated from German). Musgrave RA, Peacock AT (1958), Classics in the Theory of Public Finance. Macmillan, London.

Maler, K.-G., Vincent, J.R., 2005. The Handbook of Environmental Economics, Valuing Environmental Changes, vol. 2. North-Holland, Amsterdam.

Mankiw, N.G., 2014. Principles of Economics, seventh ed. Cengage Learning, Stamford, CT.

Manne, A.S., Richels, R.G., 1999. The Kyoto protocol: a cost-effective strategy for meeting environmental objectives? Energy J. 20 (Special Issue), 1–23.

Mas-Colell, A., Whinston, M.D., Green, J.R., 1995. Microeconomic Theory. Oxford University Press, Oxford.

Mauzerall, D., Sultan, B., Kim, N., Bradford, D.F., 2005. NO_x emissions from large point sources: variability in ozone production, resulting health damages and economic costs. Atmos. Environ. 39, 2851–2866.

Mendelsohn, R., 1980. An economic analysis of air pollution from coal-fired power plants. J. Environ. Econ. Manag. 7, 30–43.

Mendelsohn, R., Neumann, J., 1999. The Impact of Climate Change on the United States Economy. Cambridge University Press, Cambridge.

Mendelsohn, R., Olmstead, S., 2009. The economic valuation of environmental amenities and disamenities: methods and applications. Annu. Rev. Resour. 34, 325–347.

McKibbin, W.J., Wilcoxen, P.J., 2002. The role of economics in climate change policy. J. Economic Perspect. 16 (2), 107–129.

Metcalf, G., 2009. Designing a carbon tax to reduce US greenhouse gas emissions. Rev. Environ. Econ. Policy 3, 63–83.

Milgrom, P., 2004. Vickrey–Clarke–Groves mechanisms. In: Milgrom, P. (Ed.), (2004) Putting Auction Theory to Work. Cambridge University Press, Cambridge.

Mises, L.V., 1949. Human Action: a Treatise on Economics. Yale University Press, New Haven, CT.

Montgomery, W.D., 1972. Markets in licenses and efficient pollution control programs. J. Economic Theory 5, 395–418.

Muller, N.Z., Mendelsohn, R., 2009. Efficient pollution regulation: getting the prices right. Am. Economic Rev. 99, 1714–1739.

Muller, N.Z., Mendelsohn, R., Nordhaus, W., 2011. Environmental accounting for pollution in the United States economy. Am. Economic Rev. 101, 1649–1675.

Musgrave, R., 1939. The voluntary exchange theory of public economy. Q. J. Econ. 53, 213–237.

Musgrave, R., 1959. The Theory of Public Finance. McGraw-Hill, New York.

Nash, J., 1950. Equilibrium points in n-person games. Proc. Natl Acad. Sci. 36, 48–49.

Nash, J., 1951. Non-cooperative games. Ann. Mathematics 54, 286–295.

Newell, R.G., Pizer, W.A., 2003. Regulating stock pollutants under uncertainty. J. Environ. Econ. Manag. 45, 416–432.

New York Times (NYT), 2009. Paul A. Samuelson, Economist, Dies at 94. December 14, 2009. NYT, New York.

New York Times (NY), 2013. Ronald H. Coase, a Law Professor and Leading Economist, Dies at 102. September 3, 2013. NYT, New York.

Nordhaus, W., 1991. To slow or not to slow: the economics of the greenhouse effects. Economic J. 101, 920−937.

Nordhaus, W., 2007. To tax or not to tax: alternative approaches to slowing global warming. Rev. Environ. Econ. Policy 1 (1), 26−44.

Nordhaus, W.D., 2008. A Question of Balance: Weighing the Options on Global Warming Policies. Yale University Press, New Haven, CT.

Nordhaus, W., 2010. Carbon taxes to move toward fiscal sustainability. Economists' Voice 7 (3), 1−5.

Nordhaus, W., 2015. Climate clubs: overcoming free-riding in international climate policy. Am. Economic Rev. 105, 1339−1370.

Nordhaus, W.D., Boyer, J.G., 1999. Requiem for Kyoto: an economic analysis of the Kyoto Protocol. Energy J. 20 (Special Issue), 93−130.

Oates, W., Baumol, W., 1975. The instruments for environmental policy. In: Mills, E.S. (Ed.), Economic Analysis of Environmental Problems. National Bureau of Economic Research, MA.

Pareto, V., 1906. In: Montesano, A., Zanni, A., Bruni, L., Chipman, J.S., McLure, M. (Eds.), Manual for Political Economy. (2014) Oxford University Press, Oxford.

Pigou, A.C., 1920. Economics of Welfare. Macmillan and Co, London.

Pizer, W., 1997. Prices vs. Quantities revisited: The Case of Climate Change. Resources For the Future (RFF), Discussion Paper 98-02. RFF, Washington, DC.

Pope, C.A., Burnett, R.T., Thun, M.J., Calle, E.E., Krewski, D., Ito, K., et al., 2002. Lung cancer, cardiopulmonary mortality, and long-term exposure to fine particulate air pollution. J. Am. Med. Assoc. 287 (9), 1132−1141.

Ridker, R., Henning, J., 1967. The determination of residential property values with special reference to air pollution. Rev. Econ. Stat. 48, 246−257.

Rosen, S., 1974. Hedonic prices and implicit markets: product differentiation in pure competition. J. Political Economy 82, 34−55.

Samuelson, P., 1954. The pure theory of public expenditure. Rev. Econ. Stat. 36, 387−389.

Samuelson, P., 1955. Diagrammatic exposition of a theory of public expenditure. Rev. Econ. Stat. 37, 350−356.

Samuelson, P., Nordhaus, W., 2009. Economics, 19th edition McGraw-Hill Education, New York.

Sandel, M., 2013. What Money Can't Buy: The moral limits of markets. Farrar, Straus and Giroux, New York.

Schmalensee, R., Stavins, R.N., 2013. The SO_2 allowance trading system: the ironic history of a grand policy experiment. J. Econ. Perspect. 27, 103−122.

Seo, S.N., 2016a. Modeling farmer adaptations to climate change in South America: a microbehavioral economic perspective. Env. Ecol. Stat. 23, 1−21.

Seo, S.N., 2016b. Microbehavioral Econometric Methods: theories, Models, and Applications for the Study of Environmental and Natural Resources. Academic/Elsevier, Amsterdam.

Seo, S.N., 2017a. The Behavioral Economics of Climate Change: adaptation Behaviors, Global Public Goods, Breakthrough Technologies, and Policy-making. Academic Press, Amsterdam.

Seo, S.N., 2017b. Beyond the Paris agreement: climate change policy negotiations and future directions. Regional Sci. Policy Pract. 9, 121−140.

Seo, S.N., 2019. Economic questions on global warming during the Trump years. J. Public. Aff. 19, 1−5. Available from: https://doi.org/10.1002/pa.1914.

Smith, V.K., 2008. Reflections on the literature. Rev. Environ. Econ. Policy 2 (2), 292−308.

Smith, V.K., Desvousges, W.H., 1986. Averting behavior: does it exist? Econ. Lett. 20, 291−296.

Stavins, R., 2007. A US Cap-and-Trade System to Address Global Climate Change. Hamilton Project Discussion Paper 2007-13. The Brookings Institution, Washington, DC.

Supreme Court of the United States (SCOTUS), 2007. Massachusetts et al. vs Environmental Protection Agency et al. Supreme Court of the United States, Washington, DC.

Thaler, R., Rosen, S., 1976. The value of saving a life: evidence from the market. In: Terleckyj, N. (Ed.), Household Production and Consumption. National Bureau of Economic Research, Cambridge, MA.

Tietenberg, T.H., 1980. Transferable discharge permits and the control of stationary source air pollution: a survey and synthesis. Land. Econ. 56 (4), 391−416.

Tietenberg, T., Lewis, L., 2014. Environmental & Natural Resource Economics, ninth ed. Routledge, New York.

Tol, R.S.J., 2002. Estimates of the damage costs of climate change—part 1: benchmark estimates. Environ. Resour. Econ. 21, 47−73.

United Nations Framework Convention on Climate Change (UNFCCC), 1997. Kyoto Protocol to the United Nations Framework Convention on Climate Change. UNFCCC, Geneva.

United States Environmental Protection Agency (USEPA), 1990. The Clean Air Act Amendments. USEPA, Washington, DC.

United States Environmental Protection Agency (USEPA) (1999) The benefits and costs of the Clean Air Act: 1990−2010. EPA Report to Congress. EPA 410-R-99-001. Washington, DC.

United States Environmental Protection Agency (USEPA), 2009. Endangerment and Cause or Contribute Findings for Greenhouse Gases under Section 202(a) of the Clean Air Act. USEPA, Washington, DC.

United States Environmental Protection Agency (USEPA), 2014. Carbon Pollution Emission Guidelines for Existing Stationary Sources: Electric Utility Generating Units. USEPA, Washington, DC.

United States House of Representatives, 2009. H.R.2454 - American Clean Energy and Security Act of 2009. US House of Representatives, Washington, DC.

Unites States House of Representatives, 2019. Resolution: Recognizing the Duty of the Federal Government to Create a Green New Deal. United States House of Representatives, February 7, 2019.

Viscusi, W.K., 1979. Employment Hazards: An Investigation of Market Performance. Harvard University Press, Cambridge, MA.

Viscusi, W.K., Aldy, J.E., 2003. The value of a statistical life: a critical review of market estimates throughout the world. J. Risk Uncertain. 5, 5−76.

Weitzman, M.L., 1974. Prices versus quantities. Rev. Economic Stud. 41, 477−491.

Weitzman, M.L., 1998. The Noah's ark problem. Econometrica 66, 1279−1298.

Weitzman, M.L., 2009. On modeling and interpreting the economics of catastrophic climate change. Rev. Econ. Stat. 91, 1−19.

Woodruff, T.J., Parker, J.D., Schoendorf, K.C., 2006. Fine particulate matter (PM2.5) air pollution and selected causes of postneonatal infant mortality in California. Environ. Health Perspect. 114, 786−790.

The economics of global-scale public goods: key challenges and theories

3

3.1 Introduction

The preceding chapter critically reviewed the core economics literature on public goods with an emphasis on historical developments of major theories and research fields. This chapter, the second chapter of Part II of the book, will continue the expositions of the economics of public goods, but this time with a focus on the applied works on the economics of public goods, which will nonetheless demonstrate that the applied works have indeed advanced the fundamental economic theories elaborated in the last chapter significantly and sometimes in a ground-breaking manner.

Although the goods and services that possess as one of their features the characteristics of a public good are numerous, it may be only a handful of such goods and services that is widely accepted as a predominantly public good problem. Prominent examples are, *inter alia*, national defense, public roads, police works, public education, public works, malaria eradication in Sub-Sahara, a nation-wide air pollution control, infectious diseases, nuclear wars and disarmaments, global warming, free trade, and asteroid collision (Sandler, 1997; Kaul et al., 2003; Seo, 2017a).

Each of these issues will be analyzed in this chapter and Chapter 7, The Economics of Globally Shared Goods, and Chapter 8, Extensions of the Economic Theory to a Basket of Globally Shared Goods, drawing on the pertinent literature for each issue. To begin with, each of the issues has its own unique characteristics, wherefore there is no single panacea solution that can be applied to resolve all of these issues at once. This will be amply illustrated through the analyses of these issues.

Most saliently, a key parameter that distinguishes one public good from another from the above-mentioned list of public goods is a scale of publicness, put differently, a scale of joint consumption (Samuelson and Nordhaus, 2009). Some goods are considered a national public good, for example, national defense or public education. Other goods are considered a global public good, for instance, global warming or asteroid collision. There are other public good issues that are relevant at different geo-political scales: police works or public works as a municipality scale public good, malaria eradication as a continental scale public good, a pollution control as a cross-boundary scale public good.

The Economics of Globally Shared and Public Goods. DOI: https://doi.org/10.1016/B978-0-12-819658-8.00003-2

An even closer look at each of these economic issues further reveals that the production technology required for successfully handling each of the aforementioned public issues must be unique and tailored as well. The task of protection of the Earth against a killer asteroid collision should rely on a different production technology from that technology relied upon for protection of the Earth against global warming catastrophes. The production technology for the provision of an eradication of Malaria in Sub-Saharan Africa should again be different from either of the above two production technologies (Hirshleifer, 1983; Nordhaus, 2006).

The most complicated situation in a public good provision arises, as will be made clear in this chapter, under the two conditions: first, the scale of publicness in consumption is global and, second, the required production technology is cumulative. In such a situation, the actions taken at the level of an individual actor located across the entire globe must add up to an aggregate action which should be sufficient to achieve the needed task at the global level. This means, among other things, that, for any shot at a successful remedy at the Planet-level, the participation rate of individual actors in a global effort should be extremely high (Nordhaus, 2008; Ellerman et al., 2016).

In the applied economic research on public goods, consequently whether a particular policy instrument from the list of instruments elaborated in the preceding chapter can outperform the other instruments in terms of the participation rate of the negotiating parties has emerged as a critical theoretical inquiry. From a slightly different angle but much connected, researchers have explored possible ways of negotiation in order to increase the participation from the parties into a global treaty or agreement (Carraro et al., 2006; Barrett, 2010; Nordhaus, 2015). The applied researches on this front were conducted with reference to the quandary of global climate change policy negotiations (Seo, 2017a,b). The negotiations and treaty enforcements on nuclear nonproliferation and disarmaments, on the other hand, have pointed to a similarly challenging negotiation issue among the parties but largely different in many aspects from the global warming negotiations (Schelling, 1966; Campbell et al., 2004).

Examined from another viewpoint, it has become increasingly evident to country negotiators that a global-scale public good policy that would reach far beyond national boundaries should end up with a greatly variant policy outcome across the negotiating parties, regardless of any policy and instrument adopted including a Pareto optimal solution for the globe (Seo, 2012). In the present international order which protects national sovereignty under the Westphalian system (Treaty of Vienna, 1969), a creation of evident winners and losers from a global public policy would make any negotiated policy solution by far more difficult and further may not even be justified (Seo, 2017a).

Another critical question that the applied economists have grappled with is how to discount the future consumption values and damages that would be realized in a far distant future, for example, as far as half a century or an entire century (Arrow et al., 1996; Weitzman, 1998). A heavy investment into the question by the economists was attributable to the awakening that there is a class of public goods not only whose pertinent spatial scale is as wide as the entire Planet but also whose pertinent time horizon is as far as many centuries. For reference, the currently unfolding global warming is defined by the scientific community at a three-century time scale (Le Treut et al., 2007).

Intriguingly, the discounting debate, which is also referred to as the debate on the rate of time preference in economics, was centered on the application of a zero discounting rate in the policy models of global warming (Stern, 2007; Nordhaus, 2007b). The present author will have an opportunity in this chapter to clarify the views of the proponents and the views of the critics of the zero-discounting proposal. In any way, it is broadly shared that the discount rate cannot be completely divorced from the interest rates that we observe today in various markets, in other words, the real rate of return to capital (Fisher, 1930).

When the appropriate time horizon for a public good policy model is as far as, say, an entire century, it is not only the choice of a discounting rate that becomes an important policy variable: an even more apparent policy feature that emerges is that all projections of many interconnected variables in the policy models made to the end of 21st century would become uncertain to varying degrees. One of such projections that received the most attention is the projection of the future climate system in a century and beyond (Le Treut et al., 2007). In the presence of an extremely high degree of uncertainty which might be at the same time ineluctable and irreducible, a policy designer would face the following question: is a benefit−cost analysis which has been a corner stone for nearly all policy-making decisions on public goods still an appropriate policy design and evaluation tool? Or is there a better policy analysis option in such extreme situations (Weitzman, 2009)?

To be specific, researchers have called into question the validity of a dynamic welfare optimization model of global warming policy decisions, the DICE model to be precise. The DICE model, short for the Dynamic Integrated Climate and Economy model, was rooted fundamentally on the concept of benefits and costs of a policy decision (Nordhaus, 1994). A surprising conclusion put forth by the preem-inent critic was that the world should spend all of its income earned today to make certain that there will be a dollar to spend in the highly uncertain future (Weitzman, 2009). The critics were quick to respond from which intense debates have ensued between the two sides of the aisle on multifaceted aspects of uncertainty (Nordhaus, 2011; Seo, 2018).

In parallel with the academic inquiries, policy negotiators as well as politi-cians who have frequented to the international roundtables of global warming came to propose a global fund whose main purpose is to assist developing coun-try parties to adapt to future changes and at the same time as a tool for increas-ing participation thereof in a globally agreed framework (UNFCCC, 2009; GCF, 2011). The Green Climate Fund (GCF), to be concrete, is a global public good fund which is established through the monetary contributions from rich devel-oped countries and disbursed to the public good projects in poor developing countries. The GCF may have played a pivotal role in achieving a global agree-ment in Paris at the end of 2015, the Paris Agreement, by the UNFCCC member parties (UNFCCC, 2015).

An array of mutually beneficial monetary transfers to be implemented across the member parties has long been recognized as an alternative option in the global warming policy designs (Schelling, 1991; Carraro et al., 2006; Barrett, 2010). Of the multiple forms proposed and the disparate goals of such transfer schemes, the GCF has taken on a specific form. The GCF has already allocated grants to more than 111 projects submitted by developing country parties. Notwithstanding the big leap policy-wise, there remains a big critical gap in the knowledge with regard to how a researcher should evaluate the global public good fund approach such as the GCF and further how she/he should assess individual grant decisions and project outcomes (Seo, 2019b).

In summary, the economics literature of global-scale public goods is extensively covered in this chapter, including the main points discussed in the above. This will be followed up by the three empirical chapters which offer three unique critiques to the theories and models of global public goods that are elaborated in this chapter. Synthesizing all the points in the preceding chapters, the present author will offer in Chapter 7, The Economics of Globally Shared Goods, the core of this book, a novel economic theory of globally shared goods.

3.2   Spatio-political scales of a public good

The concept of a public good was defined and then established, as explained in the previous chapter, by Samuelson and other scholars (Bowen, 1943; Samuelson, 1954; Buchanan, 1965). When the theory surfaced in the middle of the 20th century, the theoreticians took it for granted that they were talking about a nation-wide public good, put differently, a public good in the context of a national economy. Samuelson and Buchanan at the times of the above-cited publications may have never imagined a public good at different scales, say, a global-level public good.

As clarified in Chapter 2, The Economics of Public Goods and Club Goods, the public good is short for the public consumption good which is again meant to be a jointly consumed good by a large number of people, more accurately, all the citizens (Samuelson, 1955). The concept is also encompassed by the term "publicness" in the consumption of a good (Buchanan, 1965). As such, there is no reason to think that the concept cannot be extended to another spatial or political scale.

In the recent editions of the book "Economics," the celebrated textbook by Paul Samuelson which was published up to the 19th edition and profoundly influenced economists during the 20th century, Samuelson and William Nordhaus, a Nobel Prize winner in 2018 for his contribution to global warming economics, describes the public goods at different political scales: a municipal public good, a state public good, a national public good, a multi-national public good, and a global public good (Samuelson and Nordhaus, 2009).

The classification of the public goods can be done by either a political unit or a spatial unit, even though the term "public" has a strong political connotation. Since the public good policies are designed and implemented by a political entity, the classification by the political unit such as the one by Samuelson and Nordhaus is rational. For a global-scale public good, however, there is no such political entity, that is to say, a global government. Further, there are situations in which the publicness of a public good does not overlap the political boundaries. In such situations, a spatial scale can turn out to be a more fitting criterion for the classification.

There can be also a public good whose appropriate scale lies between two political levels. In other words, a joint consumption of the public good may be carried out by a political level higher than a single State but lower than a nation. Similarly, it can be carried out by a political level higher than a nation but lower than a regional union, say, the EU. A trans-state air pollutant is an example for the former while a trans-national air pollutant is an example for the latter. A classification of the whole array of public goods on the criterion of a political scale is summarized in Table 3.1.

The public goods at the national level in the table include a national defense system, a national road system, and a public education system. Once the national defense system is provided, the consumption of one citizen does not diminish the consumption by another of the national defense system. Neither is it possible to exclude an individual from the consumption of the national defense already provided. A national government is the political entity that should provide the national defense system.

A public road system such as the US interstate highway system is another national public good. Every citizen enjoys the benefit of the national road system, that is, no one can be excluded from walking on the roads. For nonrivalry, however there is some degree of rivalry in the national road system attributed to the congestion that can be caused by too many drivers on the same road at the same time (Brown, 1973).

A public education system can be a national public good if it is provided to all citizens up to a certain age free of charges. In all developed countries, it is legally required that the government should provide free education up to the completion of a high school, that is, a secondary school in the United States. Once the free public

Table 3.1 A classification of public goods by a political scale.

Types of goods	Political levels	Goods and services

Public goods	Municipal
	State
	National
	Multi-national/
	  continental
	Global
		Public works
		Police works
		National defense, public roads, and public education
		Infectious diseases (malaria, polio, small pox, and
		  measles), trans-national air pollution
		Global warming, asteroid collision, nuclear
		  disarmaments, Ozone layer protection, artificial
		  intelligence, and strangelets

education system is established, it is not possible to exclude an individual from attending a public school. Nor does the consumption by one student diminish the consumption by other students of the public education system. Again, though, the congestion/crowding effects can occur in, for example, a crowded classroom.

Such a free education system will not be provided solely by the market system. It should be provided by the government via a national taxation and expenditure. In the United States, however, private schools and public schools coexist and, as such, parents can opt out of the public school system and choose a private school for their child.

An example of a municipal public good listed in the table is public works. The department of public works constructs and maintains public spaces and facilities such as municipal buildings, roads, bridges, parks, water supply, sewage system, and wastes collection and disposal. These works are carried out not at the Federal level but at the municipal level.

An example of a state-level public good listed in the table is police works. In the United States, the Constitution gives, under the 10th amendments, each of the 50 States the power to have a police force which enforces the law, protects lives, and prevents crimes in the State (US Senate, 2019). By contrast, the Constitution gives the Federal government the power to deal with foreign affairs and interstate affairs. The rationale for the State-level police force is that it is more efficient and effective to manage the police activities at the State level than at the Federal level. One of the reasons for this is that the State-level police department can have more detailed knowledge of the State's unique characteristics, people, and activities.

For a global-level public good, the publicness of its consumption reaches as far as the entire Planet. Put differently, a global public good is consumed jointly by all the citizens on Earth. In the classical economic analysis, such a good may have been unthinkable. Consider, for your confirmation, the classical books such as Samuelson's Foundations of Economic Analysis or Friedman's Capitalism and Freedom (Samuelson, 1947; Friedman, 1962).

Let us examine first an asteroid collision problem. An asteroid is a small planet in the solar system, most of which reside in the Asteroid Belt located in the region between Mars and Jupiter (Chapman and Morrison, 1994). A collision with an asteroid whose diameter is larger than one kilometer is assessed by the scientific community to have the potential to wreak a global-scale damage (NRC, 2010). The humanity has certainly experienced such a catastrophic asteroid 66 million years ago. The asteroid that wiped out the dinosaurs from the Planet hit the Yucatan Peninsula at the end of the Cretaceous, whose size is estimated to be 7.5-mile (about 10 km) wide in diameter (Kaiho and Oshima, 2017).

A protection of Earth against such a large asteroid's strike is a global-scale public good. The enjoyment of the benefits of such a planetary protection has the characteristics of nonexcludability and nonrivalry at the global level (Seo, 2018). This is especially so for a killer asteroid that has the potential to destroy Earth or kick it off the solar orbit permanently. The technologies for diverting such an asteroid are believed to be available now, although costly and never tested in a real situation (NRC, 2010).

For another example, let's consider a global warming or a global climatic shift. The present author may frame its core policy problem as an increase in carbon dioxide concentration in the global atmosphere, although other ways of framing are possible. Although every air pollutant is released from a local source, a carbon dioxide molecule is special because it is quickly mixed in the atmosphere and stays there for as long as a hundred years. It has, in other words, a residence time of as long as 200 years. The consequence is that a locally released carbon dioxide molecule would end up changing the global atmosphere and, as a result, "damaging" the global economic activities and ecosystems (IPCC, 1990).

Preventing a "dangerously" high level of carbon dioxide concentration in the global atmosphere as to threaten the stability of the Earth's climate system is a global-scale public good (UNFCCC, 1992). The benefits of such prevention would fall upon all countries and citizens on the Planet. The enjoyment of the benefits has the conspicuous characteristics of the public good: nonrivalry and nonexcludability (Nordhaus, 1994). On the other hand, the actions needed for containing the global climate system are costly. There are not a few reasons that an individual country may seek to free ride on other nations' costly abatement actions (Nordhaus, 2010; Seo, 2012).

Of the basketful of public goods listed in Table 3.1, this chapter lays, so does this book, a special emphasis on the public goods at a global scale. This is because the failures of the public good provisions and the challenges of providing them efficiently first foreseen by Samuelson et al. are by far amplified when it comes to an economic analysis of global-scale public goods. As such, the theory of public goods cannot be written satisfactorily without a sensible remedy for the conundrums of the global-scale public goods elucidated (Seo, 2017a).

Other than the two phenomena described in the above, there are other politically prominent global-scale public goods, some of which are also addressed by the global community through an international treaty or another (Sandler, 1997). A nuclear nonproliferation and disarmaments is one of such cases tackled by the Treaty on Non-Proliferation of Nuclear Weapons, commonly known as the NPT (UNODA, 2017).

Another example is the protection of the Ozone layer in the Earth's atmosphere, the depletion of which causes severe damages on human health including skin cancer (Molina and Rowland, 1974). The Ozone layer protection may be a global public good, that is, it benefits all people on Earth. The Montreal Protocol on Substances that Deplete the Ozone Layer was signed in 1987 and the Kigali Amendment to the Montreal Protocol, extending the Montreal Protocol to Earth-heating gases, was signed in 2016 (UNEP, 2016).

Of the public goods that are often mentioned as a global public good, some can be better thought of as a continental public good or a subcontinental public good than a global-scale public good. Consider Malaria eradication in Sub-Saharan Africa. Although Malaria was nearly eradicated in many parts of the globe, the mosquito-borne infectious disease is still active in Sub-Sahara. In 2017, Africa accounted for 93% of Malaria deaths in the globe (WHO, 2016). Since the Malaria virus is carried easily from one person to another person and from one country to another country in Sub-Sahara, it has not been possible to eradicate Malaria occurrences in the continent. As long as there is a country or even a local area with a Malaria patient, the virus can quickly spread to outside the locality. An eradication of the disease would provide a public good, that is, the benefit of eradication, predominantly to the African continent.

It might be possible that the Malaria virus spreads to other parts of the globe in the future carried by a traveler to the African continent. However, a Malaria vaccination, which is highly effective, is available to the travelers, so is a quarantine at the ports of entry for infected travelers, both of which makes a global outbreak of Malaria at a future time a highly unlikely event.

An eradication of other once-much-feared diseases such as polio, small pox, and measles, can be similarly analyzed as a continental or subcontinental public good. The eradication rate of polio is 99% as of 2019 and the global eradication of smallpox was certified in 1980 (Barrett, 2010).

3.3 Global public goods

Of the five levels of the public goods listed in Table 3.1, public policy challenges are certainly higher in the provision of a global-scale public good. The experiences on global warming policy negotiations led by the United Nations during the past several decades amply demonstrate that it is an elusive endeavor to have all stakeholder nations agreed on a single treaty and be committed to it (Nordhaus, 2010; Seo, 2017a). The treaty on nuclear arms nonproliferation and disarmaments, another global-scale public good, is also an on-going negotiation process with not a few pitfalls (Campbell et al., 2004).

What makes the provision of a global public good most elusive of all the public goods? There are a host of reasons, some of which can be drawn directly from the fundamental concept while others are well documented by the researchers and negotiators. The first evident challenge is absence of the government that is elected by the constituents to design a relevant policy and implement it. For the Federal, State, and municipal public goods, there is a government as such: the Federal government, the State government, and the municipal government.

In the current international law and order, national sovereignty is protected and guaranteed. An international body cannot infringe upon the sovereignty of an individual nation. As such, when an international treaty is agreed upon, it may become unenforceable when it conflicts with the national sovereignty, say, the decision by the people of the nation.

That an international treaty on a global public good may collide with individual national interests and there is no "global government" empowered to enforce the global treaty against the sovereignty of individual nations is referred to as a Westphalian Dilemma. It refers to the Treaty of Westphalia in 1648 that ended recurrent territorial disputes and conflicts in Europe and drew the national boundaries of today in Europe (Treaty of Vienna, 1969).

The second salient feature of the provision of global public goods is the range and depth of heterogeneity across the individual stakeholders and nations. There is an array of variables with regard to which individual countries across the globe are vastly different, including average annual income, political ideology, religion, endowments of oil and natural gas, altitude above sea level, an island or landlocked territory, and climate.

For an illustration of the heterogeneity, let us take a look at a 30-year average temperature, called a temperature normal, which is one component of the climate system. Globally, the hottest countries are Burkina Faso and Mali, two Sub-Saharan tropical countries, where it reaches slightly above $+28°C$. The coldest countries are Russia and Canada where it falls below $-5°C$. For the temperate climate zones, the average temperature is about $11°C$ in the countries such as South Korea, Japan, and France, and about $9°C$ in the United States (Harris et al., 2014). The range of the temperature normal across the Planet is $33°C$.

For the basket of national public goods mentioned in Table 3.1, the degree of heterogeneity would be smaller. In other words, an individual nation is more homogeneous than the community of all nations with regard to any of the aforementioned variables. For any nation, the range of average temperature across the country would be smaller than $33°C$. A similar exercise can be done for each of the above-referenced variables of heterogeneity, that is, the income level, politics, and so forth.

The third salient feature is a conspicuous role of technological innovations, for which there are two sides. Technological innovations are often a cause for the creation of a global public good, for the most drastic example, a singularity catastrophe from computing revolutions or a strangelet catastrophe from high risk scientific experiments (Kurzweil, 2005; Ellis et al., 2008). On the other hand, technological breakthroughs also often provide a powerful remedy for the problem of a global public good. Consider global warming. The set of technological solutions suggested by the scientific community includes many existing and future technological breakthroughs: sunlight reflectors such as a stratospheric aerosol layer or a marine cloud brightening, a carbon-capture-storage, ocean fertilization, solar energy, electric vehicles, nuclear fusion, and new ways of lighting (NRC, 2015a,b; Seo, 2017a). Notwithstanding the bunch of technologies available or possible, the scale of implementation of each of these technologies as well as the risk of implementing it should be global (NRC, 2015a,b).

A pivotal importance of technological options can be stated even more clearly for the asteroid collision prevention, the solution set for which is predominantly technology-driven. After detecting a killer asteroid which has the potential to wreak havoc at a global scale, the Planetary defense team should deflect the asteroid through either of the two technological options in the outer space: a kinetic impactor or a gravity tractor (NASA, 2014).

3.4 Production technologies

A production function is a technological relationship between quantities of inputs, that is, factors of production, and quantities of outputs. The production of a global public good may take on a particular technological relationship while that of another global public good may take on another technological relationship. In particular, we can identify three different production technologies from the productions of the list of global public goods listed in Table 3.1: cumulative, best-shot, and weakest-link technologies (Hirshleifer, 1983).

A generic production function is written as follows, with Q being the output and X_i being a factor of production:

$$Q = f(X_1, X_2, \ldots, X_n). \tag{3.1}$$

To continue with the technologies for the global public goods, let E_i be the effort by an individual country to provide the global public good under consideration and Q the level of the public good provided. Then, a production function with a cumulative production technology can be written as follows, which states that individual countries' efforts add up to produce the global good:

$$Q = f\left(\sum_{i=1}^{n} E_i\right). \tag{3.2}$$

The weakest-link technology refers to the production function whose level of the output is determined by the least-effort factor, that is, the effort of the country, of all the countries, that made the least effort. The better efforts are of no meaning in this technology. We can express the weakest-link production technology by the Leontief production function or the fixed proportions production technology (Mas-Colell et al., 1995). Let δ_i be the quality of the unit effort and E_i be the quantity of effort. Then, the weakest-link production technology is expressed as:

$$Q = \min\{\delta_1 E_1, \delta_2 E_2, \ldots, \delta_n E_n\}. \tag{3.3}$$

The third type of the production technology is the best-shot technology. The production function is defined by the best effort and the lesser efforts are of no meaning in this production technology. Same as before, let δ_i be quality of the unit effort and E_i be the amount of effort. Then, the production function of the best-shot technology takes on the following form:

$$Q = \max\{\delta_1 E_1, \delta_2 E_2, \ldots, \delta_n E_n\}. \tag{3.4}$$

The three production technologies are immediately applicable to the productions of the public goods introduced in the previous two sections (Nordhaus, 2006; Barrett, 2010). For the global warming, the production function takes on a cumulative technology because each country's reduction of carbon dioxide emissions should add up to the total global aggregate reduction which would eventually determine the level and success of a global warming policy or response.

The production technology for the asteroid collision prevention is a best-shot: the best-shot of all the efforts made determines the success or failure of the provision. The lesser efforts, including the second best effort, are meaningless. An outcome from the best technology is what determines the ultimate outcome.

The weakest-link technology is often referred to for the production of a coastal wall in preparation against the climate change caused sea level rises and subsequent inundations. Another frequently cited weakest-link production technology is eradication of an infectious disease such as Malaria in the Sahel. In these public goods, as long as there is the weakest point in the wall construction or the Malaria eradication effort where there is a crack in the wall or a remnant virus, the entire effort will fail to provide the intended public goods. A success or failure of the policy to provide the public good hinges on the state of the weakest point.

3.5 A globally harmonized carbon price or tax

Of the three types of the global public good as per its production technology, the thorniest policy challenge belongs to the provision of a global-scale public good with a cumulative production technology. The nature of the challenge is, briefly stated, a universal participation, as far as the theory is concerned: all countries on the Planet should participate in a global policy effort, whose aggregate efforts should also be sufficient for achieving a global goal.

What is the most rational policy option for providing a global public good with a cumulative technology? Slightly narrowly, what is the optimal/efficient policy instrument for achieving the successful provision thereof? To answer these questions, we can extend the analyses of the three policy instruments conducted in the previous chapter: a price-based policy, a quantity-based policy, and a hybrid.

A careful examination of the policy negotiations during the past nearly three decades and the notable agreements/treaties on global warming, a salient example of a global public good with a cumulative technology, will reveal that the three policy instruments have all been heavily analyzed and discussed. In addition, these policy options were adopted in one form or another to address the problem of global warming in one context or another.

Let me elaborate the last point. The Kyoto Protocol of 1997, the only international treaty on the topic, adopted a quantity-based limit on the level of greenhouse gas emissions. The Protocol chose the 1990 level of emissions of greenhouse gases as the threshold limit (UNFCCC, 1997; Nordhaus and Boyer, 1999; Manne and Richels, 1999). The Cancun Agreements of 2010 adopted the concept of a global temperature ceiling at 2°C (UNFCCC, 2010).

The European Union's Emissions Trading Scheme which was launched in 2005 is an example of a hybrid approach, more specifically, a quantitative cap on the total emissions coupled with trading of emissions permits across the firms (Ellerman et al., 2016; EC, 2016). The Waxman-Markey Bill proposed during the

Obama Presidency attempted unsuccessfully to legislate a cap-and-trade program for the United States (Stavins, 2007; US House of Representatives, 2009).

As analyzed in depth in the previous chapter in the context of a national public good, the most efficient as well as socially optimal policy instrument of the three is a price-based policy, barring exceptional cases. For the context of a global public good, this point was pioneered through a globally harmonized carbon tax which has been elucidated by William Nordhaus who was awarded the Nobel Memorial Prize in Economic Science in 2018 for his contributions to the economics of climate change (Nordhaus, 1982, 1994, 2018).

Although the carbon tax was never adopted as a global climate policy, it was chosen at a national and a subnational level, albeit, even at that limited level, only in a partial manner (Tietenberg, 2013). A national carbon tax was introduced in Sweden in 1991, which charges all fossil fuels in proportion to their carbon content (Hammar and Akerfeldt, 2011). A national carbon tax policy was announced at the end of 2018 by the Canadian government, which was entitled the Greenhouse Gas Pollution Pricing Act (ECCC, 2019).

The carbon price has been recognized as an inevitable element of either the quantity-based policy or the hybrid cap-and-trade program (Montgomery 1972). Put differently, the threshold imposed on the total emissions as well as the total number of permits to be issued cannot be determined satisfactorily without the essential knowledge of the social cost of carbon, that is, the price of carbon. It is not an exaggeration to say that the globally harmonized carbon tax has been a benchmark in the economics of global warming (Seo, 2017a).

As such, all global warming policy dialogues must grapple with the central question of the price of carbon, more accurately, the price of carbon dioxide and other greenhouse gases (Pearce et al., 1996, Stern, 2007; NASEM, 2017). From this point on, the present author will succinctly explain the concept of the socially optimal price of carbon as well as the analytical model which was developed to calculate the globally harmonized price of carbon empirically. The latter is often called the DICE model, short for the Dynamic Integrated Climate and Economy model (Nordhaus, 1994). The DICE is one of the social welfare optimization models developed for global warming policy decisions but is the only dynamic welfare optimization model (Manne et al. 1995; Nordhaus and Sztorc, 2013).

The DICE model assumes that the global community's objective is to maximize its welfare which is defined as the present value of a stream of the world community's utilities over an appropriate time horizon (Nordhaus, 1994). Let U_t be the society's utility at time t. The society's objective function of the DICE model is written as follows:

$$\omega = \sum_{t=0}^{\infty} U_t \, (1+\rho)^{-t}. \tag{3.5}$$

A key economic parameter in Eq. (3.5) is ρ, a social rate of time preference, which determines how the DICE model discounts the utilities obtained in the future periods. The larger the value of this parameter, the more the society discounts the future utilities. The smaller the value of the parameter, the less the society discounts the future utilities. What is the correct discount rate to use in the DICE model has been a contentious point of debate, but it should be some positive fractional value which hinges on other factors in the economy such as consumption growth rate, elasticity of marginal utility of consumption, and the market interest rate (Arrow et al., 1996; Weitzman, 1998; Stern, 2007; Nordhaus, 2007a).

The world community's utility function at time period t, one component of Eq. (3.5), needs to be defined. In the DICE model, it is specified as the individual's utility function multiplied by the total world population (*POP*). The individual's utility function is defined as a Bernoulli utility function, a nonlinear function of the consumption per capita (c), whose shape is determined by the world community's aversion to inequality (η) (Nordhaus, 2008; Weitzman, 2009):

$$U_t = POP_t \cdot \left(\frac{c_t^{1-\eta}}{1-\eta} \right). \tag{3.6}$$

In the DICE model, the population trajectory of the world should be modeled exogenously, for which the projections by such specialized population research centers as the United Nations' Population Program and the International Institute for Applied Systems Analysis (IIASA) (Lutz et al., 2014) are referred to. The latter provides a probabilistic population projection which is the most advanced population projection methodology that incorporates many behavioral changes in the future (IIASA, 2007).

The utility function is shaped by the inequality aversion parameter, another hotly debated parameter among the researchers. The value of one of this parameter, that is, $\eta = 1$, means that the world community is neutral to economic inequality; the value greater than one, that is, $\eta > 1$, means that it is averse to economic inequality; and the value smaller than one, that is, $\eta < 1$, means that it is accepting economic inequality (Nordhaus, 1994).

It should be pointed out that the choice of η is not arbitrary. That is, the choice of one value for the parameter must force other parameters in the model to be changed, the point that many researchers in the literature failed to grasp (Stern, 2007; Weitzman, 2009). To mention one example, the choice of a specific parameter value for the social aversion to inequality should alter the value of the social rate of time preference, given the market interest rate (Nordhaus, 2007a). Nordhaus presented the DICE model calibrated to $\eta = 2$ as well as that calibrated to $\eta = 1$.

To complete the economy module of the DICE model, typical relationships among economic variables are defined, following the framework of the classical economic growth theory (Solow, 1956): (1) The total consumption is determined by total production (Q_t) minus saving (=investment, I_t); (2) Saving rate is determined exogenously; (3) The capital of the global economy (K_t) is assumed to depreciate annually following a perpetual inventory method with an exponential depreciation rate (δ_t) while it increases with the investment (Kamps, 2004); and

(4) The production function takes the form of a Cobb Douglas function with labor (L_t) and capital (K_t) as inputs and the Total Factor Productivity (A_t) as a multiplicative factor (Hulten, 2000). It assumes a Hicks-neutral technological change (Hicks, 1932).

The phenomenon of global warming and climate change, which is a global public good or, more precisely, a global public bad, will affect the global economic production and subsequently the global consumption. In the macroeconomic growth model that integrates the global warming phenomenon, the production function takes on the Cobb-Douglas function and further it integrates both the damage from global warming on economic production (Ω) and the cost of abatement of carbon dioxide and other greenhouse gases (Θ). The abatement cost is incurred when a meaningful global warming policy is implemented, which forces carbon abatements. Adding two global warming-induced costs multiplicatively, the DICE model production function is written as follows:

$$Q_t = [1 - \Theta_t] \cdot [1 + \Omega_t]^{-1} \cdot A_t \cdot K_t^{\tau} \cdot L_t^{1-\tau}. \tag{3.7}$$

Of the two economic costs resulting from the climate change, the abatement cost is estimated statistically from the family of empirical abatement cost data obtained from the firms and firm units. Alternatively it can be estimated through a bottom—up process with an engineering approach (Fischer and Morgenstern, 2006). The statistical approach finds that the abatement cost function is a power function of the control rate (μ), whose shape is determined by the exponent, θ_2 (Nordhaus and Boyer, 2000):

$$\Theta_t = \theta_{1t} \cdot \mu_t^{\theta_{2t}} \tag{3.8}$$

The abatement cost is bounded by the existence of a backstop technology. A backstop technology is the technology that can provide energy indefinitely at a fixed price with near zero emissions of carbon dioxide (Nordhaus, 1973). Examples of a backstop technology may be energy generations from nuclear fusion or solar radiation. As far as stopping global warming is concerned, it can be a solar radiation reflection technology or a carbon capture from the atmosphere (NRC, 2015a, b). The marginal cost of abatement at the 100% abatement of carbon emissions is the marginal cost of abatement by a backstop technology. In other words, the marginal cost of abating one ton of carbon emissions will keep increasing as ever larger amounts of emissions are abated, but it cannot increase beyond the marginal abatement cost of a backstop technology.

The other cost resulting from the climate change phenomenon is the economic damage that a change in the climate system inflicts on the global economy. Put straightforwardly, the question of how harmful the impacts of the global warming and climate change will be on the numerous economic activities on the Planet has been the most contentious field of the climate change economics but at the same time has swayed policy negotiations profoundly (Mendelsohn and Neumann, 1999;

Tol, 2009; Seo, 2016a,b). The DICE model has maintained its initial specification of a quadratic damage function, Ω_t, of a global average atmospheric temperature increase from the preindustrial global average atmospheric temperature (T_t^{ATM}):

$$\Omega_t = \tau_1 \cdot T_t^{ATM} + \tau_2 \cdot \left(T_t^{ATM}\right)^2. \tag{3.9}$$

Faced with the two costs that result from the global warming phenomenon, the global community must consider the following trade-off: either reduce the emissions of greenhouse gases to minimize the global warming damage or let the emissions increase unabated to minimize the cost of reducing the emissions. Put differently, it would be better to let one ton of carbon dioxide released into the atmosphere if the cost of abating one ton of emissions exceeds the damage induced by the tone of emissions.

By forcing the global community to make a decision faced with this trade-off, the DICE model calculates a trajectory of the optimal level of abatement decade by decade for the Planet. This was referred to as the optimal control rate in Eq. (3.8), that is μ_t. From the trajectory of the optimal control rate, the trajectory of the optimal price of carbon is calculated through Eq. (3.8) or Eq. (3.9), which is also referred to as the social cost of carbon.

The price of a ton of carbon dioxide or carbon efficiently determined is the heart of the DICE model as well as the host of climate change policy models. The policy model determines the single price of carbon which should then be imposed on any emission activities across the globe. Economic actors, small and large, will incorporate the price of carbon when they make myriad economic decisions, the consequences of which will be the control rate of the global carbon emissions in Eq. (3.8) to be achieved by the global community.

The emissions of the greenhouse gases (e_t) is then determined by the economic production, control rate, and the carbon intensity of the economy. The carbon intensity (φ_t) is expressed as the tons of carbon emissions per US\$ 1000 economic production.

$$e_t = \varphi_t \cdot \left(1 - \mu_t\right) \cdot Q_t. \tag{3.10}$$

$$e_t = e_t^{industrial} + e_t^{natural}. \tag{3.11}$$

The carbon intensity of the advanced economy has been falling since the early 20th century owing primarily to technological changes and to some minor degree because of increased environmental concerns. The carbon intensity of developing countries such as China and India is more than two times larger than that of the United States at the present time, but is expected to decline in the coming decades in a similar historical trend witnessed in developed countries. The carbon intensity is a key policy variable of contention among the national negotiators. The China's proposal to the Paris Agreements, for your reference, is centered around this variable (UNFCCC, 2015; Seo, 2017a).

The total amount of greenhouse gas emissions is again composed of two components, as in Eq. (3.11) (GCP, 2017). One is the emissions from industrial sectors ($e^{industrial}$) and the other is the emissions from natural resource sectors ($e^{natural}$). The emissions from the natural resource sectors are carbon dioxide emissions from, *inter alia*, tree cutting, soil tillage, methane emissions from ruminant animals and wetlands, and ocean sinks (Schlesinger, 1997; Houghton, 2008).

To complete the description of the DICE model, the present author needs to explain the nature module of the model. The economy module of the DICE is what is explained in Eqs. (3.5)–(3.11). The nature module comprises a set of causal relationships between changes in greenhouse gas emissions and changes in the atmospheric, oceanic, and climate systems.

First, the nature module can begin with the total amount of carbon emissions that can be emitted by the global society, which is bounded by the maximum amount of fossil fuels that the Planet possesses and can be economically extracted by the humanity indefinitely. This amount is nearly fixed, which is set at 6000 GtC in the DICE model, because fossil fuels such as oil, natural gas, and coal, are formed through geological and chemical processes that take millions of years and, as such, exhaustible resources (Hotelling, 1931; Nordhaus and Sztorc, 2013; BP, 2019).

Second, the carbon dioxide emitted from various anthropogenic activities are, unlike the other Earth-heating gases, mixed quickly in the atmosphere, which is the most salient physical characteristic of the molecule thereof that renders the phenomenon of climate change to become a global public good. It does not matter where the carbon dioxide is emitted, that is, from which country the chemical compound is released. It is quickly mixed in the global atmosphere equalizing the atmospheric concentration of carbon dioxide across the globe (Keeling et al., 2005). Further the carbon dioxide once released into the atmosphere stays there for many decades and even many centuries, thereby accumulates in the atmosphere. More formally, the residence time of carbon dioxide is from many decades to centuries (Le Treut et al., 2007).

Third, the atmospheric carbon is absorbed in part by the oceans and land-based ecosystems that are in turn appropriated by the human society as well as the other sentient beings, through which process carbon is released into the atmosphere again. This process of carbon compounds moving from one ecosystem to another is called the carbon cycle (Schlesinger, 1997). The DICE model simplifies the carbon cycle through a three-reservoir model in which the transfers of carbon are made among the three reservoirs: atmosphere, upper ocean, and deep ocean (Schneider and Thompson, 1981; Schlesinger and Jiang, 1990).

Fourth, through the carbon cycle, carbon dioxide accumulates in the atmosphere, which then increases the Radiative Forcing (RF) (IPCC, 1990). The RF caused by carbon compounds is additional radiation incident on the Earth surface induced by the greenhouse effects caused by carbon accumulation. Besides the carbon, other factors can increase or decrease the RF. For example, an increase in aerosols in the atmosphere decreases the RF while an increase in nitrous oxides (N_2O) or methane (MH_4) increase the RF. The key statistic in this chain is the RF caused by the doubling of carbon dioxide concentration in the atmosphere, which is equivalent to 3.8 W/m^2 (Watts per square meter) (Le Treut et al., 2007).

Finally, the changes in the RF, that is, the amount of radiation received by Earth, leads to changes in atmospheric temperature and deep ocean temperature. An increase in the RF caused by an increase in carbon dioxide concentration in the atmosphere leads to the phenomenon of global warming. The key statistic in this chain is the equilibrium temperature sensitivity, that is, the magnitude of the increase in global average temperature in response to the doubling in carbon dioxide concentration from 280 ppm (parts per million) to 560 ppm. Following the climate science literature reported by the IPCC, it is set at 3°C in the DICE model (Nordhaus, 2008; IPCC, 2014).

This completes the description of the nature module of the DICE model, which, coupled with the economy module explained previously, also completes the description of the DICE model. Fig. 3.1 summarizes the major components of the DICE model with key statistics for each component: economy, atmospheric concentration of carbon dioxide, carbon cycle, RF, and climate system. Since the DICE model integrates all of these components into a single decision-making framework, it is called an Integrated Assessment Model of climate change.

Before we close this section, a succinct description of the RICE model, short for the Regional Dynamic Integrated model of Climate and Economy, an extension of the DICE, is very much called for. The RICE model was developed in order to explain regional differences in preference, economy, technology, and carbon emissions, which was impossible in the DICE model (Nordhaus and Yang, 1996). The two models have the same equations for the geophysical aspects of the models. The only difference in the RICE model is the world economy which is decomposed into 12 regional economies (Nordhaus and Boyer, 2000).

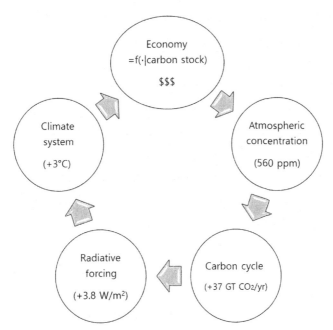

Figure 3.1 Major components of the climate and economy model.

As such, the two models by and large arrive at the same policy conclusions for global warming policy designs. From a modeling perspective, it is far more complicated, more specifically, data-intensive. Besides that, there is an additional theoretical element added to the RICE model: the Negishi welfare weights through which marginal utilities are equated across the world regions as well as across the time periods as a dynamic optimality condition of the RICE model (Negishi, 1960). More specifically, the global welfare function is written as a Bergson-Samuelson social welfare function which encompasses multiple regions:

$$\Gamma = \sum_{t=1}^{t_{max}} \sum_{i=1}^{N} \xi_{i,t} \cdot U^{i \cdot} \left[1 + \rho_t^i \right]^{-1}. \qquad (3.12)$$

The Negishi weights, $\xi_{i,t}$, are specified for each region and each time period. The Negishi algorithm in the RICE model sets the Negishi weights in a way that the marginal utility of consumption is equalized across all regions and all time periods. This ensures the global welfare function in Eq. (3.12) is maximized in the optimal solution.

This completes the succinct description of the climate and economy model, the DICE. It arrives at one price of carbon across all countries and regions of the globe at each time period. The is the optimal price of a public good, or equivalently a public bad, described in Chapter 2, The Economics of Public Goods and Club Goods. The DICE model provides an empirical economic model through which researchers can measure the optimal price of the global public good.

3.6   Economics of the value of time

The economics of public goods cannot be satisfactorily established without a theory of the value of time. The reason is that the costs and the benefits from a provision of a public good are earned at the present time and in the future time periods, in some cases very far into the future. In the modeling of global warming described in the previous section, the damages and benefits of a policy or a no policy would unravel over a timescale of a century.

How we should value today the dollars earned in the future time is one of the fundamental inquiries in the economics literature (Fisher, 1930). Most basically, in the financial markets, one dollar earned, say, 10 years later is not the same as one dollar earned today because of the interest rate that can be earned over the 10-year period. One dollar today is equal to one dollar plus an interest to be accrued in the future time. With r an annual interest rate, t the number of years from today, and q the dollars saved today, the value at the future date (FV) is as follows with a discrete discounting:

$$FV = q * (1 + r)^t. \qquad (3.13)$$

Why is there an interest rate in the financial markets? Economists explain the existence and size of the interest rate via multiple factors: impatience of individuals on the future, round about ways of production, and technological advances over time, all of which factors are traded in the market for money (Fisher, 1930; Bohm-Bawerk, 1959).

The relationship between the interest rate and these factors can be expressed succinctly in a mathematical equation assuming a competitive market. Let g be a constant rate of consumption growth, η be a constant elasticity of marginal utility of consumption, and ρ be the pure rate of time preference. An optimization of the social welfare function leads to the following Ramsey equation at the equilibrium (denoted by $*$) in the competitive market (Ramsey, 1928; Nordhaus, 2007b):

$$r^* = \rho + \eta \, g^*. \tag{3.14}$$

The r^* is the equilibrium interest rate. Of the three parameters on the right side of Eq. (3.14), the most controversial one is ρ, the pure social rate of time preference, which was explained in Eq. (3.5). In the climate economics literature, the value of this parameter has been varied from 0% to 3% depending upon the models and researchers. The higher the rate, the more impatient the society is, preferring the current dollar more strongly to the future dollar.

As shown in Eq. (3.14), however, a researcher cannot choose the value of this parameter entirely arbitrarily. The choice of this parameter is subject to the Ramsey equation. More concretely, at 6% real interest rate, 2% consumption growth, and the elasticity of marginal utility of consumption of 2, the social rate of time preference should be set to 2%. Alternatively, at 4% real interest rate, 2% consumption growth, and the elasticity of marginal utility of consumption of 1.5, the social rate of time preference should be set to 1%.

A heated debate on the choice of a discount rate for a global warming policy model such as the DICE broke out in the past decade. Some argued that the social rate of time preference should be set to zero in the global warming policy models (Stern, 2007). The primary argument is grounded on ethical considerations. Ethicists argued that it is immoral to discount the damage inflicted on future generations since the value of the future generation is not different from the value of the current generation (Broome, 1992, 1994). The damage in the future should be treated as the same value as the damage that is inflicted today.

This ethical viewpoint, however, overlooks the other side of morality embedded in discounting and interest rate. That is, a dollar earned today which is left to the future generation would become in the future a dollar plus a stream of interest payments to the future date. Imagine that you purchase a bond with the dollar whose expiration date is the future date and leave it to the future generation. Because of the interest rate in the financial market, a larger sum of money than one dollar will be left to the future generations. This aspect is of course well encapsulated in Eqs. (3.14) and (3.15).

The social rate of time preference is not directly observed in the market. A researcher may therefore argue in one way or another that it should be set at a high level or at a low level, depending upon the problem under consideration. However, the choice must be anchored at Eq. (3.15). Then, the important empirical question boils down to the market interest rate.

What should be the real interest rate that the DICE and similar models should rely upon? The data in Table 3.2 were put together from three data sources: (1) the estimated real returns of various capital assets by Arrow et al. for the IPCC Report; (2) the online data compiled by Shiller for his book entitled Irrational Exuberance (Arrow et al., 1996; Shiller, 2005, 2019); and (3) The real estate investment trust (REIT) index data by REIT (2019). The Shiller data cover the most recent period as well as the entire history in the case of the S&P500 Index.

The table shows that the US equities earned 6.5% real return per annum from 1925 to 1992, that is, the nominal return minus the inflation rate. According to the Shiller's book, for the entire period of the S&P500 Index, the real return amounted

Table 3.2 Estimated real returns to capital investments.

Assets	Sources	Time period	Real return (%)
(1) United States			
Equities	Arrow et al. (1996)	1925−1992	6.5
S&P500	Shiller (2019)	Entire history: 1926−2018	6.98
All private capital, pretax	Arrow et al. (1996)	1963−1985	5.7
Corporate capital, capital, posttax	Arrow et al. (1996)	1963−1985	5.7
Real estate	Arrow et al. (1996)	1960−1984	5.5
Real estate (Case-Shiller real home price index)	Shiller (2019)	1953−2018	0.66
Real estate (FTSE U.S. REIT)	REIT (2019)	1972−2018	7.63
Farmland	Arrow et al. (1996)	1947−1984	5.5
Treasury bills	Arrow et al. (1996)	1926−1986	0.3
(2) Other high income countries			
Equities	Arrow et al. (1996)	1960−1984	5.4
Bonds	Arrow et al. (1996)	1960−1984	1.6
Nonresidential capital	Arrow et al. (1996)	1975−1990	15.1
Government short-term bonds	Arrow et al. (1996)	1960−1990	0.3
(3) Developing countries			
Primary education	Arrow et al. (1996)	various	26
Higher education	Arrow et al. (1996)	various	13

to 6.98% per annum from 1926 to 2018 (Shiller, 2019). In the high-income industrial countries, nonresidential capital earned a real return of 15.1% per annum during the period from 1975 to 1990 while equities earned 5.4% real return over 1960−1984.

The real return for the real estate investments vary by the property type. The Case-Shiller Real Home Price Index shows an annual real return of 0.66% during the 1953−2018 period (Shiller, 2019). On the other hand, the FTSE U.S. REIT Index shows 7.3% annual real return during the 1972−2018 period (REIT, 2019). The real return for the real estate investments in the United States for the past 20 years, covering the period from 1999 to 2018, outperformed the equity return in the United States, with about 7.2% real return per annum. The table shows that even the farmland has a high rate of return at about 5.5% annually from 1947 to 1984.

Government short-term bonds in the high-income industrial countries and the US Treasury bills earned the lowest returns, about 0.3% per annum. Commercial bonds earned 1.6% real return in high-income countries.

In developing countries, it is estimated that the real return from investments in education is very high, especially so for primary education. The primary education earned 26% real return per annum while the higher education earned 13% of real return annually.

The estimates of the real returns of various types of assets summarized in Table 3.2 can be averaged with a different weight assigned to each asset type to construct a real interest rate that can be used by global warming policy models, that is, the r^* in Eq. (3.14). In turn, the choice of the real interest rate should guide researchers in choosing the discount rate, that is, ρ in Eq. (3.14).

Another point of contention in the discount rate debate is whether the real interest rate in the future time periods should be assumed to be the same as the today's real interest rate (Ainslie, 1991; Weitzman, 1998; Cropper and Laibson, 1999; Nordhaus, 2008). Will the future interest rates rise or fall? An examination of the 200-year history of the market interest rates for the U.S. long-term government bonds finds a long-term trend of a steady decrease in the interest rate, which started at over 7% interest rate 200 years ago to around 3% by the 1990s. However, the history also shows repeated up-and-down swings in the rates. The U.S. long-term government bonds represent the highest quality, lowest risk asset, whose market investments are consistently available in the United States over the past 200 years (Newell and Pizer, 2001).

The discount rate that is declining steadily over time is called a hyperbolic discounting in contrast to an exponential discounting in which the discount rate remains constant over the future time periods (Ainslie, 1991; Cropper and Laibson, 1999). In an exponential discounting, the dollar in a future time period is discounted exponentially. Let k be a parameter of the degree of discounting. Then, the discount factor, f, is as follows:

$$f(t) = \$1 \times e^{-kt}. \tag{3.15}$$

For the exponential discounting, the discounting between two adjacent time periods remains the same, regardless of how far or near in the future we choose the two periods:

$$\frac{f(t+1)}{f(t)} = \frac{e^{-k(t+1)}}{e^{-kt}} = e^{-k}, \text{ for any } t. \tag{3.16}$$

The discount factor for the hyperbolic discounting is defined by a hyperbolic function. For the \$1 at t:

$$g(t) = \$1 \times \frac{1}{1+kt}. \tag{3.17}$$

For the hyperbolic discounting, the discounting between the two adjacent time periods depends on how far in the future the two periods are happening:

$$\frac{g(t+1)}{g(t)} = \frac{\frac{1}{1+k(t+1)}}{\frac{1}{1+kt}} = \frac{1}{1 + \frac{k}{1+kt}}. \tag{3.18}$$

From Eq. (3.18), it is easy to verify that the ratio goes to one when t goes to infinity. That is, there is nearly no discounting between the two time periods in the extreme case. When $t = 0$, the ratio is $1/(1 + k)$, which is less than 1. This can be contrasted to Eq. (3.16), the exponential discounting, in which the discounting between the two time periods remains unchanged regardless how far in the future the two periods are considered.

Theorists for the hyperbolic discounting argue that individuals make decisions as if the farther the future events considered by them, the lower the discount rate they choose (Ainslie, 1991). However, an individual with hyperbolic preferences should make exactly the same decisions as the individual with a conventional exponential discounting. They argue that both discounting methods discount the future at the rate equal to the rate of return to capital. The only difference is how the two discounting methods understand today's decisions on the future events (Laibson, 1997; Cropper and Laibson, 1999).

In Fig. 3.2, discount factors from both the exponential discounting and the hyperbolic discounting are put together for the 100-year time period from today. In the figure, $k = 0.04$ is assumed for both discounting methods, that is, 4% discount rate in the case of the former. A clear difference in the trajectories of the two discount factors is demonstrated. The discount factor in the exponential discounting declines at a much faster rate and falls to about 0.15 in 50 years and to near 0 in 100 years. On the other hand, the discount factor in the hyperbolic discounting declines at a slower rate and falls to 0.4 in 50 years and to about 0.25 in 100 years.

The two discount factors are about the same magnitude in the first 10 years, but depart substantially in the final 50 years of the time period considered in the figure. By 100 years, the hyperbolic discount factor remains high at 0.25 while the

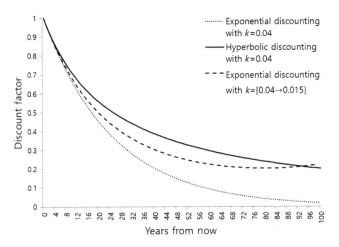

Figure 3.2 Hyperbolic discounting versus exponential discounting.

exponential discount factor falls to near zero. As such, the two discounting methods have very different implications on the economic outcomes that would occur far in the future.

However, the two discounting methods can lead to a similar trajectory of the discount factor, which is demonstrated by the third line in Fig. 3.2. The dashed line is drawn with the exponential discounting with the discount rate, k, assumed to decline linearly from 0.04 to 0.015. The trajectory of the discount factor of the dashed line is by far closer to the trajectory of the discount factor from the hyperbolic discounting.

In the end, the two discounting methods can be calibrated to yield about the same trajectory of the two discount factors, as in Fig. 3.2. More critically, such calibrations would be possible by assuming that an individual should apply a lower discount rate for a farther away future event. Put differently, the solid line and the dashed line in Fig. 3.2 are possible under the same behavioral assumption.

An important behavioral economic research question is whether an individual actually discounts a dollar reward with a lower discount rate, the farther away in time the reward is earned (Thaler, 1981; Ainslie, 1991). However, even if researchers can find some individuals make decisions according to the hyperbolic discounting, there remains the question of whether such decisions are consistent with an economically optimal decision-making (Laibson, 1997). That is, the individuals will end up with monetary losses if the real interest rates in the economy keep deviating from the discount rates determined by the hyperbolic decision-making.

Another way to approach the discounting debate is to ask whether there is a theoretical ground to believe that the real interest rate in the economy, that is, the real return from investments, should keep declining over the future time periods (Newell and Pizer, 2001). A pessimist would reach such a conclusion based on, among other things, limitations of land and natural resources, for example, the limits of growth report by the Rome Club or zero-growth/degrowth proponents

(Meadows et al., 1972; Speth, 2012). However technological enthusiasts would counter that new possibilities for growth always exist through technological innovations such as oil discovery, automobiles, space explorations, personal computers, smartphones, and artificial intelligence that were observed since the dawn of the 20th century.

3.7   Uncertainty, catastrophe, and precautionary principle

The social welfare optimization framework of the DICE model explained in Section 3.5 provides a foundational economic answer to the question of provision of a global public good, which is encapsulated by the trajectory of the efficient price of the public good. However this fundamental framework would become less forceful intellectually, the larger the uncertainty around the efficient price thus determined, which is the ultimate policy variable that is produced from the model. Furthermore, in the extreme uncertainty, the framework would certainly be no longer meaningful, which is the principal point put forth by the uncertainty critics (Weitzman, 2009).

Before getting to the theory upon which the uncertainty critics are standing, let me begin by describing the elements of uncertainty in the global warming policy-making which exist in many policy-relevant variables, both economic and geophysical, of global warming. The first and most debated is the uncertainty in future climate change predictions (Le Treut et al., 2007). According to the most recent assessment by the Intergovernmental Panel on Climate Change (IPCC), a global temperature increase by the end of the 21st century is predicted to be in the range from no change at all to an 8°C increase. The projected global precipitation changes, another indicator of climate change, are even more uncertain, with the range from a 7% decrease to an 18% increase by the end of this century (IPCC, 2014).

The uncertainty about future changes in the climate variables is even further magnified at the smaller geo-political levels. To give you an idea, predicted changes in the Arctic winter temperature by the end of the 21st century are in the wide range from a 5°C decrease to an 18°C increase. Further, predicted changes in the Arctic summer precipitation fall in the wide range from 10% decrease to 70% increase from the baseline precipitation by the end of this century. Antarctic climate changes are predicted to be equally uncertain (IPCC, 2014).

The large uncertainty on the future climate change predictions can be attributed to many factors, one of which is the basketful of climate change prediction models. Each of these models, which is called an Atmospheric Oceanic General Circulation Model (AOGCM) in the climate literature, rely on different assumptions and relationships among the variables included in the model (IPCC, 2014; Le Treut et al., 2007). The runs of the AOGCM call for a super computer capacity, as such, there are only about a dozen AOGCMs available in the world. The collaborative research effort to compare the programs and outcomes across the AOGCMs is called in the

Table 3.3 Selected models from the climate model intercomparison project 5 (CMIP5).

Modeling center	Country of origin	Model name
Canadian Centre for Climate Modelling and Analysis	Canada	CanESM2; CanCM4; CanAM4
National Center for Atmospheric Research	US	CCSM4
Centro Euro-Mediterraneo per I Cambiamenti Climatici	Italia	CMCC-CESM; CMCC-CM; CMCC-CMS
Centre National de Recherches Météorologiques / Centre Européen de Recherche et Formation Avancée en Calcul Scientifique	France	CNRM-CM5; CNRM-CM5-2
Commonwealth Scientific and Industrial Research Organization	Australia	CSIRO-Mk3.6.0
NOAA Geophysical Fluid Dynamics Laboratory	US	GFDL-CM3; GFDL-ESM2G; GFDL-HIRAM-C180
NASA Goddard Institute for Space Studies	US	GISS-E2-H; GISS-E2-R
Met Office Hadley Centre	UK	HadCM3; HadGEM2-CC; HadGEM2-ES; HadGEM2-A
Atmosphere and Ocean Research Institute (The University of Tokyo), National Institute for Environmental Studies, and Japan Agency for Marine-Earth Science and Technology	Japan	MIROC4h; MIROC5
Meteorological Research Institute	Japan	MRI-AGCM3.2 H; MRI-CGCM3; MRI-ESM1

literature the Climate Model Intercomparison Project (CMIP). The climate models examined by the CMIP5, shown in Table 3.3, include the CCCMA, NCAR, CMCC, CNRM, CSIRO, GFDL, GISS, MOHC, MIROC, and MRI (Taylor et al., 2012).

Another major source of uncertainty lies in the growth of the world economy through the end of this century which by and large determines the amount of greenhouse gas emissions, especially carbon dioxide emissions, to be released during the timeframe. In fact, a pool of future possibilities is nearly unlimited with regard to the changes in the economy, society, culture, and technology. For the purpose of predicting the future climate, the IPCC researchers adopt a storyline (scenario) approach (Nakicenovic et al., 2000). Th set of scenarios defined by the IPCC were called the emissions scenarios by the Special Report on Emissions Scenarios (SRES) by the international organization. The four families of storylines put forward by the Special Report are A1, A2, B1, and B2 (Fig. 3.3).

Of the four scenarios, the A-scenario family is developed in contrasts with the B-scenario family on the criterion of the assumptions on the fossil fuel intensity of the future economic growth. In the A-scenarios, the world economy is assumed to

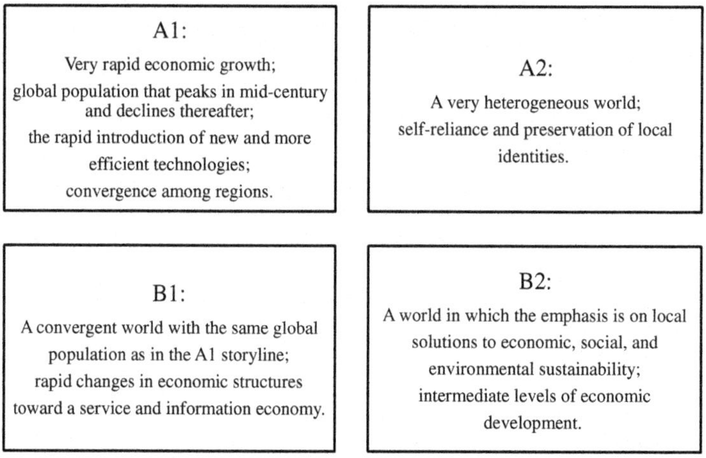

A1:	A2:
Very rapid economic growth; global population that peaks in mid-century and declines thereafter; the rapid introduction of new and more efficient technologies; convergence among regions.	A very heterogeneous world; self-reliance and preservation of local identities.

B1:	B2:
A convergent world with the same global population as in the A1 storyline; rapid changes in economic structures toward a service and information economy.	A world in which the emphasis is on local solutions to economic, social, and environmental sustainability; intermediate levels of economic development.

Figure 3.3 Families of emissions scenarios by the IPCC.

grow in more or less the same way as today's, that is, relying predominantly on fossil fuels. In the B-scenarios, the world economy is assumed to grow in a more environmentally friendly way, for example, relying on low-carbon energy sources.

The four scenario families can also be differentiated into the 1-scenario family and the 2-scenario family by the assumptions on the economic convergence of the global economies (Barro and Sala-i-Martin, 1992). The 1-scenarios assume that the world's national economies should develop in a globally convergent way while the 2-scenarios assume that the world's national economies should develop in a regionally convergent way. Plainly, the economic convergence assumption is that the national economies will catch up with the most advanced economy at the present time and eventually all economies in a particular region or the world will converge.

Each of the four scenario families is further divided into multiple subscenarios by the aforementioned IPCC Special Report. For example, the A1 family can be further refined into A1F1, A1T, and A1B. These subscenarios are distinguished by alternative directions in the technological developments in the energy system. The A1F1 scenario assumes high reliance on the energy technologies based on fossil fuels; The A1T scenario assumes high reliance on energy produced from nonfossil energy sources such as solar, wind, hydro, and geothermal; The A1B scenario assumes a balance between fossil fuels-driven energy technologies and nonfossil fuels-driven energy technological developments.

The most recent IPCC report replaces the SRES scenario (storyline) approach with a Representative Concentration Pathways (RCP) approach (IPCC, 2014). There are four RCPs suggested by the IPCC: RCP 2.6, RCP 4.5, RCP 6.0, and RCP 8.5. Each of these pathways corresponds to the GHG emissions trajectory that results in the RF of 2.6, 4.5, 6.0, and 8.5 W/m^2, respectively.

The RCP approach takes the heavy burden of the climate researchers off of describing the future world's changes such as economic growth, regional geopolitics, technological changes, population changes, and social behavioral changes. At the same time, however, it hides the complexity of the future worlds, economic and social, that must go into any serious climate change modeling.

The third element of the uncertainty is technological changes, especially with regard to breakthrough technologies. Will a nuclear fusion energy production become successful by the middle of this century at a commercial scale (ITER, 2015)? Will solar PV technologies replace fossil fuels-based energy productions as a dominant source of electricity generations (Heal, 2010; MIT, 2015)? Will a direct air carbon-capture-storage technology become an effective technology for a large geographical scale application (Lackner et al., 2012; NRC, 2015b)? Will a solar radiation reflector technology provide an effective method at relatively lower costs for reducing the amount of solar radiation that falls on the Earth and, if so, by which timeframe and by what environmental side-effects (NRC, 2015a)? Will the genetic science make it possible for humans to cure heat-related human and animal diseases that have been regarded fatal up until now (Aksoy et al., 2014)? These are some, but not all, of the technology-related questions that remain uncertain in the discussions of global warming.

The fourth major source of the uncertainty lies in the size of monetary damages of global warming which again hinges on the impacts thereof on ecosystems and humans. The damage estimates suggested by economists are varied widely, which can be attributed to several elements in the impact analysis models (Mendelsohn and Neumann, 1999; Tol, 2009). The first is the uncertainty on how productivities of various ecosystems will undergo changes given the realizations of global warming (Ainsworth and Long, 2005; Denman et al., 2007). The second is the uncertainty on how individuals and societies will adapt to changes in the climate system and ecosystems (Mendelsohn et al., 1994; Seo, 2006, 2016b). The third is the array of impact estimation methodologies which often yield disparate predictions (Adams et al., 1990; Schlenker and Roberts, 2009; Seo, 2015a, 2016a).

Considering the seemingly vast extent of uncertainty, a dismal theoretical outcome was derived by Weitzman based on the assumption of the extreme uncertainty in a global warming policy decision (Weitzman, 2009). In plain terms, he argues that the global average temperature is predicted by some climate models to increase by as much as 20°C by the end of the 21st century, notwithstanding that the average of all the models' predictions is about 2.5°C, and this extreme prediction cannot be reduced by whatever efforts humanity may undertake and therefore should not be excluded from the economic modeling. As such, the end of Planetary civilizations caused by a future global warming cannot be excluded from a list of plausible outcomes of global warming when a climate researcher builds a climate policy model such as the DICE. Under such circumstances, it follows that the world community should stop releasing Earth-heating gases immediately and completely, which is the straightforward and unequivocal policy recommendation from the dismal theorists.

The argument was presented by Weitzman through a more formal terminology: the economic damage from global warming has a fat-tailed distribution, for which reason the willingness to pay by the world citizens for a global warming policy program that purports to avert such a fat-tail outcome is infinite. The fat-tail distribution, which is at the heart of the argument, is a statistical probability distribution which has often been associated with an analysis of catastrophic events (Cropper, 1976; Schuster, 1984; Mandelbrot, 2001).

The essence of the dismal theorem proposed by its creator is expressed by the following simple equation. For any given n and k, the amount of present consumption that the world would be willing to give up in the present period to obtain one sure unit of consumption in the future period, M below, is unbounded (Weitzman, 2009):

$$\lim_{\lambda \to \infty} E[M|\lambda] = + \infty. \tag{3.19}$$

The M defined as above is a stochastic discounting factor. At any given moment, the parameters n and k are fixed. The former is roughly the number of available data (information) and the latter is the number of prior data (information), both of which are essential information needed to narrow down the uncertainty in a global warming policy decision described in the above. The parameter λ is the Value of Statistical Life (VSL) like parameter (Viscusi and Aldy, 2003). It is interpreted as the VSL on Earth as we know it. This value is certainly very large, that is, overwhelmingly larger than the global income per annum. With these parameters, the Eq. (3.19) states that the world would be willing to sacrifice unlimitedly to survive on this Planet if the M has a fat-tail distribution.

The dismal theorem in Eq. (3.19), as it was named as such, can be held only with several limiting assumptions which were clarified by critiques soon after its publication (Nordhaus, 2011; Yohe and Tol, 2012). At the heart of the failure of the dismal theorem as a policy model, as the present author pointed out earlier, lies the omission of adaptation behaviors and systems in the model. This omission is very common in the literature of catastrophe and chaos theories, of which the dismal theorem is another manifestation (Seo, 2018). More concretely, the catastrophe theory does not include an adaptative mechanism that may slow down the march toward the bifurcation point or tipping point (Thom, 1975). In the fractal theories, there is no mechanism that links the fractal relationship to the human and economic systems (Mandelbrot, 2001).

To be more formal, Eq. (3.19) is only valid when the damage distribution from global warming has a fat-tail distribution. Let Z be the damage from global warming whose distribution is a fat-tailed distribution, also called in various names such as a power-law distribution, a Pareto principle, a Zipf's law, or a Pareto-Levy-Mandelbrot (PLM) distribution (Pareto, 1896; Zipf, 1949). It can be written as a countercumulative distribution function as well as a probability density function:

$$\begin{aligned} P[Z > z] &\sim z^{(-\varphi)}; \\ P[Z = z] &= kz^{-(1+\varphi)} \end{aligned} \tag{3.20}$$

The PLM distribution has a power-law tail whose shape is defined by the shape parameter, φ, which takes on nonnegative values. The larger the φ, the closer the tail of the PLM distribution to the Normal (Gaussian) distribution. The closer the φ to zero, the fatter the tail of the PLM distribution becomes.

Fig. 3.4 will give readers a good idea of why the fat-tail distribution would be instrumental for a policy analysis of catastrophic events. The figure draws a fat-tail distribution against a medium-tail distribution such as a Normal distribution. The top panel draws a non fat-tailed distribution and the bottom panel draws a fat-tailed distribution. In each panel, a countercumulative distribution function for each is drawn (see Eq. 3.20).

A catastrophic event is marked in the figure by the threshold value in Z denoted as a tipping point. The tipping point is set at 10 and the range of Z is from 1 to 21. Readers may relate the tipping point to a 10°C change in the global climate system. In a medium-tail distribution (top panel), even if the catastrophic event were considered a possibility, the probability of its realization is "so low" that it wouldn't matter much in the calculation of the expected damage from the range of possible events. Statistically, it approximates zero.

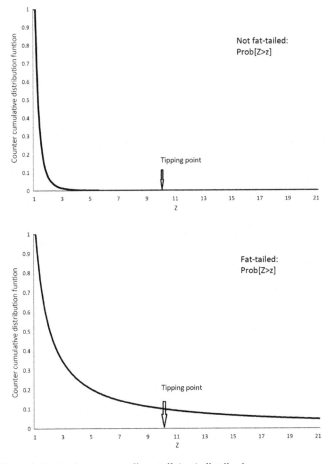

Figure 3.4 Fat-tail (bottom) versus medium-tail (top) distribution.

On the contrary, as depicted in the bottom panel, the probability of the catastrophe event remains "high" in the fat-tailed distribution. Statistically speaking, it does not approximate zero. The consequence is that the expected damage from the range of possible events would be dominated by the magnitude of the tipping point event. Interpreted in the context of global climatic changes, a possibility of a tipping point event would overwhelm any consideration of the expected damage from a range of possibilities as well as any benefit–cost analysis.

The core of the dismal theorem can be rewritten, with the tipping point or the threshold event being T_c, by the expected damage from the event:

$$\Omega\left(T_c\right) = z(T_c) * P\left(Z = z(T_c)\right) \tag{3.21}$$

The first term on the right-hand side of the equation is the damage and the second term is the probability density. Note that, for the sake of simplicity, Eq. (3.21) is written with regard to only the tipping point event. Adaptation behaviors by individuals and systems affect both the first term and the second term. We can write the equation with the adaptation parameter ξ and can show that the omega is bounded by a constant, h:

$$\Omega(T_c, \xi) = z\left(T_c, \xi_1\right) * P\left(Z = z, \xi_2\right) < h. \tag{3.22}$$

The Eq. (3.22) would hold in multiple circumstances. Let me explain two extreme cases here for the sake of clarity and more general situations in the Appendix of this book. The first case is that adaptation behaviors offset nearly all effects of physical changes through a power-law reaction:

$$z\left(T_c, \xi_1\right) = z(T_c)T_c^{-\xi_1}. \tag{3.23}$$

The second case is that the adaptation behaviors force the fat-tail distribution in Eq. (3.20) to approximate a medium-tail distribution through, again, a power-law reaction:

$$P\left(Z = z, \xi_2\right) = kz^{-(1+\varphi)}z^{-\xi_2}. \tag{3.24}$$

The empirical evidence of Eq. (3.23) is found in the literature. That is, many studies find that adaptation behaviors and strategies make the damage estimate from global warming far smaller than those predicted by the studies with the assumption of no adaptation (Seo, 2016a,b). Eq. (3.23) proposes that the impact of such adaptation behaviors on the damage estimate is fat-tailed, but again this is not an essential assumption as far as the disproof of the dismal theorem is concerned (refer to the Appendix of this book for the disproof).

The empirical evidence for Eq. (3.24) is also handily found. Many studies document that the host of technological options makes it far less likely that the global temperature will cross past the threshold level, say, 10°C increase from the present level (NRC, 2015a,b; ITER, 2015). Eq. (3.24) proposes that the impact of such technological options on the temperature increase is fat-tailed, but once again it is not an essential assumption (refer to the Appendix).

Readers may ask why adaptation behaviors and strategies should take on the power-law responses as in Eqs. (3.23) and (3.24). Adaptation behaviors will be a focus of the ensuring chapters of the book, especially Chapter 4, A Critique of the Economics of Global Public Goods: A Microbehavioral Theory and Model, and Chapter 7, The Economics of Globally Shared Goods, where the present author will have an opportunity to explain a set of empirical studies which revealed the strong mitigating effects of adaptation behaviors on both the magnitude of economic damage and the degree of global warming. The power-law responses are, however, not essential in Eqs. (3.23) and (3.24), put differently, other functional forms can be used instead to make the same point of this section.

In the Appendix of this book, the present author formally provides a mathematical disproof of the dismal theorem. The disproof shows that even if the fat-tail distribution exists in the global warming policy, an account of adaptation "deltas" in the damage function and the probability density function will make the conclusion of the dismal theorem to fail to hold (refer to the Appendix).

3.8   Optimal mutually beneficial monetary transfers

The Section 3.5 presented a globally optimal economic policy model that can be applied to the policy decisions on global warming. This was followed by Section 3.6 which addresses the question of the value of time and the discount rate, and Section 3.7 which addresses the question of uncertainty and a fat-tailed catastrophe.

A salient feature of a globally optimal welfare policy framework such as the DICE is that any agreement or treaty which might be achieved by the international conferences, say, the Kyoto Protocol, or the Paris Agreement, or else, is certain to yield distinct winners and losers from the implementation of the agreement (Seo, 2012). Under such situations of disparate policy consequences across sovereign nations, the chance of achieving an agreement at the global scale would be quite slim, so would be the chance of making any agreed policy sustainable.

This raises another possibility: is it possible to couple the globally optimal global warming policy such as a globally harmonized carbon tax with a set of optimal monetary transfers from the winner nations to the loser nations in an effort to increase the possibility of the loser nations joining an international agreement as well as to improve the sustainability of the agreed policy (Carraro et al., 2006; Seo, 2019b)?

Put differently, the globally harmonized carbon price described in Section 3.5 offers a socially optimal solution, but the policy assumes that there will be global cooperation among the nations. If, however, loser nations were to lose big or the impacts of the carbon pricing across the nations were to be disparate, such a cooperative policy framework would not be materialized (Seo, 2012). This may explain a low participation rate in a global warming treaty (Nordhaus, 2015). To overcome this, a second-best policy can be designed by coupling an array of monetary transfers from the winners to the losers with the harmonized carbon pricing. Although a second-best, a well-designed transfer mechanism would improve the global welfare from the state of a business-as-usual (BAU) policy if it should induce a global cooperative policy action (Carraro et al., 2006; Chan, 2019).

The global welfare, ω^*, at the global cooperative solution is the sum of individual nation's welfare at a certain time, U_{kt}. Let c_{kt} be a per capita consumption and POP_{kt} be a total population of the country k. Then, the global welfare without monetary transfers can be expressed as follows:

$$\sum_{t=0}^{\infty} \sum_{k} \frac{U_{kt}(c_{kt}^*, POP_{kt}) \cdot POP_t}{(1+\rho)^t}. \tag{3.25}$$

Let ω^{BAU} be the global welfare under the BAU scenario and ω^{mt} be the global welfare with a family of monetary transfers coupled with the global cooperative solution. The monetary transfer mechanism purports to achieve the following second-best outcome:

$$\omega^* > \omega^{mt} > \omega^{BAU}. \tag{3.26}$$

Let the net monetary transfer to country k at time t be m_{kt}, assuming that the set of transfers is performed annually, which must sum up to zero at the global level:

$$\sum_{k} \sum_{t} m_{kt} = 0. \tag{3.27}$$

The after-transfer global welfare is expressed as follows, assuming independence of the monetary transfers from changes in productions and populations of individual nations:

$$\omega^{mt} = \sum_{t=0}^{\infty} \sum_{k} \frac{U_{kt}(c_{kt}^* + m_{kt}, POP_{kt}) \cdot POP_t}{(1+\rho)^t}. \tag{3.28}$$

The theoretical question of the coupled carbon price and monetary transfer mechanism then boils down to the following: Does the $\{m_{kt}, \forall k\}$ exist that satisfies Eq. (3.26) and, if it does, what is the value of the $\{m_{kt}, \forall k\}$? Notice that the m_{kt} must be found for each country and each time period in the optimization model.

As of November 2019, the present author is able to point to a real-world monetary transfer scheme implemented as part of a global warming policy agreement. The UN-led climate conferences announced a GCF in 2009 at a scale of US$ 100 billion per annum from which the first batch of allocations of the Fund was made in November 2015 (UNFCCC, 2009; GCF, 2011). A careful examination of the 111 + GCF-funded projects through the end of 2019 shows that the GCF funding programs do not answer the two aforementioned theoretical questions (Seo, 2019b).

The impossibility of finding such a transfer scheme, that is, $\{m_{kt}, \forall k\}$, can be illustrated intuitively via several transfer scenarios (Seo, 2019b). In the first scenario, a rich country suffers little from global warming while a poor country suffers a great deal from global warming (Mendelsohn et al., 2006). In this scenario, the poor country "should" transfer money to the rich country if the poor country wants to give an incentive to the rich country for a globally agreed action. This is of course nearly absurd politically.

In the second scenario, the marginal productivity of the funding recipient in the transfer recipient country is smaller than the marginal productivity of the donor in the transfer donor country. The transfer will then lower the global welfare. The larger the difference in the marginal productivity between the two countries, the larger the decrease in the global welfare. If the monetary transfer mechanism were to end up with a large-scale transfer from a family of high marginal productivity countries to a family of low marginal productivity countries, the world welfare would suffer substantially from the transfer scheme itself.

The third scenario is when the series of wealth transfers planned by the global organization such as the GCF alters the greenhouse gas emission behaviors by the recipient country (Chan, 2019). The changes in the behaviors of funding recipients can take many forms. In one case, the funding may give the recipient an incentive to stick to a vulnerable enterprise or a high emissions enterprise. In another case, the funding may give the recipient an incentive to switch to a more vulnerable enterprise or a heavier emitter of greenhouse gases (Seo, 2019b).

3.9 The public sector for global public goods

The final topic of the present author's extensive descriptions of the economics of public goods through Chapter 2, The Economics of Public Goods and Club Goods and Chapter 3, The Economics of Global-Scale Public Goods: Key Challenges and Theories, is the public sector that should, according to all the theories discussed so far, take on the responsibility to provide a variety of public goods. For a national public good, the appropriate public sector is a federal government. For a state public good, it is a state government.

For the global public goods, the public sector that should assume the responsibility for the provision thereof does not exist. There is no public organization at the global level that is equivalent to a national government that is given the power by its people to govern and enforce laws and regulations of the country. The question has been raised about which organization or country should take the lead in providing a global public good or another.

For the range of global public goods such as, *inter alia*, nuclear nonproliferation, asteroid protection, and global warming, an international treaty signed by the members of the United Nations on each of these issues is given the legal force, when entered into force, that is nearly equivalent to national laws and regulations. For each treaty, a secretariat is established to enforce the treaty.

Table 3.4 summarizes the major international treaties and agreements. The treaties include the Treaty on the Non-Proliferation of Nuclear Weapons (NPT), the Montreal Protocol on Substances that Deplete the Ozone Layer, the Kyoto Protocol, and the Marrakesh Agreement (UNEP, 2016; UNODA, 2019; UNFCCC, 1997; WTO, 2019). The Paris Agreement was signed in 2015 and entered into force the following year, but is not a treaty that has a binding legal force (UNFCCC, 2015). There is neither an international treaty nor an agreement on artificial intelligence or asteroid collisions (Seo, 2018).

Table 3.4 International treaties, secretariats, and organizations for global public goods.

Treaties/agreements	Signed/entry into force	Secretariat	Organization
Treaty			
The Treaty on the Non-Proliferation of Nuclear Weapons	1968/1970	The International Atomic Energy Agency	United Nations
The Montreal Protocol on Substances that Deplete the Ozone Layer	1987/1989	Ozone Secretariat, United Nations Environment Programme	United Nations
The Kyoto Protocol	1987/2005	United Nations Framework Convention on Climate Change	United Nations
The Marrakesh Agreement	1994/1995	World Trade Organization Secretariat	World Trade Organization
Agreement			
The Paris Agreement	2015/2016	United Nations Framework Convention on Climate Change (UNFCCC)	United Nations
No Treaty or Agreement			
Asteroid collision/ planetary defense Artificial Intelligence/ singularity			

The table also lists the secretariats and organizations that are given primary responsibilities in implementing the treaties and agreements. The table demonstrates a predominant power and authority given to the United Nations as far as the global public goods and affairs are concerned. As it stands now, the United Nations in fact provides global governance in dealing with the global affairs and concerns.

The preeminence of the United Nations in addressing global challenges can be traced back to the Charter of the United Nations signed in 1945 after the two catastrophic world wars during the first half of the 20th century (UN, 1945). Although the Charter declared the foremost purpose of the United Nations to be the maintenance of international peace and security, the Article 1 of the Charter also declared the international cooperation on numerous international economic, social, cultural, and humanitarian issues as one of the purposes for the establishment of the United Nations. The Article 1 resulted in the creations of two dozen affiliated organizations and programs of the United Nations including the United Nations Environment Programme (UNEP), the United Nations Framework Convention on Climate Change (UNFCCC), the International Atomic Energy Agency (IAEA), all listed in Table 3.4 (Seo, 2019b).

Two critical challenges to the role of the United Nations have emerged and become increasingly acknowledged. One is the limited power of the United Nations. Unlike a national government, the United Nations does not have the authority to tax its citizens, nor does it have the authority to infringe upon national sovereignty by interfering national decisions. This means that despite the graveness of the UN-led activities and initiatives on social and economic issues such as those listed in Table 3.4, the United Nations does not have sufficient power and resources to make any of the treaties and agreements forceful.

On the other hand, resistance to the UN-led social and economic initiatives has surged recently as many countries came to the realizations that many of the initiatives are against the nation's interests and pressing issues, even though there can be global benefit from implementing them. Touting an "America First" policy, President Trump withdrew from the Paris Agreement in June 2017 (Seo, 2019a). Australia also removed greenhouse gas emission reduction requirements from its energy policy which was designed in accordance with the commitments to the Paris Agreement. The Kigali Amendment to the Montreal Protocol entered into force in January 2019, but major stakeholders have not ratified it, including India, China, and the United States (UNEP, 2016).

The two challenges are both rational responses and at the same time point to the same conclusion: when it comes to providing a global public good, there will be no easy way to overcoming the governance issues. It will not be easy to reach an agreement at a global scale on a social or economic issue and even harder to implement it.

3.10 Conclusion

Along with Chapter 2, The Economics of Public Goods and Club Goods, this chapter completes the descriptions of the economic theories on public goods. Chapter 2, The

Economics of Public Goods and Club Goods, focused on the core theories of public goods and this chapter concentrated on the theories and issues that arose in tandem with the emergences of the global-scale public goods. The array of topics that are addressed in this chapter includes types of global-scale public goods, production technologies, a globally optimal economic policy model, choice of a discount rate, a fat-tail catastrophe, a basket of mutually beneficial monetary transfers, and global governance.

This completes the Part 2 of the book which is the presentation of the theories of public goods and global-scale public goods. The next three chapters constitute the Part 3 of the book, which is the presentation of the three primary critiques by the present author of the economic theories reviewed thus far.

The next three chapters will reorient the readers rather drastically to the empirical models and analyses with regard to a global public good or another, a global warming policy in particular. These empirical studies will reveal that the theories described thus far either fail to resolve the issues to be presented in each of the next three chapters or are lacking the finesse to capture the behaviors to be described thereof. The analyses in the next part of the book consisting of Chapters 4, 5, and 6 will render a clear motivation to redirect the theories of the global-scale public goods in consideration of the behavioral responses of individuals and societies to be described in the next part of the book.

The three critiques have the following central arguments: Chapter 4, A Critique of the Economics of Global Public Goods: A Microbehavioral Theory and Model, will show how an individual decision-maker will respond to a global public bad in an efficient manner, thereby minimizing the damage from it as well as maximizing the potential benefit from it (Seo, 2016b). Chapter 5, A Critique of the Economics of Global Public Goods: Economics of Noncooperative Games, will provide an analysis of why the countries in the negotiating position for a global public good provision will have an incentive to non-cooperation (Seo, 2017a). Chapter 6, A Critique of the Economics of Global Public Goods: The Economics of a Global Public Good Fund, will explain how a large array of monetary transfers designed to deliver a global public good will fail to achieve its goal owing to, among many other reasons, the impossibility of predicting behavioral responses of individuals and communities (Seo, 2015b,b).

References

Adams, R., Rosenzweig, C., Peart, R.M., Ritchie, J.T., McCarl, B.A., Glyer, J.D., et al., 1990. Global climate change and US agriculture. Nature 345, 219–224.
Ainslie, G., 1991. Derivation of 'rational' economic behavior from hyperbolic discount curves. Am. Econ. Rev. 81, 334–340.
Ainsworth, E.A., Long, S.P., 2005. What have we learned from 15 years of free-air CO_2 enrichment (FACE)? A meta analysis of the responses of photosynthesis, canopy properties and plant production to rising CO_2. N. Phytologist 165, 351–372.

Aksoy, S., Attardo, G., et al., 2014. Genome sequence of the tsetse fly (Glossina morsitans): vector of African trypanosomiasis. Science 344 (6182), 380–386.

Arrow, K.J., Cline, W., Maler, K.G., Munasinghe, M., Squitieri, R., Stiglitz, J., 1996. Intertemporal equity, discounting, and economic efficiency. In: Bruce, J.P., Lee, H., Haites, E.F. (Eds.), Climate Change 1995: Economic and Social Dimensions of Climate Change, Intergovernmental Panel on Climate Change. Cambridge University Press, New York.

Barrett, S., 2010. Why Cooperate?: The Incentive to Supply Global Public Goods. Oxford University Press, Oxford.

Barro, R.J., Sala-i-Martin, X., 1992. Convergence. J. Political Econ. 100, 223–251.

Bohm-Bawerk, E.V., 1959. Capital and interestIn: Huncke, G.D., Sennholz, H.F. (Eds.), Libertarian Press, South Holland, IL.

Bowen, H.R., 1943. The interpretation of voting in the allocation of economic resources. Q. J. Econ. 58 (1), 27–48.

British Petroleum (BP), 2019. BP Energy Outlook, 2019 edition BP, London.

Broome, J., 1992. Counting the Cost of Global Warming. The White Horse Press, Cambridge.

Broome, J., 1994. Discounting the future. Philosophy Public. Aff. 23, 128–156.

Brown, K.M., 1973. Welfare implications of congestion in public goods. Rev. Soc. Econ. 31, 89–92.

Buchanan, J.M., 1965. An economy theory of clubs. Economica 32, 1–24.

Campbell, K.M., Einhorn, R.J., Reiss, M.B. (Eds.), 2004. The Nuclear Tipping Point: Why States Reconsider Their Nuclear Choices. Brookings Institution Press, Washington, DC.

Carraro, C., Eyckmans, J., Finus, N., 2006. Optimal transfers and participation decisions in international environmental agreements. Rev. Int. Organ. 1, 379–396.

Chan, N.W., 2019. Funding global environmental public goods through multilateral financial mechanisms. Environ. Resour. Econ. 73, 515–531.

Chapman, C.R., Morrison, D., 1994. Impacts on the Earth by asteroids and comets: assessing the hazard. Nature 367, 33–40.

Cropper, M., 1976. Regulating activities with catastrophic environmental effects. J. Environ. Econ. Manag. 3, 1–15.

Cropper, M.L., Laibson, D., 1999. The implications of hyperbolic discounting for project evaluation. In: Portney, P.R., Weyant, J.P. (Eds.), Discounting and Intergenerational Equity. Resources for the Future, Washington, DC.

Denman, K.L., Brasseur, G., Chidthaisong, A., et al., 2007. Couplings between changes in the climate system and biogeochemistry. In: Solomon, S., et al., (Eds.), Climate Change 2007: The Physical Science Basis. The Fourth Assessment Report of the Intergovernmental Panel on Climate Change. Cambridge University Press, Cambridge.

Ellerman, A.D., Marcantonini, C., Zaklan, A., 2016. The European Union emissions trading system: ten years and counting. Rev. Env. Econ. Policy 10, 89–107.

Ellis, J., Giudice, G., Mangano, M., Tkachev, I., Wiedemann, U., 2008. Review of the safety of LHC collisions. J. Phys. G: Nucl. Part. Phys. 35 (11).

Environment and Climate Change Canada (ECCC), 2019. How We're Putting a Price on Carbon Pollution. Government of Canada, Gatineau, QC.

European Commission, 2016. EU ETS Handbook. European Commission, Brussels.

Fischer, C., Morgenstern, R.D., 2006. Carbon abatement costs: why the wide range of estimates? Energy J. 27, 73–86.

Fisher, I., 1930. The Theory of Interest. Macmillan, New York.

Friedman, M., 1962. Capitalism and Freedom. The University of Chicago Press, Chicago, IL.

Global Carbon Project (GCP), 2017. Global Carbon Budget 2017. Available at: <http://www.globalcarbonproject.org/carbonbudget/index.htm>.

Green Climate Fund (GCF), 2011. Governing Instrument for the Green Climate Fund. GCF, Songdo City, South Korea.

Hammar, H., Akerfeldt, S., 2011. Carbon taxation in Sweden: 20 years of experience and looking ahead. Ministry of Finance, Sweden.

Harris, I., Jones, P.D., Osborn, T.J., Lister, D.H., 2014. Updated high-resolution grids of monthly climatic observations – the CRU TS3.10 Dataset. Int. J. Climatol. 34, 623−642.

Heal, G., 2010. Reflections: the economics of renewable energy in the United States. Rev. Environ. Econ. Policy 4, 139−154.

Hicks, J.R., 1932. The Theory of Wages. Macmillan, London.

Hirshleifer, J., 1983. From weakest-link to best-shot: the voluntary provision of public goods. Public. Choice 41, 371−386.

Hotelling, H., 1931. The economics of exhaustible resources. J. Political Econ. 39 (2), 137−175.

Houghton, R.A., 2008. Carbon flux to the atmosphere from land-use changes: 1850−2005. In: Trends, A. (Ed.), Compendium of Data on Global Change. Carbon Dioxide Information Analysis Center. Oak Ridge National Laboratory, U.S. Department of Energy, Oak Ridge, TN.

Hulten, C.R., 2000. Total Factor Productivity: A Short Biography. National Bureau of Economic Research (NBER) Working Paper Series 7471, Cambridge, MA.

Intergovernmental Panel on Climate Change (IPCC), 1990. Climate Change: The IPCC Scientific Assessment. Cambridge University Press, Cambridge.

Intergovernmental Panel on Climate Change (IPCC), 2014. Climate Change 2014: The Physical Science Basis, The Fifth Assessment Report of the IPCC. Cambridge University Press, Cambridge.

International Institute of Applied Systems Analysis (IIASA), 2007. Probabilistic projections by 13 world regions, forecast period 2000−2100, 2001 revision. Available online at: <http://www.iiasa.ac.at/Research/POP/proj01/>.

International Thermonuclear Experimental Reactor (ITER), 2015. ITER: The world's largest Tokamak. Available at: <https://www.iter.org/mach>.

Kaiho, K., Oshima, N., 2017. Site of asteroid impact changed the history of life on Earth: the low probability of mass extinction. Sci. Rep. 7, 14855. Available from: https://doi.org/10.1038/s41598-017-14199-x.

Kamps, C., 2004. New Estimates of Government Net Capital Stocks for 22 OECD Countries 1961−2001. IMF Working Paper 04/67. Washington, DC.

Kaul, I., Conceicao, P., Goulven, K.L., Mendoza, R.U. (Eds.), 2003. Providing Global Public Goods: Managing Globalization. Oxford University Press, Oxford.

Keeling, C.D., Piper, S.C., Bacastow, R.B., Wahlen, M., Whorf, T.P., Heimann, M., et al., 2005. Atmospheric CO_2 and $^{13}CO_2$ exchange with the terrestrial biosphere and oceans from 1978 to 2000: observations and carbon cycle implications. In: Ehleringer, J.R., Cerling, T.E., Dearing, M.D. (Eds.), A History of Atmospheric CO_2 and Its Effects on Plants, Animals, and Ecosystems. Springer Verlag, New York, pp. 83−113.

Kurzweil, R., 2005. The Singularity is Near. Penguin, New York.

Lackner, K.S., Brennana, S., Matter, J.M., Park, A.A., Wright, A., Zwaan, B.V., 2012. The urgency of the development of CO_2 capture from ambient air. Proc. Natl. Acad. Sci. 109 (33), 13156−13162.

Laibson, D., 1997. Golden eggs and hyperbolic discounting. Q. J. Econ. 112 (2), 443−477.

Le Treut, H., Somerville, R., Cubasch, U., Ding, Y., Mauritzen, C., Mokssit, A., et al., 2007. Historical overview of climate change. In: Solomon, S., Qin, D., Manning, M., Chen, Z., Marquis, M., Averyt, K.B., Tignor, M., Miller, H.L. (Eds.), Climate Change 2007: The physical science basis. Contribution of working group I to the fourth assessment report of the intergovernmental panel on climate change. Cambridge University Press, Cambridge.

Lutz, W., Butz, W., Samir, K.C. (Eds.), 2014. World Population and Global Human Capital in the 21st Century. Oxford University Press, Oxford.

Mandelbrot, B., 2001. Scaling in financial prices: I. tails and dependence. Quant. Financ. 1, 113−123.

Manne, A.S., Mendelsohn, R. &, Richels, R., 1995. MERGE: a model for evaluating regional and global effects of GHG reduction policies. Energy Policy 23 (1), 17−34.

Manne, A.S., Richels, R.G., 1999. The Kyoto Protocol: a cost-effective strategy for meeting environmental objectives? Energy J. 20 (Special Issue), 1−23.

Massachusetts Institute of Technology (MIT), 2015. The Future of Solar Energy: An Interdisciplinary MIT Study. MIT, Cambridge, MA.

Meadows, D.H., Meadows, D.L., Randers, J., Behrens, I.I.I., William, W., 1972. The Limits to Growth: A Report for the Club of Rome's Project on the Predicament of Mankind. Universe Books, New York.

Mendelsohn, R., Dinar, A., Williams, L., 2006. The distributional impact of climate change on rich and poor countries. Env. Dev. Econ. 11, 1−20.

Mendelsohn, R., Neumann, J., 1999. The Impact of Climate Change on the United States Economy. Cambridge University Press, Cambridge.

Mendelsohn, R., Nordhaus, W., Shaw, D., 1994. The impact of global warming on agriculture: a Ricardian analysis. Am. Economic Rev. 84, 753−771.

Molina, M.J., Rowland, F.S., 1974. Stratospheric sink for chlorofluoromethanes: chlorine atom-catalysed destruction of ozone. Nature 249, 810−812.

Montgomery, W.D., 1972. Markets in licenses and efficient pollution control programs. J. Econ. Theory 5, 395−418.

Nakicenovic, N., Davidson, O., Davis, G., Grübler, A., Kram, T., La Rovere, E.L., et al., 2000. Emissions Scenarios, A Special Report of Working Group III of the Intergovernmental Panel on Climate Change. IPCC, Geneva.

National Academies of Sciences, Engineering, and Medicine (NASEM), 2017. Valuing Climate Damages: Updating Estimation of the Social Cost of Carbon Dioxide. The National Academies Press, Washington, DC. Available from: https://doi.org/10.17226/24651.

National Aeronautics and Space Administration (NASA), 2014. NASA's Efforts to Identify Near-Earth Objects and Mitigate Hazards. IG-14−030. NASA Office of Inspector General, Washington, DC.

National Research Council, 2010. Defending Planet Earth: Near-Earth-Object Surveys and Hazard Mitigation Strategies. National Academies Press, Washington, DC.

National Research Council (NRC), 2015a. Climate Intervention: Reflecting Sunlight to Cool Earth. Committee on Geoengineering Climate: Technical Evaluation and Discussion of Impacts. The National Academies Press, Washington, DC.

National Research Council (NRC), 2015b. Climate Intervention: Carbon Dioxide Removal and Reliable Sequestration. The National Academies Press, Washington, DC.

Negishi, T., 1960. Welfare economics and existence of an equilibrium for a competitive economy. Metroeconomica 12, 92−97.

Newell, R., Pizer, W., 2001. Discounting the Benefits of Climate Change Mitigation: How Much Do Uncertain Rates Increase Valuations? Pew Center, Washington, DC.

Nordhaus, W., 1973. The allocation of energy resources. Brook. Pap. Econ. Act. 1973, 529—576.

Nordhaus, W., 1982. How fast should we graze the global commons? Am. Econ. Rev. 72, 242—246.

Nordhaus, W., 1994. Managing the Global Commons. MIT Press, Massachusetts.

Nordhaus, W.D., 2006. Paul Samuelson and Global Public Goods. In: Szenberg, M., Ramrattan, L, Gottesman, A.A., (eds) Samuelsonian Economics and the Twenty-First Century. Oxford Scholarship Online.

Nordhaus, W., 2007a. To tax or not to tax: alternative approaches to slowing global warming. Rev. Environ. Econ. Policy 1 (1), 26—44.

Nordhaus, W., 2007b. A review of the stern review on the economics of climate change. J. Econ. Lit. 55, 686—702.

Nordhaus, W.D., 2008. A Question of Balance: Weighing the Options on Global Warming Policies. Yale University Press, New Haven, CT.

Nordhaus, W., 2010. Economic aspects of global warming in a post-Copenhagen environment. Proc. U.S. Natl. Acad. Sci. 107 (26), 11721—11726.

Nordhaus, W., 2011. The economics of tail events with an application to climate change. Rev. Environ. Econ. Policy 5, 240—257.

Nordhaus, W., 2015. Clim. Clubs: Overcoming Free-Riding Int. Clim. Policy. Am. Econ. Rev. 105 (4), 1339—1370.

Nordhaus, W.D., 2018. Climate change: the ultimate challenge for economics. Prize Lecture. NobelPrize.org. <https://www.nobelprize.org/prizes/economic-sciences/2018/nordhaus/lecture/>.

Nordhaus, W., Yang, Z., 1996. A regional dynamic general-equilibrium model of alternative climate change strategies. Am. Econ. Rev 86, 741—765.

Nordhaus, W.D., Boyer, J.G., 1999. Requiem for Kyoto: an economic analysis of the Kyoto Protocol. Energy J. 20 (Special Issue), 93—130.

Nordhaus, W., Boyer, J., 2000. Warming the World: Economic Models of Global Warming. MIT Press, Cambridge, MA.

Nordhaus, W., Sztorc, P., 2013. DICE 2013: Introduction and User's Manual. Yale University, New Haven, CT.

Pareto, V., 1896. Cours d'Economie Politique. Librairie Droz, Geneva.

Pearce, D., Cline, W.R., Achanta, A., Fankhauser, S., Pachauri, R., Tol, R., et al., 1996. The social costs of climate change: greenhouse damage and benefits of control. In: Bruce, J., Lee, H., Haites, E. (Eds.), Climate Change 1995: Economic and Social Dimensions of Climate Change. Cambridge University Press, Cambridge.

Ramsey, F.P., 1928. A mathematical theory of savings. Econ. J. 38, 543—559.

REIT, 2019. FTSE Nareit U.S. Real Estate Index Historical Values & Returns. Accessed from: <https://www.reit.com/data-research/reit-indexes/ftse-nareit-us-real-estate-index-historical-values-returns>.

Samuelson, P.A., 1947. Foundations of Economic Analysis. Harvard University Press [Enlarged edition published in 1983].

Samuelson, P., 1954. The pure theory of public expenditure. Rev. Econ. Stat. 36, 387—389.

Samuelson, P., 1955. Diagrammatic exposition of a theory of public expenditure. Rev. Econ. Stat. 37, 350—356.

Samuelson, P., Nordhaus, W., 2009. Economics, ninteenth ed McGraw-Hill Education, New York.

Sandler, T., 1997. Global Challenges: An Approach to Environmental, Political, and Economic Problems. Cambridge University Press, Cambridge.

Schelling, T.C., 1966. Arms and Influence. Yale University Press, New Haven, CT.

Schelling, T.C., 1991. Greenhouse Effect. Presidential Address at 103 Annual Meeting, American Economic Association, Washington, DC.

Schlesinger, W.H., 1997. Biogeochemistry: An Analysis of Global Change, 2nd ed Academic Press, San Diego, CA.

Schlesinger, M.E., Jiang, X., 1990. Simple model representation of atmosphere-ocean GCMs and estimation of the timescale of CO_2-induced climate change. J. Clim. 3, 12−15.

Schneider, S.H., Thompson, S.L., 1981. Atmospheric CO_2 and climate: importance of the transient response. J. Geophys. Res. 86, 3135−3147.

Schuster, E.F., 1984. Classification of probability laws by tail behavior. J. Am. Stat. Assoc. 79 (388), 936−939.

Seo, S.N., 2006. Modeling Farmer Responses to Climate Change: Climate Change Impacts and Adaptations in Livestock Management in Africa. Ph.D. dissertation. Yale University, New Haven, CT.

Seo, S.N., 2012. What eludes global agreements on climate change? Econ. Aff. 32, 73−79.

Seo, S.N., 2015a. Micro-behavioral Economics of Global Warming: Modeling Adaptation Strategies in Agricultural and Natural Resource Enterprises. Springer International Publishing, Springer.

Seo, S.N., 2015b. Helping low-latitude poor countries with climate change. Regulation. Winter 2015−2016: 6−8.

Seo, S.N., 2016a. Modeling farmer adaptations to climate change in South America: a micro-behavioral economic perspective. Environ. Ecol. Stat. 23, 1−21.

Seo, S.N., 2016b. Microbehavioral Econometric Methods: Theories, Models, and Applications for the Study of Environmental and Natural Resources. Academic Press (Elsevier), Amsterdam, The Netherlands.

Seo, S.N., 2017a. The Behavioral Economics of Climate Change: Adaptation Behaviors, Global Public Goods, Breakthrough Technologies, and Policy-Making. Academic Press (Elsevier), Amsterdam, the Netherlands.

Seo, S.N., 2017b. Beyond the Paris areement: climate change policy negotiations and future directions. Regional Sci. Policy Pract. 9, 121−140.

Seo, S.N., 2018. Natural and Man-Made Catastrophes: Theories, Economics, and Policy Designs. Wiley-Blackwell, Hobokken, NJ.

Seo, S.N., 2019a. Economic questions on global warming during the Trump years. J. Public. Aff. 19, e1914. Available from: https://doi.org/10.1002/pa.1914.

Seo, S.N., 2019b. The Economics of Global Allocations of the Green Climate Fund: An Assessment From Four Scientific Traditions of Modeling Adaptation Strategies. Springer Nature.

Shiller, R.J., 2005. Irrational Exuberance, second ed. Princeton University Press, Princeton, NJ.

Shiller, R., 2019. Online Data for Rebert Shiller. Yale University, New Haven, CT, Accessed from: <http://www.econ.yale.edu/~shiller/data.htm>.

Solow, R.M., 1956. A contribution to the theory of economic growth. Q. J. Econ. 70 (1), 65−94.

Speth, G., 2012. Manifesto for a post-growth economy. YES! Magazine, WA. <https://www.yesmagazine.org/new-economy/Manifesto-for-a-post-growth-economy-james-gustaves-speth>.

Stavins, R., 2007. A US Cap-and-Trade System to Address Global Climate Change. Hamilton Project Discussion Paper 2007-13, The Brookings Institution, Washington, DC.

Stern, N., 2007. The Economics of Climate Change: The Stern Review. Cambridge University Press, New York.

Taylor, K.E., Stouffer, R.J., Meehl, G.A., 2012. An overview of CMIP5 and the experiment design. Bull. Am. Meteorological Soc. 93, 485–498.

Thaler, R.H., 1981. Some empirical evidence on dynamic inconsistency. Econ. Lett. 8 (3), 201–207.

Thom, R., 1975. Structural Stability and Morphogenesis. Benjamin-Addison-Wesley, New York.

Tietenberg, T., 2013. Reflections – carbon pricing in practice. Rev. Environ. Econ. Policy 7, 313–329.

Tol, R., 2009. The economic effects of climate change. J. Econ. Perspect. 23, 29–51.

Treaty of Vienna, 1969. Vienna Convention on the Law of Treaties (with Annex). Concluded Vienna on May 23, 1969. <https://treaties.un.org/doc/Publication/UNTS/> Volume% 201155/volume-1 155-I-18232-English.

United Nations, 1945. Charter of the United Nations and Statue of the International Court of Justice. UN, San Francisco, CA.

United Nations Environmental Programme (UNEP), 2016. The Kigali Amendment to the Montreal Protocol on Substances That Deplete the Ozone Layer. UNEP, Kigali, Rwanda.

United Nations Framework Convention on Climate Change (UNFCCC), 1992. United Nations Framework Convention on Climate Change. UNFCCC, New York.

United Nations Framework Convention on Climate Change (UNFCCC), 1997. Kyoto Protocol to the United Nations Framework Convention on Climate Change. UNFCCC, New York.

United Nations Framework Convention on Climate Change (UNFCCC), 2009. Copenhagen Accord. UNFCCC, Geneva.

United Nations Framework Convention on Climate Change (UNFCCC), 2010. Cancun Agreements. UNFCCC, New York.

United Nations Framework Convention on Climate Change (UNFCCC), 2015. The Paris Agreement. Conference of the Parties (COP) 21. UNFCCC, Geneva.

United Nations Office for Disarmament Affairs (UNODA), 2019. Treaty on the Non-Proliferation of Nuclear Weapons. Available at: <http://www.un.org/disarmament/WMD/Nuclear/NPT.shtml>.

United States House of Representatives, 2009. H.R.2454 - American Clean Energy and Security Act of 2009. US House of Representatives, Washington, DC.

United States (US) Senate, 2019. Constitution of the United States. US Congress, Washington, DC.

Viscusi, W.K., Aldy, J.E., 2003. The value of a statistical life: a critical review of market estimates throughout the world. J. Risk Uncertain. 5, 5–76.

Weitzman, M.L., 1998. Why the far-distant future should be discounted at its lowest possible rate. J. Environ. Econ. Manag. 36, 201–208.

Weitzman, M.L., 2009. On modeling and interpreting the economics of catastrophic climate change. Rev. Econ. Stat. 91, 1–19.

World Health Organization (WHO), 2016. Global atlas of infectious diseases. WHO, Rome, Italy. Available at: <http://apps.who.int/globalatlas/>.

World Trade Organization (WTO), 2019. Marrakesh Agreement Establishing the World Trade Organization. WTO, Geneva, Switzerland.

Yohe, G.W., Tol, R.S.J., 2012. Precaution and a dismal theorem: implications for climate policy and climate research. In: Helyette, G. (Ed.), (ed.) Risk Management in Commodity Markets. Wiley, New York.

Zipf, G.K., 1949. Human Behavior and the Principle of Least Effort. Addison-Wesley, Cambridge, MA.

A critique of the economics of global public goods: a microbehavioral theory and model

4

4.1 Introduction

This chapter begins the description of the microbehavioral economics of global-scale public goods which will be continued in Chapter 5, A Critique of the Economics of Global Public Goods: Economics of Noncooperative Games, and Chapter 6, A Critique of the Economics of Global Public Goods: The Economics of a Global Public Good Fund. These chapters will pave the way for the author to present a novel and enhanced economic theory on the provision of globally shared goods in Chapter 7, The Economics of Globally Shared Goods, the core chapter of this book, from the microbehavioral perspectives, that is, through an individual-level decision analysis and microbehavioral adaptations and incentives.

For the grand task of this book, the present author starts with a presentation of a microbehavioral econometric model which was developed to quantify behavioral changes in response to or in anticipation of global warming (Seo, 2006, 2010a, Seo and Mendelsohn, 2008a). This line of research is often referred to as a climate adaptation research. The readers who read through Chapter 2, The Economics of Public Goods And Club Goods, and Chapter 3, The Economics of Global-Scale Public Goods: Key Challenges and Theories, may be swiftly struck by the realization that the theories and debates presented in the preceding review chapters barely touched on this critical domain of research concerning global-scale public good provisions.

The three types of global-scale public goods were introduced in Chapter 3, The Economics of Global-Scale Public Goods: Key Challenges and Theories, with reference to a production technology: a best-shot, a weakest-link, and a cumulative technology (Hirshleifer, 1983; Nordhaus, 2006). The description in this chapter of the microbehavioral models of global-scale public goods will be provided with an emphasis on a cumulative technology. Nonetheless, it should not be hard to comprehend that the microbehavioral analyses presented in this chapter are also apposite in the provision of the public goods with the other types of production technologies, which the present author will come back to elaborate in the final chapter of this book.

Be reminded that the economics of global public goods has concerned itself primarily on the question of how the world community as a whole should determine its actions in order to address the market failures in providing a global public good or another (Nordhaus, 1994). As such the literature has predominantly concentrated

The Economics of Globally Shared and Public Goods. DOI: https://doi.org/10.1016/B978-0-12-819658-8.00004-4

on a global-level decision. The major theoretical components explained in Chapter 2, The Economics of Public Goods and Club Goods, and Chapter 3, The Economics of Global-Scale Public Goods: Key Challenges and Theories, including a globally harmonized price of a public good, a social rate of time preference, a catastrophic fat-tail event, and global governance are all elaborated at the global decision level (Nordhaus, 2008; Stern, 2007; Weitzman, 2009). Even a finer level analysis, if possible at all, has only the resolution of the world's geopolitical or geoeconomic regions (Nordhaus and Yang, 1996; Sandler, 1997; Carraro et al., 2006; Barrett, 2010).

Considering this historical background, it is not a surprise that the microbehavioral models and empirical studies of global warming decisions would reveal vast amount of new information that has been either hidden in or ignored by the climate change literature (Seo, 2016a, 2017a). Further it may not be unexpected that the microbehavioral studies would come to a different conclusion on many contentious points of debate in the literature surveyed in Chapter 3, The Economics of Global-Scale Public Goods: Key Challenges and Theories.

How do we define a microbehavioral model and its empirical analysis? It is an analysis where the unit of analysis is an individual decision-maker and whose objects of analysis are choices made by the individuals and differential economic outcomes from such choices. Further it is an empirical analysis based on the observed market data of the behaviors of the individuals and monetary values. The origin of the microbehavioral model and empirical economics can be traced back to the dissertation entitled "Modeling Farmer Responses to Climate Change" published in 2006 (Seo, 2006, 2016a).

In the historical developments of the economics of global public goods and climate change, the microbehavioral studies were treated as a niche market primarily because they are neither directly concerned about nor do provide a direct input to a global policy negotiation such as a global carbon tax, a carbon dioxide emissions reduction target, or a temperature ceiling (Nordhaus, 2008, 2013; Wagner and Weitzman, 2015). The microbehavioral analyses were nearly absent in the foundational works of the field such as Samuelson's and Buchanan's (Samuelson, 1954; Buchanan, 1965).

The pendulum of the economics and policy concerning the literature has, however, swung the other way. With the establishment of the Green Climate Fund (GCF) in 2010 and its disbursements of the funds to over a hundred adaptation projects submitted by the developing country parties that began in November 2015, the microbehavioral studies are increasingly perceived by policy scientists and negotiators as the core intellectual element of the economics and policy designs (Seo, 2019a).

This drastic shift in the recognition of the microbehavioral modeling efforts can be attributed to the following two realizations. One is scientific, and the other is practical. The scientific realization is that the array of adaptation behaviors at the micro level is very vast, and the effects of such behavioral changes are profound (Seo, 2010a, 2016a, 2017b, 2018b). The practical realization is that repeated attempts to have a global treaty that can be shared by all the countries on Earth have instead revealed that the countries do indeed selfishly care about the impacts of the treaty on their countries, disparate impacts across different constituents within each country, and potential false-reporting and exaggeration of impacts by others (Nordhaus, 2010; Seo, 2015a, 2019b).

This chapter will provide a thorough description of the microbehavioral econometric method that was developed to quantify behavioral changes of individuals and their economic consequences in response to and in anticipation of changes in the global climate, that is, a global public good (Seo, 2016a). The description is divided into two parts. The first part is allocated to the economic theory and model of the microbehavioral studies. The second part is allocated to the presentation of the results from the applications of the microbehavioral model to the different micro decision data sets.

4.2   A theory of the microbehavioral economics of globally shared goods

The microbehavioral economics in the analysis of global-scale public goods has two salient theoretical features (Seo, 2016a). First, like the microeconomics, it grapples with the question of how an individual producer or a consumer makes its decisions rationally (Samuelson, 1947; von Neumann and Morgenstern, 1947; Nash, 1951; Mas-Colell et al., 1995). The motive of the individual's decisions is assumed to be a profit maximization from their decisions that would have long-term effects (Faustmann, 1849; Hotelling, 1931; Koopmans, 1951, 1965).

The second prominent feature is its focus on behavioral changes of an individual decision-maker such as a selection of a portfolio, diversification, integration, and land uses and how such changes by the individual manager lead to changes in economic outcomes for the manager. This has been a central inquiry, most prominently, of resource economics and financial economics (Ricardo, 1817; von Thunen, 1826; Markowitz, 1952; Kahneman and Tversky, 1979; Shiller, 2005).

For a quantitative analysis of the microbehavioral economic models, researchers have developed a family of quantitative methodologies making use of the essential toolbox of the microeconometric methods (Seo, 2006, 2010a, 2016b,c). Particularly pertinent of the microeconometric methods are binary and multinomial choice models (Bliss, 1934a,b, Berkson, 1944; McFadden, 1974), discrete-continuous econometric models and selection bias (Heckman, 1979; Lee, 1983; Dubin and McFadden, 1984), mixed models and simulation methods (Geweke, 1989; Hajivassiliou and McFadden, 1998; McFadden and Train, 2000), and spatial spillover effect models (Moran, 1950a,b, Anselin, 1988).

The microbehavioral model starts with an individual farm as the unit of analysis. The farm is assumed to manage its portfolio of products in order to maximize the expected profit that would be earned over the future periods. The factors that determine the farm profit earned from the portfolio of choice are many, one of which is a global public good. The global public good here is a global climate system. A global warming phenomenon which disturbs the climate system and consequently farm profits may be seen as a global public bad. This is how we can establish the nexus between the microbehavioral economic model and the global public good, as shown in the diagram of Fig. 4.1. Although this is not the only nexus, as will be clarified later on in this chapter, this is the foundation of the microbehavioral economics of the global public goods (Seo, 2006, 2016a).

A substantial literature, both scientific and agronomic, is available which associates changes in the global climate system with changes in physical productivities of farm products such as crops, livestock, and forest products (Ainsworth and Long, 2005; Hahn et al., 2009). The changes in physical productivities, along with other changes, underlie the changes in farm profits, the essential variable of the microbehavioral models.

Another nexus exists in the opposite direction, as depicted in Fig. 4.1. The optimization behaviors of the farms would have consequences on the amount of greenhouse gases emitted into the atmosphere, which then affect the global climate system, that is, the global public good of concern. Farming activities release all of the greenhouse gases, directly and indirectly, to some degree: carbon dioxide, nitrous oxides, methane, and fluorinated gases. However, farming activities are also a sink of the greenhouse gases: farm soils store carbon; trees absorb carbon dioxide through photosynthesis; and grasses protect soil carbon and absorb atmospheric carbon (Houghton, 2008; Smith et al., 2008; Schaefer et al., 2016).

Of the two nexuses, the first is the evident link denoted by black arrows in Fig. 4.1, and the second is the roundabout link denoted by white arrows in Fig. 4.1. In other words, the causal link from the changes in the global climate system to the changes in farm behaviors and profits is direct and occurring at the level of an individual farm. On the other hand, the causal link from the changes in farm behaviors to the changes in the global climate system cannot be established at the individual

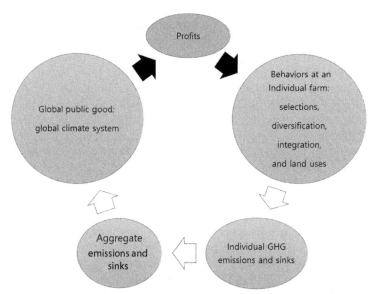

Figure 4.1 A schematic diagram of the microbehavioral economics of a global public good.

farm level. That is, an individual farm's actions do not impact the global climate system at all but only the aggregate of the farms' actions, for example at the national level, does make an impact.

The microbehavioral economics causally associates the changes in the global climate system with the changes in the farm profit and the changes in farm behaviors through a cross-sectional analytical framework. That is, the changes in the farm profit across the space are associated with the changes in the climate system across the space which is one cross-section of time (Mendelsohn et al., 1994). Similarly the changes in the farm behaviors such as selection of a portfolio, diversification, and integration across the space are associated with the changes in the climate regime across the space. After controlling other factors that vary across the cross-section, a researcher can single out the impact of a change in the climate system on the farm profit and the farm choices (Seo, 2006, 2010a).

Therefore, for a microbehavioral analysis, the larger the variation in the climate system across the cross-section, the easier it becomes to identify the climate effects in behavioral and economic outcomes. Similarly, the larger the variation in economic outcomes and behaviors, the easier it becomes to identify the climate effects on these economic and behavioral variables. Considering this, the microbehavioral models were developed and applied to a continental-scale data, that is, not a national-scale data, such as the Africa-wide farm survey (Seo and Mendelsohn, 2008a; Seo, 2010a; Kurukulasuriya et al., 2011).

Once the relationships between the climate system and the economic outcomes and behavioral changes are established, the impacts of a change in the climate system on the economic outcomes and farm behaviors are measured by the differences in the values of these variables before the change and after the change in the climate system. The impacts are calculated assuming that the other non-climate variables remain unchanged. However, it is also possible to calculate the impacts of the non-climate variables through the microbehavioral models.

In addition to the assumption of a profit maximization by an individual actor, the microbehavioral model assumes that the individual is fully informed of the range of climate regimes and the array of economic options she can rely on in different climate regimes. It may be argued by the critics that since the individual farmer is only accustomed to the climate system where s/he is in, she does not have the full knowledge of the other climate regimes and economic options. However, it is highly likely that past experiences, scientific research, and information services make individuals far more informed when it comes to these options. Otherwise, the transition cost of learning by repeated failures could be incurred (Kelly et al., 2005).

Another key distinction to be made in the microbehavioral theory is that it does not assume that the individual farmer is fully capable of predicting the weather variations from one year to another. Nor does it assume that the impacts of such variations can be measured. The microbehavioral economic theory is only concerned about the climate system which is defined as the average of 30-year weather variations, that is, the long-term weather system where the farms are located. This is consistent with the climate science literature which focuses on the climate system, put differently, climate normals (Le Treut et al., 2007).

As such, what the microbehavioral models can reveal is the changes in farm behaviors and monetary outcomes caused by the changes in the climate system. To put differently, they do not show the changes in these economic variables caused by a weather variation in a specific year (Deschenes and Greenstone, 2007; Lobell et al., 2011; Fisher et al., 2012; Seo, 2013a).

4.3   The microbehavioral economic model

Henceforth the present author describes the microbehavioral model of an individual's adaptation behaviors to the global climate change. Let us assume that a natural resource manager (*n*), or equivalently a farmer, located in a particular climate regime chooses one portfolio (*j*) from the family of agricultural and natural resource portfolios (*J*) with the goal of maximizing the expected long-term profit (*π*), given a range of immutable factors that determines the fam income such as the climate and soils. The decision problem by the farmer (*n*) can be stated succinctly:

$$ArgMax_j\{\pi_{n1}, \pi_{n2}, \ldots, \pi_{nJ}\}. \tag{4.1}$$

What constitutes the choice set of agricultural and natural resource portfolios in Eq. (4.1)? Of the wide array of crops, farm animals, and trees that farmers manage, climate researchers identified the seven portfolios as shown in Fig. 4.2: a crops-only, a livestock-only, a forests-only, a crops-livestock, a crops-forests, a livestock-forests, and a crops-livestock-forests (Seo, 2010c, 2012a).

The choice set is encompassing of all the options available to the natural resource manager. As an illustration, let us consider the portfolios of assets owned by South American farmers (Seo and Mendelsohn, 2008b, Seo, 2012a). In the continent, a large number of crops, animals, and forest products in different varieties and species is managed by the rural managers. The major crops widely planted across the continent include the class of cereals such as wheat, maize, rice, millet, and sorghum; the class of oil seeds such as soybeans, peanuts, canola, and sunflowers; the class of vegetables such as potatoes, cassavas, tomatoes, onions, broccoli, garlic, carrots, lettuce, cabbage, spinach, and many others; and the class of specialty crops such as cotton, tobacco, mushrooms, sugarcane, and coffee (Mata et al., 2001).

Saliently in South America, the livestock management outweighs crop farming in many aspects in many regions. The ratio of the land size of pasturelands over

$$A\ rural\ economy \sim \begin{cases} \begin{cases} A\ crops-only\ portfolio \\ A\ livestock-only\ portfolio \\ A\ forest-only\ portfolio \end{cases} \sim Specialized \\ \begin{cases} A\ crops-livestock\ portfolio \\ A\ crops-forest\ portfolio \\ A\ livestock-forest\ portfolio \end{cases} \sim Diversified \\ \{A\ crops-livestock-forest\ portfolio \quad \sim Integrated \end{cases}$$

Figure 4.2 The choice set.

that of croplands is in the range from four to eight (Baethgen, 1997). Also, South America leads the world in cattle export among the six continents in the globe (Steiger, 2006). Along with different varieties of beef cattle which are dominant farm animals in the continent, most frequently raised animals are dairy cattle, chickens, pigs, goats, and sheep (Seo et al., 2010).

In addition to the crops and farm animals, forests and forest products are a vital component of the rural economy in South America. The continent is the world leader among the six continents in terms of the percentage of the land area covered by dense forests (WRI, 2005). The magnificent Amazonia covers 7.5 million km^2 and is the world's largest pluvial forest (Mata et al., 2001). Most common trees planted by rural farms include mango, pineapple, cashew, citrus, cacao, banana, palm, shea nut, apple, Kola, peach, almond, prune, apricot, avocado, cherry, hickory, eucalyptus, lemon, Brazil nut, rubber, mahogany, logwood, jacaranda, and flamboyant (Seo, 2012a).

The first three portfolios in Fig. 4.2 are specialized portfolios. The farm that owns one of these specialized portfolios will be called henceforth a specialized enterprise. The middle three portfolios are diversified portfolios: each of these portfolios comprises two of the three specialized portfolios. The last one is the fully integrated enterprise in that it contains all three components of the rural economy, that is, crops, livestock, and forests.

Having chosen one of the portfolios in Fig. 4.2, the natural resource manager will employ a host of technologies and practices to achieve the maximum profit from the chosen enterprise, which includes, inter alia, fertilizers, machineries, irrigation technologies, extension services, intercropping, and trained workers.

Let us assume that the long-term profit of enterprise j be written as the sum of the observable component and the unobservable component. Further assume that the observable component can be written as a linear function of the set of explanatory variables (X) (McFadden, 1974). For enterprise 1, with μ being the unobservable component,

$$\pi_{n1} = X_n\beta_1 + \mu_{n1}. \tag{4.2}$$

Statisticians cannot estimate Eq. (4.2) directly because of the manager's selection of a portfolio from the choice set which will make the parameter estimates of Eq. (4.2) biased (Heckman, 1979). The π denotes the observed profit of the farm which is observable only when the portfolio was actually chosen by the farm. Otherwise, there is no observed value for π_{n1} and X_{n1}.

However, even if the farmer did not choose the portfolio, it does not mean that the profit that can be earned from the portfolio is zero. It only means that the profit from the portfolio is smaller than that from another portfolio which is chosen. The π^* denotes the latent profit, that is, the profit expected of a portfolio if the portfolio were to be managed by the farm (n), regardless of it being actually chosen or not. The latent profit equations for J enterprises of farm n can then be estimated as follows:

$$\pi^*_{nj} = Z_n\gamma_j + \eta_{nj}, \quad \text{where } j = 1, 2, \ldots, J. \tag{4.3}$$

Unlike the vector X in Eq. (4.2) which is the set of the explanatory variables that is pertinent only to the first enterprise, the vector Z is the set of explanatory variables pertinent to all the enterprises in the model. The η_n is an error term, which will be defined shortly.

The vector of explanatory variables (Z) include a set of climate variables. The climate subvector includes both a set of climate normals and a set of climate risk normals (Seo, 2012b). Further, seasonal climate variables are entered to capture seasonal changes in the climate system and seasonal changes in farming and resource activities (Mendelsohn et al., 1994). The seasons in the Southern Hemisphere are opposite to the seasons in the Northern Hemisphere. Frequently there are no distinct four seasons in the tropical or low-latitude countries (Seo and Mendelsohn, 2008b). In the monsoon climate regime, the seasons can be distinguished by a monsoon season and a non-monsoon season (Seo, 2016c).

Assuming that $\eta_{nj}'s$ are independently and identically Gumbel distributed (McFadden, 1974) and further that spatial neighborhood effects are accounted for by a resampling of the original spatial data (Anselin, 1988; Beron and Vijberberg, 2004; Seo, 2011b, 2016a), we can write the probability of the first natural resource enterprise being chosen by the farmer succinctly as a Logit probability or a mixed Logit probability (Berkson, 1944; McFadden and Train, 2000; Train, 2003):

$$P_{n1} = \frac{\exp\,(Z_n\gamma_1)}{\displaystyle\sum_{k=1}^{K} \exp\,(Z_n\gamma_k)}. \tag{4.4}$$

Eq. (4.4) can be estimated for each of the alternatives in the model, which would give us the key knowledge that can be obtained from the microbehavioral models, that is, the adaptation behaviors. Eq. (4.4) tells us how farmers choose each natural resource enterprise given the climate system and how they switch to another enterprise if the climate system were to be shifted.

Having chosen enterprise 1, for example, a crops-only enterprise, the manager should make numerous decisions efficiently regarding a bundle of inputs and outputs to be employed as well as a basket of farming practices in order to maximize the profit from the chosen enterprise. An estimation of the profit equation of each of the enterprises is the second core knowledge of the microbehavioral models.

As stated above, a direct estimation of Eq. (4.2) does not yield unbiased estimates of the parameters of the model, with the standard assumption of the independent and identically distributed error term such as follows:

$$E\big(\mu_{n1}|X,Z\big) = 0, \, Var\big(\mu_{n1}|X,Z\big) = \sigma^2. \tag{4.5}$$

A direct estimation of Eq. (4.2) will result in biased parameter estimates because of the selection decision that precedes the other management decisions (Heckman, 1979). To obtain consistent parameter estimates of the profit function, selectivity, commonly called the selection bias, must then be corrected (McFadden, 1999).

For a multinomial, or equivalently polychotomous, choice model, there are several selection bias correction methods that have been proposed since the Heckman's seminal paper. Of those, the Lee's generalized method, the Dahl's semi-parametric method, and the Dubin-McFadden's method are most widely discussed and used in applications (Lee, 1983; Dubin and McFadden, 1984; Dahl, 2002). It can be shown that the Dubin-McFadden's method outperforms the other two methods, with a few exceptional cases aside, because the other methods place severe restrictions on the correlation structure of the choice alternatives, as will be clarified shortly (Schmertmann, 1994; Bourguignon et al., 2004; Seo, 2016b).

The microbehavioral models relied on the Dubin and McFadden method, the DM method henceforth, for the selection bias correction in a multinomial choice situation (Dubin and McFadden, 1984). Allowing for a markedly more flexible correlation pattern than the other selection bias correction methods which assumes the identity of the J correlation coefficients, the DM method assumes the following linearity condition, which states that the correlation coefficient (λ_{ij}) between the enterprise i profit and the enterprise j profit adds up to one across j for each i :

$$\sum_{j=1}^{J} \lambda_{ij} = 1, \quad \text{where} \quad \lambda_{ij} = corr(\mu_i, \eta_j). \tag{4.6}$$

A second-stage outcome equation is then estimated after incorporating the selectivity bias correction. The conditional profit equation for enterprise i is estimated as follows with the selection bias correction term that is expressed as a mapping of the estimated probabilities, P_{nj}, from Eq. (4.4):

$$\pi_{ni} = X_n \varphi_i + \sigma_i \sum_{k \neq i}^{J} \lambda_{ik} \left[\frac{P_{nk} \ln P_{nk}}{1 - P_{nk}} + \ln P_{ni} \right] + \delta_{ni}. \tag{4.7}$$

All the parameters and variables are as defined before while δ is a white noise error with its mean being zero. For each of the seven enterprises, the above outcome equation is estimated. For example, a conditional long-term profit equation for the crops-only enterprise, the crops-livestock enterprise, the livestock-only enterprise, and the other enterprises can be estimated by constructing the selection bias correction term accordingly.

The second term on the right-hand side of Eq. (4.7) is the set of selection bias correction components. Note that the selection bias correction term includes the choice probabilities of all enterprises in the model, that is, $P_1, P_2, P_3, ..., P_7$. This means that the estimation of the second-stage outcome equation in Eq. (4.7) takes into account the selections of all seven alternatives in the model. This is not the case in the other selection bias correction methods, which explains the preference of the DM method over the others by statisticians (Bourguignon et al., 2004).

Why does the selection bias correction term take the specific form shown in the second term on the right-hand side of Eq. (4.7)? In brief, it naturally follows from the linearity assumption in Eq. (4.6). A mathematical derivation of the DM selection bias term was explained by the present author elsewhere, relying on earlier works (Dubin and McFadden, 1984; Bourguignon et al., 2004; Seo, 2016a).

In estimating Eqs. (4.4) and (4.7), a simultaneous estimation of the system of equations, that is, the set of the choice equation and the profit equations, is called for, as such, the parameters in the model should be identified (Fisher, 1966; Manski, 1995; Johnston and DiNardo, 1997). In nontechnical terms, the identification problem in statistical estimations is the problem of one equation or a combination of equations determines another equation, which should be avoided. The parameters of the microbehavioral model can be identified nonparametrically with an exclusion condition. More concretely, an identification strategy is to exclude from the profit equations and the identification variables that are entered in the choice equation (Seo and Mendelsohn, 2008a, Seo, 2010a).

The second-stage equations in Eq. (4.7) give us the knowledge about the profit equation of each enterprise. The third stage of the microbehavioral model combines the choice probabilities in Eq. (4.4) and the profit equations in Eq. (4.7) to construct the expected (long-term) profit of the farm. The expected long-term profit, or equivalently land value, of the farm is the sum across the seven enterprises the estimated probability of each natural resource enterprise being chosen times the conditional profit of the enterprise. Put differently, it is the weighted average of the enterprise-specific land values where the weights are the choice probabilities of the corresponding enterprises.

Formally let E be the vector of climate variables. Then the expected long-term profit of the farm (Π) is derived as follows, with the component after the vertical bar inside the parentheses implying the other explanatory variables than the climate:

$$\Pi_n(E|.) = \sum_{j=1}^{J} P_{nj}(E|.) * \pi_{nj}(E|.) \tag{4.8}$$

Having the expected land value estimated through Eq. (4.8) for each farm, we can now calculate the impact of a change in the climate system on the expected long-term profit of the farm. Let us pick a climate change scenario, from the ensemble of scenarios provided by the Intergovernmental Panel on Climate Change (IPCC), in which the vector E takes on the value of E_0 at the present time and E_1 at the future time (IPCC, 2014). The change in the expected profit, $\Delta\Pi_n$, attributed to the materialization of the scenario can be measured as the difference in the value after and before the change, with dropping the vertical bars for the sake of simplicity:

$$\begin{aligned}\Delta\Pi_n &= \Pi_n(E_1) - \Pi_n(E_0) \\ &= \sum_{j=1}^{J} P_{nj}(E_1) * \pi_{nj}(E_1) - \sum_{j=1}^{J} P_{nj}(E_0) * \pi_{nj}(E_0).\end{aligned} \tag{4.9}$$

The change in the expected land value in Eq. (4.9) captures both the changes in the choice probabilities of all possible enterprises and the changes in the conditional land values of them. As we saw above, the changes in the enterprise choice probabilities are calculated through Eq. (4.4). The changes in the conditional land values are calculated through Eq. (4.7). Eq. (4.9) combines both changes.

The degree to which the estimate in Eq. (4.9) is uncertain is calculated by the confidence interval, for example, 95% confidence interval. A parametric confidence interval of Eq. (4.9) is difficult to derive because of many parameters in the single equation. If the sample size is sufficiently large, however, a bootstrapping method can be used to calculate the standard error estimate based on a large number of sub-samples drawn randomly from the original sample (Efron, 1981; Seo and Mendelsohn, 2008a). The standard errors for the changes in choice probabilities in Eq. (4.4) and for the changes in conditional land values in Eq. (4.7) can be calculated similarly by applying the bootstrapping method.

The structure of the microbehavioral model is fully explained by the Eqs. (4.1)−(4.9). For the explanation of the full content of the model, however, two additional questions should be addressed. One is the vector of explanatory variables (Z), and the other is the subvector of climate variables (E) that should enter the model.

First, the vector of explanatory variables in the microbehavioral modeling is composed of the subvector of climate variables and that of nonclimate variables. The latter vector comprises soils, topography, hydrology (water flows and runoff), market access (travel hours to major markets for exports, sales, or inputs), household characteristics (gender, education, number of family members, etc.), policy variables (extension service), and country dummies (Seo, 2011b, 2016a).

The vector of climate variables is of primary interests to the readers of this book. The climate variables can come from either satellite data or ground weather station data (NASA, 2018; UAH, 2018). Nonclimate explanatory variables are obtained from various geographically referenced data sources, which will be explained in detail in the empirical section, such as the dominant soil map of the world by the Food and Agriculture Organization (FAO) (FAO, 2003). The farm-related data are obtained directly from the household survey conducted in the African continent or the South American continent (Kurukulasuriya et al., 2006; Seo and Mendelsohn, 2008b).

As per the second question, the microbehavioral model, like other economic models, was initially developed to measure the impacts of changes in climate normals. A climate normal is defined to be a 30-year average of weather realizations for a concerned variable, which was declared to be the primary variable of concern by climate scientists (UNFCCC, 1992). The most frequently used indicators in climate science are temperature normals and precipitation normals. A temperature normal is a 30-year average of daily temperature while a precipitation normal is a 30-year average of daily precipitation.

More recently, scientists increasingly started to argue that an increase in climate risk may be of graver concern than the changes in climate normals (Rahmstorf and Coumou, 2011; Hansen et al., 2012). The crux of their arguments is that the variability of yearly weather may increase significantly, even if the average climate were to remain the same, so is the within-year weather variability. The microbehavioral researchers have followed suit to shift the focus of the model to climate risks (Seo, 2012b, 2016c, 2018a).

The present author developed three indicators of climate risk, to be explained presently. Before they are introduced to the readers, it should be emphasized that the climate risk is not the same as the weather risk (Udry, 1995; Dai et al., 2004; Deschenes and Greenstone, 2007; Lobell et al., 2011). For example, an African village may suffer from occasional weather shocks such as a severe drought or a severe flooding, but it can still be located in a low climate risk zone if such occurrences are not frequent or intense in the timeframe of many decades. In this sense, the indicators introduced below are climate risk normals.

With this point in mind, a long-term variability of daily rainfall, that is, a precipitation risk normal, can be captured by the coefficient of variation in precipitation (CVP) measured from the rainfall observations for the 30-year period from 1961 to 1990 (Seo, 2012b). The CVP is a measure of rainfall dispersion that does not depend on the size of average rainfall and can be defined as follows, with R_{jk} being monthly average precipitation in month j in year k ($K = 30$) and $\overline{R_j}$ being the 30-year average rainfall for month j:

$$\text{CVP}_j = \frac{sd_j}{\overline{R_j}}, \quad \text{with} \quad sd_j = \sqrt{\frac{\sum_{k=1}^{K} \left(R_{jk} - \overline{R_j}\right)^2}{K - 1}}. \tag{4.10}$$

Of particular importance is that the CVP measure can identify a large variability of precipitation owing to a regional rainfall pattern which exhibits a decadal or multidecadal swing in yearly average rainfall caused by, for example, a change in an ocean current circulation. Such ocean current circulations include the Atlantic multidecadal oscillation (AMO) that affects the rainfall regime of Sub-Sahara (Janowiak, 1988; Hulme et al., 2001), the El Nino Southern Oscillation (ENSO) that affects the Pacific Rim countries, and the Pacific Decadal Oscillation (PDO) that affects South Asia and the Pacific Rim countries (Curtis et al., 2001; Biondi et al., 2001).

The second source of risk from global climate changes is temperature variability. A climate system might exhibit a more frequent occurrence of extremely hot or cold days or a higher variability from a year to another. Agricultural researchers have argued that an increase in daily maximum temperature or daily minimum temperature affects crop growth significantly (Easterling et al., 2000; Welch et al., 2010).

The temperature variability can be measured by the diurnal temperature range (DTR) (New et al., 2002; Seo, 2012b). The diurnal temperature range variability (DTRV) can be defined as the variability of the average diurnal temperature over a 30-year period. Let $T_{k,m,j,\max}$ be daily maximum temperature in day j, month m, and year k. Let $T_{k,m,j,\min}$ be defined in the same way for daily minimum temperature. The DTRV for a particular month is defined as follows:

$$DTRV_m = \frac{\sum_{k=1}^{K} \sum_{j=1}^{J} \left(T_{k,m,j,\max} - T_{k,m,j,\min}\right)}{K * J}. \tag{4.11}$$

The third measure of climate risk can be constructed to capture the risk caused by a monsoon climate regime (Seo, 2016c). The monsoon climate regime is characterized as a regional climate regime in which an extremely heavy rainfall during the monsoon season is followed by an extremely low rainfall during the nonmonsoon season, vice versa (Chung and Ramanathan, 2006; Meehl and Hu, 2006; Christensen et al. 2013). The monsoon regime is particularly strong in South Asian countries such as India, Bangladesh, and Thailand (Kala, 2015; Seo, 2019c).

The monsoon risk can be defined by a monsoon precipitation ratio normal (MPRN), which is averaged for a 30-year period. Let the monsoon season aggregate precipitation be PR_{ms}, and the nonmonsoon season aggregate precipitation be PR_{nm}. The monsoon precipitation ratio (MPR) is PR_{ms}/PR_{nm}. Then the MPRN is defined:

$$MPRN_t = \frac{1}{30} \sum_{k=t}^{k=t+30} \frac{PR_{ms,k}}{PR_{nm,k}}. \tag{4.12}$$

The MPRN is the mean of MPR and another risk measure can be constructed by the variability of the MPR across the time period. More specifically the monsoon variability index (MVI) can be defined as the coefficient of variation in the MPR (Seo, 2016c, 2019c):

$$MVI_t = \frac{sd(MPR_t)}{MPRN_t}. \tag{4.13}$$

4.4   Empirical analyses of the microbehavioral model

An empirical analysis of the microbehavioral model began with the World Bank supports of the climate change projects in Africa and Latin America. The first complete description of the model described in the previous section is found in Seo (2006) and Seo and Mendelsohn (2008a) who applied the model to African livestock data. The fully developed model is found in Seo (2010a, 2016a,b) with an application to the agricultural and natural resource data and the land value data in Latin America.

The World Bank's African climate change project interviewed and collected filled-out surveys from more than 11,000 farms located in 11 African countries (Kurukulasuriya et al., 2006; Seo, 2006; Dinar et al., 2008). The eleven countries cover geopolitical regions of Africa: North Africa, West Africa, Central Africa, East Africa, and Southern Africa. Southern African countries in the survey are South Africa, Zambia, and Zimbabwe; East African countries are Kenya and Ethiopia; A Central African country is Cameroon; West African countries are Ghana, Niger, Burkina Faso, and Senegal; A North African country is Egypt. The sampled farms also cover the five major agroecological zones of Africa: deserts, arid, semiarid, subhumid, and humid zones (Dudal, 1980; FAO, 2005).

The World Bank's Latin American climate change project interviewed and collected filled-out surveys from more than 2500 households located in seven countries (Seo and Mendelsohn, 2008b, Seo, 2010a). Of the seven, three countries were from the Andean region: Venezuela, Colombia, and Ecuador. Four countries were from the Southern Cone region of South America: Argentina, Uruguay, Brazil, and Chile.

The farm household surveys in the two continents asked farm managers detailed questions on farming activities during the years of the surveys. The survey questions were organized into multiple sections: farm outputs, farm inputs, land characteristics, market access, household characteristics, perceptions of climate change, credit/subsidy, and identification variables of the respondent's farm.

The farm-level activities were then coupled with other georeferenced data, and the most important of which are climate data, climate change prediction data, soils, hydrology, and geography data. These data are made available by various research organizations at the level of a grid cell whose size can be 1 by 1 degree or at a finer resolution of a 10 arc-minute cell (FAO, 2003; Strzepek and McCluskey, 2006; Danielson and Gesch, 2011; Seo, 2013b).

For the microbehavioral model of global warming, the explanatory variables of primary concern are the climate data and the climate change prediction data. The climate data can be constructed from either weather station records or satellite records. For the latter, the data are available from the middle of 1980s (Basist et al., 1998; New et al., 2002; UAH, 2018).

A projection of the future climate system is done through a supercomputer simulation of the Atmospheric Oceanic General Circulation Model (AOGCM). As of June 2019, there are more than a dozen AOGCMs in the world (Taylor et al., 2012; IPCC, 2014). The most frequently used AOGCMs for the microbehavioral economic models have been the Goddard Institute for Space Studies (GISS) model by the NASA, the Geophysical Fluid Dynamics Laboratory (GFDL) model by the NOAA, the Hadley center Climate Model (HadCM) by the UK Meteorology Office (UKMO), the Canadian Center for Climate Modeling and Analysis (CCCMa) model, the Commonwealth Scientific and Industrial Research Organization (CSIRO) model in Australia (Taylor et al., 2012; Gordon et al., 2000; Schmidt et al., 2005).

From the microbehavioral data thus compiled, we can associate farmers' behaviors with the climate normals and risks. The two figures of Fig. 4.3 depict how the climate normals and risks influence the ecosystems of Sub-Saharan Africa (Seo et al., 2009; Seo, 2010c). Across the sixteen AEZs, the figures show a range of values for each of the climate variables.

The temperature normal is very high in the continent compared to the global temperature normal which is about 14°C. In the lowland semiarid zone, it reaches as high as 27°C while in the lowland dry savannah, it reaches 26°C. By contrast, the lowland humid-forest and the lowland subhumid zones have the lowest diurnal temperature range normal (DTRN).

As for precipitations, the desert has the precipitation normal as low as 10 mm/month. The lowland semiarid has the second lowest precipitation normal with

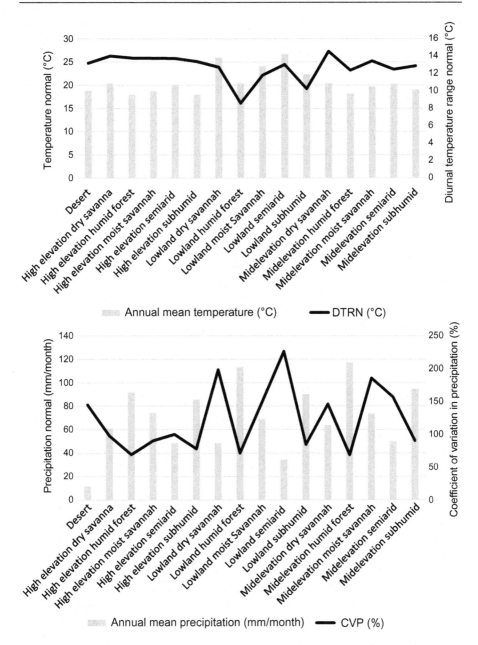

Figure 4.3 Climate normals versus climate risks across the agroecological zones of Sub-Sahara.

35 mm/month. The semiarid zones in midelevations and high elevations, along with the lowland dry savannah, have a very low precipitation normal with about 45 mm/month. By contrast a high precipitation normal can be observed in midelevation humid forest zones and lowland humid forests.

In addition to the extremely low rainfall, the Sahelian arid zones suffer from a large variation in precipitation across the years. The lowland semiarid zone has the CVP value of about 230% while the lowland dry savannah zone has the value of about 200%. By contrast, high rainfall zones such as the lowland humid forests and the lowland subhumid zones have the smallest variation in the precipitation with the CVP value of about 70%−80%.

The adversity faced by Sub-Saharan farmers owing to harsh climate conditions has received much attention from agricultural and development researchers, and Fig. 4.3 clearly summarizes this adversity via the four climate variables (World Bank, 2008, 2009; Byerlee and Eicher, 1997).

One of the key contributions of the microbehavioral models is that the differences in the climate regime across the continent, as shown in Fig. 4.3, cause Sub-Saharan farmers to adopt one farm portfolio or another. This can be demonstrated in Fig. 4.4 which plots adoption percentages of the three farm portfolios for each of the five AEZs (Seo, 2014a). The three farm portfolios are a crops-only, a mixed crops-livestock, and a livestock-only.

The AEZ classification in Fig. 4.4 is a simpler one, also the original, with the five AEZs. The AEZ classification, both for that used in Figs. 4.4 and 4.3, is based on the concept of the length of growing period (LGP) for crops which is the number of days in a year which are suitable for crop growth (Dudal, 1980; FAO, 2005).

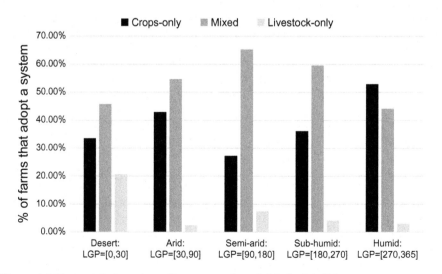

Figure 4.4 Farmers choices given climate normals and risks in Sub-Sahara.

The five AEZs are a desert, an arid zone, a semiarid zone, a subhumid zone, and a humid zone. The LGP range for each of these AEZs is in order [0,30], [30,90], [90,180], [180,270], and [270,365], respectively, as noted in the figure, expressed as the number of days in a year.

The figure shows that the larger the LGP, the more likely a crops-only portfolio is adopted. More precisely the crops-only portfolio is chosen most often in the humid zones. In the semiarid zones, the mixed crops-livestock portfolio is most preferred, in fact, dominates other portfolios. A majority of the livestock-only portfolio farms is located in the desert AEZ.

A more refined analysis of the Sub-Saharan data done at the level of animal species further reveals that the farmers in the desert zones, also arid zones, of the continent rely on the ownership of goats and sheep as a primary source of income and livelihood (Seo and Mendelsohn, 2008a; Seo, 2014a).

An application of the spatial Logit model to the farm data in Fig. 4.4 and the climate data in Fig. 4.3 confirms the observational evidence in Fig. 4.4 and shows statistically that the farmers in Africa have switched from the crops-only system to a mixed crops-livestock system or a livestock-only system in response to an increase in average temperature (Seo, 2010b, 2011a).

The farmers' adaptation behaviors in response to a change in other climate normal and risk variables such as a precipitation normal, the coefficient of variation in precipitation, and the DTRN can be readily modeled and explained through the statistical models described in the previous section (Seo, 2012b). The next section of this chapter will focus on those adaptation behaviors and strategies of the farmers which were revealed by the African and Latin American analyses.

The second stage of the microbehavioral model statistically explains the changes in the long-term profit, specifically, the land value, in response to the changes in the climate normal and risk variables. Since the land value data are only available from the Latin American analyses, we shift our focus from the African continent to the Latin American continent while maintaining the focus on the three agricultural systems (Seo, 2016a).

Fig. 4.5 draws the change in the land value of each of the three agricultural systems as a result of the change in the climate system according to one of the most widely used AOGCMs. Specifically, the figure relies on the Goddard Institute of Space Studies (GISS) ER scenario for the time period of 2046−2065. This scenario predicts about 2°C increase in average temperature and about 3% increase in average precipitation for the above-mentioned period on the sampled farm locations (Schmidt et al., 2005; Seo, 2016a).

The figure shows that the expected loss under the scenario is disparate across the three agricultural portfolios. More aptly, although some portfolios suffer significantly from a climate change, the figure shows that the other portfolios may suffer much less or even benefit from the climate change. Again this is one of the salient features of the microbehavioral economic modeling that is distinct from the theory of global-scale public goods presented in Chapter 2, The Economics of Public Goods and Club Goods, and Chapter 3, The Economics of Global-Scale Public Goods: Key Challenges and Theories.

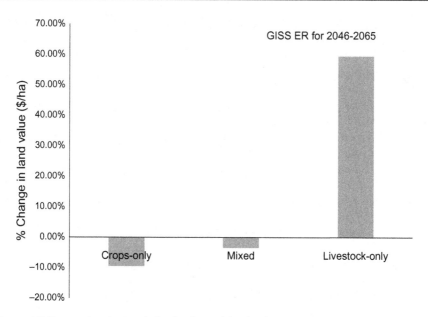

Figure 4.5 Percentage changes in land values of the three systems in Latin America.

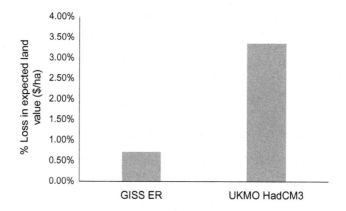

Figure 4.6 Percentage loss in the expected land value for Latin America by midcentury.

The crops-only portfolio is predicted to suffer the damage in the long-term profit, that is, land value, by about 8% under the GISS scenario. On the other hand, the mixed portfolio is predicted to suffer much less, that is, by only about 3% of the land value. Further the livestock-only portfolio is predicted to even get benefits from the climate change scenario, by about 60% of the land value.

With the changes in choice probabilities and the changes in land values of the three agricultural portfolios estimated as above, we can measure the changes in the expected long-term profit (land value) of Latin American agriculture, as described in the previous section. In Fig. 4.6, the present author shows two predictions from two AOGCM scenarios by the middle of this century: the aforementioned GISS ER scenario and the United Kingdom Met Office (UKMO) HadCM3 (Hadley center Climate Model) scenario. The HadCM3 scenario predicts a warming of about 2.4°C and a 5% reduction in summer and winter precipitations (Gordon et al., 2000).

The changes in the expected land value shown in Fig. 4.6 tell only modest, if not insignificant, damage on agricultural and natural resource sector of Latin America if the two climate model predictions were to be realized. The damage is predicted to be about 0.5% of the land value under the GISS scenario and about 3.5% of the land value under the UKMO scenario (Seo, 2016a,b).

As Fig. 4.6 reveals, the predictions of the microbehavioral model of global warming depart sharply from the predictions from other modeling traditions that are lacking or limited in accounting for behavioral adaptations of farmers (Seo, 2019a). To mention a few examples, statistical models of crop growth predict as much as 50%−80% reductions in major crops such as wheat, maize, rice, soybeans in the US and South Asia (Schlenker and Roberts, 2009; Welch et al., 2010). The microbehavioral model predictions also sharply deviate from the catastrophic agricultural damages forecasted by the IPCC (IPCC, 2014; Seo, 2014b).

The modest damages predicted by the microbehavioral model can be attributed to the farmers' experiences and capacities to deal with and adapt to the changes in the climate regime which are fully accounted for by the microbehavioral model. Put differently, there are more resilient systems of agriculture or portfolios and the farmers and natural resource managers can switch to them if the current climate regime were to be shifted. In the next section, we will review these resilient portfolios and systems that the farmers rely upon as an adaptation option.

4.5 Adaptation behaviors and strategies in the microbehavioral model

4.5.1 Adopting livestock species

The seminal microbehavioral model began with an examination of how African farmers choose farm animals in the varied climate regimes in the continent (Seo and Mendelsohn, 2008a). They raise more than two dozen farm animals across Africa frequently: the most frequently raised are beef cattle, dairy cattle, goats, sheep, and chickens and the less frequently favored by African farmers at the continental level include donkeys, horses, camels, pigs, beehives, dogs.

The initial application of the microbehavioral economic model elaborated in the above resulted in one of the most prominent empirical findings in the climate change economics literature. It showed that some farm animals are in fact favored in climatically adverse regions, for example, a hot or an arid climate zone. Further it showed that different animals are favored by African farmers in different climate regimes.

More concretely, the distributions of adoption probabilities of the five major farm animals show that the hotter the temperature normal, the higher the probability of a farmer adopting a goat or a sheep. By contrast, the hotter the temperature normal, the lower the probability of a farm adopting cattle or chickens (Seo and Mendelsohn, 2008a). It was suspected by the authors that goats and sheep may be more heat tolerant than the other farm animals (NRC, 2015).

Estimated probabilities of adoption of the five animals are drawn in Fig. 4.7. The number attached to each animal in the figure is the mean temperature of the farms that adopted the corresponding animal. The mean temperature is as high as 24°C for either goats or sheep while it is as low as 19°C for cattle. For chickens it is 21°C. Be aware that the mean temperature for either goats or sheep is about 10°C higher than the global temperature normal during the 20th century (NASA, 2018). Further the mean temperature for either goats or sheep is 5°C higher than that for cattle.

The second important revelation was that some animals are more favored by farmers in high precipitation zones while other animals are favored in arid and semiarid zones of Sub-Sahara. African farmers are found to adopt either goats or chickens, especially goats, more often in higher rainfall zones while either cattle or sheep are more frequently adopted in more arid zones of the continent. Estimated probabilities of adoption of the five major animals across the precipitation normal in Africa are shown in Fig. 4.8. Again, the number attached to each animal is the mean precipitation of the farms that adopted the corresponding animal.

This result may indicate that goats are genetically more resilient to high precipitation and humidity conditions, which is important to note because such climate conditions have often led to the prevalence of livestock diseases such as trypanosomiasis (commonly called sleeping sickness) carried by tsetse flies which in some

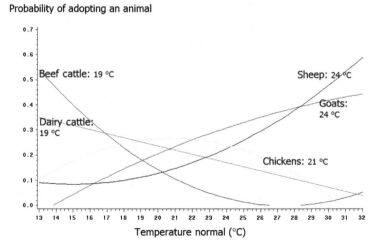

Figure 4.7 Probability of adopting a farm animal over temperature normal in Africa.

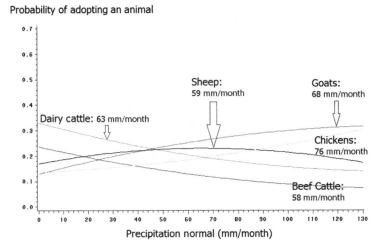

Figure 4.8 Probability of adopting a farm animal over precipitation normal in Africa.

years kills millions of cattle in Sub-Sahara (Ford and Katondo, 1977). An increase in the preference for goats by farmers in high precipitation zones is also reported in India where a monsoon climate regime is dominant (Seo, 2016d).

This result was also revealing at the time of its publication in that agricultural and development experts had long been concerned almost exclusively on the harmful effects of recurrent drought events and an arid climate regime of Sahelian countries (World Bank, 2009). Under the arid climate regime in the Sahel, however, this result showed that livestock management is adopted more frequently and relied upon by African farmers than crop farming, especially through the management of either cattle or sheep, which seems to increase the profits of the farms thereof and make them more resilient against adverse climate conditions.

4.5.2   Switching agricultural systems

Other than the major farm animals analyzed in the above subsection, farmers manage a large number of crops in different varieties. Some farms may own only livestock while others may cultivate only certain crops. We can classify the entire range of farms into a crops-only farm, a livestock-only farm, and a mixed crops-livestock farm. A farmer's adoption of one farm system over the others can be examined by the microbehavioral model and would provide much insight into how farmers respond to changes in the climate system.

In Fig. 4.4 the present author already depicted how the three agricultural systems are chosen in the five different agroecological zones in Africa. The results from the applications of the microbehavioral model to these choices are shown in Table 4.1. The top panel is from the African research, and the bottom panel is from the Latin American research.

Table 4.1 Changes in adoption probabilities of agricultural systems in Africa and Latin America.

	Crops-only	Mixed	Livestock-only
(1) Africa			
% Point changes under +1°C	− 0.65%	+ 1.63%	− 0.99%
% Point changes under +1% precipitation	+ 0.05%	+ 0.05%	− 0.10%
(2) Latin America			
% Point changes under CCCma 2060	− 4.14%	+ 2.10%	+ 2.04%
% Point changes under PCM 2060	+ 1.81%	+ 2.54%	− 4.35%

For Africa, an increase in temperature normal by 1°C causes African farmers to switch away from the specialized systems to the mixed system. The probability of adoption increases by 1.63% points for the mixed system. This occurs simultaneously with the decreases in adoption probabilities of the specialized systems.

An increase in precipitation by 1% by the middle of this century causes African farmers to switch away from the specialized livestock system to either a crops-only system or a crops-livestock system (Seo, 2010b).

For Latin America, the predictions based on two climate scenarios are presented: the CCCma (Canadian Center for Climate Modeling and Analysis) and the PCM (Parallel Climate Model) scenarios for 2060. Under the CCCma 2060 scenario which predicts a hotter and drier climate regime, the probability of adoption of a specialized crop system is predicted to fall by 4.1% points. By contrast, the adoption probability of a mixed crops-livestock system is predicted to increase by 2.1% points, and the probability of adoption of a specialized livestock system is predicted to increase by 2.0% points.

Under the PCM 2060 scenario which predicts a mildly hotter climate regime with higher precipitation, the probability of adoption of a livestock-only system is predicted to fall by 4.35% points. On the other hand, the adoption probability of a crops-livestock system is predicted to increase by 2.5% points while that of a crops-only system to increase by 1.8% points.

These empirical results point to strong behavioral responses by African and Latin American farmers to the changes in climate variables. In a hotter climate regime by the latter half of the 21st century, farmers are expected to make a switch to the mixed crops-livestock system in order to cope with the change. In a hotter and more arid climate regime, they are expected to make a switch to both the mixed system and the livestock-only system.

4.5.3   Switching agricultural systems under increased climate risk scenarios

A deeper look at the choice behaviors of the farmers of the three agricultural portfolios reveals an even more fascinating aspect of the microbehavioral economic models. That is, the adoptions of the agricultural systems are a primary strategy by farmers to deal with increased climate risks (Seo, 2012b).

In the theory section, we already encountered with the rationale for the microbehavioral models that incorporate the climate risk variables and were presented with the four indicators of climate risk: the CVP, the DTRN, and the monsoon precipitation ratio normal (MPRN), and the monsoon variability index (MVI).

In Fig. 4.9, the present author draws the prediction results from two climate risk scenarios on the adoptions of the three agricultural portfolios using the African research (Seo, 2012b). The first scenario is a 30% increase in the CVP index from the present level, and the second scenario is a 3°C increase in the DTRN index. From the table appeared in Seo (2012b), only the statistically significant predictions are highlighted in Fig. 4.9 while setting aside the statistically insignificant predictions.

First, it is evident in the figure that the increased precipitation risk captured by the CVP increase is harmful to the crops-only portfolio which is predicted to decline by 6% points under the assumed scenario. The hardships and harms caused by the rainfall variability in Africa have been well-documented by researchers and policy experts, which is confirmed in Fig. 4.9 (Udry, 1995; Kazianga and Udry, 2006; World Bank, 2009).

What has not been known to the researchers and policy-makers is also depicted in Fig. 4.9, which is that African farmers have adapted to the climate adversity through an increase in the mixed crops-livestock system. The system is predicted to increase by 7% points under the assumed precipitation risk scenario (Seo, 2012b).

A more recent literature on increased climate risks focuses on the changes in the daily maximum temperature and the daily minimum temperature, especially an

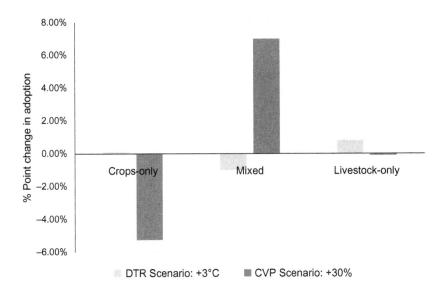

Figure 4.9 Farmer behaviors under increased climate risk scenarios.

increase in the daily minimum temperature, whose impacts were argued to be very harmful to crop growth and yields (Easterling et al., 2000; Welch et al., 2010). As expected, Fig. 4.9 shows that the increase in the diurnal temperature range by 3°C is predicted to decrease the adoption of the mixed crops-livestock system by about 1% while there is no significant effect on the crops-only system.

Even with this alternative climate risk increase scenario, it stands out in the figure that the livestock-only system is predicted to increase across Africa if the diurnal temperature variation were to increase.

What if the climate change should cause changes in both climate risk indicators? If the increase in DTR by 3°C and the increase in the CVP by 30% were to occur concurrently, the above-cited research predicts that the crops-only system would be severely hit with the adoption of the system declining by 4.9% across Sub-Sahara. On the other hand, the mixed system would gain largely, with its adoption increasing by 6.3% across the continent. Put differently, farmers in Sub-Sahara will switch from the crops-only portfolio to the mixed portfolio in order to adapt to the joint increases in the two climate risk indicators.

4.5.4 Switching to natural resource intensive enterprises

The microbehavioral model can be applied more broadly to the natural resource sector which includes the agricultural sector (Seo, 2012a). In fact, rural areas around the globe engage in many nonagricultural natural resource management activities. A prime example is forestry as well as the production of nontimber forest products in Latin American countries. Beyond Latin America, forest-related productive activities are also prominent in South Asian countries, for example, Indonesia, and other continents.

To give you an idea of the importance of forests in Latin America, the continent ranks first in the world in terms of the coverage area (in percentage) of densely forested zones, that is, the forested zones where the forest coverage is greater than 40%. About 48% of the land area of Latin America is covered by dense forests (WRI, 2005). A survey of Latin American countries reports that a basket of forest-related activities accounts for as much as 22% of rural income in Latin America (Vedeld et al., 2007).

Reflecting on this, a natural resource sector microbehavioral model was first developed with Latin American rural data (Seo, 2012a). A rural natural resource manager has the following basket of seven options in the model: a crops-only enterprise, a livestock-only enterprise, a forest-only enterprise, a crops-livestock enterprise, a crops-forests enterprise, a livestock-forests enterprise, and a crops-livestock-forests enterprise. Note that this choice set or the classification of rural production activities was already explained in the theory section of this chapter.

At present, choices of these enterprises are varied across the range of climate zones in Latin America. How will these choices be altered in the future if the present climate system were to be shifted to a future climate system? Fig. 4.10 provides an answer to this question assuming a future climate scenario made available by the UK Met Office, the HadCM3 (Hadley Center Coupled Model) A2 scenario

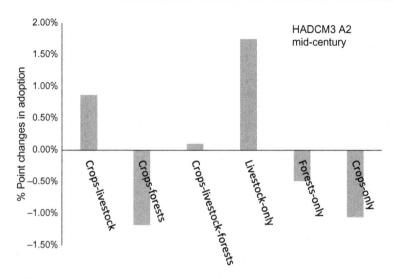

Figure 4.10 Adaptation through natural resource enterprises in Latin America.

(Gordon et al., 2000). The A2 scenario is one family of storylines proposed by the IPCC, which foretells a high degree of warming owing to the fast rate economic growth fueled by extensive fossil fuel uses and divergent regional growth (Nakicenovic et al., 2000). The HadCM3 predicts about 2.5°C increase in temperature by about 2060. It also predicts a 13 mm/month decrease in summer precipitation.

Assuming the future climate system as forecasted by the HadCM3, changes in choices of the natural resource enterprises are calculated, whose results are shown in Fig. 4.10 (Seo, 2016b). With the hotter and more arid HadCM3 scenario, the livestock-inclusive enterprises are all predicted to expand by the middle of this century due to the climatic change: the livestock-only, the crops-livestock, the crops-livestock-forest enterprise. The expansion is large for the livestock-only enterprise, so is for the crops-livestock enterprise.

By contrast, forests-containing enterprises and crops-containing enterprises are losers from the assumed climate system. As shown in the figure, the crops-forests enterprise, the crops-only enterprise, and the forests-only enterprise are all predicted to shrink by the middle of this century. In a more arid climate regime that is foretold by the HadCM3 scenario, crop farming and forestry may lose its competitiveness in many areas of the continent because of deficiency of sufficient summer rainfall needed for crop and tree growth.

On the other hand, a decrease in summer precipitation may help the livestock-containing enterprises by limiting the outbreaks and spreads of vector-borne livestock diseases such as the above-referenced sleeping sickness (Ford and Katondo, 1977). Farm animals may be also more resilient under a hotter climate regime than crops and trees owing to internal heat regulation mechanisms as well as animals' mobility (Hahn et al., 2009).

4.5.5 Public adaptations

The development of the microbehavioral models has pointed to two types of adaptation: a private adaptation and a public adaptation. Up to this point, we focused on the private adaptation. The public adaptation can be defined as an adaptation action that is taken by either a community (group) of individuals or the public sector.

The microbehavioral literature revealed that an adaptation action can be provided in part by a private individual and in part by the public sector (Seo, 2011a). A prime example is irrigation for crop farming which is an important adaptation strategy. There are many methods for irrigating a farmland, some of which are privately supplied and others are supplied by a public agency. Irrigation techniques include surface water irrigation, ground water irrigation, sprinkler irrigation, drip irrigation, and other precision irrigation techniques (Schoengold and Zilberman, 2007).

A study of the Latin American farm households' irrigation behaviors reveals that 65% of the farms rely on rainfed agriculture, that is, with no irrigation. Many of these unirrigated farms are likely livestock managers or forest managers. Of the 35% that have irrigated, 21% relied on a public water scheme and 14% relied on private irrigations (Seo, 2011a).

Fig. 4.11 draws the mean temperature of each of the three irrigation schemes in the top panel and the mean precipitation of each scheme in the bottom panel. More precisely, it shows the temperature normal (or precipitation normal) in the farms that chose each of the three irrigation systems. Both summer season and winter season statistics are presented.

The top panel reveals that the temperature normal in the public irrigation farms is lower than the temperature normal in the private irrigation farms and also lower than the temperature normal in the rainfed farms. The temperature normal in the private irrigation farms is nearly equal to that in the rainfed farms.

This can be interpreted that when the climate gets warmer, farmers adapt either by irrigating privately or by switching to the enterprises that rely on natural rainfall, for example, a pastoral livestock system. Alternatively, it can be said that the public irrigation system has failed to respond to the higher temperature risk in agriculture (Seo, 2011a). This point will be made clearer by the bottom panel of the figure.

The bottom panel yields additional intriguing observations. First, the rainfed agriculture is adopted when precipitation normal is high. Second, when summer rainfall is "sufficient" in the farms, farmers choose to irrigate privately. Third and most interestingly, the public irrigation system has been provided to the regions where summer rainfall is "deficient" for crop growth. As shown in the figure, precipitation normal in the public irrigation system is only 1/3 of that in the rainfed system. Fourth, an application of the microbehavioral model to the choice data summarized in Fig. 4.11 further reveals, although not shown in Fig. 4.11, that when precipitation normal falls, the choice probability of the public irrigation scheme increases at a much faster rate than that of the private irrigation scheme (Seo, 2011a).

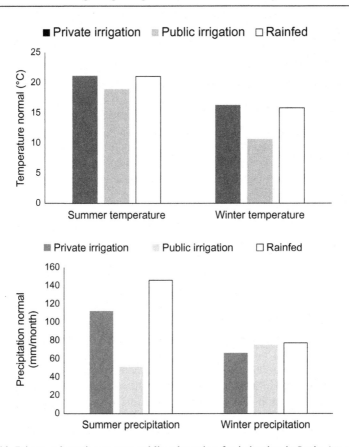

Figure 4.11 Private adaptation versus public adaptation for irrigation in Latin America.

Taken together, the irrigation analysis seems to unravel two important insights into a public adaptation. First, the public agency may have only limited knowledge and consequently responds to one stress, for example, rainfall shortage, but fails to respond to a more complex set of stresses, for example, a hot temperature stress, that constrains agriculture.

Second, the public agency may overprovide the public good, that is, the public irrigation scheme in this example, against the efficient level. If we interpret that the provision of a private irrigation is made efficiently, then it can be argued that the public provision of irrigation in Latin America is made inefficiently, that is, at the level beyond the efficient level. It is inefficient in the sense that the public irrigation scheme is provided even to the areas where such provision is no longer helpful to farmers. Note in Fig. 4.11 that the public irrigation is provided in the areas where summer precipitation is on average 50 mm/month, which can be contrasted to the private irrigation which is provided at summer precipitation of on average 110 mm/month.

4.6   Microbehavioral models in the economics of global public goods

To the readers who have read through Chapter 2, The Economics of Public Goods and Club Goods, and Chapter 3, The Economics of Global-Scale Public Goods: Key Challenges and Theories, that dealt with the theories and concepts of the public goods developed during the seven decades since Samuelson's seminal papers, this chapter may have come as a total surprise to some and a refreshing perspective to others (Samuelson, 1954). The microbehavioral theory, models, and applications elucidated in this chapter certainly provide an alternative, thought-provoking theory on the economic problems of public goods.

At the core, the traditional theories of public goods, also presently predominant, are centered around the creation of a correct price, often referred to as a shadow price, for the public good that is under consideration (Samuelson, 1954; Buchanan, 1965). The price should be enforced across the macro economy through a legal vehicle, which will ultimately resolve the problem of the public good itself, national or global, that is, restore a Pareto optimality of the economy.

As such the variables and parameters of the empirical models of the classical theories such as the dynamic integrated climate and economy (DICE) model are all macro-level variables and parameters: to name some, global welfare, global rate of time preference, global production, global damage, global abatement cost, global average temperature, and global emissions of carbon dioxide (Nordhaus, 1994).

In an utterly counterintuitive and surprising manner, the microbehavioral model clarified in this chapter builds a theory and model of a global-scale public good whose central character is an individual who is forced to make numerous optimal decisions for the management of her resources (Seo, 2006, 2016a). This chapter has shown, especially through the empirical applications, that the microbehavioral decisions can play a pivotal role in addressing the problems of a global-scale public good. More specifically, the host of microbehavioral decisions explained in this chapter provides one of the mechanisms through which the humanity can cope with the problems of a global public good, that is, a global climatic change.

A critic and a traditional theorist may ask: will the microbehavioral decisions such as the ones described in this chapter be sufficient for the humanity's dealing with the problems of global warming efficiently? Although this chapter does not provide a satisfactory answer, it does indicate the possibility and even present the roads which ultimately would lead to the answer. The ensuing chapters, especially Chapter 7, The Economics of Globally Shared Goods, will prove quantitatively that an ensemble of microbehavioral decisions can successfully handle the problems of global warming.

The microbehavioral theory and model of global public goods are counterintuitive, as such, largely overlooked in the economics literature for the past seven decades, because the problem of a public good by definition occurs at the public level and therefore the intuition tells that it should be solved at the public level. For this obvious reason, the classical theorists of public goods have all taken the macro economy approach (Nordhaus, 2008; Weitzman, 2009; Barrett, 2010).

Take for example the polycentric governance approach for the commons by Elinor Ostrom (Ostrom, 1990). In the study directed at the local commons, she reported a local governance, that is, a rule or a custom, set up by a local community for dealing with the problem of the commons in the locality. In her approach, the local commons problem is solved by the local community through a pool of collective actions. The local governance approach, therefore, lacks an individual decision-maker whose decisions are, when added up across the individuals, powerful enough to ultimately address the problem of the public good.

The microbehavioral theory can be compared with the Ronald Coase's bargaining approach for the social cost problems (Coase, 1960). The highly acclaimed Coase theorem, which was awarded the Nobel Prize in economics in 1991, encapsulates the thoughts of the Chicago School of economics and the following previously quoted paragraph from Milton Friedman (Friedman, 1962):

> *An obvious example is the pollution of a stream. The man who pollutes a stream is in effect forcing others to exchange good water for bad. These others might be willing to make the exchange at a price. But it is not feasible for them, acting individually, to avoid the exchange or to enforce appropriate compensation.*

The bargaining solution is only effective when there is a limited number of polluters (upstream) and a limited number of victims (downstream), continuing with the language in the above quote. When there is either a large number of polluters or a large number of victims, a voluntarily negotiated solution to the pollution problem becomes nearly impossible. This is perhaps the reason why the Coase theorem is pertinent to the negative externality problem but not to the problem of a public good which by definition involves a great large number of individuals.

A bargaining solution is certainly impossible for the problem of a global public good, more concretely, that of global warming. The number of polluters as well as the number of victims are truly large. The microbehavioral theory and model, by contrasts, is developed to address the problem of a global public good and therefore may be less effective, as far as the explanatory power is concerned, in the problems of negative externalities such as the upstream polluter problem in the above.

At this point, I presume that the readers are greatly intrigued by the presentation in this chapter and especially in this section regarding the microbehavioral model of a global public good. The full arguments of the present author and of this book will be made explicit by Chapter 7, The Economics of Globally Shared Goods, of this book. A swift reader, however, would not have to wait until Chapter 7, The Economics of Globally Shared Goods, to figure out why the microbehavioral theory and model may provide a satisfactory remedy to the problem of a global public good. A short description in the next section would suffice to give her ample insights and unmissable clues to the arguments.

4.7   Mitigation and sinks in the microbehavioral model

As is unambiguously depicted in Fig. 4.1, the economic problems of global warming in the microbehavioral theory/model consist of two dimensions: climate change impacts and adaptations on the one hand and carbon emissions and mitigation on the other hand. The descriptions up to this point in this chapter have concentrated on the former.

On the latter, that is, the dimension of carbon emissions and mitigation, the microbehavioral theory and model has indeed a lot to offer, although it is not well grasped by the researchers in the literature (NRC, 2015). A satisfactory account of this dimension is certainly necessary for the microbehavioral model to have any chance of offering an economic remedy to the problems of global warming. Here the present author will give a couple of examples of microbehavioral decisions that have a bearing on the mitigation and sinks of greenhouse gases. A full and complete description will be presented in Chapter 7, The Economics of Globally Shared Goods.

The clearest connection between a microbehavioral decision in the natural resource sector and the reduction in greenhouse gases is found in the forest sector. The forest sector engages primarily in two production activities: timber productions and nontimber forest products (NTFP) productions (Peters et al., 1989). The forest sector in the rural areas of Latin America is reported to generate about a quarter of rural income in the continent (Vedeld et al., 2007).

The amount of carbon dioxide that can be reduced by the forest management can be emphatically shown by Fig. 4.12. The figure plots the net carbon flux from the land use changes in the United States from 1850 to 2005 provided by Houghton

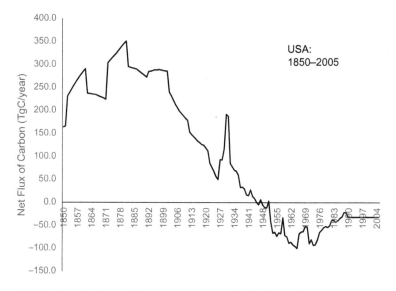

Figure 4.12 Carbon dioxide sink by land use changes in the United States.

from the Woods Hole Research Center (Houghton, 2008). The positive value is the total net amount of carbon emissions while the negative value is the total net amount of carbon reductions.

The figure shows that the net carbon flux in the United States peaked at 350 teragram of carbon (TgC)/year, equivalent to about 350 million ton per year, during the 1880s and turned to the net negative values around the 1950s. The net carbon flux was about -100 TgC/year during the 1970s, meaning that the land uses in the US became a net sink of carbon dioxide owing to, most prominently, increased forests including old growth forests.

The microbehavioral models have shown that farmers in Africa as well as Latin America are switching to forest and NTFP productions in a hotter climate regime, especially, coupled with increased precipitation. As already discussed, African farmers favor a crops-forest enterprise in the humid agroecological zones of Africa (Seo, 2010c). Latin American natural resource managers are shown to switch to forest activities when the climate regime turns to a hotter and larger-precipitation regime by adopting a specialized forest enterprise, a crops-forests enterprise, a crops-livestock-forests enterprise (Seo, 2012a, 2016c).

These microbehavioral decisions will certainly have a clear relationship with the amount of greenhouse gases that a country will emit annually. As such, it is unmistakable that the member countries of the UNFCCC were trying to take the full advantage of the mitigation potentials from the forest sector when they voluntarily submitted the intended nationally determined contribution (INDC) to the eventual Paris Agreement in 2015 (UNFCCC, 2015). This was especially the case for the countries with the largest forest resources such as Brazil, Indonesia, Viet Nam, China, etc. (Seo, 2017a).

The second connection, which is subtler, can be made about the grasslands. Latin America, for example, is gifted with large iconic grasslands such as the Pampas grasslands and the Llanos grasslands (Seo, 2016a). The Pampas is a lowland grassland covering 750,000 km^2 while the Llanos is a highland tropical grassland whose size is about 570,000 km^2. Other iconic grasslands on the globe include the Mongolian-Manchurian steppe, the North American prairie that includes the Great Plains, and the Australian rangelands (Seo, 2015b).

Given the richness of grasslands across the globe, it would be comforting to know that various types of grasses are carbon sinks, that is, absorb carbon dioxide from the atmosphere. A meta analysis of experimental studies including the Free-Air Carbon Enrichment (FACE) experiments and laboratory-based agronomic experiments confirm this (Ainsworth and Long, 2005). Further, grasslands keep soil carbons from being released into the atmosphere and, conversely, soil carbons are released when grasslands are converted to croplands (Smith et al., 2008).

In Fig. 4.13, the present author summarizes the results from the meta analysis of the FACE experiments concerning the carbon dioxide uptakes by grasses and other vegetations (Ainsworth and Long, 2005). The figure confirms that trees are the best carbon sink: the CO_2 update by trees increases by 47% under the enhanced carbon dioxide concentration. The grasses are the next best carbon sink, with its carbon dioxide uptake increased by about 40%. The increase in CO_2 uptake is about 20%

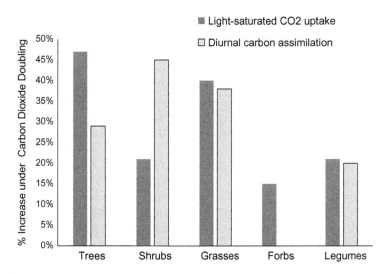

Figure 4.13 Increased carbon dioxide uptake by trees and grasses.

for legumes and shrubs, 15% for forbs. By the other indicator, that is, diurnal carbon assimilation shown in the figure, the increase amounts to 29% for trees and to 38% for grasses.

These scientific results are of much importance to the interpretations of the microbehavioral theory/model whose primary finding, among other crucial findings, is that a switch from a crops-only system of agriculture to a mixed crops-livestock system and/or a livestock-only system is an efficient and effective adaptation strategy of farmers to changes in the climate system. The livestock systems are by and large reliant on grassland ecosystems, for example, the Pampas grasslands that support livestock management in Latin America and the rangelands that support Australian livestock management.

The two connections offer a glimpse on how this book may establish the microbehavioral model as a foundation for an effective mitigation strategy. A fuller description of this subject is reserved for Chapter 7, The Economics of Globally Shared Goods, where the present author will analyze, among other things, a much-spotlighted aspect in the climate change policy circles: an increase in methane emissions from farm animals (Gerber et al., 2013; Schaefer et al., 2016; NASEM, 2018).

References

Ainsworth, E.A., Long, S.P., 2005. What have we learned from 15 years of free-air CO_2 enrichment (FACE)? A meta-analytic review of the responses of photosynthesis, canopy properties and plant production to rising CO_2. New Phytol. 165, 351–371.

Anselin, L., 1988. Spatial Econometrics: Methods and Models. Kluwer Academic Publishers, Dordrecht.

Baethgen, W.E., 1997. Vulnerability of agricultural sector of Latin America to climate change. Clim. Res. 9, 1–7.

Barrett, S., 2010. Why Cooperate?: The Incentive to Supply Global Public Goods. Oxford University Press, Oxford.

Basist, A., Peterson, N., Peterson, T., Williams, C., 1998. Using the special sensor microwave imager to monitor land surface temperature, wetness, and snow cover. J. Appl. Meteorol. 37, 888–911.

Berkson, J., 1944. Application of the logistic function to bio-assay. J. Am. Stat. Assoc. 39, 357–365.

Beron, K.J., Vijberberg, W.P.M., 2004. Probit in a spatial context: a Monte Carlo approach. In: Anselin, L., Florax, R.J.G.M., Rey, S.J. (Eds.), Advances in Spatial Econometrics: Methodology, Tools and Applications. Springer-Verlag, Heidelberg, Germany, pp. 169–192.

Biondi, F., Gershunov, A., Cayan, D.R., 2001. North Pacific decadal climate variability since 1661. J. Clim. 14, 5–10.

Bliss, C.I., 1934a. The method of probits. Science 79, 38–39.

Bliss, C.I., 1934b. The method of probits. Science 79, 409–410.

Bourguignon, F., Fournier, M., Gurgand, M., 2004. Selection Bias Corrections Based on the Multinomial Logit Model: Monte-Carlo Comparisons. DELTA working paper no. 20. Département et Laboratoire d'Economie Théorique et Appliquée (DELTA), Paris.

Buchanan, J.M., 1965. An economy theory of clubs. Economica 32, 1–24.

Byerlee, D., Eicher, C.K., 1997. Africa's Emerging Maize Revolution. Lynne Rienner Publishers Inc., USA.

Carraro, C., Eyckmans, J., Finus, N., 2006. Optimal transfers and participation decisions in international environmental agreements. Rev. Int. Organ. 1, 379–396.

Christensen, J.H., Kumar, K.K., Aldrian, E., An, S., Cavalcanti, I.F.A., de Castro, M., et al., 2013. Climate phenomena and their relevance for future regional climate change. Climate Change 2013: The Physical Science Basis. Cambridge University Press, Cambridge.

Chung, C.E., Ramanathan, V., 2006. Weakening of North Indian SST gradients and the monsoon rainfall in India and the Sahel. J. Clim. 19, 2036–2045.

Coase, R., 1960. The problem of social costs. J. Law Econ. 3, 1–44.

Curtis, S., Adler, R.F., Huffman, G.J., Nelkin, E., Bolvin, D., 2001. Evolution of tropical and extratropical precipitation anomalies during the 1997 to 1999 ENSO cycle. Int. J. Climatol. 21, 961–971.

Dahl, G.B., 2002. Mobility and the returns to education: testing a Roy model with multiple markets. Econometrica 70, 2367–2420.

Dai, A., Trenberth, K.E., Qian, T., 2004. A global dataset of Palmer Drought Severity Index for 1870–2002: relationship with soil moisture and effects of surface warming. J. Hydrometeorology 5, 1117–1130.

Danielson, J.J., Gesch, D.B., 2011. Global Multi-Resolution Terrain Elevation Data 2010 (GMTED2010). US Geo-Logical Survey Open-File Report 2011–1073, 26 p.

Deschenes, O., Greenstone, M., 2007. The economic impacts of climate change: evidence from agricultural output and random fluctuations in weather. Am. Econ. Rev. 97, 354–385.

Dinar, A., Hassan, R., Mendelsohn, R., Benhin, J., 2008. Climate Change and Agriculture in Africa: Impact Assessment and Adaptation Strategies. EarthScan, London.

Dubin, J.A., McFadden, D.L., 1984. An econometric analysis of residential electric appliance holdings and consumption. Econometrica 52 (2), 345–362.

Dudal, R., 1980. Soil-Related Constraints to Agricultural Development in the Tropics. International Rice Research Institute, Los Banos, The Philippines.

Easterling, D.R., Evans, J.L., Groisman, P.Y., Karl, T.R., Kunkel, K.E., Ambenje, P., 2000. Observed variability and trends in extreme climate events: a brief review. Bull. Am. Meteorol. Soc. 81, 417−425.

Efron, B., 1981. Nonparametric estimates of standard error: the jackknife, the bootstrap and other methods. Biometrika 68, 589−599.

FAO, 2005. Global agro-ecological assessment for agriculture in the twenty-first century (CD-ROM). FAO Land and Water Digital Media Series. FAO, Rome.

Faustmann, M., 1849. On the determination of the value which forest land and immature stands possess for forestry. In: Gane, M. (Ed.), (1968) Martin Faustmann and the Evolution of Discounted Cash Flow. Oxford Institute, p. 42.

Fisher, F.M., 1966. The Identification Problem in Econometrics. McGraw-Hill, New York.

Fisher, A.C., Hanemann, W.M., Roberts, M.J., Schlenker, W., 2012. The economic impacts of climate change: evidence from agricultural output and random fluctuations in weather: comment. Am. Econ. Rev. 102, 3749−3760.

Food and Agriculture Organization (FAO), 2003. The Digital Soil Map of the World (DSMW) CD-ROM. FAO, Rome.

Ford, J., Katondo, K.M., 1977. Maps of tsetse fly (Glossina) distribution in Africa, 1973, according to subgeneric groups on a scale of 1: 5000000. Bull. Anim. Health Prod. Afr. 15, 187−193.

Friedman, M., 1962. Capitalism and Freedom. The University of Chicago Press, Chicago, IL.

Gerber, P.J., Steinfeld, H., Henderson, B., Mottet, A., Opio, C., Dijkman, J., et al., 2013. Tackling Climate Change Through Livestock: A Global Assessment of Emissions and Mitigation Opportunities. Food and Agriculture Organization (FAO), Rome.

Geweke, J., 1989. Bayesian inference in econometric models using Monte Carlo integration. Econometrica 57, 1317−1339.

Gordon, C., Cooper, C., Senior, C.A., Banks, H.T., Gregory, J.M., Johns, T.C., et al., 2000. The simulation of SST, sea ice extents and ocean heat transports in a version of the Hadley Centre coupled model without flux adjustments. Clim. Dynamics 16 147−168.

Hahn, G.L., Gaughan, J.B., Mader, T.L., Eigenberg, R.A., 2009. Chapter 5: Thermal indices and their applications for livestock environments. In: DeShazer, J.A. (Ed.), Livestock Energetics and Thermal Environmental Management. American Society of Agricultural and Biological Engineers, St. Joseph, MI.

Hansen, J., Sato, M., Reudy, R., 2012. Perception of climate change. In: Proceedings of the National Academy of Sciences of the United States of America 109: E2415−2423.

Hajivassiliou, V., McFadden, D., 1998. The method of simulated scores for the estimation of LDV models. Econometrica 66, 863−896.

Heckman, J., 1979. Sample selection bias as a specification error. Econometrica 47, 153−162.

Hirshleifer, J., 1983. From weakest-link to best-shot: the voluntary provision of public goods. Public Choice 41, 371−386.

Hotelling, H., 1931. The economics of exhaustible resources. J. Political Econ. 39 (2), 137−175.

Houghton, R.A., 2008. Carbon flux to the atmosphere from land-use changes: 1850−2005. Trends: A Compendium of Data on Global Change. Carbon Dioxide Information Analysis Center, Oak Ridge National Laboratory, U.S. Department of Energy, Oak Ridge, TN.

Hulme, M., Doherty, R.M., Ngara, T., New, M.G., Lister, D., 2001. African climate change: 1900−2100. Clim. Res. 17, 145−168.

Intergovernmental Panel on Climate Change (IPCC), 2014. Climate Change 2014: The Physical Science Basis. The Fifth Assessment Report of the IPCC. Cambridge University Press, Cambridge.

Janowiak, J.E., 1988. An investigation of interannual rainfall variability in Africa. J. Clim. 1, 240−255.

Johnston, J., DiNardo, J., 1997. Econometric Methods, fourth ed. McGraw-Hill, New York.

Kahneman, D., Tversky, A., 1979. Prospect theory: an analysis of decision under risk. Econometrica 47, 263−291.

Kala, N., 2015. Ambiguity Aversion and Learning in a Changing World: The Potential Effects of Climate Change From Indian Agriculture. Ph.D. Dissertation. Yale University, New Haven, CT.

Kazianga, H., Udry, C., 2006. Consumption smoothing? Livestock, insurance, and drought in rural Burkina Faso. J. Dev. Econ. 79, 413−446.

Kelly, D.L., Kolstad, C.D., Mitchell, G.T., 2005. Adjustment costs from environmental change. J. Environ. Econ. Manag. 50, 468−495.

Koopmans, T.C., 1951. Efficient allocation of resources. Econometrica 19, 455−465.

Koopmans, T.C., 1965. On the concept of optimal economic growth. Acad. Sci. Scr. Varia 28 (1), 1−75.

Kurukulasuriya, P., Mendelsohn, R., Hassan, R., et al., 2006. Will African agriculture survive climate change? World Bank. Econ. Rev. 20, 367−388.

Kurukulasuriya, P., Kala, N., Mendelsohn, R., 2011. Adaptation and climate change impacts: a structural Ricardian model of irrigation and farm income in Africa. Clim. Change Econ. 2, 149−174.

Le Treut, H., Somerville, R., Cubasch, U., Ding, Y., Mauritzen, C., Mokssit, A., et al., 2007. Historical overview of climate change. In: Solomon, S., et al., (Eds.), Climate Change 2007: The Physical Science Basis. The Fourth Assessment Report of the IPCC. Cambridge University Press, Cambridge.

Lobell, D., Schlenker, W., Costa-Roberts, J., 2011. Climate trends and global crop production since 1980. Science 333, 616−620.

Manski, C.F., 1995. Identification Problems in the Social Sciences. Harvard University Press, Cambridge, MA.

Markowitz, H., 1952. Portfolio selection. J. Financ. 7, 77−91.

Mas-Colell, A., Whinston, M.D., Green, J.R., 1995. Microeconomic Theory. Oxford University Press, Oxford.

Mata, L.J., Campos, M., et al., 2001. Latin America. In: McCarthy, J.J., Canziani, O.F., Leary, N.A., Dokken, D.J., White, K.S. (Eds.), Climate Change 2001: Impacts, Adaptation, and Vulnerability. The IPCC. Cambridge University Press, Cambridge.

McFadden, D.L., 1974. Conditional logit analysis of qualitative choice behavior. In: Zarembka, P. (Ed.), Frontiers in Econometrics. Academic, New York, pp. 105−142.

McFadden, D., 1999. Sampling and selection. Lecture Note. University of California, Berkeley, CA.

McFadden, D., Train, K., 2000. Mixed MNL models for discrete response. J. Appl. Econ. 15, 447−470.

Meehl, G.A., Hu, A., 2006. Megadroughts in the Indian monsoon region and southwest North America and a mechanism for associated multidecadal Pacific sea surface temperature anomalies. J. Clim. 19, 1605−1623.

Mendelsohn, R., Nordhaus, W., Shaw, D., 1994. The impact of global warming on agriculture: a Ricardian analysis. Am. Econ. Rev. 84, 753–771.

Moran, P.A.P., 1950a. Notes on continuous stochastic phenomena. Biometrika 37, 17–23.

Moran, P.A.P., 1950b. A test for the serial dependence of residuals. Biometrika 37, 178–181.

Nakicenovic, N., Davidson, O., Davis, G., Grübler, A., Kram, T., La Rovere, E.L., et al., 2000. Emissions Scenarios. A Special Report of Working Group III. The IPCC, Geneva.

Nash, J., 1951. Non-cooperative games. Ann. Mathematics 54 (2), 286–295.

National Academies of Sciences, Engineering, and Medicine (NASEM), 2018. Improving Characterization of Anthropogenic Methane Emissions in the United States. The National Academies Press, Washington, DC. Available from: https://doi.org/10.17226/24987.

National Aeronautics and Space Administration (NASA), 2018. Missions: Earth Observing System (EOS). NASA, Washington, DC, Accessed from: <https://eospso.nasa.gov/mission-category/3>.

National Research Council (NRC), 2015. Critical Role of Animal Science Research in Food Security and Sustainability. National Academies of Sciences, Engineering, and Medicine (NASEM), Washington, DC.

New, M., Lister, D., Hulme, M., Makin, I., 2002. A high-resolution data set of surface climate over global land areas. Clim. Res. 21, 1–25.

Nordhaus, W., 1994. Managing the Global Commons. MIT Press, Cambridge, MA.

Nordhaus, W.D., 2006. Paul Samuelson and global public goods. In: Szenberg, M., Ramrattan, L., Gottesman, A.A. (Eds.), Samuelsonian Economics and the Twenty-First Century. Oxford Scholarship Online.

Nordhaus, W.D., 2008. A Question of Balance-Weighing the Options on Global Warming Policies. Yale University Press, New Haven, CT.

Nordhaus, W., 2010. Economic aspects of global warming in a post-Copenhagen environment. Proc. U.S. Natl Acad. Sci. 107 (26), 11721–11726.

Nordhaus, W., 2013. The Climate Casino: Risk, Uncertainty, and Economics for a Warming World. Yale University Press, New Haven, CT.

Nordhaus, W., Yang, Z., 1996. A regional dynamic general-equilibrium model of alternative climate change strategies. Am. Econ. Rev. 86, 741–765.

Ostrom, E., 1990. Governing the Commons: The Evolution of Institutions for Collective Action. Cambridge University Press, Cambridge.

Peters, C.M., Gentry, A.W., Mendelsohn, R.O., 1989. Valuation of an Amazonian rainforest. Nature 339 (6227), 655–656.

Rahmstorf, S., Coumou, D., 2011. Increase of extreme events in a warming world. In: Proceedings of the National Academy of Sciences of the United States of America 108: 17905–17909.

Ricardo, D., 1817. On the Principles of Political Economy and Taxation. John Murray, London.

Samuelson, P.A., 1947. Foundations of Economic Analysis. Harvard University Press [Enlarged edition published in 1983].

Samuelson, P., 1954. The pure theory of public expenditure. Rev. Econ. Stat. 36, 387–389.

Sandler, T., 1997. Global Challenges: An Approach to Environmental, Political, and Economic Problems. Cambridge University Press, Cambridge.

Schaefer, H., Fletcher, S.E.M., Veidt, C., et al., 2016. A 21st century shift from fossil-fuel to biogenic methane emissions indicated by $^{13}CH_4$. Science 352, 80–84.

Schlenker, W., Roberts, M., 2009. Nonlinear temperature effects indicate severe damages to crop yields under climate change. Proc. Natl Acad. Sci. U.S.A. 106 (37), 15594−15598.

Schmertmann, C.P., 1994. Selectivity bias correction methods in polychotomous sample selection models. J. Econ. 60, 101−132.

Schmidt, G.A., Ruedy, R., Hansen, J.E., et al., 2005. Present day atmospheric simulations using GISS ModelE: comparison to in-situ, satellite and reanalysis data. J. Clim. 19, 153−192.

Schoengold, K., Zilberman, D., 2007. The economics of water, irrigation, and development. In: Evenson, R., Pingali, P. (Eds.), Handbook of Agricultural Economics, vol. 3, 2933−2977.

Seo, S.N., 2006. Modeling Farmer Responses to Climate Change: Climate Change Impacts and Adaptations in Livestock Management in Africa. Ph.D. Dissertation. Yale University, New Haven.

Seo, S.N., 2010a. A microeconometric analysis of adapting portfolios to climate change: adoption of agricultural systems in Latin America. Appl. Econ. Perspect. Policy 32, 489−514.

Seo, S.N., 2010b. Is an integrated farm more resilient against climate change? A microeconometric analysis of portfolio diversification in African agriculture? Food Policy 35, 32−40.

Seo, S.N., 2010c. Managing forests, livestock, and crops under global warming: a microeconometric analysis of land use changes in Africa. Aust. J. Agric. Resour. Econ. 54, 239−258.

Seo, S.N., 2011a. An analysis of public adaptation to climate change using agricultural water schemes in South America. Ecol. Econ. 70, 825−834.

Seo, S.N., 2011b. A geographically scaled spatial analysis of adaptation to climate change by agricultural systems in Africa. J. Agric. Sci. 149, 437−449.

Seo, S.N., 2012a. Adapting natural resource enterprises under global warming in South America: a mixed logit analysis. Econ.: J. Lat. Am. Caribb. Econ. Assoc. 12, 111−135.

Seo, S.N., 2012b. Decision making under climate risks: an analysis of Sub-Saharan farmers' adaptation behaviors. Weather Clim. Soc. 4, 285−299.

Seo, S.N., 2013a. An essay on the impact of climate change on US agriculture: weather fluctuations, climatic shifts, and adaptation strategies. Clim. Change 121, 115−124.

Seo, S.N., 2013b. Refining spatial resolution and spillovers of a microeconometric model of adapting portfolios to climate change. Mitig. Adapt. Strateg. Glob. Change 18, 1019−1034.

Seo, S.N., 2014a. Evaluation of agro-ecological zone methods for the study of climate change with micro farming decisions in sub-Saharan Africa. Eur. J. Agron. 52, 157−165.

Seo, S.N., 2014b. Adapting sensibly when global warming turns the field brown or blue: A comment on the 2014 IPCC Report. Econ. Aff. 34, 399−401.

Seo, S.N., 2015a. Helping low-latitude, poor countries with climate change. Regulation. Winter 2015−2016: 6−8.

Seo, S.N., 2015b. Adapting to extreme climates: raising animals in hot and arid ecosystems in Australia. Int. J. Biometeorol. 59, 541−550.

Seo, S.N., 2016a. Microbehavioral Econometric Methods: Theories, Models, and Applications for the Study of Environmental and Natural Resources. Academic Press, Amsterdam, The Netherlands.

Seo, S.N., 2016b. Modeling farmer adaptations to climate change in South America: a microbehavioral economic perspective. Environ. Ecol. Stat. 23, 1−21.

Seo, S.N., 2016c. The micro-behavioral framework for estimating total damage of global warming on natural resource enterprises with full adaptations. J. Agr. Biol. Environ. Stat. 21, 328–347.

Seo, S.N., 2016d. Untold tales of goats in deadly Indian monsoons: adapt or rain-retreat under global warming? J. Extreme Events. Available from: https://doi.org/10.1142/S2345737616500019.

Seo, S.N., 2017a. The Behavioral Economics of Climate Change: Adaptation Behaviors, Global Public Goods, Breakthrough Technologies, and Policy-Making. Academic Press (Elsevier), Amsterdam, The Netherlands.

Seo, S.N., 2017b. Measuring policy benefits of the cyclone shelter program in the North Indian Ocean: protection from intense winds or high storm surges? Clim. Change Econ. 8 (4), 1–18.

Seo, S.N., 2018a. Natural and Man-Made Catastrophes: Theories, Economics, and Policy Designs. Wiley-Blackwell, Hoboken, NJ.

Seo, S.N., 2018b. Two tales of super-typhoons and super-wealth in Northwest Pacific: will global-warming-fueled cyclones ravage East and Southeast Asia? J. Extreme Events 5. Available from: https://doi.org/10.1142/S2345737618500124.

Seo, S.N., 2019a. The Economics of Global Allocations of the Green Climate Fund: An Assessment From Four Scientific Traditions of Modeling Adaptation Strategies. Springer Nature, Switzerland.

Seo, S.N., 2019b. Economic questions on global warming during the Trump years. J. Public. Aff. 19, e1914. Available from: https://doi.org/10.1002/pa.1914.

Seo, S.N., 2019c. Will farmers fully adapt to monsoonal climate changes through technological developments? An analysis of rice and livestock production in Thailand. J. Agric. Sci. 157, 97–108.

Seo, S.N., Mendelsohn, R., 2008a. Measuring impacts and adaptations to climate change: a structural Ricardian model of African livestock management. Agric. Econ. 38, 151–165.

Seo, S.N., Mendelsohn, R., 2008b. A Ricardian analysis of the impact of climate change impacts on South American farms. Chil. J. Agric. Res. 68, 69–79.

Seo, S.N., Mendelsohn, R., Dinar, A., Hassan, R., Kurukulasuriya, P., 2009. A Ricardian analysis of the distribution of climate change impacts on agriculture across agro-ecological zones in Africa. Environ. Res. Econ. 43, 313–332.

Seo, S.N., McCarl, B., Mendelsohn, R., 2010. From beef cattle to sheep under global warming? An analysis of adaptation by livestock species choice in South America. Ecol. Econ. 69, 2486–2494.

Shiller, R.J., 2005. Irrational Exuberance, second ed. Princeton University Press, Princeton, NJ.

Smith, P., Martino, D., Cai, Z., et al., 2008. Greenhouse gas mitigation in agriculture. Philos. Trans. R. Soc. B 363, 789–813.

Steiger, C., 2006. Modern beef production in Brazil and Argentina. Choices Mag. 21, 105–110.

Stern, N., 2007. The Economics of Climate Change: The Stern Review. Cambridge University Press, Cambridge.

Strzepek, K., McCluskey, A., 2006. District level hydroclimatic time series and scenario analyses to assess the impacts of climate change on regional water resources and agriculture in Africa. Centre for Environmental Economics and Policy in Africa (CEEPA) Discussion Paper No. 13. University of Pretoria, Pretoria.

Taylor, K.E., Stouffer, R.J., Meehl, G.A., 2012. An overview of CMIP5 and the experiment design. Bull. Am. Meteorol. Soc. 93, 485–498.

Train, K., 2003. Discrete Choice Methods With Simulation. Cambridge University Press, Cambridge.

Udry, C., 1995. Risk and saving in Northern Nigeria. Am. Econ. Rev. 85, 1287–1300.

United Nations Framework Convention on Climate Change (UNFCCC), 1992. United Nations Framework Convention on Climate Change. UNFCCC, New York.

United Nations Framework Convention on Climate Change (UNFCCC), 2015. The Paris Agreement. Conference of the Parties (COP) 21. UNFCCC, New York.

University of Alabama in Huntsville (UAH), 2018. Global Temperature Record. The Earth System Science Center. UAH. Available from: https://www.nsstc.uah.edu/climate/.

Vedeld, P., Angelsen, A., Bojø, J., Sjaastad, E., Kobugabe, G.K., 2007. Forest environmental incomes and the rural poor. For. Policy Econ. 9, 869–879.

von Neumann, J., Morgenstern, O., 1947. Theory of Games and Economic Behavior, second ed. Princeton University Press, Princeton, NJ.

von Thunen, J.H., 1826. Der Isolierte Staat in Beziehung auf Landwirtschaft und Nationalökonomie, Hamburg, Perthes. (English trans. by Wartenberg CM (1996) The Isolated State. Pergamon Press, Oxford.

Wagner, G., Weitzman, M., 2015. Climate Shock: The Economic Consequences of a Hotter Planet. Princeton University Press, Princeton, NJ.

Weitzman, M.L., 2009. On modeling and interpreting the economics of catastrophic climate change. Rev. Econ. Stat. 91 (1), 1–19.

Welch, J.R., Vincent, J.R., Auffhammer, M., Moya, P.F., Dobermann, A., Dawe, D., 2010. Rice yields in tropical/subtropical Asia exhibit large but opposing sensitivities to minimum and maximum temperatures. Proc. Natl Acad. Sci. U. S. A. 107, 14562–14567.

World Bank, 2008. World Development Report 2008: Agriculture for Development. World Bank, Washington, DC.

World Bank, 2009. Awakening Africa's Sleeping Giant: Prospects for Commercial Agriculture in the Guinea Savannah Zone and Beyond. World Bank and FAO, Washington, DC.

World Resources Institute (WRI), 2005. World Resources 2005: The Wealth of the Poor— Managing Ecosystems to Fight Poverty. WRI, Washington, DC.

A critique of the economics of global public goods: economics of noncooperative games

5

5.1 Introduction

To refresh your memory, the present author provided a comprehensive review of the economics literature of public goods in Chapter 2, The Economics of Public Goods and Club Goods, and Chapter 3, The Economics of Global-Scale Public Goods: Key Challenges and Theories. In Chapter 4, A Critique of the Economics of Global Public Goods: A Microbehavioral Theory and Model, I offered a broad critique of the literature by way of a novel development in the literature, the microbehavioral economic theory and model on the provision of global-scale public goods which is founded on a quantitative modeling of individuals' choices and their economic consequences. This chapter will level the second critique of the literature while the next chapter the third.

The critique in this chapter may be referred to as the economics of noncooperation, which is in contrast with the presumption of global cooperation implicitly embedded in the theories of the public goods presented in Chapter 2, The Economics of Public Goods and Club Goods, and Chapter 3, The Economics of Global-Scale Public Goods: Key Challenges and Theories. The critique will show why there would be no-cooperation among the nations for a global public good provision and further why no-cooperation is inherent, that is, makes sense economically for each nation considering all contingencies (Seo, 2012).

The presumption of global cooperation in the literature, although implicit, has taken on multiple forms: a globally uniform limit on greenhouse gas emissions, a globally harmonized carbon price approach, an international cooperative game theoretic solution, or a precautionary threshold principle for a global challenge (Nordhaus, 1994; UNFCCC, 1997; Sandler, 1997; Barrett, 2003; Weitzman, 2009).

For a national-level public good, the problem of noncooperation does not arise and, even if it does, is not a severe obstacle. Once the national public good, for example, national defense, is provided to the public, all citizens must bear the burden of the public good provision by paying the tax to the government. There is no option for a citizen to reject the tax-payer responsibility. The constitution of the nation imposes this responsibility which is enforced through the government.

For a global-scale public good provision, a low rate of cooperation emerges as the biggest obstacle to any global policy effort (Nordhaus, 2010a, 2011). For the policy issue of global warming, international efforts to reach a globally participating legal protocol have failed repeatedly in Kyoto in 1997, Copenhagen in 2009,

The Economics of Globally Shared and Public Goods. DOI: https://doi.org/10.1016/B978-0-12-819658-8.00005-6

and Paris in 2015 because many countries objected to participating in any proposed global treaty in each negotiation (UNFCCC, 1997, 2009, 2015). For the issue of nuclear nonproliferation, for another example, many nuclear-weapon nations did not sign the United Nations treaty while there remains strong possibility that many nonnuclear nations may reconsider and withdraw from the UN nuclear nonproliferation treaty in the future (Campbell et al., 2004).

The repeated failures in policy negotiations which were broadcasted heavily through the global media, have motivated both researchers and policy-makers to devise a mechanism that can compel negotiating parties to an agreement. The proposed mechanisms include a tariff to nonparticipating countries, a monetary compensation mechanism to loser nations, technology and other physical transfers, a deferment of implementation given to certain countries, and a global public good fund (UNFCCC, 1997; Carraro et al., 2006; GCF, 2011; Nordhaus, 2015).

However, these remedies did not solve the problem of noncooperation successfully but rather ironically may further encourage negotiating members to object to any proposal document in the hopes of receiving the largest concession possible from the process. Such concessions to a country often amount to nonparticipation of the country even if the country would join an international agreement. In other words, the concessions would allow the country to sacrifice nothing under the agreed framework for the provision of the global public good.

Therefore these remedies have not solved the problem of a low participation rate in a global public good agreement. Neither do these remedies seem to have increased the possibility of a global agreement. At the fundamental level these augmented policy models do not address the presumption of global cooperation inherent in the public good theories.

This chapter will provide an empirical analysis of noncooperation in the problem of a global public good by showing that some countries will lose big financially under a globally optimal economic policy and consequently will have no options but to reject it even if some countries were to win financially and consequently push enthusiastically for a global treaty (Seo, 2012). The analysis will be provided by considering multiple policy scenarios and showing that big-loser countries under one policy scenario may turn out to be big-winner countries under another policy scenario. This will constitute the second major critique by the present author of the classical economics of public goods.

For the analysis, the present author will introduce the empirical global public good policy model developed by William Nordhaus referred to as the Dynamic Integrated Climate and Economy (DICE) model (Nordhaus, 1994). As you may recall, the theoretical aspects that support the DICE model were at the heart of Chapter 3, The Economics of Global-Scale Public Goods: Key Challenges and Theories, and fully explained there. For the empirical policy evaluations in this chapter, the present author needs to elaborate the empirical contents of the DICE model such as its major parameters, functions, policy variables, and country specifications (Nordhaus, 2008).

The analysis in this chapter may be replicated by other integrated assessment models (IAM) of climate change such as the MERGE (A Model for Evaluating

Regional and Global Effects of GHG Reduction Policies), FUND (The Climate Framework for Uncertainty, Negotiation and Distribution), or PAGE (A Policy Analysis of the Greenhouse Effect) (Manne et al., 1995; Tol, 1997; Hope, 2006). However, the DICE is superior to these alternative models because it is explicitly a dynamic optimization model of the social welfare (Nordhaus and Sztorc, 2013).

The analysis in this chapter will make clear, first, what a globally optimal economic policy that should be agreed upon by member countries is like and, second, how negotiating parties must face disparate incentives and economic outcomes regardless of any policy option from the family of options would be agreed upon. This chapter will offer a rationale for why international negotiations have failed repeatedly in the past and may continue to turn out the same way in the future negotiations, which constitutes the economic fundamentals for noncooperation for a global public good provision, the central theme of this chapter.

5.2   The premise of cooperation in the theory of global public goods

The most difficult theoretical policy question with regard to a public good provision is what should be the goal in a governmental intervention and through which policy instrument such a goal can be achieved. If there were to be no reason to worry about noncooperation, for example, by the constituents of the country on a governmental policy, the above questions would be the most important ones that should be answered before a legal implementation of the policy thus adopted.

The theories explained in Chapter 2, The Economics of Public Goods and Club Goods, and Chapter 3, The Economics of Global-Scale Public Goods: Key Challenges and Theories, can be regarded as intellectual endeavors to offer an answer to the above questions. The present author will begin a policy analysis in this chapter with a visual presentation in Figs. 5.1 and 5.2 of the answers offered by the theorists on the above-posed two questions. The analysis in this chapter will be performed in the context of a global warming and climate change policy.

The above-referenced DICE model and a small basket of other integrated assessment models purport to address the phenomenon of global warming in a socially optimal manner, which is the ultimate goal of the global community embedded in these models. This goal can be visually depicted by an optimal transition trajectory of the global average temperature projected by each of these models (Nordhaus, 1992). This is the trajectory of the global climate system expected under an efficient management of the problem by the global community.

The trajectory proposed by the most recent DICE model is drawn in Fig. 5.1. In the globally optimal policy (GOP) scenario, the temperature anomaly from the pre-industrial normal climate is increasing gradually over the 21st century to about 2.7°C. After reaching the peak, it stabilizes during the early 22nd century and eventually starts to fall through the 22nd century (Nordhaus, 2008).

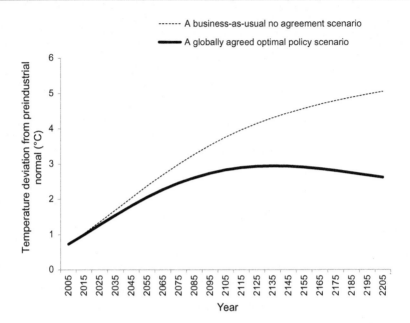

Figure 5.1 The goal of global cooperation through a globally optimal policy.

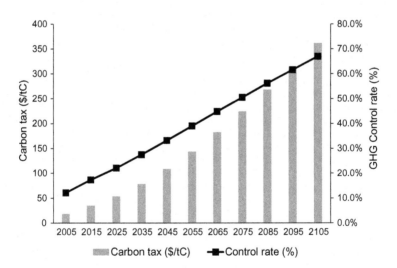

Figure 5.2 Policy variables of a global optimal policy scenario.

The goal of a global climate policy agreement as represented by the thick black line in Fig. 5.1 can be contrasted with the business-as-usual (BAU) no agreement policy scenario which is shown as another trajectory in the dotted line in Fig. 5.1. The BAU scenario assumes no policy agreement internationally, no policy actions nationally, and the fossil-fuel based economies of the 20th century to be continued in the future periods. With the BAU scenario, the global average temperature is projected to increase throughout the 21st century almost linearly. The rate of increase would slow down in the early 22nd century but the global average temperature increase would still reach above 5°C by the end of the century (Le Treut et al., 2007). Compared with the ensemble of climate change predictions published by the most recent assessment of the IPCC, the DICE model which adopts a simplistic three-reservoir climate change module predicts a slightly larger temperature increase than the IPCC suggested range of 0.5°C−4.5°C (IPCC, 2014).

The goal of the efficient/optimal global climate policy (GOP) which is well-documented and widely accepted in the economics literature is to transition the world economy from the BAU trajectory of the global climate system in Fig. 5.1 to the GOP trajectory in the same figure. It is also worth noting that the GOP trajectory is very similar to the expressed goal of the Intergovernmental Panel on Climate Change (IPCC) and the United Nations conferences such as Cancun Agreements and Paris Agreements, that is, containing the increase of global temperature by 2°C, even though the peak temperature in the GOP scenario is slightly above the 2°C threshold declared by the UN conferences (UNFCCC, 2010, 2015; Nordhaus, 2013).

For the UN-led climate conferences, the global climate change target similar to the GOP trajectory in Fig. 5.1, say, the 2°C limit, has been the final word on the world's ambition to be agreed upon. However, for an efficient policy, the climate change trajectory in Fig. 5.1 must be presented in tandem with a policy instrument which must be agreed upon by the international community. As you are all familiar with at this point, that policy instrument is the trajectory of carbon dioxide price (tax) (EAERE, 2019). Put differently, it is the trajectory of the social cost of carbon.

The efficient carbon price trajectory is drawn in Fig. 5.2 for the period of the 21st century, which is based on the most recent version of the DICE model coupled with the present author's calibrations of the model parameters such as the climate damage functions to be explained shortly (Nordhaus and Sztorc, 2013). The efficient carbon tax is about US\$ 40 per ton of carbon (tC) at 2015. The carbon tax increases nonlinearly. It rises to US\$ 60 per tC in 2025, US\$ 140 per tC in 2055, and US\$ 350 per tC in 2105.

For an efficient solution, the world community should agree on the carbon tax trajectory in Fig. 5.2 or a similar one to it. Notwithstanding, the global community, including policy negotiators, environmental activists, and the general public, has long been skeptical about the carbon pricing. Many academics even blamed the carbon pricing for the climate crisis we are in (Refer to the responses to the award of Nobel Prize in economics in 2018). Notwithstanding, there is ample indication that the world community has increasingly realized that a satisfactory solution to the global climate change problem will not come about without pricing carbon emissions. Most recently, the statement by the European Association of Environmental and Resource Economists (EAERE) on carbon pricing endorses the carbon price approach (EAERE, 2019).

For reference, Canada passed the Greenhouse Gas Pollution Pricing Act in February 2018, which created the Federal carbon pollution pricing system to begin operation in 2019 (DOJ, 2018). According to the Act, the carbon tax would start at 20 Canadian dollars (Can$) per ton of carbon dioxide equivalent in 2019, which increases linearly to 50 Can$ in 2022. The carbon tax will stay at that level until a further legislation. You may even get the feeling that the carbon pricing in Canada was anchored by the efficient carbon tax trajectory drawn in Fig. 5.2.

Fig. 5.2 overlays another climate policy variable, the rate of control of greenhouse gas emissions from the BAU baseline emissions. In the optimization model such as the DICE, the trajectory of carbon tax determines the global rate of control. Put differently, as the price of carbon dioxide rises, carbon polluters will be forced to rely increasingly less on fossil fuels and other greenhouse gas emitting activities, which would lead to the reductions in the total emissions from the BAU economy. Therefore the trajectory of the carbon pollution control rate drawn in Fig. 5.2 is implied and indeed determined by the trajectory of carbon tax in the figure.

The control rate starts at about 18% in 2015, which rises to 25% in 2025, 40% in 2055, and about 67% by 2105. This trajectory can be compared with the national commitments made voluntarily for the Paris Agreement (UNFCCC, 2015). The EU's intended nationally determined contribution (INDC) under the Paris Agreement is to reduce greenhouse gas emissions by at least 40% by 2030 compared to the 1990 level. The INDC submitted by the United States is to cut greenhouse gas emissions by 26%−28% by 2025 from the 2005 level (Seo, 2017a).

The host of optimal global warming policy models such as the DICE provides the world community with the invaluable information on the policy goal shown in Fig. 5.1 and policy instruments shown in Fig. 5.2, which are in essence the economic solutions to the global public good problem. Notwithstanding, these optimization policy models presumed that the global community will without doubt agree on the policy goal and instrument as suggested in Figs. 5.1 and 5.2. Or, perhaps it is fairer for me to say that the modelers were not concerned about and set aside the conundrum of how to make all the parties in negotiation to reach an agreement on an economic solution to a global public good provision.

In the ensuing sections, the present author will first explain the parameters and functional relationships in the DICE model, many of which are without doubt contentious, that underlie the model which produces the outcomes in Figs. 5.1 and 5.2. This will be followed by an empirical analysis of why some countries will not have an incentive to participate in an agreement while others will as well as why countries will reverse their initial positions when another agreement is considered.

We will conduct the analysis of nonparticipation with the very economic and policy outcomes that are projected by the DICE model. The DICE model—which is a standard-bearer of the global cooperative economic policy models—will be shown in this chapter to be a harbinger of global noncooperation in the global public good provisions.

5.3 The parameters of contention in the cooperative DICE model

The set of empirical analyses to be presented in this chapter will be conducted within the framework of the most recent version of the DICE model (Nordhaus and Sztorc, 2013). The details of the model were also explained by the present author recently (Seo, 2017a), so interested readers may refer to either of these publications. This section will clarify the economic parameters in the DICE model that are critical as well as contentious and are particularly pertinent to the analysis of noncooperation by negotiating parties, including those that are strongly hinged on the future realizations of the climate system.

To begin with, we choose the values for the two key economic parameters, following the recommendations from the above-referenced DICE version. The first is the rate of social time preference, ρ in Chapter 3, The Economics of Global-Scale Public Goods: Key Challenges and Theories, is set to 1.5%. The second is the rate of inter-generational inequality aversion, α in Chapter 3, The Economics of Global-Scale Public Goods: Key Challenges and Theories, to 2. But, the present author must emphasize that the analysis in this chapter can be performed with different numerical values of the two parameters without altering the primary conclusion of this chapter (Newell and Pizer, 2001; Nordhaus, 2007; Stern, 2007).

Another important clarification that is called for before we proceed further is the world population growth. This chapter relies on the world population projections by either the United Nations Population Fund or the International Institute of Applied Systems Analysis (IIASA), especially the latter (IIASA, 2007; Lutz et al., 2014). Both projections, widely accepted in the economics modeling, predict a stabilization of the world population by the end of the 21st century.

In the analysis that ensues, the players in the game of a global public good treaty are 13 world regions: the US, EU, China, India, Africa, Latin America and the Caribbean, Russia, Japan, Middle East, Eurasia, other high-income countries, other Asian countries, and Oceania. This classification follows the specification of the regional DICE model but adds Oceania as another unique player (Nordhaus and Yang, 1996). The Oceania classification captures Australia and New Zealand as a unique region of the world.

The first set of contentious economic parameters—probably the most contentious of all—belongs to the climate change damage function for the globe as well as for each region. The present author specifies the climate damage function for each of the 13 players (Ω_i) as a quadratic function of a global temperature increase (T_t^{ATM}) at time t:

$$\Omega_{it} = \tau_{i1} \cdot T_t^{ATM} + \tau_{i2} \cdot \left(T_t^{ATM}\right)^2. \tag{5.1}$$

The calibration by this chapter of the climate damage function for each region is summarized in Table 5.1. The table shows the value of the linear coefficient and

Table 5.1 The calibration of the climate damage function for each player.

Players	Vulnerability index	Expected damage from carbon doubling (% of GDP)	Linear coefficient of the damage function: τ_1	Quadratic coefficient of the damage function: τ_2
EU	High damage	2.5% loss	0	0.00278
India	High damage	2.5% loss	0	0.00278
Africa	High damage	2.5% loss	0	0.00278
Latin America and the Caribbean	High damage	2.5% loss	0	0.00278
Middle East	High damage	2.5% loss	0	0.00278
Other Asian countries	High damage	2.5% loss	0	0.00278
Oceania	High damage	2.5% loss	0	0.00278
US	Medium damage	1.25% loss	0	0.00139
Japan	Medium damage	1.25% loss	0	0.00139
Other high-income countries	Medium damage	1.25% loss	0	0.00139
China	Low damage	0.4% loss	0	0.00037
Eurasia	Low damage	0.4% loss	0	0.00037
Russia	Beneficiary	1.25% gain	0	-0.00139

that of the quadratic coefficient of the damage function in Eq. (5.1) for each player. The 13 players are identified by the vulnerability index of each player: high damage, medium damage, low damage, beneficiary. For each of the vulnerability index, the present author assigned the quadratic coefficient uniquely, which you can verify from the table.

The quadratic coefficient for each vulnerability index is determined in accordance with a simple rule specified in the third column of the table: the carbon doubling will lead to a 2.5% loss in the GDP for the high damage country, to a 1.25% loss for the medium damage country, to a 0.4% loss for the low damage country, and to the gain of a 1.25% of the GDP for the beneficiary country. The carbon doubling, more precisely, the doubling of the carbon dioxide concentration in the global atmosphere, leads to about 2.5°C increase in global average temperature in the DICE model.

The calibration of the damage function from carbon doubling are based on the economic literature on climate change damage. For reference, the DICE model assumes about 1.5%−2% loss in the output globally (Nordhaus, 2008). A survey of the economic damage literature shows that the estimates vary widely across the economic models and modelers while the average of the estimates is about 1.5% loss in economic output globally (Mendelsohn et al., 2006; Mendelsohn and Williams, 2007; Tol, 2009).

In Table 5.1, the present author assigns a 2.5% loss in the economic output for the high damage countries, a half of that for the medium damage countries (1/2*2.5%), and a third of the medium damage estimate for the low damage countries (1/3*1.25%). The beneficiary country gains by about 1.25% of its output.

The medium damage countries are the US, Japan, and other high-income countries because of their economic size and the temperate climate regime at the present time in these countries. The low damage countries are China and Eurasia because of large areas of these regions being in cold climate zones. The beneficiary country is Russia owing to the predominantly cold climate regime, including the permafrost, before the predicted climatic shift.

The second set of contentious parameters belongs to the abatement cost function of carbon dioxide equivalent. The abatement cost function specifies the total cost of abating the tons of carbon dioxide equivalent utilizing the existing technologies at the time of abatement. In Chapter 3, The Economics of Global-Scale Public Goods: Key Challenges and Theories, the abatement cost function was described as a power function of the control rate (μ), whose shape depends on the exponent, θ_2, of the power function, and the player-specific abatement cost function (Γ_i) can be written as follows (Nordhaus and Boyer, 2000):

$$\Gamma_{it} = \theta_{1it} \cdot \mu_t^{\theta_{2it}} \tag{5.2}$$

As explained in Chapter 3, The Economics of Global-Scale Public Goods: Key Challenges and Theories, the abatement cost for each marginal ton of carbon dioxide equivalent is bounded by the cost of a backstop technology. A backstop is defined as a technology that can provide energy nearly infinitely to humanity with near zero emissions of carbon dioxide at a constant price (Nordhaus, 1973). This means that the marginal cost of abatement at a 100% abatement of carbon dioxide equivalent emissions should be equal to the marginal cost of abatement by a backstop technology (Devarajan and Fisher, 1981).

Following the Intergovernmental Panel on Climate Change (IPCC) estimates and the Nordhaus' estimate, we assume the cost of the backstop technology at the present time is US$ 1200 per ton of carbon removed (Nordhaus, 2008; IPCC, 2014). In Chapter 7, The Economics of Globally Shared Goods, a detailed presentation of the backstop technologies and their estimated costs will be provided (NRC, 2015a,b). Since a zero-carbon economy is easier to achieve for some countries than others, we assume different marginal costs of the backstop technologies. The point here is that a highly industrialized country may be deeply embedded with fossil-fuel based economic activities, which makes a complete decoupling of its economy from fossil fuels more costly to realize.

Table 5.2 summarizes the details of the calibration of the abatement cost function for each of the 13 regions. First, the exponent of the abatement cost power

Table 5.2 The calibration of the region-specific abatement cost function.

Players	Exponent of the abatement cost function (θ_2)	Marginal cost of a backstop technology, \$/tC	Ratio of asymptotic price to current backstop price
US	2.8	1200	1/2
EU	2.8	1200	1/2
Japan	2.8	1200	1/2
Middle East	2.8	1200	1/2
India	2.8	792	1/2
Africa	2.8	792	1/2
Latin America	2.8	792	1/2
Other high-income countries	2.8	792	1/2
Other Asian countries	2.8	792	1/2
Oceania	2.8	792	1/2
China	2.8	720	1/2
Eurasia	2.8	720	1/2
Russia	2.8	600	1/2

function, θ_2 in Eq. (5.2), is set to 2.8, following the Nordhaus estimate. Second, the cost of the backstop technology for each region is assumed to decline over time owing to technological advances to the asymptotic level which is 1/2 of the present level by the end of the 21st century. The cost of solar energy generations or that of nuclear fusion/fission energy generations, for example, will continue to fall through the 21st century (Heal, 2010).

Third, the present author assumes that the marginal cost of abatement for the backstop technology to be US\$ 1200 for the US, EU, Japan, and the Middle East; US\$ 792 (about 2/3*1200\$) for Africa, India, Latin America, other Asian countries, other high-income countries, Oceania; US\$ 720 (3/5*1200\$) for China and Eurasia; US\$ 600 (about 1/2*1200\$) for Russia.

The third set of contentious economic parameters in the DICE modeling is the rate of technological changes in the economy, in particular, those which work to help reduce carbon emissions in the economy. These technologies are different from the low-carbon technologies which are being developed specifically for the purpose of reducing carbon emissions and concentration (Hulten, 2000; Keeling et al., 2005). This type of technological changes is often called an exogenous technological change which may or may not be a Hicks-neutral technological change. The rate of change for this type of technological progresses is captured in the DICE model by the carbon intensity which is expressed as the amount of carbon dioxide equivalent emissions per US\$ 1000 worth of economic outputs.

The carbon intensity in the developed countries' economies has fallen dramatically over the past five decades. For example, the carbon intensity of the US economy has decreased by about 40% from the baseline of 1980 in a nearly linear trend (Nordhaus and Boyer, 2000; Seo, 2017a). More concretely, the US economy emitted 220 tons of carbon dioxide equivalent for each 1 million dollars of Gross Domestic Product (GDP) in 1980, which has declined to 130 tons of carbon dioxide equivalent in 2005.

Table 5.3 summarizes the calibrations of the region-specific carbon intensity parameters that will be used for the analysis in this chapter. Note that the carbon intensity is much lower in the developed economies than the developing economies. As of 2005, carbon intensity of the US is 133 tons of carbon dioxide per one million dollar GDP while it is as high as 305 tons of carbon dioxide per one million dollar GDP in China. It is lowest in the EU and Japan with 90 tons of carbon dioxide per one million dollar GDP (Nordhaus and Boyer, 2000).

For the US economy, the carbon intensity fell by 18% during the 1970s, by 26% during the 1980s, and by 17% during the 1990s (EIA, 2004, 2014). The carbon intensities of the developing countries such as China, India, and Russia started to fall only recently in the past decade, especially so for China, and are projected to fall further at a faster rate as these economies continue to grow in the coming decades (Fan et al., 2007).

A projection of the future carbon intensity in each region is captured by the (negative) growth rates of the carbon intensity, as presented in the third column of Table 5.3. For the fast developing economies such as China and India, the carbon intensity is projected to decline faster than those of the developed economies. Note

Table 5.3 The calibration of the carbon intensity parameters.

Players	Carbon intensity in 2005 (tons of CO2/US$ 1000)	Growth rate of carbon intensity (per decade)
EU	0.090	−0.1196
Japan	0.091	−0.2249
Latin America	0.093	−0.1397
Other Asian countries	0.128	−0.1469
US	0.133	−0.1748
Africa	0.141	−0.2212
India	0.142	−0.2458
Other high-income countries	0.176	−0.1368
Oceania	0.176	−0.1368
Middle East	0.210	−0.1263
Eurasia	0.268	−0.2800
Russia	0.280	−0.2727
China	0.305	−0.2286

that the carbon intensity of a regional economy cannot decline infinitely to near zero because this parameter only captures an exogenous technological change, that is, does not include the emission reductions resulting from an array of climate mitigation policies including the backstop technologies. As such, although not shown in Table 5.3 for the sake of clarity of the table, the present author further assumed that the negative growth rate of the carbon intensity shown in the third column of Table 5.3 will decline over time (Nordhaus and Boyer, 2000).

The fourth set of contentious economic parameters is the land use emissions of carbon dioxide and other Planet-heating gases. As highlighted at the end of Chapter 4, A Critique of the Economics of Global Public Goods: A Microbehavioral Theory and Model, many types of land use are a source of carbon dioxide and other greenhouse gases but at the same time a sink of these chemicals (Denman et al., 2007). Such land uses as a carbon sink either absorb carbon dioxide from the atmosphere or prevent the releases of emissions from the lands or both.

Table 5.4 shows the amount of land use emissions of carbon for each player minus the amount of land use sinks of carbon, which is the amount of net emissions of carbon per decade (Nordhaus and Boyer, 2000). The amount of net land use emissions varies widely across the regions. It is as high as 6 giga tons of carbon emissions (GtC) per decade for Latin America and the Caribbean countries (Seo, 2010a). It is also high in other Asian countries, which include forest-rich countries such as Indonesia, with 6.2 GtC per decade. The large amounts of emissions are largely attributed to the deforestations in these regions for timber productions and sales (WRI, 2005). The amount of net land use emissions is about 2.6 GtC for Africa which has vast resources of Central African forests (Seo, 2010b; CAFI, 2015).

Table 5.4 Net land use emissions of carbon.

Players	Net land use emissions of carbon (GtC/decade)	Notes
Other Asian countries	6.197	Includes Indonesian forests
Latin America and the Caribbean countries	6.064	Includes the Amazon rainforests
Africa	2.624	Includes the Central African forests
Russia	0.200	
Other high-income countries	0.176	
India	0	
Japan	0	
Middle East	0	
Eurasia	0	
Oceania	0	
China	−0.129	
EU	−0.180	
US	−0.320	

Intriguingly, the amount of net land use emissions of carbon is negative for the US, EU, and China. For the US, the net land use emissions amounted to -0.320 GtC/decade (Houghton, 2008). In particular, the Chinese net land use emissions is negative at -0.129 GtC/decade. For these players, the amount of carbon sinks primarily through increased forests and grasslands exceeds the amount of carbon emissions primarily through deforestations during the past several decades (USEPA, 2015). Unlike Latin America and Indonesia, the deforestation rate is very low in the US and EU and even negative with additional lands are reforested or are made protected lands.

5.4   An analysis of noncooperation: disparate incentives of parties under a business-as-usual scenario

An analysis of noncooperation in a global public good provision can begin with the question of why some countries are more willing to have a global agreement on a global public good policy than other countries that may even be averse to it. In all the major treaties and agreements on global warming such as the Rio Earth summit, Kyoto Protocol, Copenhagen Accord, and Paris Agreements, it has been repeatedly observed that there are countries that always push for a deal and a more ambitious agreement while there are other countries that resisted to such a deal.

A country's push for a more ambitious agreement can be explained by many factors, of which the following three are outstanding most often. The first is that the push country may perceive that the country will be more vulnerable than others to climatic shifts. Although the country alone cannot stop the global warming trend, it can push others to take a unified action to stop or slow down the trend.

The second factor is that the push country may be able to reduce the emissions of greenhouse gases at a lower cost than the other countries, which may be attributable to more advanced technological capabilities of the push country such as nuclear energy, solar energy, and electric vehicles. Or, the push country may have low-cost nontechnological options to abate greenhouse gases such as forestry, hydroelectric energy, and methane capture.

The third factor is a noneconomic one or may even be a purely political one. Any global warming treaty would create an unprecedented global governance with an associated global political power club. This governance will operate independently of the national governments founded on the concept of national sovereignty and democracy and may become a higher layer of governance in the global affairs. To be cautious, there may be other political motives than this, for example, the need for additional tax revenue by an autocratic government.

The political and governance aspect of a global public good policy has not been lucidly presented in the literature, as such, deserves more attention and an incisive analysis by researchers. Unlike other global affairs, as emphasized in the theory chapters of this book, a global warming treaty is likely to impose significant burdens on every decision an individual makes and an individual country makes today.

To give you an idea, a carbon pricing scheme that must set the price level every 10 years or so and distribute the tax revenue at the entire global scale would turn out to be a monumental political maneuver and power play, to say the least.

Let's take the first of these factors for a closer analysis. In Fig. 5.3, the present author draws a trajectory of the economic damage expected of each player during the 21st century for each of the nine players. For each player, a percentage loss in the GDP attributable to an unfolding global warming is projected. This projection is made with the assumption of the BAU economy and the BAU climate system, that is, the dashed line in Fig. 5.1.

By 2045, the damage estimates of the world regions remain modest, less than 0.5% loss in the regional GDP even in the most heavily impacted region. In addition, the damage estimate does not vary greatly across the regions. By the middle of the century, however, the damage estimates start to diverge noticeably. By the end of the century, the damage estimates are divergent greatly from one region to another, ranging from 3.5% loss in the GDP to 0.5% gain.

The clear loser players are the usual suspects such as Africa, Latin America, and India but also surprisingly the EU. The EU is predicted to lose about 3.5% of the GDP under the BAU scenario. Africa, Latin America, and India are all predicted to suffer about 1.5%–2% loss in the GDP. These regions are labeled as Group 1 in the figure.

The Group 2 countries would experience the impact of global warming quite differently under the BAU scenario. For China and Japan, the damage would be small,

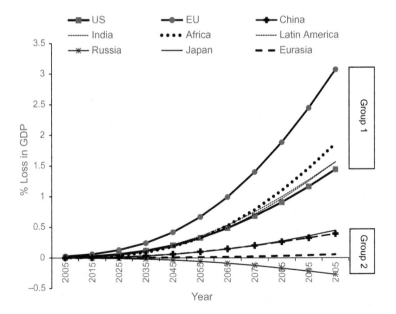

Figure 5.3 Divergence of incentives under the business-as-usual scenario.

amounting to about 0.3% loss in the GDP even at the end of the 21st century. Eurasia would not notice any impact of global warming on its GDP throughout the century, at least in the aggregate output of the region. Russia—on the other hand—would slightly benefit from global warming because a large permafrost area and Siberia would become suitable for vegetation growth as well as natural resource extractions.

The Group 1 members should have an incentive to push for a global climate policy which aims at slowing down or preventing the increase of global temperature through cooperative actions of all world nations. On the other hand, the Group 2 members would certainly do not feel an urgent need to reach a global deal on global warming, considering the policy and economic burdens that such a treaty will impose on the national economies. The figure places the US in the middle of the two groups.

This figure can provide a rationale behind the eagerness of the EU and other regions such as Africa and Latin America in breaking away from a BAU approach and seeking vigorously a global climate policy regulation (Nordhaus, 2001, 2010a). It also explains why China, Russia, Eurasia, and Japan would be at best reluctant participants in the negotiations. It is also interesting to notice that India, despite belonging to the Group 1, has not been an ambitious participant in climate negotiations (Seo, 2017a,b). The figure also lends a rationale for the US swinging back and forth from one policy position to an opposite policy position on global negotiations (White House, 2017, Seo, 2019b).

Fig. 5.3 informs that, given the disparate impacts of a shift in the global climate system across the countries, a global grand deal will be onerous to be reached. However, it does not tell us definitively that reaching a global climate deal is impossible. What the BAU analysis in Fig. 5.3 reveals is that it would not be an easy task for the Group 1 countries to persuade the Group 2 countries to join an international climate policy. Put differently, as long as the damages from global warming to their countries remain modest as in Fig. 5.3, the Group 2 countries may not object to a global climate regulation which would reduce the damages of global warming on the Group 1 countries.

Having said that, for a country to decide its position in international policy negotiations, Fig. 5.3 provides only partial information on the country's economic welfare changes that may arise from an alteration in the climate system. More specifically, the country needs to be informed of the impacts of an international climate policy, if achieved at all, on its economy, which is the subject of the next section, to make a national decision.

This is also where the cost of abatement, the second motive introduced in the beginning of this section, comes to being an important factor for a country's participation decision. The non Group 1 countries, for example, Japan or the US, may be inclined to a global climate regulation being aware of their superior technological/engineering capabilities through which novel abatement technologies can be developed and eventually sold to other countries (Heal, 2000; ITER, 2015; NRC, 2015a,b).

5.5   An analysis of noncooperation: alterations of incentives under a globally optimal policy scenario

For a continued analysis of countries' incentives to cooperate or noncooperate in a global treaty, let us shift our focus to a globally optimal climate policy (GOP) scenario in which the carbon pricing (tax) is implemented globally as described in Chapter 3, The Economics of Global-Scale Public Goods: Key Challenges and Theories, whose level is updated dynamically every decade.

Under the GOP scenario, the level of carbon price per ton of carbon should be agreed upon by the conference of international negotiators and further should be updated through the conferences. The determination of the carbon price level by international negotiators would be made in consideration of both the mitigation levels of carbon dioxide equivalent emissions, as shown in Fig. 5.2, and the levels of global temperature change, as shown in Fig. 5.1. From an alternative angle, the internationally agreed carbon price should force each member country to decide upon efficient abatement actions.

An analysis of the impact of the GOP policy on each member country of the treaty has to take into account the following three cost elements: economic damage, abatement cost, and carbon tax. The first is a decrease in economic damage attributable to a reduced global warming that results from the GOP. This is equivalent to the difference between the economic damage under the BAU economy shown in Fig. 5.3 and the economic damage under the GOP economy.

The second element is the cost of abatement. A global treaty means that an individual country should accept the internationally determined price of carbon and further charge each carbon emitter in the country for each ton of carbon emissions with the price. The carbon emitter's efficient decisions will lead to the level of carbon abatement that each emitter will be forced to achieve under the GOP treaty in its attempt to minimize the carbon tax payment. The abatement cost is a fresh new cost element to each emitter, that is, an individual firm or an individual country, that is to be given birth by the treaty.

The third element is the carbon tax that should become the legal burden of each emitter in the country to pay to the government. It is equivalent to the amount of carbon emissions that is unabated by the emitter times the internationally determined price of carbon. The tax burden is also fresh, new cost to each firm or country under the GOP treaty.

The tax revenue can be redistributed to low-income tax-payers or other national economic programs as long as it is in the hands of the government (Metcalf, 2009; Nordhaus, 2010b). On the other hand, the redistribution of the tax revenue to low-income families will in a large percentage end up being spent for increasing their consumption of food and other necessities. This will increase the nation's carbon emissions, contrary to the goal of the GOP treaty, offsetting the abatement achieved by the carbon tax. In an extreme case, the offset will be exactly the same as the abatement induced by the policy. In the worst case, the offset will be even larger than the policy-induced abatement if such reallocations are associated with low-technology sectors.

In addition, the imposition of carbon tax will lead to an increase in the size of the government bureaucracy. This size increase may turn out to be remarkable, if not overbearing, to the economy and micro economic decisions owing to the pervasiveness of carbon emitting activities in the economy. That every activity an individual performs in the economy is a carbon pollution may not be an exaggeration considering that all living beings are made of carbon (Schlesinger, 1997). The bureaucracy effect may result in efficiency loss in the national economy.

To sum up, the total net cost to an individual player at each time period of a GOP implemented through the carbon tax can be expressed as follows:

$$\Psi_{it} = \Delta\Omega_{it}\left(T_t^{ATM}\right) + \Gamma_{it}\left(\mu_{it}\right) + P_t^* e_{it}, \tag{5.3}$$

where P_t^* is the carbon price per ton, e_{it} is the amount of carbon emissions for the region determined under the GOP policy, μ_{it} is the rate of control (or abatement) for the region, and T_t^{ATM} is the degree of global warming. The trajectory of the global atmospheric temperature increase under the GOP scenario is shown in Fig. 5.1. The trajectory of the carbon price under the GOP scenario is shown in Fig. 5.2. The trajectory of the emissions control (abatement) rate is also shown in Fig. 5.2, but at the global level only.

A calculation of the Ψ_{it} for each time period of the 21st century can be done by running the DICE model embedded with the calibrations of the four sets of contentious parameters as described in Section 5.3. The results of such calculations are presented in Fig. 5.4 for the seven selected regions of the model, for the sake of

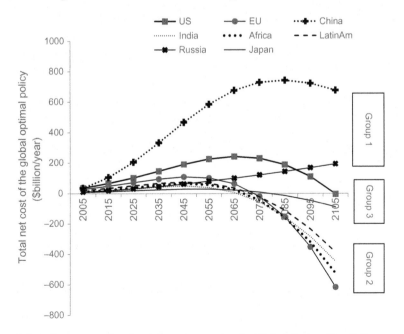

Figure 5.4 A divergence of national incentives under the Global Carbon Tax Policy.

avoiding the heavy clutter in the figure when all 13 regions' results are packed in. The y-axis is the total net cost in US$ billions per year.

The most striking aspect of the figure is that there emerges a clear winner group as well as a clear loser group from an adoption of the GOP treaty. The winner group includes the EU, Africa, India, and Latin America. The clear loser group includes China, Russia, Eurasia, and the US. Also, the figure reveals that there is another group, Group 3, for which the cost of the GOP policy nearly equals the benefit of the policy.

China is the biggest loser from an adoption of the GOP treaty. The total net cost to China would reach US$ 240 billion (in 2015 dollars) per year by 2025, which would rise further to US$ 720 billion per year by the middle of this century, and even further to US$ 960 billion per year by 2080. The figure reveals that the monetary loss to China starts as soon as the policy goes into effects and will continue to grow until the end of the century. The annual loss to China by the end of this century is as large as about 9% of the current GDP of China in 2015, so by no means a small loss even to the mighty Chinese economy. For clarification, the dollar amounts cited from now on are all 2015 dollars (World Bank, 2019).

Russia is another big loser from an adoption of the GOP treaty. In Fig. 5.3, the present author showed that Russia would be a big winner from a BAU no policy scenario. When the BAU approach is rejected and the GOP treaty is adopted by the parties of negotiation, the country will immediately turn into a net financial loser and the size of its loss will continue to grow to US$ 240 billion (in 2015 dollars) per year by the end of this century.

The Group 2 countries, by contrasts, are predicted to enjoy the financial benefits from the implementation of the GOP policy throughout the 21st century. We already saw in Fig. 5.3 that the Group 2 countries will be harmed financially from an unfolding of global warming if there would be no international policy action. If the GOP treaty were to be adopted, the Group 2 countries will still be a financial loser because of their mitigation obligations, but the financial loss owing to mitigation actions would be much smaller than the monetary cost under the BAU scenario which is equal to the economic damage from unmitigated global warming. Note that even if the Group 2 countries were to take abatement actions of carbon emissions during the first half of the century in accordance with the globally optimal policy, there would be only minor total net cost incurred to these countries during the first half of the century if the avoided damage cost of global warming under the BAU policy were subtracted.

By the middle of this century, the Group 2 countries will start to reap the financial benefits of a global climate treaty designed based on the GOP carbon tax. The financial gains that will fall upon these regions will be as large as US$ 600 billion to 720 billion (in 2015 dollars) per year by the century's end. The large economic gains to the Group 2 countries are ascribable to the reduced economic damage which is again owing to a reduction in the degree of global warming made possible by the internationally cooperative efforts through the GOP treaty.

The figure sends a clear signal that there will be a great tension between the winner group and the loser group in policy negotiations among the parties. There is ample empirical evidence of such tension in the history of climate negotiations. The Kyoto Protocol left out China and India, and faced resistance from Russia that in the end endorsed the Protocol, but saw the US withdrawing from the Protocol (Nordhaus, 2001). The Copenhagen conference failed to reach a grand agreement owing to the split between developing countries such as China, India, and Russia and developed countries (Nordhaus, 2010a; Seo, 2012). At the end of the first phase of the Kyoto Protocol in 2012, the US, Japan, Australia, Russia, and Canada all withdrew from the Kyoto Protocol (Seo, 2017b). At the Paris Agreement, the EU and the developing countries such as Africa, Latin America, and India all joined the agreement, but the US withdrew from it (Seo, 2019b).

The past alliances and divisions during the above-described major negotiations bring our attention to the striking position of the US and Japan depicted in Fig. 5.4. The present author put them together into Group 3, which may be called a reluctance group. For Japan, a GOP-founded treaty would impose little on the nation's economy through the end of the century. The additional cost of the GOP treaty will be seen trivial against the economic giant of Japan.

The US case is somewhat different. The additional cost of the GOP treaty will be immediate although small during the first several decades of the treaty. The cost will be growing, however, from about US\$ 120 billion by 2030 to about US\$ 360 billion (in 2015 dollars) per annum by 2065. Compared against the overall size of the US economy, this is perhaps not a big cost. Furthermore, even this modest cost starts to fall quickly during the last two decades of the 21st century. By the end of the 21st century, the additional cost of the GOP treaty, that is, the quantity in Eq. (5.3), will be near zero.

The net cost trajectory of the US drawn in Fig. 5.4, however, should be interpreted against the damage cost trajectory of the country shown in Fig. 5.3 under the BAU no policy scenario. More specifically, there will be additional cost on the US economy on top of the cost in Fig. 5.4, that is, the damage cost of a global climate change under the GOP treaty, which is predicted to become sizeable by the latter half of the century even though smaller than the damage cost expected under the BUA scenario.

The reluctance group countries will likely take a position of 'wait-and-see' in policy negotiations. They will be engaged in the negotiations but reluctant to commit to a climate treaty, especially a stringent one. They will strongly resist any policy proposal that is projected to benefit other countries at the expense of their countries. The US withdrawals from the Kyoto Protocol and the Paris Agreements can be interpreted in this context (Nordhaus, 2001; Seo, 2019b; White House, 2017). The withdrawals from the second phase of the Kyoto Protocol and also from the Paris Agreements by Japan and Australia can be understood from this perspective (SMH, 2011; DW, 2018).

A complementary analysis of the control rates of greenhouse gases required of the players under the GOP treaty would offer additional insight. Considering that the players are concerned about more than the control (abatement) rates, this does not give as comprehensive analysis as the first analysis captured in Fig. 5.4 on disparate incentives of the players in a global climate policy negotiation.

Fig. 5.5 draws the trajectory of the control rate of carbon dioxide equivalent emissions called for for each region with the implementation of the GOP-based treaty, which is efficiently determined by each player taking the internationally harmonized carbon tax as given. By 2015, the control rate across the regions lies within 15%−20% of each region's total baseline emissions, implying that gaps in the control rate among the regions are not large. The baseline emissions is the level of emissions under the BAU economy. The gaps, however, are gradually widened over the course of the 21st century. By the end of the century, the gap between the abatement rate in the most ambitious and that in the least ambitious is as large as almost 30%.

By the century's end, Russia and Eurasia will have to abate 85% of its emissions in an optimal decision for the country under the GOP-based treaty in place. The China's control rate comes next with a 77% required reduction. The control rates for Africa, India, Latin America, and other Asia are equivalent to 73% of the baseline emissions. The control rates for developed countries such as the US, EU, Japan, and Oceania are the least ambitious with 59% of abatement by the end of this century.

By the nearer term of the mid-century, the GOP-based treaty will force Russia to reduce its emissions by about 50% from the baseline, China by about 44%, Africa/ Latin America/India by 42%. By contrast, the carbon tax will force the US, EU, and Japan to cut its emissions by only 33%.

The control rate trajectory for the US drawn in Fig. 5.5 is lower than the US ambitions declared by the Intended Nationally Determined Contribution (INDC) for the Paris Agreement which is 26%−28% reduction by 2030 from the 2005

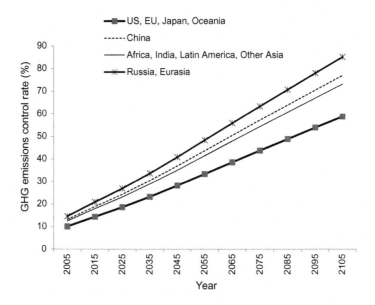

Figure 5.5 Disparity in GHG control rates under the Global Carbon Tax Policy.

emissions level. The US control rate trajectory is far lower than the EU's INDC proposal of a 40% reduction by 2030 and the region's net zero emissions goal by 2050 (Seo, 2017a; UNFCCC, 2015).

The analysis so far of the control rates of the players indicates that a GOP-like treaty may be far advantageous for the developed nations than the Paris Agreement and far disadvantageous for the developing nations such as China, India, Russia, Africa, and Latin America. From another angle, the Paris Agreement is far more favorable to the developing nations than the GOP policy (Seo, 2017b).

5.6   Optimal monetary transfers or a climate club

The analyses up to this point encapsulates the conundrum of global warming policy negotiations: while the globally optimal policy would improve the welfare of the global community at large, there are not a few rational reasons based on which each player in the negotiations would seek to deviate from a global cooperative solution. More dramatically stated, the economics of global public goods, which is the gold standard in the economics corpus, leads the world community ineluctably to a dramatic failure in adopting the globally optimal policy espoused by the economics. There is certainly the economics of noncooperation.

A most direct analysis of the noncooperation conundrum, similar to the ones provided in the previous sections, in the economics context of global public goods may have been made by the present author (Seo, 2012). However, economists had been increasingly aware of this problem by the time of the Copenhagen conference disarray which was widely broadcasted by the global media (Nordhaus, 2010a). Although without a direct analysis of noncooperation such as the one provided in this chapter, economists were more concerned with the generic question of how to make cooperation possible in global talks and treaties regarding global public goods, the question which was also broadly shared among climate scientists and negotiators (Barrett, 2003). Stated more concretely, the mechanisms for enhancing cooperation by developing country parties were one of the core elements in the UN-led global conferences, which were often expressed and referred to as the Clean Development Mechanism (CDM) (UNFCCC, 1992, 1997).

In the literature on cooperation for a global public good provision, an emphasis has been laid on designing an international monetary transfer scheme which establishes an array of monetary transfers among the parties (GCF, 2011; Seo, 2019a; Chan, 2019). An economic analysis would help to design the scheme as well as to quantify the consequences of such transfers in terms of both economic performances and carbon dioxide outcomes.

A sub-literature of the monetary transfer scheme is a coalition and transfer model (Barrett, 1994; Carraro et al., 2006). Another sub-literature is a climate club model (Nordhaus, 2015). A climate coalition may be formed, which would take a unified action to address global warming. Within the club, monetary transfers may or may not be made among the members 'optimally' in order to share the economic gains from the coalition from the winners with the financial losers within the club. In the climate club model, an economic sanction is imposed on the nonclub members through a tariff.

In an analysis of environmental coalitions, Barrett emphasizes a self-enforcing, that is, a credible treaty in which individual rationality for each country party and collective rationality for the group are combined. He emphasizes the difficulties of reaching an agreement on a global public good when there is a large number of participants owing to the incentives for free-riding. He finds that stable climate coalitions have few members and that as the number of countries increases, the fraction of global emissions covered by the coalition declines (Barrett, 1994, 2003). There is a small coalition paradox in a global public good provision.

Nordhaus proposes instead a top-down approach to a coalition formation in contrast to a bottom-up coalition such as the Barrett's. In the climate club model, the club is optimized 'from the top' to attract a large number of participants and achieve a high level of abatement. Then the club forces other countries to decide to join or not. Nordhaus proposes a trade tariff for non-participants (Nordhaus, 2015). The top-down approach is found in the Bretton Woods institutions such as the International Monetary Fund (IMF) and the World Trade Organization (WTO).

The results from the coalition as well as the club theory can be anticipated from our analyses in the previous sections as captured in Figs. 5.4 and 5.3. More specifically, the coalition, if it had any chance of being meaningful, must include the big loser countries from the GOP-like treaty, that is, China and Russia. Then, the monetary transfers within the club/coalition must be made from the EU, Africa, Latin America, and India to China and Russia.

Unlike the coalition and the club model, the economics of noncooperation presented in this chapter arrives at the conclusion that there is no-cooperation even in the BAU policy: there are winners and losers from the BAU. Extending this conclusion, the noncooperation economics finds that there will be no-cooperation in any policy proposal from an entire range of policy options for a global public good provision (Seo, 2012).

With this foresight in mind, we can proceed to examine the empirical simulation results put forth by the coalition theorists which shed light on the nature of the coalition and monetary transfers, which is summarized by the present author in Table 5.5 (Carraro et al., 2006). They built a model with six members: US, EU, China, Japan, Former Soviet Union (FSU), and Rest of the World (ROW). The time period used for their projections is 1990−2300. The authors defined the economic welfare as the present discounted value of the future consumptions for the time period considered by the optimization model.

They run the full cooperation model, the partial cooperation models, and the no-cooperation model, based on which economic and climate outcomes are compared. The authors rely on the game theory equilibrium concepts, more specifically, a subgame perfect Nash equilibrium (Nash, 1950; Harsanyi and Selten, 1988; Sandler, 1997). The full cooperation model outcomes are set to the index value of 100 and the no-cooperation model outcomes are set to the index value of zero, and the partial cooperation model outcome is presented as a number that lies between the full cooperation model outcome and the no-cooperation model outcome.

Table 5.5 Simulations from a coalition and monetary transfer model.

Coalition scenario	Coalition membership	Coalition size	Economic welfare	Reduction in atmospheric carbon content	Reduction in cumulative emissions of carbon
Full cooperation					
1	US, EU, China, JPN, FSU, ROW	6	100	100	100
Partial cooperation and optimal transfers within the club					
2	US, EU, China, ROW	4	94.50	81.96	83.13
3	EU, China, FSU, ROW	4	91.17	72.26	73.61
4	JPN, EU, China, ROW	4	89.41	69.75	71.53
5	US, EU, FSU, ROW	4	68.96	61.20	62.01
6	US, JPN, EU, ROW	4	66.80	59.47	60.54
7	US, JPN, FSU, ROW	4	64.67	48.90	50.21
8	EU, JPN	2	0.60	0.20	0.30
No cooperation					
9	No cooperation	0	0	0	0

Source: Modified from Carraro, C., Eyckmans, J., Finus, N., 2006. Optimal transfers and participation decisions in international environmental agreements. Rev. Int. Organ. 1, 379–396.

Relative to the full cooperation model, the coalition that consists of the US, EU, China, and ROW has the potential to become an effective coalition, a club for climate policy. This club would achieve 95% of the economic welfare, 82% of reduction in the atmospheric carbon content, and 83% of reduction in cumulative carbon emissions, all relative to the full cooperation model.

Of the six partial coalition scenarios (from scenario 2 to scenario 7), the first three coalition scenarios are by and large effective, reaching more than 90% of the economic welfare from the full coalition model. However, the last three coalition scenarios are much less effective, achieving only about two-thirds of the economic welfare and about 50%–60% reduction in the cumulative carbon emissions as well as in the atmospheric carbon content, relative to the full cooperation model.

Note that the decisive factor in the partial cooperation models that distinguishes the first three scenarios from the last three scenarios is the participation of China. In the coalition scenario 5 with US, EU, FSU, and ROW as the members, for example, the economic welfare falls to 69% from the full cooperation model and reduction in the cumulative emissions to 60%.

The coalition Scenario 8 is a coalition of the EU and Japan, which is close to the Kyoto Protocol's first implementation period. The results show that the coalition, and the Kyoto Protocol, is nearly of no effect at all, especially with the environmental outcome indicators being close to the bottom of the scale: the reduction of atmospheric carbon content is only 0.2%. This is, loosely put, the only scenario that we can judge the coalition model outcomes in Table 5.5 against the realized policy outcomes, that is, the outcomes from the first phase of the Kyoto Protocol (Ellerman et al., 2016; Nordhaus, 2011). The noncooperation scenario is Scenario 9 in the table.

Does this coalition and transfer mechanism provide a solution for the problem of noncooperation in the global public good provision? The answer is no, for which many reasons can be laid out. To begin with, the six-region model shown in Table 5.5 is too simplistic to be a meaningful analysis on a climate policy negotiation. Specifically, the ROW in the model includes India, Latin America, Africa, Other Asia, Canada, Oceania, Eurasia which all face different realities, as revealed in Figs. 5.3 and 5.4. Note that the partial coalition models in Table 5.5 all include the ROW as the member, for which reason the results in Table 5.5 are too optimistic about the effectiveness of a climate coalition. A more realistic network of stakeholders (players) that could be adopted by the coalition model would make it exponentially harder to find a stable and effective coalition. To give a numerical example, the number of international transactions to be considered in the six-player model is 36 ($=6*6$) but increases to 169 ($=13*13$) in the more realistic 13-player model used for the analyses in the preceding sections. Stated succinctly, the larger the scale of a public good, the harder the problem of noncooperation becomes and the harder a meaningful coalition to emerge and hold.

Second, the coalition theory authors fixed policy outcomes of the noncooperation scenario (scenario 9) to the index value of zero. However, in reality, there can be countries that benefit from a BAU global warming as well as countries that are more or less unaffected economically under such a scenario, as shown in Fig. 5.3. In such a country, the values for the policy indices in Table 5.5 for noncooperation can be more than 100 for the country at the national (regional) level. In such a situation, the country would oppose to any global climate policy proposal to begin with. Under the coalition theory, the country should be either left outside the coalition or be enticed to join the coalition by financial compensation. Both of these options available to the country are inconsistent with the coalition theory (Seo, 2017a).

If the country were to be left out, the country has every intention to increase the emissions of greenhouse gases because such emissions will benefit the country. This will make the coalition ineffective. If, on the other hand, the country were to be enticed into the coalition by financial compensation, the coalition will have to compensate the lost global warming benefits to the country plus the cost of abatements to be undertaken by the country plus the total carbon tax to be paid by the country. This compensation package will likely overwhelm any effective coalition, especially when such countries are multiple.

Third, the effective coalitions such as coalition scenario 2, 3, or 4 assume that the optimal monetary transfers will be made among the member countries once the coalition is formed. Given the regional net total costs presented by the present author in Fig. 5.5 under the globally optimal policy, it would be a monumental task to agree on the matrix of transfers. The coalition theory does not answer how these transfers can be possible, determined, and implemented over the time frame of many centuries. There is no theory as of yet on the optimal matrix of monetary transfers (Seo, 2017a; Chan, 2019).

Note that the matrix size is nearly 200 by 200. To be more concrete, the number of monetary transfers needed in the six-player model is 36 while it is 169 in the more realistic 13-player model, as already stated. The United Nations Framework Convention on Climate Change (UNFCCC) has 197 members as of 2019, for which the number of monetary transactions needed is 38,809 ($=197*197$). These many transactions must be made annually for three centuries.

Fourth, a country's incentive to defect the coalition increases, that is, not decreases in the presence of a climate coalition or club (Hart and Kurz, 1983; Barrett, 1994). By defecting, a country would leap the benefit of a global climate control implemented among the club members while the country would no longer be held accountable for the expensive mitigation actions required when it should remain within the club. The incentive to defect would be especially large for a country that is required by the coalition to sacrifice hugely by taking expensive mitigation activities. Put differently, the coalition theory does not solve the issue of free riding in the global public good provisions (Nordhaus, 2008, 2015).

Fifth, the coalition theory is conceptualized at the level of the six world regions, which may be expanded by the researchers to a 13-region model. However, any global warming treaty needs to attend to disparate incentives not only internationally but also intra-nationally. This means that the global warming treaty and the coalition must also design monetary transfers among the citizens within each nation or, for example, among the States within the US. For an insight, you can refer to the Canadian greenhouse gas pricing act of 2018 in which the revenues from the carbon tax are redistributed to government-designated groups of individuals (Metcalf, 2009; DOJ, 2018). The consideration of the intra-national disparities under a coalition-led global optimal climate policy will make the coalition theory exponentially untenable.

Besides the five essential critiques, there are other issues which are more minor. One of them is the long-term perspective that is needed for a coalition to work. In the above coalition model, all countries should have a 200-year planning horizon. Second, over such a long-time horizon, how trustworthy or uncertain are the monetary estimates used in the coalition model? The third is a political one: can the coalition order India to transfer a large sum of money to Middle East, order Africa to transfer money to China, order Latin America to transfer funds to Russia, or order the US to transfer funds to Middle East for a climate change coalition? Given other geopolitical issues to be considered by the countries than a climate treaty, say, nuclear arms, terrorism, and trade, such monetary transfers may be politically impossible even for a single year.

5.7 Concluding remarks

This chapter provided the second critique of the economics literature of global public goods from the angle of the assumption of cooperation among the parties under negotiation. In the provision of the global public good with a cumulative production technology, it showed that the assumption of global cooperation lies at the heart of the economic theory and its policy recommendation.

The presumption of a cooperative solution is perhaps sound in an economic theory of the provision of a national public good for which national laws force the constituents to comply with the national legislation. However, for the provision of a global public good for which there is no global 'government' to legislate and enforce a law pertaining to its provision, the presumption of cooperation would make a global public good policy model look like a purely conceptual framework devoid of the doses of reality.

Furthermore, it is poorly grasped by the researchers that the larger the geo-or-political scale of a public good, the higher the probability of noncooperation in its provision becomes; the larger the geo-or-political scale of a public good, the larger the disparities in the incentives across the negotiating parties for its provision. Extending this logic, we arrive at the point that the economics core of the global public good provision is noncooperation itself.

This chapter provides an empirical analysis of the economics of noncooperation in the provision of a global public good. The empirical model has several essential components, the first of which is to describing what must be agreed upon and cooperated upon by the negotiating parties who are 13 regional players: a future trajectory of global warming and a trajectory of global carbon tax. The second essential component is the calibration of the four sets of contentious economic parameters: global warming damages, abatement cost, carbon intensity, and land use emissions. The trajectory of each of these variables was determined for each of the 13 regional players in the world. The third component is the calculation of the total net economic cost of a treaty which is defined in this chapter as the sum of net economic damages, abatement cost, and carbon tax payment. The fourth component is the analysis of divergent incentives for noncooperation conducted under two, or more, policy situations: (1) a business-as-usual (BAU) economy with a continuation of the global warming as predicted by the ensemble of climate prediction models; and (2) a globally optimal climate policy (GOP) to slow down the rate of global warming.

In the BAU policy scenario, the noncooperative club would include Africa, India, and Latin America, all of which expect substantial economic damages from the global warming scenarios. In the GOP scenario, the noncooperative club would include China, Russia, and Eurasia while the reluctance group would include the US and Japan. For the noncooperation group, the total net cost of a globally agreed global warming treaty is high forcing the members of the group to nonparticipate.

In the light of the analysis of noncooperation in this chapter, the coalition theory is correct in predicting that China's participation will determine the effectiveness of any stable coalition for the global public good provision. However, given the coalition model is too simplified, in a more realistic model, the players other than China will also become a crucial member to be included in the coalition, for example, India, Africa, Latin America, South Asia. Second, the coalition theory relies on the assumption of a set of optimal monetary transfers among the members in order to build a strong coalition. This assumption is, however, as strong as the presumption of cooperation in the global public good models. Transferring a large sum of dollars from one country to another year after year would be a politically thorny issue, to say the least. This problem would become exponentially disruptive if it is taken into account that any effective coalition should be very large and simultaneously sustained for two centuries. Third, the coalition theory would become of, nearly, no theoretical consistency if a group of countries can continually benefit from noncooperation and a BAU economy.

This completes the analysis of the economics of noncooperation in the global public good provisions. What next? Readers may ask. This book will offer the third critique of the economics of global public goods in the next chapter from the perspective of a global public good fund. In Chapter 7, The Economics of Globally Shared Goods, the book will provide a comprehensive novel theory of the global-scale public goods integrating the discussions in Chapters 2−6.

References

Barrett, S., 1994. Self-enforcing international environmental agreements. Oxford Econ. Papers 46, 878−894.

Barrett, S., 2003. Environment and Statecraft: The Strategy of Environmental Treaty. Oxford University Press, Oxford.

Campbell, K.M., Einhorn, R.J., Reiss, M.B. (Eds.), 2004. The Nuclear Tipping Point: Why States Reconsider Their Nuclear Choices. Brookings Institution Press, Washington, DC.

Carraro, C., Eyckmans, J., Finus, N., 2006. Optimal transfers and participation decisions in international environmental agreements. Rev. Int. Organ. 1, 379−396.

Central African Forest Initiative (CAFI), 2015. CAFI- Joint Declaration. CAFI Secretariat, UNDP, Châtelaine, Switzerland.

Chan, N.W., 2019. Funding global environmental public goods through multilateral financial mechanisms. Environ. Resour. Econ. 73, 515−531.

Denman, K.L., Brasseur, G., Chidthaisong, A., Ciais, P., Cox, P.M., Dickinson, R.E., et al., 2007. Couplings between changes in the climate system and biogeochemistry. In: Solomon, S., et al., (Eds.), Climate Change 2007: The Physical Science Basis. The Fourth Assessment Report of the Intergovernmental Panel on Climate Change. Cambridge University Press, Cambridge.

Department of Justice (DOJ), 2018. Greenhouse Gas Pollution Pricing Act. S.C. 2018, c. 12, s. 186. DOJ, Canada. Accessed from: <https://laws-lois.justice.gc.ca/eng/acts/G-11.55/page-1.html>.

Deutsche Welle (DW), 2018. Australia Ditches Greenhouse Gas Emissions Target. Published on 20 August, 2018.

Devarajan, S., Fisher, A.C., 1981. Hotelling's "Economics of exhaustible resources": fifty years later. J. Econ. Lit. 19, 65−73.

Ellerman, A.D., Marcantonini, C., Zaklan, A., 2016. The European Union emissions trading system: ten years and counting. Rev. Environ. Econ. Policy 10, 89−107.

European Association of Environmental and Resource Economists (EAERE), 2019. Endorse the Economists' Statement on Carbon Pricing by Signing It!. EAERE.

Fan, Y., Liu, L., Wu, G., Tsai, H., Wei, Y., 2007. Changes in carbon intensity in China. Empirical findings from 1980−2003. Ecol. Econ. 62, 683−691.

Harsanyi, J.C., Selten, R., 1988. A General Theory of Equilibrium Selection in Games. MIT Press, Cambridge, MA.

Hart, S., Kurz, M., 1983. Endogenous formation of coalitions. Econometrica 51 (4), 1047−1064.

Heal, G., 2010. Reflections: the economics of renewable energy in the United States. Rev. Environ. Econ. Policy 4, 139−154.

Hope, C., 2006. The marginal impact of CO_2 from PAGE2002: an integrated assessment model incorporating the IPCC's five reasons for concern. Integrat. Assess. J. 6, 19−56.

Houghton, R.A., 2008. Carbon flux to the atmosphere from land-use changes: 1850−2005. TRENDS: A Compendium of Data on Global Change. Carbon Dioxide Information Analysis Center, Oak Ridge National Laboratory, U.S. Department of Energy, Oak Ridge, TN.

Hulten, C.R., 2000. Total Factor Productivity: A Short Biography. National Bureau of Economic Research (NBER). Working Paper Series 7471, Cambridge, MA.

Intergovernmental Panel on Climate Change (IPCC), 2014. Climate Change 2014: The Physical Science Basis, The Fifth Assessment Report of the IPCC. Cambridge University Press, Cambridge.

International Institute of Applied Systems Analysis (IIASA), 2007. Probabilistic projections by 13 world regions, forecast period 2000−2100, 2001 revision. Available online at: <http://www.iiasa.ac.at/Research/POP/proj01/>.

International Thermonuclear Experimental Reactor (ITER), 2015. ITER: the world's largest Tokamak. Available at: <https://www.iter.org/mach>.

Keeling, C.D., Piper, S.C., Bacastow, R.B., Wahlen, M., Whorf, T.P., Heimann, M., et al., 2005. Atmospheric CO_2 and $^{13}CO_2$ exchange with the terrestrial biosphere and oceans from 1978 to 2000: observations and carbon cycle implications. In: Ehleringer, J.R., Cerling, T.E., Dearing, M.D. (Eds.), A History of Atmospheric CO_2 and Its Effects on Plants, Animals, and Ecosystems. Springer Verlag, New York, pp. 83−113.

Le Treut, H., Somerville, R., Cubasch, U., Ding, Y., Mauritzen, C., Mokssit, A., et al., 2007. Historical overview of climate change. In: Solomon, S., et al., (Eds.), Climate Change 2007: The Physical Science Basis. The Fourth Assessment Report of the Intergovernmental Panel on Climate Change. Cambridge University Press, Cambridge.

Lutz, W., Butz, W., Samir, K.C. (Eds.), 2014. World Population and Global Human Capital in the 21st Century. Oxford University Press, Oxford.

Manne, A.S., Mendelsohn, R., Richels, R., 1995. MERGE—A model for evaluating regional and global effects of GHG reduction policies. Energy Policy 23 (1), 17−34.

Mendelsohn, R., Dinar, A., Williams, L., 2006. The distributional impact of climate change on rich and poor countries. Environ. Dev. Econ. 11, 1−20.

Mendelsohn, R., Williams, L., 2007. Dynamic forecasts of the sectoral impacts of climate change. In: Schlesinger, M., Kheshgi, H., Smith, J., de la Chesnaye, F., Reilly, J.M., Wilson, T., Kolstad, C. (Eds.), Human-Induced Climate Change: An Interdisciplinary Assessment. Cambridge University Press, Cambridge.

Metcalf, G., 2009. Designing a carbon tax to reduce US greenhouse gas emissions. Rev. Environ. Econ. Policy 3, 63−83.

Nash, J., 1950. Equilibrium points in n-person games. Proceedings of the National Academy of Sciences 36 (1), 48−49.

National Research Council (NRC), 2015a. Climate Intervention: Reflecting Sunlight to Cool Earth. Committee on Geoengineering Climate: Technical Evaluation and Discussion of Impacts. The National Academies Press, Washington, DC.

National Research Council (NRC), 2015b. Climate Intervention: Carbon Dioxide Removal and Reliable Sequestration. The National Academies Press, Washington, DC.

Newell, R., Pizer, W., 2001. Discounting the Benefits of Climate Change Mitigation: How Much Do Uncertain Rates Increase Valuations? Pew Center, Washington, DC.

Nordhaus, W., 1973. The Allocation of Energy Resources. Brookings Papers on Economic Activities, pp. 529−576.

Nordhaus, W., 1992. An optimal transition path for controlling greenhouse gases. Science 258, 1315−1319.

Nordhaus, W., 1994. Managing the Global Commons. MIT Press, Cambridge, MA.

Nordhaus, W., 2001. Global warming economics. Science 294, 1283−1284.

Nordhaus, W., 2007. A review of the Stern review on the economics of climate change. J. Econ. Lit. 55, 686−702.

Nordhaus, W.D., 2008. A Question of Balance—Weighing the Options on Global Warming Policies. Yale University Press, New Haven, CT.

Nordhaus, W., 2010a. Economic aspects of global warming in a post-Copenhagen environment. Proc. U.S. Nat. Acad. Sci. 107 (26), 11721−11726.

Nordhaus, W., 2010b. Carbon taxes to move toward fiscal sustainability. Econ. Voice 7 (3), 1−5.

Nordhaus, W., 2011. The architecture of climate economics: designing a global agreement on global warming. Bull. Atom. Sci. 67 (1), 9−18.

Nordhaus, W., 2013. The Climate Casino: Risk, Uncertainty, and Economics for a Warming World. Yale University Press, New Haven, CT.

Nordhaus, W., 2015. Climate clubs: overcoming free-riding in international climate policy. 105(4), 1339−1370.

Nordhaus, W., Boyer, J., 2000. Warming the World: Economic Models of Global Warming. MIT Press, Cambridge, MA.

Nordhaus, W., Sztorc, P., 2013. DICE 2013: Introduction and User's Manual. Yale University, New Haven.

Nordhaus, W., Yang, Z., 1996. A regional dynamic general-equilibrium model of alternative climate change strategies. Am. Econ. Rev 86, 741−765.

Sandler, T., 1997. Global Challenges: An Approach to Environmental, Political, and Economic Problems. Cambridge University Press, Cambridge.

Schlesinger, W.H., 1997. Biogeochemistry: An Analysis of Global Change, second ed. Academic Press, San Diego, CA.

Seo, S.N., 2010a. A microeconometric analysis of adapting portfolios to climate change: adoption of agricultural systems in Latin America. Appl. Econ. Perspect. Policy 32, 489−514.

Seo, S.N., 2010b. Managing forests, livestock, and crops under global warming: a micro-econometric analysis of land use changes in Africa. Aust. J. Agr. Resour. Econ. 54 (2), 239–258.

Seo, S.N., 2012. What eludes global agreements on climate change? Econ. Affairs 32, 73–79.

Seo, S.N., 2017a. The Behavioral Economics of Climate Change: Adaptation Behaviors, Global Public Goods, Breakthrough Technologies, and Policy-Making. Academic Press, Amsterdam, the Netherlands.

Seo, S.N., 2017b. Beyond the Paris agreement: climate change policy negotiations and future directions. Reg. Sci. Policy Pract. 9, 121–140.

Seo, S.N., 2019a. The Economics of Global Allocations of the Green Climate Fund: An Assessment From Four Scientific Traditions of Modeling Adaptation Strategies. Springer Nature, Switzerland.

Seo, S.N., 2019b. Economic questions on global warming during the Trump years. J. Public Aff. 19, e1914. Available from: https://doi.org/10.1002/pa.1914.

Stern, N., 2007. The Economics of Climate Change: The Stern Review. Cambridge University Press, Cambridge.

Sydney Morning Herald (SMH), 2011, Kyoto Deal Loses Four Big Nations. SMH, published on May 11, 2011.

Tol, R., 2009. The economic effects of climate change. J. Econ. Perspect. 23, 29–51.

Tol, R.S.J., 1997. On the optimal control of carbon dioxide emissions: an application of FUND. Environ. Model. Assess. 2, 151–163.

United Nations Framework Convention on Climate Change (UNFCCC), 1992. United Nations Framework Convention on Climate Change. UNFCCC, New York.

United Nations Framework Convention on Climate Change (UNFCCC), 1997. Kyoto Protocol to the United Nations Framework Convention on Climate Change. UNFCCC, New York.

United Nations Framework Convention on Climate Change (UNFCCC), 2009. Copenhagen Accord. UNFCCC, New York.

United Nations Framework Convention on Climate Change (UNFCCC), 2010. Cancun Agreements. UNFCCC, New York.

United Nations Framework Convention on Climate Change (UNFCCC), 2015. The Paris Agreement. Conference Of the Parties (COP) 21. UNFCCC, New York.

United States Energy Information Administration (US EIA), 2004. Emissions of Greenhouse Gases in the United States 2003. DOE/EIA-0573. Department of Energy (DOE), Washington, DC.

United States Energy Information Administration (US EIA), 2014. Annual Energy Outlook 2014. US EIA, Department of Energy, Washington, DC.

United States Environmental Protection Agency (US EPA), 2015. Inventory of US Greenhouse Gas Emissions and Sinks: 1990–2013. EPA, Washington, DC.

Weitzman, M.L., 2009. On modeling and interpreting the economics of catastrophic climate change. Rev. Econ. Stat 91, 1–19.

White House, 2017. Statement by President Trump on the Paris Climate Accord. White House, Washington, DC.

World Bank, 2019. Inflation, GDP Deflator: Linked Series (annual %), World Bank Development Indicators. World Bank, Washington, DC.

World Resources Institute (WRI), 2005. World Resources 2005. The Wealth of the Poor: Managing Ecosystems to Fight Poverty. WRI, Washington, DC.

A critique of the economics of global public goods: the economics of a global public good fund

6

6.1 Introduction

Previous two chapters leveled two encompassing critiques on the economics literature of global public goods. The critique in Chapter 4, A Critique of the Economics of Global Public Goods: A Microbehavioral Theory and Model, was anchored at the microbehavioral economics and that in Chapter 5, A Critique of the Economics of Global Public Goods: Economics of Noncooperative Games, was anchored at noncooperative games. This chapter offers the third critique from the vantage point of the economics of a global public good fund. The present author will describe multifaceted economic aspects of a public good fund as an alternative policy approach for a public good provision, based upon which a series of empirical evaluations will be conducted to determine the approach's effectiveness and efficiency.

To many readers, a public good fund may sound rather unfamiliar. A public good fund can be defined as a fund generated by a voluntary group of members of the public for the purpose of providing a public good to the public. It can be thought of as an alternative approach for the provision of a public good to the efficient and socially optimal policy approach detailed in Chapter 2, The Economics of Public Goods and Club Goods, and Chapter 3, The Economics of Global-Scale Public Goods: Key Challenges and Theories, that is, the policy of efficient prices, for example, a carbon pricing or its variants such as a cap-and-trade system (Samuelson, 1954; Nordhaus, 1992, 2008).

In fact, there are many examples of a public good fund whose contributions are sought and then disbursed at a global scale, although they may not be named as such and many of them do not even explicitly express their purpose as a public good provision or another (Seo, 2019a). A majority of the public good funds sprung from the treaty that established the United Nations and its roles in global affairs after the two world wars (UN, 1945). There are also not a few international funds originated from the private sector that purport to contribute to a public good or another.

The Charter of the United Nations declared as one of its goals the promotion of cooperation among member nations on, besides global security and peace-keeping, social and economic issues. From the UN Charter, it was only matter of time that many international funds were established. To name some of them: The United

The Economics of Globally Shared and Public Goods. DOI: https://doi.org/10.1016/B978-0-12-819658-8.00006-8

Nations' Children's Relief Fund (UNICEF), the World Food Programme (WFP), the United Nations Environment Programme (UNEP), the United Nations Development Programme (UNDP), the United Nations International Strategy for Disaster Reduction (UNISDR), and the United Nations Framework Convention on Climate Change (UNFCCC) (UNSCEB, 2018). These programs rely on the member countries' donations to the funds which are subsequently disbursed globally to a multitude of selected projects to achieve the goals of each of these funds.

The public good funds originated from the private sector are also as far-reaching in their goals and as resourceful in their coffers as the United Nations' aforementioned numerous funds. To give you an idea, the Médecins Sans Frontieres (MSF), also known as Doctors Without Borders, of the French origin has an annual expenditure of approximately US$ 1.9 billion and with more than 30,000 employees as of 2017 (MSF, 2017). The Save the Children Fund of the UK origin in 1919 and the Tzu Chi Foundation's international disaster relief of the Taiwan origin are two of the most active private sector public good funds.

Continuing from the previous two chapters our analyses of the economic literature on global public goods, this chapter will shed a spotlight on the international fund that was created specifically to address the conundrums in the provision of a global climate treaty, that is, the Green Climate Fund (GCF) (Seo, 2019a). The GCF emerged in 2009 from the international climate policy negotiations led by the United Nations climate convention and became the primary financial instrument for the UNFCCC and the Paris Agreement soon afterwards (UNFCCC, 2009, 2015; GCF, 2011).

The GCF offers economists a rare opportunity for conducting a particularly stimulating as well as rigorous analysis of a global public good fund for a number of reasons to be described presently. The Fund has a specified fund-raising goal, specifically US$ 100 billion per annum, and the members of the UNFCCC are the donors of the GCF (GCF, 2011, 2019d). The GCF funds are then given out to the host of projects submitted by the member countries each of which proposes to perform specific activities concerning climate change mitigation or adaptation (GCF, 2019e). The funds are given only to selected projects by the GCF Board based on the investment criteria defined by the Board. The selected projects must specify the primary areas of activities, the proposed amount of carbon emissions reduction, and]the expected number of beneficiaries from implementing the projects (GCF, 2019b,c). There have been 111 projects approved for funding by the GCF and the total funding size is US$ 2.4 billion, including both grants and loans but mostly grants, as of July 2019 (GCF, 2019a).

We will track down these quantitative data mostly open to the public by the GCF and perform an economic analysis of the data, for which the present author will be based on the three fundamental economic theories that have the potential to lend rationales for the existence and actions of the global fund (Seo, 2019a). The first is the theory of public expenditure for the public goods (Samuelson, 1954, 1955; Nordhaus, 1994). The second is the theory of efficiency in land and resource uses (Ricardo, 1817; von Thunen, 1826; Pareto, 1906). The third is the theory of public adaptations versus private adaptations (Mendelsohn, 2000; Hanemann, 2000; Seo, 2011).

The global public good fund approach for a public good provision has certainly arisen from the reality of repeated failures by international negotiators and enthusiast politicians in arriving at a global agreement and treaty which could be called a landmark or a turning point (UNFCCC, 2009; Seo, 2015b). As elaborated in the previous chapter, economists have sought the means and strategies, other than the global public good fund, that can force member countries to agree on a globally optimal policy or another (Barrett, 2003). The first of these is a revenue-neutral carbon tax scheme (Metcalf, 2009). The second is the bundle of optimal monetary transfers coupled with a globally optimal policy (Carraro et al., 2006; Chan, 2019). The third is a climate club model in which nonclub members are punished through one form of penalty such as trade tariffs or another, which can be broadened in principle to include a negative penalty to club members (Nordhaus, 2015).

The three modified schemes devised to increase participation of member countries into a globally agreed policy can be considered as a harbinger of the emergence of the GCF. However, the GCF and more broadly the global public good fund approach has many distinct features that make it a unique policy proposal different from the others. To allude to just a few of them, the GCF, like many other private funds, is generated by voluntary member donations which are not tied to any country party's climate policy. For another, the allocations of the GCF funds to selected projects in selected countries are not explicitly tied to any of the above-mentioned three policy mechanisms, that is, revenue neutrality, optimal transfers, no-club penalties.

From another angle, it can be said that the theoretical foundation of the global public good fund is weaker than that of the globally optimal policy of carbon tax, which will be elaborated in this chapter. Notwithstanding, political ambitions and enthusiasm about the GCF are unmatched, as evidenced by the realized and planned sizes of the funds from the GCF which may top US$ 1 trillion per year (Economic Times of India, 2015; GEF, 2017). Will such ambitions and sacrifices bear fruit in the end for the Planet or just end up running the world to another big financial mess? This chapter will provide an initial answer to this question and many others on the global public good fund (Seo, 2019a).

6.2   Global public good funds

6.2.1   Types of a public good fund

A fund is a sum of money, saved or collected, which is set aside for a particular purpose. A public good fund can be defined as a sum of money collected for the purpose of provision of a particular public good. A global public good fund is then such money set aside for provision of a particular global public good.

A public good fund can be established by one of the five ways, depending on the donors and originators of the fund: (1) a single individual donor and originator; (2) a group of donors from the private sector with an originator from the private sector; (3) a group of donors from the private sector with an originator from the public sector; (4) a group of donors from the public sector with an originator from the public sector; and (5) a group of donors from both the private and public sector with an originator from the public sector.

As shown in Table 6.1, most of the public good funds are type 2, type 4, or type 5. The type 2 funds are Greenpeace, Save the Children Fund, and Tzu Chi Relief Fund. The type 4 funds are such as the UNDP, UNEP, and the Global Environmental Facility (GEF), which are funded entirely by the member country contributions. The type 5 funds are such as the UNICEF, World Food Programme (WFP), and the Green Climate Fund, which are mostly funded by the member country contributions but also receive donations from the private enterprises and individuals. Of the type 2 funds, some of the crowdfunding, such as GoFundMe, projects are initiated for providing a particular public good or another, many of which are collecting donations for natural disaster victims such as earthquakes, hurricanes, flooding, and famine (GoFundMe, 2017; Seo, 2019a).

Across all the public good funds, a fundamental question is whether a public good fund is endowed with a sufficiently large sum of money to carry out its specified activities and to provide an intended public good. The size of the funds listed in Table 6.1 is in the range of US$ 10 million for the private sector funds to around US$ 6 billion for several public funds: US$ 5.6 billion in annual budget for the

Table 6.1 Types of a public good fund.

Type	Originators	Donors	Examples	Fund size
1	Private sector	A single individual	Gates foundation	
2	Private sector	A group of individuals	Greenpeace, Save the Children Fund, Tzu Chi Relief Fund, some of crowdfunding projects.	About US$ 0.4 billion/year for Greenpeace
3	Public sector	A group of individuals		
4	Public sector	Public sector	UNDP, UNEP (Environment Fund), Global Environmental Facility	US$ 5.6 billion/ year for UNDP
5	Public sector	Private and public sector	UNICEF, World Food Programme, Green Climate Fund	US$ 5.4 billion/ year for UNICEF; US$ 6.8 billion/ year for WFP; US$ 100 billion/ year for GCF.

UNDP, US\$ 5.4 billion in annual expenses for the UNICEF, and US\$ 6.8 billion in annual contributions for WFP (UNICEF, 2018; UNDP, 2018; WFP, 2018; Seo, 2019a). In the criterion of the fund size, the GCF is a transcendent public good fund with its target annual allocation of funds of US\$ 100 billion from 2020 (GCF, 2011; UNFCCC, 2015). As of July 2019, the total donations committed to the GCF amounted to US\$ 5.2 billion.

The GCF is also an extraordinary public good fund in terms of the pervasiveness of its intended activities. The GCF funding activities are in fact unlimited, that is, any mitigation and adaptation activities taken place anywhere in the Planet can be considered for its funding. Specifically, 197 member countries of the UNFCCC can receive grants from the GCF for which each funded project should carry out proposed and approved activities. Notice that nearly all activities of a human being, an animal, or a plant have consequences on carbon emissions as well as adaptation to climatic systems.

Because of the ground-breaking size and the pervasiveness of the GCF, the economics of a global public good fund that this chapter sets out to elucidate has become far more realistic as well as policy-pertinent. If the GCF fund size were to increase to US\$ 1 trillion per year as some reports and environmental activists have argued, the GCF may even be considered for an alternative to the globally optimal policy or its variants discussed in the previous chapters.

6.2.2   Green climate fund

From this point on, the present author will provide a comprehensive but succinct introduction to the GCF and proceed to the economics of it in the next section. The GCF has first emerged in an abrupt fashion at the Copenhagen Conference of the UNFCCC in 2009. That was the first year of the Obama presidency and the first year of operation of the GCF was 2016, the last year of the Obama presidency. It may even be said that the GCF is the biggest international legacy of President Obama (NYT, 2016).

What happened in Copenhagen in 2009? After the Kyoto Protocol entered into force in 2005 excluding the United States, China, and India, and the first phase of the Protocol began in 2008, the parties of the conference, that is, the negotiators at the UN conferences, agreed through the Bali Road Map in 2007 to adopt a binding agreement that includes all developing country parties as well as all developed country parties at the Copenhagen Conference in 2009, which would be called a Kyoto II or an extended Kyoto Protocol (UNFCCC, 2007).

The conference in Copenhagen started with high expectations but turned into shambles by its closing because of deep disagreements between the developing country parties and the developed country parties. Hilary Clinton, representing Present Obama as the Secretary of State, arrived at the last minutes of the Conference and announced an adaptation fund with the size of US\$ 100 billion per year which the United States would provide, surprising everyone (NYT, 2009a,b). In the formal document, it became inscribed as the Copenhagen Green Climate Fund (UNFCCC, 2009).

The following years witnessed the establishment of the institution and legal framework of the GCF. At the Cancun Conference in 2010, the GCF was formally established with the creation of the transitional committee and the appointment of the interim trustee, the World Bank (UNFCCC, 2010). At the Durban Conference in 2011, the governing instrument for the Fund developed by the transitional committee was approved (UNFCCC, 2011; GCF, 2011). At the Doha Conference in 2012, Songdo City in the Republic of Korea was selected and endorsed as the host city of the GCF Secretariat (UNFCCC, 2012).

The GCF Secretariat is responsible for day-to-day operations of the Fund and is headed by the Executive Director, first appointed in 2013 and second in 2017, and senior management officials. As of July 2019, the Secretariat had 224 staff members who came from 63 + countries, in addition to a large number of consultants. The second Executive Director abruptly stepped down in September 2018, possibly because of a failure to raise the funds after the United States withdrawal from the Paris Agreement (White House, 2017). The Secretariat services and is accountable to the Governing Board.

The Governing Board governs the GCF and is accountable to the United Nations. It is composed of 24 board members who are equally chosen from the developing country parties and the developed country parties, that is 12 from the former and 12 from the latter. It makes decisions based on the consensus of the board members (GCF, 2011).

In 2014, the Fund began its initial resource mobilization period of 2015−2018, with zealous supports from both UN Secretary General Ban Kimoon and President Obama. It raised about US\$ 10 billion equivalent in the first year of campaigning, about 80% of which came from the five countries: The United States (US\$ 3 billion), Japan (US\$ 1.5 billion), United Kingdom (US\$ 1.2 billion), France (US\$ 1 billion), and Germany (US\$ 1 billion). As of July 2019, the fund size remained unchanged from the first year total commitment while the United States pledges were withdrawn (GCF, 2019d).

In November 2015, the first batch of projects was awarded the GCF grants, timed for the Paris Conference. Two projects were awarded from the Latin America and the Caribbean (Peru, Mexico), one project from the Asia Pacific (Bangladesh), two projects from the Alliance of Small Island States (AOSIS) (Maldives, Fiji), and three projects from Africa (Malawi, Senegal, Rwanda).

In December 2015, with the historic Paris Agreement by 195 members, the GCF became the primary financial instrument of the Paris Agreement (UNFCCC, 2015). The following year marked the first year of the GCF's full operation with additional 29 projects approved by the Governing Board. As of July 2019, 111 projects were awarded either a grant or a loan and the total funding for the projects under implementation amounted to US\$ 2.4 billion (GCF, 2019e).

6.2.3 Allocating the green climate fund: investment criteria

With the Fund thus established, the GCF Board should decide on which projects from a pool of proposals should receive the funding and how much money should be allocated to each selected project. For the Board's funding decisions, the GCF offers a set of investment criteria that the public and participants should refer to (GCF, 2019b,c). These criteria are essential information for the researchers who seek to analyze the organization's funding decisions and their economic and climate consequences, which is the central question of this chapter.

The GCF's investment framework is formulated as a set of parallel criteria. Each criterion is composed of a set of subcriteria, each of which is again explained by a family of assessment indicators. The six parallel investment criteria are, in the order presented by the GCF document, impact potential, paradigm shift potential, sustainable development potential, needs of the recipient, country ownership, and effectiveness and efficiency (GCF, 2019b,c).

A summary of the investment framework is presented in the two tables below: Tables 6.2 and 6.3. The salient feature of the GCF investment framework is that there is no single encompassing indictor that tells to the public decisively which project is more or less important in the Board's selection decision. The single investment indicator may be constructed by assigning individual weights to each of the six investment criteria formulated by the GCF, but such an attempt is not made at least for now. Under the current framework, we cannot tell which of the six criteria was more or less important in the Board's funding decisions, as such, we should interpret the six criteria parallel, that is, given equal weights.

The second feature of the investment framework is that although the Board is required to make its funding decision on a consensus basis, the funding documents do not reveal how a funded project scored on each of the six criteria. Neither do they reveal a combined, weighted or not, score that a funded project received. So, analysts cannot dig empirically into the funding decisions yet.

As summarized in Table 6.2, the impact criterion is divided into two coverage areas: mitigation and adaptation. The subcriterion for the mitigation impact coverage area is formulated as a "contribution to the shift to low-emission sustainable development pathways." The indicators for the subcriterion are called the indicative assessment factors which include (1) expected tons of carbon dioxide equivalent emissions to be reduced or avoided; (2) degree to which activity avoids lock-in of

Table 6.2 Investment criteria: mitigation and adaptation impacts.

Criteria	Coverage area	Activity specific subcriteria	Indicative assessment factors
Impact potential	Mitigation impact	Contribution to the shift to low-emission sustainable development pathways	Expected tons of carbon dioxide equivalent to be reduced or avoided.
	Adaptation impact	Contribution to increased climate-resilient sustainable development	Expected total number of direct and indirect beneficiaries.

Table 6.3 Investment criteria other than mitigation and adaptation impacts.

Criteria	Coverage area	Indicative assessment factors/subcriteria
Paradigm shift potential	Potential for scaling up and replication	Opportunities for targeting innovative solutions, new market segments, developing or adopting new technologies, business models, modal shifts and/or processes.
	Potential for knowledge and learning	Existence of a monitoring and evaluation plan and a plan for sharing lessons.
	Contribution to the creation of an enabling environment	Sustainability of outcomes and results beyond completion.
	Contribution to the regulatory framework	Degree to which the project or programme advances the national/local regulatory or legal frameworks.
	Overall contribution to climate-resilient development pathways (Adaptation only)	Scaling up the scope and impact of the intended project/programme without equally increasing the total costs of implementation.
Sustainable development potential	Environmental cobenefits	Positive environmental externalities such as air quality, soil quality, conservation, and biodiversity.
	Social cobenefits	Externalities in areas such as health and safety, access to education, improved regulation and/or cultural preservation.
	Economic cobenefits	Positive externalities in areas such as expanded and enhanced job markets, job creation and poverty alleviation for women and men.
	Gender-sensitive development impact	Correct prevailing inequalities in climate change vulnerability and risks.
Needs of the recipient	Vulnerability of the country	Intensity of exposure to climate risks and the degree of vulnerability.
Country ownership	Vulnerable groups and gender aspects Economic and social development level Absence of alternative sources of financing Need for strengthening Institutions/capacity Existence of a national climate strategy Coherence with existing policies Capacity of accredited entities or executing entities to deliver Engagement with civil society organizations and other relevant stakeholders	

(Continued)

Table 6.3 (Continued)

Criteria	Coverage area	Indicative assessment factors/ subcriteria
Efficiency and effectiveness	Cost-effectiveness and efficiency regarding financial and nonfinancial aspects	1. Proposed financial structure is adequate ... to achieve the proposal's objectives; 2. The proposed financial structure provides the least concessionality needed to make the proposal viable; 3. The Fund's support ... will not crowd out private and other public investment; 4. Estimated cost per tCO_2eq
	Amount of cofinancing Programme/project financial viability	Economic and financial rate of return with and without the fund's support.
	Industry best practices	

long-lived, high-emission infrastructure; and (3) expected increase in the number of households with access to low emission energy. In the table, only the first is shown, for the sake of simplicity for the readers' review.

For the adaptation impact coverage area, the subcriterion is formulated as a "contribution to increased climate-resilient sustainable development." The indicative assessment factors include (1) expected total number of direct and indirect beneficiaries through either reduced vulnerability or increased resilience; and (2) number of beneficiaries relative to total population, particularly the most vulnerable groups. Again, only the first of the two is shown in the table.

The other investment criteria than the mitigation and adaptation impact potentials are summarized in Table 6.3. The table is somewhat lengthy but I guarantee that it is worthwhile to read through the table just once. First, the paradigm shift potential criterion is formulated as five coverage areas: (1) potential for scaling up and replication, and its overall contribution to global low-carbon development pathways being consistent with a temperature increase of less than 2-degree celsius; (2) potential for knowledge and learning; (3) contribution to the creation of an enabling environment; (4) contribution to the regulatory framework and policies; and (5) overall contribution to climate-resilient development pathways consistent with a country's climate change adaptation strategies and plans.

Each coverage area is further elaborated by subcriteria and indicative assessment factors of which only the most essential ones are presented in the table to give readers a glimpse of how they are formulated. The coverage area of "potential for knowledge and learning" is further explained by the indicative assessment factor specified as an "existence of a monitoring and evaluation plan and a plan for sharing lessons." The coverage area of "contribution to the creation of an enabling environment" is further elaborated by "sustainability of outcomes and results beyond the project's completion" as an indicative assessment factor. The coverage area of "contribution to the regulatory framework" is attached by the assessment factor specified as "degree to which the project or programe advances the national/local regulatory or legal frameworks."

Next, for the sustainable development potential criterion, the coverage areas are (1) environmental cobenefits; (2) social cobenefits; (3) economic cobenefits; and (4) gender-sensitive development impact. The environmental cobenefits coverage area is further elaborated as the indicative assessment factor of the "degree to which the project or programme promotes positive environmental externalities such as air quality, soil quality, conservation, biodiversity, etc." The social cobenefits are elaborated by "potential for externalities in the form of expected improvements, for women and men as relevant, in areas such as health and safety, access to education, improved regulation and/or cultural preservation." The economic cobenefits are further explained as "potential for externalities in the form of expected improvements in areas such as expanded and enhanced job markets, job creation and poverty alleviation for women and men, increased and/or expanded involvement of local industries." The coverage area of gender-sensitive development impact is further elaborated as "explanation of how the project activities will address the needs of women and men in order to correct prevailing inequalities in climate change vulnerability and risks."

That the concept of sustainable development plays an important, if not essential, role in the formulation of the GCF and its works were highlighted in the book recently published by the present author (Seo, 2019a). Notice that not only the concept of sustainable development is adopted as one of the investment criteria, the coverage areas expressed as cobenefits in various aspects are extensive, as shown in Table 6.3. Second, notice that the mitigation impact criterion as well as the adaptation impact criterion are defined by the subcriteria of sustainable development, as shown in Table 6.2. Third, the GCF Board requests any proposal to the Board to indicate one of the millennium sustainable development goals declared in the United Nations' Millennium Declaration that the proposal addresses (UN, 2000).

The above-referenced book emphasized that the policy problems of global warming and climate change as a global public good are starkly different from the problems of sustainable development, therefore, it is misguided to rely on the remedies developed for the latter to design the solutions for the former (Solow, 1974, 1993; Hartwick, 1977). To put it more directly, the many cobenefits described above do not cause climate policy-pertinent mitigation and adaptation activities, nor such mitigation and adaptation activities lead to these cobenefits in any meaningful manner for a global climate policy.

The next investment criterion is the "needs of the recipient" whose coverage areas are formulated as (1) vulnerability of the country; (2) vulnerable groups and gender aspects; (3) economic and social development level of the country; (4) absence of alternative sources of financing; and (5) need for strengthening institutions and implementation capacity.

At first glance, the criterion and coverage areas look uninteresting or not unseemly. However, this criterion may best capture the true identity of the GCF if a careful examination of the 111 funded projects were performed. This point will be clarified empirically later in this chapter. The key point is that the GCF funding allocations are truthful to the principle of "common but differentiated responsibilities" declared in the foundation document of the United Nations Framework Convention on Climate Change (UNFCCC, 1992). This principle in turn can be traced back to the first United Nation's conference on human environment held in Stockholm two decades earlier (UN, 1972).

The next criterion is the country ownership with the following coverage areas: (1) existence of a national climate strategy; (2) coherence with existing policies; (3) capacity of accredited entities or executing entities to deliver; and (4) engagement with civil society organizations and other relevant stakeholders.

Finally, the last investment criterion added to the end of the document is efficiency and effectiveness with the following coverage areas: (1) cost-effectiveness and efficiency regarding financial and nonfinancial aspects; (2) amount of cofinancing; (3) programme/project financial viability and other financial indicators; and (4) industry best practices.

To the readers of this book, it would be, at least at first sight, the most interesting criterion of them all. The criterion of "efficiency and effectiveness" is, however, formulated not in the economic sense as surveyed in the theory chapters. Chapter 2, The Economics of Public Goods and Club Goods, and Chapter 3, The Economics of Global-Scale Public Goods: Key Challenges and Theories, of this book but rather in the sense of financial adequacy of a grant or a loan to be given to a particular project. As you can verify in Table 6.3, the three assessment indicators of the coverage area of "cost-effectiveness and efficiency" simply ask, in one way or another, whether a GCF funding will be sufficient for a particular project.

The fourth assessment indicator of the first coverage area is "estimated cost per tCO_2eq as defined as total investment cost/expected lifetime emission reductions, and relative to comparable opportunities." To the GCF's credit, it is a rudimentary conceptualization of efficiency compared with either that of the microbehavioral economics in Chapter 4, A Critique of the Economics of Global Public Goods: A Microbehavioral Theory and Model, or that of the global optimal climate policy in Chapter 5, A Critique of the Economics of Global Public Goods: Economics of Noncooperative Games. A comprehensive indicator of efficiency should compare the net benefit of a project under consideration against the net benefits obtainable by alternative projects (Seo, 2016d). The net benefit is the total benefit minus the total cost. The total benefit includes not only the benefit from a ton of CO_2eq emission reduction but also other benefits. The total cost of a project is most often different from the investment cost.

Second, the estimate of the cost per tCO_2eq reduction is, however, not included in any of the GCF proposals or project documentations and there is a good reason for this omission. It would be a daunting task for the project initiator to estimate this cost especially because it should be separated out from other economic measures such as farm profits, costs, loans, and external costs.

Third, neither is there any discussion in any project documentations about a set of alternative projects to the project undertaken and funded, for which there is also a good reason. The proposal submitter does not have the precise knowledge on the full set of alternatives on her lands, especially under the altered climate systems in the decades to come.

6.2.4   Funding models of the green climate fund

The survival of a fund hinges on whether the fund initiator can generate the money sufficient to achieve the goal declared by the fund. A funding model is a method and strategy for generating the resources for a fund. There are many funding models including private donations, crowdfunding, on-line crowdfunding, business contributions, public sector contributions, and international organization resources (Mollick, 2014).

In the case of the GCF, it started as a voluntary contribution of the rich countries of the UN climate convention to assist poor countries to adapt to climatic changes (UNFCCC, 2009). The voluntary pledge approach is still the backbone of the GCF funding model, but from its original form of member nation contributions, it has been expanded to include private donations as well as business contributions (GCF, 2019d).

Soon after the Paris Agreement, generating the resources for the GCF has gradually surfaced as the biggest challenge facing its future. With the first year of resource mobilization in 2015 securing pledges of US$ 10 billion before the Paris Conference, there have been nearly no new pledges and contributions to the GCF while the United States withdrawal from the Paris Agreement meant a reduction of the Fund's size by US$ 2 billion.

It will soon dawn, if it has not already, on the GCF and UN climate negotiators that the current funding model is highly defective and will, with no revisions, come to render the Fund meaningless and in turmoil. The most obvious defect is that member contributions to the Fund are not tied to any climate change policy goal or variable. Further, since member contributions are voluntary and without legal liabilities, there will be no way, as it seems presently, that the GCF will achieve its funding goal of US$ 100 billion per year.

The current status of the GCF coffer is shown in Fig. 6.1 where major contributors and their pledges and commitments to the Fund are drawn. There are 14 countries that pledged over US$ 100 million and four countries that pledged over US$ 1 billion. The total contribution is about US$ 10 billion. The figure shows two countries in gray bars: the United States and Australia. The United States initially pledged US$ 3 billion but it withdrew from the Paris Agreement after committing only US$1 billion (White House, 2017). An Australia's contribution to the Fund, after abandoning its carbon emissions targets in the National Energy Guarantee (NEG) developed to meet the Paris Agreement as well as replacing the Prime Minister who supported it, remains in doubt (DW, 2018).

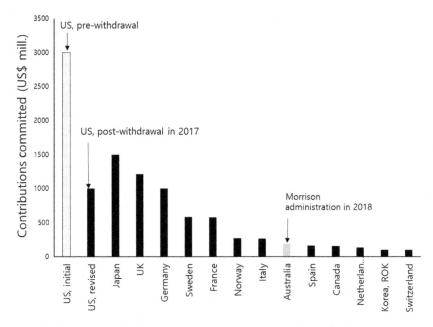

Figure 6.1 Member contributions committed (grants only) as of July 2019.

6.3   The economics behind the green climate fund as a policy alternative

The existence and activities of the GCF as a policy alternative in dealing with the problems of global warming and climate change may be justified by sound economic theories that are widely accepted in the literature. The discussions in this section will reveal that at least some activities of the GCF can be justified soundly to some degrees.

6.3.1   Economics of public expenditure

The first of such economic theories in the theory of public expenditure (Samuelson, 1954; Buchanan, 1965). We reviewed this theory extensively in Chapter 2, The Economics of Public Goods and Club Goods, so there is no need for repetition here. The crux of the theory in the context of the GCF is that there are some goods in the society that are consumed jointly by the public which cannot be supplied efficiently by the market forces alone. The public sector should supply this type of goods through determining the prices of these goods right (Muller and Mendelsohn, 2009). Depending upon the joint good considered, the public sector can be the Federal government, a State government, or a local municipality. In the GCF context, the public sector is a global governance, that is, the GCF.

Interpreted this way, the GCF collects the donations from national governments, businesses, and private individuals, which are then distributed to a large array of activities that provide a global public good. The public good is the emissions reduction of carbon dioxide and other Planet-warming gases that would eventually cause a "stable" climate system for humanity and the Planet.

A fatal weakness of this interpretation is evident. In collecting the donations from various entities, the GCF does not charge all the activities that lead to greenhouse gas emissions, nor does it cover all the entities that need to be accounted for. Neither does it charge a correct price, regardless of however it may be defined.

A flaw on the spending side of the GCF activities is also severe, but slightly less so than the revenue side. It gives a grant or a loan to a greenhouse gas emission reduction activity, which is perhaps fine and justifiable. Many questions, however, arise inevitably: (1) Are the grants/loans given to the project that achieves the largest emission reduction among a basket of alternative projects?; (2) Can the GCF awards as a whole achieve the provision of a global public good, in this case, a "stable" global climate?; and (3) Are the funding of the GCF efficient in that it achieves its goal with the least cost? The present author will answer these questions empirically in the next section making use of the data sets provided by the GCF project documentations and other sources (Seo, 2019a).

6.3.2   Economics of efficient land and resource uses

The second theoretical justification of the GCF activities can be made from the standpoint of efficiency in land and natural resource uses, whose concepts can be traced far back to Ricardo and von Thunen in the early 19th century (Ricardo, 1817; von Thunen, 1826). This theory is more pertinent to the analysis of the GCF than the first theory because it pertains to the analysis of an individual manager of a land or natural resources while the public good theory is predominantly concerned about the efficiency at the national economy level (Pareto, 1906).

The essence of the theory is that an individual land owner will utilize her land by adopting an activity among an array of activities which gives her the largest long-term profit from the land, that is, the present discounted value of the stream of rents that are generated over time from the land (Hartwick and Olewiler, 1997; Seo, 2016a). Looked across a large geographical landscape, a motley of land uses will be seen by observers as each parcel of land is allocated to a unique land use efficiently determined by a land manager.

Applied to the GCF decisions, the GCF Board can consider possible efficiency distortions in the current land uses caused by negative externalities through the emissions of greenhouse gases from a particular parcel of land and positive externalities through the sinks of greenhouse gases from the parcel of land (Pigou, 1920; Coase, 1960). The existence of externalities will give economic advantages or disadvantages to one type of land use over other possible types of land use, thereby distort an efficient use of the land.

Table 6.4 clarifies how the distortion that arises from negative externalities leads to an inefficient land use by a land owner. There are three types of land use: LU1, LU2, and LU3. The profit for each land use is α, $\alpha + 1$, and $\alpha + 2$, respectively.

Table 6.4 An inefficient land use caused by negative externalities.

Lan use choices	Present value of profits	Negative externalities	An inefficient land use because of negative externalities	An efficient land use when negative externalities are internalized
LU1	α	0		
LU2	$\alpha + 1$	0		Chosen
LU3	$\alpha + 2$	-1.5	Chosen	

Table 6.5 An inefficient land use caused by positive externalities.

Lan use choices	Present value of profits	Positive externalities	An inefficient land use because of positive externalities	An efficient land use when positive externalities are internalized
LU1	α	0		
LU2	$\alpha + 1$	$+1.5$		Chosen
LU3	$\alpha + 2$	0	Chosen	

The negative externalities exist in only LU3, whose size is -1.5. The land owner will choose LU3 because negative externalities are not charged in the market. But, the LU3 is an inefficient land use from the society's viewpoint. If the externalities were accounted for, that is, were internalized, the land owner would choose the LU2, an efficient land use. To internalize the negative externalities, the GCF Board may ask the land owner to pay for the negative externalities in the form of a tax.

It is nearly impossible, however, that the GCF Board will be able to charge land owners for their negative externalities and the land owners will be willing to comply with the requests by the GCF Board, a foreign entity operating on a foreign land. A more likely situation is described in Table 6.5 which is the same table as the previous one but with the positive externalities. This table may explain a large portion of the GCF funding decisions, at least at the conceptual level.

Again, the land use types and their profits remain the same as before. The positive externalities are occurring from the LU2 with the size of $+1.5$. The land owner's choice in the presence of the positive externalities is LU3 because the positive externalities are not internalized, that is, not rewarded in the market. The LU3 is an inefficient land use, though. The efficient land use is LU2, which would be chosen by the land owner when the positive externalities are rewarded in some way.

The GCF Board can reward the land owner with the grant of $+1.5$, which would force the land owner to switch from its current land use to LU2, an efficient land use. Unlike the tax imposed in the case of negative externalities, the GCF Board will find "no difficulties" in awarding a grant to the land owner justified on the ground of positive externalities. Further, the land owners will comply with the GCF activities as long as they are promised financial rewards.

Extending this logic to the negative externality situation in Table 6.4, the GCF Board can make its funding decisions realistic even in the situation in Table 6.4: It can grant the land owner a credit on the condition that the land owner uses the credit to remove the negative externality from the current land use, either employing new technologies or switching its land use to another.

The 111 projects that received a grant or loan from the GCF Board during the period of November 2015−July 2019 may be justified on the efficiency ground at the conceptual level. From another point of view, however, this justification has a glaring weakness: it does not explain where and how the funds that should be given out to selected projects can be generated in the first place. The funds should be generated through voluntary contributions or government-level taxations and the GCF at present relies on the former. However, the voluntary contribution funding model to the GCF funds is conceptually inconsistent and fragile.

Another big hurdle in applying the land use efficiency justification is to define the negative externalities and positive externalities that should be addressed by the GCF as well as to determine the monetary sizes of the externalities. The hurdles can even become unsurmountable if the negative and positive externalities were bargained away voluntarily among the concerned parties and such bargains cannot be traced by analysts at the GCF (Coase, 1960). Such negotiations, even if only partially, can be occurring at the community level in an informal community rule, custom, or history (Ostrom, 1990).

Beyond the GCF funds, the externality-efficiency argument has a strong basis in the climate policies adopted at the present moment around the world. Let us take a look at the climate policy in the State of California: Assembly Bill (AB) 32, the California Global Warming Solutions Act of 2006 which began the implementation of the cap-and-trade program in January 2013 (Goulder, 2007; NYT, 2012). As part of the cap-and-trade system, offset credits are offered to the following activities: forest timber management, Ozone depleting substances, methane emissions from livestock, urban tree planting projects, marine methane capture, and rice cultivation (Conte and Kotchen, 2010; CARB, 2019). An even larger list of offset programs is found in the European Union's Emissions Trading System (ETS) (Ellerman et al., 2016; EC, 2018).

Fig. 6.2 shows the number of offset credits offered to the offset programs in both compliance and early action stages by the AB 32 of California. The forest offset is the dominant offset program which was awarded 125 million credits. The next is the offset program in Ozone depleting substances with 20 million credits, which is followed by the livestock offset and the marine methane capture offset, both with about 6 million credits each. In total, the offset credit amounts to 157 million credits, which can be compared with the total number of allowances issued by the cap-and-trade program under the AB 32, about 350 million tons of CO_2eq in 2019.

6.3.3 Economics of public adaptation

The third theory that may be applicable to the justification of the GCF is the concept of a public adaptation. A private adaptation is an adaptation activity by an individual manager while a public adaptation is an adaptation activity by a group of

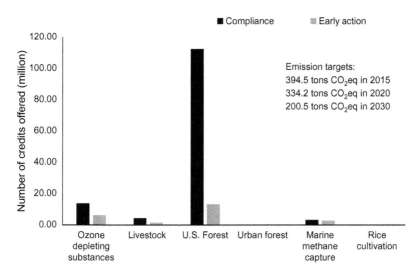

Figure 6.2 Offset credits in the cap-and-trade program in California (July 2019).

individuals where the group can be a village, a municipality, neighboring munici-palities, or a State (Mendelsohn, 2000; Hanemann, 2000; Seo, 2011).

This theory shares an element with the theory of public goods as well as with the theory of efficient land/resource uses. Similar to the former, a public adaptation is a jointly produced good by a group of individuals which is consumed jointly. Similar to the latter, a public adaptation takes place when a public provision of a good is more efficient than a private provision of a good. When a large number of upstream factories pollute the river to a downstream town, the river cannot be cleaned up by a single factory.

The theory of public adaptation, however, has also quite a few distinct features from the two theories. Unlike the theory of public goods, a public adaptation alone is not a sufficient response to a challenge, that is, a global warming challenge. A public adaptation must be undertaken in tandem with a private adaptation. For example, an efficient adaptation in agriculture to water resource constraints imposed by climatic changes must include both individual farmers' irrigations and public irrigation systems (Seo, 2011).

Unlike the theory of efficient land/resource uses, a public adaptation is a group (of individuals) response than a private response. Also, it involves public lands (resources) or resources of a group of individuals. A construction of a coastal wall for protection against the sea level rise caused by climatic changes would involve public and private lands along the coast as well as citizens and local municipalities (Yohe and Schlesinger, 1998; Ng and Mendelsohn, 2006).

In Fig. 6.3, one of the critical findings from an empirical study of private versus public adaptation is presented (Seo, 2011). The study examined the three types of irrigation adopted by seven South American countries' farmers (Dinar et al., 1992; Schoengold and Zilberman, 2007). The seven countries are Argentina, Brazil,

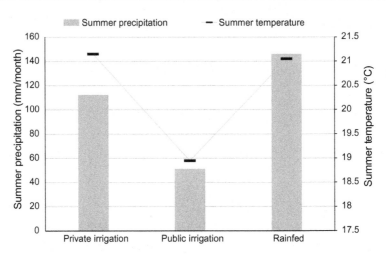

Figure 6.3 Private versus public irrigation in South America.

Uruguay, and Chile from the Southern Cone region and Colombia, Ecuador, and Venezuela from the Andean region. The figure summarizes the average temperature of where each irrigation system is adopted.

Surprisingly, the private irrigation and the public irrigation are shown to be adopted in different climate zones. The public irrigation adaptation has taken place in response to precipitation shortages. The average precipitation is only 50 mm/month in places where the public irrigation scheme is adopted whereas it is about 110 mm/month in places where the private irrigation scheme is adopted. In the rainfed system, that is, no irrigation at all, the average precipitation is as high as 140 mm/month.

On the other hand, the private irrigation adaptation has taken place in response to a hotter temperature regime. The average summer temperature in the farms where the private irrigation scheme is adopted is 21.2°C while the average summer temperature in the farms where the public irrigation scheme is adopted is 19°C.

The results in Fig. 6.3 may mean that South American farmers know more than the public agency about the irrigation needs in different climate conditions, which is why farmers take private irrigation measures in the places where the public irrigation system is not provided and they do not take private irrigation measures in the places where the public irrigation system is provided. The results may also imply that some measures of adaptation can be provided more efficiently by the public sector while other measures can be provided more efficiently by the private sector (Seo, 2011).

Of the three economic theories described thus far, the public adaptation theory is most directly related with the GCF's works. Applying the theory of public adaptation, it would be concluded that the GCF should support a public adaptation project and should not support a private adaptation project. The GCF grant should be directed to the public adaptation project when it is concluded that private (individual) adaptations cannot provide the needed goods and services to the public.

A couple of examples would make this conclusion clearer. If the GCF should decide to support agricultural irrigation efforts in a local town in India, it should not give out grants to individual farmers to purchase pumps and other irrigation instruments, but rather support the efforts to build a community pond/reservoir to which all community members have access (Seo, 2019a).

For another example, if the GCF should decide to support a shift of an energy system in a province in Peru from a fossil fuel-based system to a solar energy-based system, it should not give out solar panels to each household in the province, but should support a solar-energy generation facility which provides electricity to the public. It goes without saying that it does not mean that an individual household cannot install her own rooftop solar panels.

Pursuing the rationale further, we can derive from the public adaptation theory a guidance on which level of the public sector should be given a grant to carry out a project efficiently (Samuelson and Nordhaus, 2009). If a public project should be carried out by a village to achieve an efficient outcome, a grant should be given to the village. A grant allocated to a provincial government in this situation would yield an inefficient outcome. Similarly, if a public adaptation project should be carried out by a provincial government for an efficient outcome, a grant should not be given to a village community or an individual farmer.

6.4   Evaluation 1: A public adaptation theory test

Having clarified the economics of the GCF through the three theories, the present author will proceed to provide an evaluation of the full batch of GCF funding decisions and projects thus far approved. I will attempt to make it as comprehensive as possible, given the limitation of space in the book, and as representative as possible, albeit with a focused attention to a set of selected projects.

Let us begin with the test of the public adaptation theory. In Table 6.6, five projects in the GCF's results area of the forests and land use to which the GCF grants were allocated are summarized. Along with the project title and accredited entity of each project, quantitative data on the expected tons of CO_2-equivalent emissions removed, funding size, and project duration are presented.

For a public adaptation theory test, the present author examines these projects from the viewpoint of whom received each grant. The funding recipients are called accredited entities and executing entities by the GCF. The three accrediting entities in the table are international organizations such as the UNDP, the Inter-American Development Bank (IDB), and the Asian Development Bank (ADB). The other two recipients are national policy organizations: The Agency for Agricultural Development of Morocco (ADA), the Peruvian Trust Fund for National Parks and Protected Areas (Profonanpe).

We ask whether each of the grants is given to an appropriate entity who can carry out a funded project in the most efficient manner. Let us first examine the project submitted by Guatemala and Mexico entitled "The Low-Emission Climate

Table 6.6 Summary data of selected GCF-funded projects for a public adaptation test.

Recipient countries/ results area	Project title	Accredited entity/ executing entity	Expected contribution (tons CO_2eq avoided)	Grant size (US$)	Project duration (years)
Ecuador/ forests and land use	Priming financial and land-use planning instruments to reduce emissions from deforestation	United Nations Development Programme (UNDP)	15 m	$84 m	5
Morocco/ forests and land use	Development of Argan Orchards in degraded environment	Agency for agricultural development of Morocco (ADA)	604.2 k	$49.2 m	5
Guatemala, Mexico/ forests and land Use	Low-emission climate resilient agriculture risk Sharing facility for MSMEs (Micro, small, medium-sized enterprises)	Inter-American development Bank (IDB)	9.2 m	$158.0 m	15
Cambodia/ forests and land Use	Climate-friendly agribusiness value chains sector project	Asian Development Bank (ADB)	240.0 k	$141.4 m	6
Peru/forests and land use	Building the resilience of wetlands in the Province of Datem del Marañón, Peru	Peruvian trust fund for National Parks and Protected Areas (Profonanpe)	2.6 m	$9.1 m	5

Note: k = thousand, m = million.

Resilient Agriculture Risk Sharing Facility for MSMEs (Micro, Small, Medium-sized Enterprises)." The recipient of the project's funding—the accredited entity in the table—is the IDB, an international developmental organization. The risk sharing facility in Guatemala and Mexico, two Central American countries, should be operational at a local level, for example, a village level or a district level, so we may judge that the IDB, an international organization, would not be an appropriate group to which the grant should be given for providing a public adaptation of the low-emissions and climate resilient agriculture's risk sharing facility for the MSMEs in the Central American countries.

A climate resilient agriculture must be tailored for a local situation under consideration, so must a low-emissions agriculture. There is no single climate resilient agriculture that can be applied across the two countries in a blanket fashion, nor is there a single low-emissions agriculture (Seo et al., 2009a,b; Seo, 2012a). Many types of the risk sharing "facility" in agriculture in developing countries that have been well-researched and widely recognized are also designed and operational at a local level, to name but a few, a community-wide irrigation scheme, a village-level risk pooling, a community banking and finance, and a locally tailored extension service (Seo, 2016a,c,d).

It is true that there can be an economy-wide risk sharing mechanism such as banking and other credit services that would target vulnerable populations under future climatic changes in the two countries (Conning and Udry, 2007). However, even in such a financial/credit mechanism, locally specific knowledge and expertise are inevitable for designing a portfolio of locally appropriate services and products which can be offered to the farmers ultimately. A large number of agricultural research and extension centers, locally based agricultural cooperatives, product-specific agricultural credit services, and region-specific agricultural support programs that we observe today in Mexico and Guatemala attests to the diversity of such services and products.

Considering these points, the IDB should not be an "efficient" institutional level to take on the proposed risk sharing activities. Further, many of the climate resilient agricultural practices and strategies are undertaken at the private farm level, so are many of the low-emissions agriculture (Seo, 2016a,c). That is, the efficient level of adaptation actions for such practices and strategies is the farm/private level.

A similar analysis can be applied with a similar conclusion to the "Climate-Friendly Agribusiness Value Chains Sector Project" submitted by a Cambodian party, whose recipient of the funding was the ADB, a comparable organization in Asia to the IDB in Latin America. Also applying the above analysis to the project submitted by an Ecuadorian party entitled "Priming Financial and Land-Use Planning Instruments to Reduce Emissions from Deforestation" whose recipient of the grant is the UNDP, we can interpret the land use planning to reduce emissions from deforestation proposed by the project submitter as one of the climate resilient and low-emissions land uses and arrive at a similar conclusion.

The public adaptation theory test yields an even stronger conclusion for some projects in Table 6.6. Let us consider the project entitled "Development of Argan Orchards in Degraded Environment" submitted by a party in Morocco whose recipient of the funding was the ADA. At the first level, it is not apparent whether the development of Argan orchards in degraded environment in Morocco should be provided by a private adaptation project or a public adaptation project. At the second level, the orchard project would not be a national-scale public adaptation for which a national level intervention through the ADA of Morocco would be most efficient, which can be verified from the literature of climate adaptations in Africa (Parry et al., 2004; Butt et al., 2005; Seo et al., 2009a; Seo, 2014a).

Take now for examination the Peruvian project entitled "Building the Resilience of Wetlands in the Province of Datem del Marañón, Peru" whose grant recipient was the Peruvian Trust Fund for National Parks and Protected Areas (Profonanpe). Since the wetlands is a major source of methane, a potent greenhouse gas, it would not be apparent to analysts whether the project can be viewed as a climate adaptation project regardless of whether it is a private or a public project (Schaefer et al., 2016).

The evaluation up to this point of the GCF projects via the public adaptation theory can be extended to the projects in the other results areas defined by the international Fund. In Table 6.6, the present author singled out the five projects selected from the results area of forests and land use to demonstrate the evaluation method most clearly.

6.5   Evaluation 2: a public expenditure theory test

The second stream of evaluations is conducted on the ground of the public goods and expenditure theory, for which the present author tabulates in Table 6.7 the pertinent information about selected GCF-funded projects. The projects listed in the table belong to the results area of the energy generation and access. The present author chooses this particular result area because the energy projects supported by the GCF offer the most clearly defined public good in the climate change economics, that is, the reduction of carbon dioxide equivalent emissions from the smokestacks of powerplants. The key statistics for the evaluations in this section are therefore the expected contribution in terms of the tons of CO_2-equivalent emissions avoided and the grant size regarding each energy project.

The energy generation and access projects by the GCF, summarized in Table 6.7, are directed toward either a potpourri of energy programs targeting carbon dioxide emissions or renewable energy sources. In the table, readers will easily encounter a popular energy nomenclature or another including solar energy, green energy, renewable energy, sustainable energy, low-carbon energy, clean cooking, and hydropower. The projects in the table are the full list of the energy projects funded by the GCF during the period from November 2015 to November 2018, that is, not a selective list by the present author. As such, the table provides a rather comprehensive picture.

The size of the grant for most projects is in the range of US\$ 100–US\$ 500 million. The minimum grant size was US\$ 26 million allocated to the multiple Pacific

Table 8.7 Summary data of selected GCF-funded projects on energy generation, access, and efficiency for a public expenditure theory test.

Recipient countries	Project title	Expected contribution (tons CO_2 avoided)	Funding size (US$)	Duration (years)
Results area: energy generation & access				
Rwanda, Kenya	KawiSafi Ventures Fund in East Africa	1.5 m tons	$110.0 m	5
Chile	Climate Action and Solar Energy Development Programme in the Tarapacá Region in Chile	3.7 m tons	$265.0 m	20
Dominica	Sustainable Energy Facility for the Eastern Caribbean	9.4 m tons	$190.5 m	8
Armenia	GCF-EBRD Sustainable Energy Financing Facilities	27.5 m tons	$1.4 b	15
Madagascar	Sustainable Landscapes in Eastern Madagascar	10.0 m tons	$69.8 m	10
Benin	Universal Green Energy Access Programme	50.6 m tons	$301.6 m	15
Mongolia	Business loan programme for GHG emissions reduction	1.2 m tons	$60.0 m	5
South Africa	SCF Capital Solutions	33.0 m tons	$34.1 m	10
Argentina	Catalyzing private investment in sustainable energy in Argentina	15.3 m tons	$653.0 m	4
Mauritius	Accelerating the Transformational Shift to a Low-Carbon Economy in the Republic of Mauritius	4.3 m tons	$191.4 m	6
Cook Islands	Pacific Islands Renewable Energy Investment Program	3.0 m tons	$26.0 m	7
Bahamas	Geeref Next	769.0 m tons	$765.0 m	5
Egypt	Egypt Renewable Energy Financing Framework	18.9 m tons	$1.0b	5
Tajikistan	Tajikistan: Scaling Up Hydropower Sector Climate Resilience	7.5 m tons	$133.0 m	5
Solomon Islands	Tina River Hydropower Development Project	2.5 m tons	$234.0 m	5
Mongolia	Renewable Energy Program #1 - Solar	306.7 k tons	$17.6 m	10
Kazakhstan	GCF-EBRD Kazakhstan Renewables Framework	12.9 m tons	$557.0 m	5
Bhutan	Bhutan for Life	35.1 m tons	$118.3 m	14
Barbados	Water Sector Resilience Nexus for Sustainability in Barbados	220.2k tons	$45.2 m	5.25
Paraguay	Poverty, Reforestation, Energy and Climate Change Project	7.9 m tons	$90.3 m	5
Argentina	Promoting risk mitigation instruments and finance for renewable energy and energy efficiency investments	9.1 m tons	$163.9 m	5

(Continued)

Table 6.7 (Continued)

Recipient countries	Project title	Expected contribution (tons CO_2 avoided)	Funding size (US$)	Duration (years)
Bangladesh	Global Clean Cooking Program – Bangladesh	2.9 m tons	$82.2 m	3.5
Rwanda	Strengthening climate resilience of rural communities in Northern Rwanda	273.7 kbeneficiaries	$33.2 m	6
Zambia	Zambia Renewable Energy Financing Framework	4.0 m tons	$154.0 m	5
India	Line of Credit for Solar rooftop segment for Commercial, Industrial and Residential Housing sectors	5.2 m tons	$250.0 m	5
Results Area: Building, Cities, Industries, and Appliances				
Mexico	Energy Efficiency Green Bonds in Latin America and the Caribbean	2.6 m tons	$184.5 m	5
El Salvador	Energy savings insurance for private energy efficiency investments by Small and Medium-Sized Enterprises	562.0 k tons	$41.7 m	5
Armenia	De-risking and scaling-up investment in energy efficient building retrofits in Armenia	1.4 m tons	$29.8 m	6
Bosnia and Herzegovina	Scaling-up Investment in Low-Carbon Public Buildings	2.0 m tons	$122.6 m	8
Paraguay	Promoting private sector investments in energy efficiency in the industrial sector in Paraguay	4.0 m tons	$43.0 m	5
Brazil	Financial Instruments for Brazil Energy Efficient Cities	17.4 m tons	$1.3 b	7
Vietnam	Scaling Up Energy Efficiency for Industrial Enterprises in Vietnam	120.0 m tons	$88.0 m	5
Nauru	Sustainable and Climate Resilient Connectivity for Nauru	535.4 k tons	$65.2 m	5
Mongolia	Ulaanbaatar Green Affordable Housing and Resilient Urban Renewal Project	7.9 m tons	$544.0 m	8.5

Note: k = thousand, m = million, b = billion.

Islands' renewable energy investment program with seven-year duration. The maximum grant size was US\$ 1.4 billion allocated to multiple countries in multiple continents with 15-year duration: Armenia, Egypt, Georgia, Jordan, Republic of Moldova, Mongolia, Morocco, Serbia, Tajikistan, and Tunisia.

The first evaluation point with regard to the theory of public expenditure is whether the GCF-funded projects in Table 6.7 provide a justification for a "government" taxation and expenditure. The justification should come from the predicted reduction in the damage on the human society and ecosystems that results from undertaking the array of GCF-funded energy projects shown in the table, which is the direct measure of the benefit from the programs (Nordhaus, 1994; Mendelsohn and Neumann, 1999; Hahn and Dudley, 2007).

In this regard, we immediately notice that Table 6.7 does not present quantitative data on climate change-induced damage or the reduction in climate change-induced damage expected from implementing a GCF-funded project. Neither do the full documentations of the GCF-funded projects available publicly through the organization's website offer such information (GCF, 2019e). There is no assessment of each project by the GCF decision-makers in terms of the avoided damage in US dollars compared against the grant given to a selected program.

An alternative but indirect measure of the benefit that is expected from a GCF-funded program is the degree of avoided global temperature increase, or put differently, the degree of reduced climate "anomalies," which is often a preferred measure of a climate policy goal by climate scientists. Take, for example, the $2°C$ temperature ceiling proposed at the Cancun Conference in 2010 (UNFCCC, 2010). In the same spirit, the United Nations emissions gap report recently published assesses the total commitment of the Intended Nationally Determined Contributions by the parties to the Paris Agreement against the $2°C$ target (UNEP, 2017). The GCF-selected projects, including those in Table 6.7, do not offer such an assessment of either an individual project or the entire GCF funding programme.

A defender of the GCF funding decisions may argue that Table 6.7 does indeed present the benefit of each project by way of the avoided CO_2-equivalent emissions. However, it should be reminded that carbon dioxide (CO_2) is itself not a harmful chemical to either a human being, an animal, or ecosystems. What is harmful is the consequences of increased carbon dioxide in the atmosphere, which may include a hotter global average temperature, a climate system with more frequent and/or intense extreme events such as hurricanes (Mendelsohn and Neumann, 1999; Tol, 2009; Seo, 2017b). An increase of carbon dioxide concentration in the atmosphere, on the contrary, is beneficial to plant and ecosystem growth by way of enhancing photosynthesis processes (Ainsworth and Long, 2005; Reich et al., 2018).

The second evaluation point with reference to the theory of public goods and expenditure is the question of whether or not each of the GCF grants and loans on the results area of the energy generation and access is allocated to the recipient who could achieve the largest gain in a policy goal, say, carbon emissions reduction, with the same amount of money allocated. Let us say that the policy goal set by the GCF is the largest greenhouse gas emissions reduction from energy generation and access activities per each dollar spent by the Board.

An examination of the table reveals that the funded projects will fail to pass this critical test for the reasons to be explained presently. It is evident in the table that all of the GCF energy-related grants are allocated to under-developed poor countries in Africa, Latin America, South Asia, Eastern Europe, and Pacific Islands. The economies of these recipient countries are growing at a low growth rate, consequently, the expected increase in the CO_2-equivalent emissions in the recipient countries within, say, the next several decades, is much smaller than the expected increases from fast-growing economies of the world (GCP, 2017).

Nevertheless, the fast-growing economies such as China, India, and the United States are awarded no grants and in fact are nearly excluded from the GCF funding. Precisely, there was only one project that received a grant, a rooftop solar installation project in India. The three countries are however, the world's top three emitters of CO_2 and other greenhouse gases at the present time and the growth of the emissions of these chemicals will continue to be larger in the three countries than in other countries (GCP, 2017). From this, we can conclude that the GCF funding programs on energy generation and access will most likely do little to reduce the increase of CO_2-equivalent emissions at the global level.

Fig. 6.4 shows the trajectory of carbon emissions from fossil fuels and cement production of the three countries and the globe from 1959 to 2015 (Boden et al., 2017). The unit is a million ton of carbon, which can be converted to a carbon dioxide unit by multiplying 3.66. Several things are immediately noticeable. First, the US carbon emissions has not increased since 1980. Second, the emissions from the

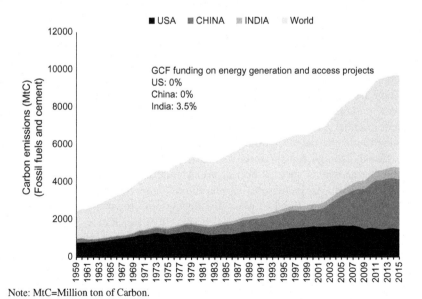

Note: MtC=Million ton of Carbon.

Figure 6.4 A history of carbon emissions from fossil fuels and cement production *vis-à-vis* GCF funding allocations. *MtC*, Million ton of Carbon.

rest of the world has not changed significantly since 1980. Third, the increase in carbon emissions from China since 1980 is remarkable and the increase in the emissions from India more recently is also notable.

The figure reveals emphatically that the carbon emissions from the energy sectors of China and India at present and in the 21st century will be a decisive factor in a global effort to cut greenhouse gas emissions from the energy generation and access activities. The force of economic growth in China and/or India will be unstoppable in the coming decades, barring unforeseeable circumstances.

Looked from a different angle, the carbon emissions from China from fossil fuels and cement production in 2017 accounted for 28% of the world total emissions, but the GCF funding to the energy projects in China was zero. The US emissions accounted for 15% of the world total while the GCF funding to energy projects in the United States was also zero. The Indian carbon emissions accounted for 7% of the global total in 2017 while the GCF funding to Indian energy projects accounted for 3.5% of the total GCF funding in the energy area.

This analysis is comparable—I hope the readers would not miss this point—to the emissions gap report by the UNEP as well as to the 1.5°C report by the Intergovernmental Panel on Climate change, the two assessments on the Paris Agreement hailed by the global media upon their publications which pointed out deficiency in the member parties' commitments (UNEP, 2017; IPCC, 2018).

The bottom panel of Table 6.3 shows the GCF-funded projects on the results area of buildings, cities, industries, and appliances (BCIA). This results area is appended to the table because the projects in this area are primarily concerned with an improvement in energy efficiency in BCIA, as you can verify from the table. The same analysis as the above can be applied to these projects.

Noting across the projects in the BCIA area, the GCF grants were awarded to the project for the energy efficient building retrofits in Armenia; Brazilian energy efficient cities; Ulaanbaatar green affordable housing and resilient urban renewal project in Mongolia; a scaling-up project of energy efficiency for industrial enterprises in Vietnam; and a sustainable and climate resilient connectivity project for the island of Nauru in Micronesia.

An improvement in energy efficiency or energy-saving in the BCIA can be achieved through various technologies: a replacement of incandescent light bulbs with the Light Emitting Diodes lamps, building rooftop solar panels, energy-efficient heating and air-conditioning systems, smart meters for gas and electricity consumption, an improvement in building insulation, heat-reflecting roofs and walls, and trees for natural cooling (Joskow, 2012; Akasaki et al., 2014; Graziano and Gillingham, 2015; DOE, 2015).

We can draw several conclusions from the BCIA energy efficiency projects, comparable to those from the energy generation and access projects. First, the grants/loans are directed without exception to under-developed countries while excluding fast-growing or advanced economies. Second, the GCF-selected projects do not specify the contribution in terms of avoided economic damage, or a reduction in temperature increase, or the degree of improvement in energy efficiency expected from undertaking each selected project.

A simple economic analysis would, however, reveal that the return from investing a dollar on the energy efficiency improvement projects would be greater in a fast-growing city than in a stagnant city (Hsu et al., 2017). In the fast-growing city, the annual energy consumption will increase at a faster rate, as such, an improvement in energy efficiency or energy-saving will lead to a larger reduction in the total energy consumption thereof.

Further, a paradox of the GCF funding may occur if the international grants should be perceived by the recipients as a foreign aid than a climate policy measure: it may increase carbon emissions rather than decrease it. The foreign grants to the buildings and cities in a stagnant country would give an incentive to property developers and politicians to construct more homes and buildings, which would increase the total carbon emissions, not decrease it, from buildings.

6.6   Evaluation 3: a land/resource use efficiency theory test

The third set of evaluations of the GCF money allocations can be conducted on the criteria of efficiency in land and resource uses. The GCF grants are not powerless, but would rather powerfully influence the ways that an individual manager of lands or natural resources makes decisions on the uses of her/his resources. Therefore, we can ask whether the GCF money allocations correct inefficient land uses or distort currently efficient land uses.

The efficiency evaluation of an individual project is, however, neither a handy nor a layman's task. It may not even be a manager's, that is, a farmer's task. A fundamental difficulty is that an evaluator should have comprehensive knowledge about which type of land use is the most profitable one of all possible types of land use in one climate system and another. Further, this knowledge should be as detailed as an efficient land use for each individual farm. On top of this, a further complication arises because the future climate system cannot be determined without uncertainty, that is, can only be predicted under a social, economic, and technological assumption which is called a "scenario" by climate scientists (Nakicenovic et al., 2000; IPCC, 2014).

Notwithstanding these obstacles, it is still possible to provide an efficiency test of an individual GCF-selected project, as will be demonstrated shortly, owing in large part to the extensive literature on land and resource uses, both agronomic and economic. For the same reason, the efficiency test is particularly adequate for an analysis of food security projects of the GCF. In Table 6.8, the present author separates the food security projects from the GCF results area of health, water, and food security.

An immediately noticeable feature in Table 6.8 is that 15 out of 16 total GCF-funded projects on food security declares the goal of the project as "resilience." For the readers' sake, the word is highlighted by the present author using a bolder font. It should surprise anyone that nearly all GCF-selected projects are agreeing on the single concept as the ultimate indicator of food security under a globally warmer world.

Table 6.8 Summary data of the GCF-funded Projects on food security for a land use efficiency theory test.

Recipient countries	Project title	Expected contribution (# of beneficiaries)	Funding size (US$)	Resilience?
Gambia	Large-scale *Ecosystem-based* Adaptation in the Gambia River Basin: developing a climate **resilient**, natural resource-based economy	57,750	$25.5 m	Yes
Sri Lanka	Strengthening the **resilience** of smallholder farmers in the Dry Zone to climate variability and extreme events through an *integrated* approach to water management	2.0 m	$52.1 m	Yes
Namibia	Climate **Resilient** Agriculture in three of the Vulnerable Extreme northern crop-growing regions	21.0 k	$10.0 m	Yes
Namibia	Empower to Adapt: Creating Climate–Change **Resilient** Livelihoods through *Community-Based* Natural Resource Management in Namibia	76.5 k	$10.0 m	Yes
Vanuatu	Climate *Information Services* for **Resilient** Development in Vanuatu	260.7 k	$21.8 m	Yes
Tanzania	Simiyu Climate **Resilient** Development Programme	3.0 m	$176.0 m	Yes
Morocco	*Irrigation* development and adaptation of irrigated agriculture to climate change in semi-arid Morocco: Providing sustainable irrigation to improve the climate **resilience** of subsistence oasis farming and larger-scale date and olive agriculture within the Boudnib Valley.	15.5 k	$93.3 m	Yes
India	*Ground Water Recharge and Solar Micro Irrigation* to Ensure Food Security and Enhance **Resilience** in Vulnerable Tribal Areas of Odisha	16.0 m	$166.3 m	Yes
Senegal	Building the Climate **Resilience** of Food-insecure Smallholder Farmers through *Integrated* Management of Climate Risks	526.5 k	$10.0 m	Yes

(Continued)

Table 6.8 (Continued)

Recipient countries	Project title	Expected contribution (# of beneficiaries)	Funding size (US$)	Resilience?
Tajikistan	Building climate **resilience** of vulnerable and food insecure communities through capacity strengthening and livelihood *diversification* in mountainous regions of Tajikistan	120.0 k	$10.0 m	Yes
Zambia	Strengthening climate **resilience** of agricultural livelihoods in Agro-Ecological Regions I and II in Zambia	3.9 m tons of CO2 Avoided	$137.3 m	Yes
Uganda, Ghana, Nigeria	Acumen **Resilient** Agriculture *Fund*	10.0 m	$56.0 m	Yes
Namibia	Improving rangeland and *ecosystem management* practices of smallholder farmers under conditions of climate change in Sesfontein, Fransfontein, and Warmquelle areas	44.4 k	$10.0 m	No
Mali	Africa *Hydromet* Program – Strengthening Climate **Resilience** in Sub-Saharan Africa: Mali	5.3 m	$27.3 m	Yes
Burkina Faso	Africa *Hydromet* Program – Strengthening Climate **Resilience** in Sub-Saharan Africa: Burkina Faso	7.0 m	$25.0 m	Yes
Morocco	Saiss *Water Conservation* Project Improving the climate **resilience** of agricultural systems in the Saiss Plain.	2.2 m	$253.6 m	Yes

Note: m = million, k = thousand.

It is also notable that what it means for food productions and consumptions to be resilient is not defined in any of the selected projects' documentations. In fact, it may be true that the term resilience does not point to the same thing across the 15 food security projects. As per the economics literature, there are more than one possible interpretations of the term. First, the term is often used in the agricultural insurance and subsidy designs in that a resilient farmer is one who can survive a threshold weather event, for example, an extreme drought or an extreme heat wave, through employing a variety of measures (Udry, 1995; Zilberman, 1998). Second, a resilient agricultural system is one that can endure the shift of the climate system from one to another with little or smaller economic loss than other systems (Seo, 2010a,b). In this definition, the shift of the climate system is a composite change rather than a singleton change, for example, an increase in global temperature in tandem with more frequent occurrences of extreme precipitation events (Seo, 2012b). The third and more drastic definition can be found in the catastrophe literature. A catastrophe system is one that cannot be recovered forever once the catastrophe strikes the system, that is, the tipping point is crossed once (Thom, 1975; Mandelbrot, 2001; Weitzman, 2009; Seo, 2018a).

In addition to the different interpretations of the term resilience adopted across the food security projects, each food security project is proposing a different strategy and technique for achieving the goal of resilience. The present author identified specific strategies and underlined them in Table 6.4. To summarize, the strategy for resilience is an "integrated" management for two GCF projects, a "diversification" for another project, a "community-based" management for another, an "ecosystem-based" management for another two projects, an "irrigation" system for another, climate "information services" for another, a creation of a "resilience fund" for another project, a "water conservation" for another, and a "hydromet" program for another two GCF projects.

Having described the pertinent details of the food security projects of the GCF, we are well-positioned to evaluate the projects on the ground of land/resource use efficiency. The most telling aspect of Table 6.8 with regard to the efficiency test is that none of the 16 food security projects is proposed on the basis of "efficiency," or "optimality," or "efficient adaptation," or "efficient uses" or "most profitable systems" or "best practices," taking into consideration the current and new climate systems (Mendelsohn et al., 1994; Seo, 2010a, 2016a,c). With absence of these rationales specified in the project documentations, we can almost certainly conclude that the GCF-funded food security projects will fail to pass the efficiency test. Stated more specifically, an individual GCF project will most likely fail to adapt efficiently—more correctly, fail to propose to adapt efficiently—to a future climate regime by switching to the most profitable practice or enterprise after a thoughtful deliberation of the new unfolding climate reality.

Empirically, we can examine the details of the GCF-selected food security projects to see if whether a grant to each of these projects was determined/allocated in a way to force the grant recipient to adopt the best, that is, optimal, system of agriculture, considering both one climate system today and another in the future. There is little, if not none, indication of such efforts across the food security projects.

The second point of evaluation is that the present author asks, by pursuing one step further the empirical examination discussed in the last paragraph, whether, rather than being an efficient and optimal strategy, each of the GCF grants creates an incentive for a recipient to take inefficient strategies and practices in responding to alterations in the climate system. The examinations reveal that many grants can create such perverse incentives. There is a strong theoretical reason for such unintended outcomes: the GCF grants are most often selectively distributed to the most vulnerable enterprises as well as the most vulnerable and impoverished populations in the recipient nations.

To clarify this point, let us consider the three grants that were awarded to the projects by Namibia, a southwestern African country whose ecosystems are dominantly arid and desert zones including the famed Namib Desert. The first project is entitled "Climate Resilient Agriculture in Three of the Vulnerable Extreme Northern Crop-growing Regions"; The second project is entitled "Empower to Adapt: Creating Climate-Change Resilient Livelihoods through Community-Based Natural Resource Management in Namibia"; The third project is entitled "Improving Rangeland and Ecosystem Management Practices of Smallholder Farmers under Conditions of Climate Change in Sesfontein, Fransfontein, and Warmquelle areas of the Republic of Namibia."

The three Namibian projects share one commonality: the GCF funding is directed to the most vulnerable region in the country, to the most vulnerable agricultural system of possible agricultural enterprises, and further to the most vulnerable population of the country. More concretely, the GCF Board chose for its grant allocations the most vulnerable northern regions of the country where the ecosystems are arid and desert-like, and chose the most vulnerable system of agriculture, that is, the crop system or the rangeland system, and further chose the smallholders of Sub-Saharan Africa (Reilly et al., 1996; Butt et al., 2005; Seo et al., 2009b; Kurukulasuriya et al., 2011).

The Sri Lankan project in Table 6.8 can be analyzed in the same way, which is entitled "Strengthening the Resilience of Smallholder Farmers in the Dry Zone to Climate Variability and Extreme Events through an Integrated Approach to Water Management." The GCF Board selected the most vulnerable zone, that is, the dry zones of the island, and chose the most vulnerable population of the country, that is, the smallholders, and further selected the most vulnerable crop system of the country, that is, the northern paddy rice system (Seo et al., 2005). The grant may end up with unintended but inefficient and distortive consequences: the international aid grant may encourage northern paddy farmers to increase the currently distressed system of agriculture.

From this analysis, we may deduce that the GCF funding principle in these projects is analogous to the principle of an agricultural insurance policy, for example, the US crop insurance and subsidy program. The purpose of the US federal agricultural subsidy is to protect the vulnerable populations of the country from recurring natural disasters that can be catastrophic to these populations (Sumner and Zulauf, 2012; Goodwin and Smith, 2014). The principle of insurance, however, should not be recommended as a principle for a climate change fund because the latter should be capable of forcing vulnerable populations to take best actions if the new climate system were to emerge. An insurance and subsidy program instead forces the recipients to remain in the present system of agriculture. This conclusion is particularly apt to the evaluation of the projects in Namibia and Sri Lanka.

The third point of evaluation is whether, with no identification of efficient actions, the GCF fund transfers would be more likely to be appropriated on nonclimate policy purposes. To be more specific, the GCF funding may end up as a development aid or an income redistribution scheme to the poor by an international organization, as such, no climate policy purposes are served.

There is some indication that such is the case. All GCF-funded projects on the results area of the health, food, and water security are classified as a "sustainable development" project (GCF, 2019e; Seo, 2019a). As such, all the food security projects funded by the GCF are regarded as a sustainable development project whose ultimate goal is a sustainable development of a recipient country. That is to say, the final goal of the GCF decisions is not a climate change policy response.

If the funding recipient should perceive the GCF monetary transfer as a foreign (development) aid to the poor countries or a justified income redistribution program to the global poor, it would drive the funding recipient to remain immovable from a current system of agriculture, for fear of losing the grants in the future, even if s/he could foretell that the current system will suffer largely in an altered climate system (Seo, 2014b, 2015b).

The fourth critical point of evaluation is whether the GCF monetary awards may force unintentionally mal-adaptation of a grant recipient. I will make this case by analyzing several funded projects. Consider the project by Morocco entitled "Irrigation Development and Adaptation of Irrigated Agriculture to Climate Change in Semi-arid Morocco." The grant to develop irrigation systems and irrigated agriculture in the semi-arid regions of Morocco would certainly lead the Moroccan farmers thereof to continue an irrigated crop system of agriculture and even switch from another agricultural system to the irrigated crop system.

Notwithstanding the predictable effects of the grant, the semi-arid climate zones in the African continent are predominantly of the ecosystem of rangelands, grasslands and deserts, which makes the regions more favorable to livestock systems of agriculture than crop systems as well as irrigated systems (Kazianga and Udry, 2006; Seo, 2010c, 2014a; Kafle et al., 2016). The international aid for the irrigation development in the semi-arid climate zones of Morocco, by compelling unwittingly the recipient farmers to reduce or remove the livestock portfolios and instead to increase irrigated crop portfolios, could make the recipient farmers more vulnerable to future climatic shifts (Byerlee and Eicher, 1997; World Bank, 2008, 2009; Seo, 2014b, 2016b). This chain of actions and responses through the GCF grant is a mal-adaptation to climate change.

Let us consider this time the project submitted by a Senegalese team entitled "Building the Climate Resilience of Food-insecure Smallholder Farmers through Integrated Management of Climate Risks." The specifics of the project are described as follows in the project documentation (GCF, 2019e):

Risk-reduction activities such as water and soil conservation measures, increased water availability, livelihood diversification and training on climate-resilient practices will be undertaken. These activities will be complemented by risk transfer through a weather index insurance programme that will transfer risk to the international market and provide farmers with compensation in case of climate shocks. The government of Senegal will contribute half the cost of the insurance premium to enrolling households.

The country of Senegal is the westernmost country of the African continent at the edge of the Sahara Desert and is highly depended on animal agriculture (Seo and Mendelsohn, 2008). The crux of the project proposal is certainly the weather index insurance which, if implemented at all, would be a massive governmental project by the Senegalese government.

The phrase "transfer risk to the international market" in the above means undoubtedly that the cost of the weather index insurance programme will be borne by the GCF and eventually by the handful of rich nations and private-sector international donors to the GCF. The project proposes that a half of the total cost of the insurance premium charged to individual participants to the program will be paid by the Senegal government, which implies that another half is paid by the GCF.

The weather index insurance programme is still a novel economic instrument, albeit old in its concept, and its successful applications to agriculture are sparse (Carter et al., 2015). As the designers hoped, the weather index insurance may force efficient adaptation behaviors of individual farmers if all index design issues were resolved, but even if such is the case, only when the participants to the program are forced to bear the consequences of their farming decisions including their weather predictions (Carter et al., 2015). These challenges are, however, monumental, to say the least.

In particular, if the premium cost of the participant would not be borne by him/herself, there would be no need for the Senegalese farmers to make efficient adaptation decisions. Many of the inefficient responses may turn out to be similar to those observed from the US crop insurance and subsidy program (Halcrow, 1949; Sumner and Zulauf, 2012). The salient difference between the Senegalese weather index insurance and the US crop subsidy is that the financial supporter of the former is not even a national government but is an "opaque" international agency.

Notwithstanding these challenges, an even more severe challenge will emerge from the program, which can be theoretically predicted. In short, the weather-index insurance program will force farmers to make farming decisions in response to yearly weather realizations while leaving aside the long-term climate system that is prevalent on the farmlands (Seo, 2013). The participants will keep making year-after-year inefficient decisions with reference to the climate system, compelled by the weather-index insurance subsidy.

Moving on, let us take a look at another program for evaluation: the Tajikistan's project entitled "Building Climate Resilience of Vulnerable and Food Insecure Communities through Capacity Strengthening and Livelihood Diversification in Mountainous Regions of Tajikistan." The proposal states that the country is witnessing increasing temperature, rainfall variability, and recurrent droughts and floods. The proposal further argues that the mountainous regions have low adaptive capacity because of inadequate climate information available and climate-sensitive sources of income. The project team proposes the following activities in return for the GCF funding:

> This initiative will introduce adaptation measures to address climate change effects leading to declines in agricultural yields, increases in food prices and reduced agricultural wages. It will focus on the most vulnerable and food insecure communities in the Rasht valley, Khatlon and Gorno-Badakhshan Autonomous Region (GBAO) regions. It will include an integrated approach to provide climate information services, capacity building, sustainable water management and resilient agriculture, and forestry.

In brief, the project will introduce adaptation measures in an integrated approach to the most vulnerable and food-insecure communities in the above-referenced regions. Evidently, the project focuses on "declines in agricultural yields" and "increases in food prices" resulting, according to the proposal, from future climatic changes. The GCF funding will therefore be appropriated to increase crop productions and crop yields in the selected region, that is, "the most vulnerable and food insecure communities" in the GBAO regions.

To proceed to an evaluation of the project, a brief background on the country is needed. Tajikistan is a landlocked, mountainous country in Central Asia in the north of Afghanistan and Pakistan. The country's geography is dominated by high mountains in the Pamir range while more than a half of the country's land area is situated above 3000 m in altitude above the sea level (Danielson and Gesch, 2011). As such, the forestry, both timber and nontimber products, is an important natural resource sector of Tajikistan.

Taking into consideration the natural and geographical conditions, the proposal seems to be a highly inefficient approach for adaptation to climate change in Tajikistan. Conditioned by the geographical and natural factors, the country has already favored noncrop agricultural investments, against crop investments, such as livestock management, forestry, precious natural resources, and specialty crops. To be more specific, only 7% of the country's land area is arable land and the country imports as much as 70% of its food consumption (FAO, 2000; WRI, 2005). For comparison, cotton, a specialty crop, is a predominant crop which accounts for 60% of agricultural production in the country and supports 75% of rural population. Of the valuable natural resources, aluminum production is the primary source of income for the country.

A GCF funding-induced redistribution of the country's investments away from these more efficient natural resource sectors to the inefficient crop sectors would make Tajikistan more insecure, that is, not less insecure, in terms of food production and income. For an analogy, imagine how inefficient it would be if an international big aid were to be given to the farmers in the Andes Mountain Ranges or in the Amazon Basin who proposed to slash and burn the forests or dam the rivers to create a vast maize growing area for food consumption in Brazil or other Andean countries (WRI, 2005; Seo, 2012a, 2016c)!

Up to this point, the present author applied the theory of land/resource use efficiency to the food security projects of the GCF to evaluate them. It goes without saying that the theory is capable of providing a solid test for the projects in other results areas defined by the Fund. To illustrate this, I will pick one project from the basket of water security projects summarized in Table 6.9. The water security projects selected for funding by the GCF are originated from small island nations such as Maldives, Fiji, and Grenada, as well as from the countries with well-recognized water-supply problems such as Bangladesh and Ethiopia.

As far as an illustration of a test of the land/resource use efficiency theory is concerned, it may suffice to end this section at this point with the completion of the evaluations of food security projects. From another vantage point, however, an

Table 6.9 Summary data on GCF-funded projects on water security for a resource use efficiency test.

Recipient countries	Project title	Expected contribution (# of beneficiaries)	Funding size (US$)	Duration (years)
Maldives	Support of Vulnerable Communities in Maldives to Manage Climate Change-Induced Water Shortages	105,000	$28.2 m	5 years
Fiji	Fiji Urban Water Supply and Wastewater Management Project	290,854	$405.1 m	7 years
Colombia	Scaling Up Climate Resilient Water Management Practices for Vulnerable Communities in La Mojana	405.6 k	$117.2 m	8 years
Ethiopia	Responding to the Increasing Risk of **Drought**: Building **Gender-responsive** Resilience of the Most Vulnerable Communities	1.3 m	$50.0 m	5 years
Grenada	Climate-Resilient Water Sector in Grenada	107.3 k	$51.6 m	6 years
Bangladesh	Enhancing adaptive capacities of coastal communities, **especially women**, to cope with climate change induced salinity	719.2 k	$33.0 m	6 years

Note: m = million, k = thousand.

evaluation of the water security projects is highly pertinent to and cannot be omitted from this chapter. This is because the water security projects will lead us to the other important global resources, beside the land-based ecosystems and resources on which the discussions of this chapter and the book have concentrated up to this point, that is, ocean-based or coastal ecosystems and resources (Emanuel, 2008; Church et al., 2013; Bakkensen and Mendelsohn, 2016). Maldives, Fiji, and Grenada are each a small island nation in the middle of a big Ocean while Bangladesh is noted for its low-lying coastal zones.

The GCF-funded water security projects in the table all expressed a clear objective of improving water security in each project-undertaking nation through enhanced access to drinking water, increased water supply, and improved sewage systems. The suggested technologies and measures for achieving this goal include harnessing rainwater and groundwater, a desalination plant, a dam, access channels to a dam, a wastewater treatment plant, solar-powered pumps, and a water tariff.

Of the six water security projects, we will have a closer look at the project in Maldives entitled "Support of Vulnerable Communities in Maldives to Manage Climate Change-Induced Water Shortages." Maldives, located in South Indian Ocean, is an archipelago consisting of 1190 small, low-lying coral islands. It is also one of the most popular tourist destinations in the world. The country is one of the smallest nations in the world with its land area of 298 km^2, which is about 1/200th of Sri Lanka (World Bank, 2019). The Maldives project is described thus (GCF, 2019e):

> There are high levels of poverty on the outer islands, which experience drinking water shortages during the dry season. . . . . . .; Groundwater becomes increasingly saline as a result of climate change-induced sea level rise (3.1 mm/year) and variable rainfall patterns. . . . . .; The project will scale up an integrated water supply system based on rainwater, groundwater, and desalinated water into a low-cost delivery system for vulnerable households. This will provide uninterrupted supply to 49 islands that currently rely on emergency water deliveries for three months of each year.

In brief, drinking water shortages occur during the dry season on the outer islands, lasting about three months each year. The increased salinity in groundwater will become increasingly problematic owing to climate change-induced sea level rise. The project will build an integrated water supply system including desalination plants. The total grant awarded for the project is US$ 28 million for 5 years.

First, it seems evident that the country's priority should rather be a construction of coastal walls to protect its citizens from sea level rises and inundations because of the country being an archipelago comprising thousands of small atolls as well as being the world's lowest-elevation country with an average elevation of 1.8 m above the sea level (Danielson and Gesch, 2011). Having said that, the construction of a multitude of coastal walls, that is, a wall for each island, would be almost unrealistic for the Maldives because the country's tourist beaches of serendipity will be gone and replaced by ugly walls while a large number of small islands makes it very costly to build even such unattractive walls (Ng and Mendelsohn, 2006).

In spite of this, considering a farther time-horizon by which the regional sea level is projected to rise by more than a meter and even as high as seven meters (Kopp et al., 2014), the proposed integrated water security project could be analyzed to be highly inefficient without the coastal protection firsthand against the rising seas.

The four desalination plants proposed in the document may appear to provide an alternative solution to the conundrum since the technology offers a way to desalinate the salt water into drinking water (Carlsbad Desalination Plant, 2016). However, the desalination approach may turn out to be highly expensive and inefficient. First, it does not provide any protection of its citizens from the threats of sea level rise and inundations. The human and ecosystem cost of such changes can be very high without coastal protections (Yohe and Schlesinger, 1998). Second, the desalination plants may be too costly to build. The Carlsbad desalination plant in San Diego, California took 14 years to construct, costing the State US$ 1 billion for a single plant. In addition, the operational cost of a desalination plant is relatively high owing to heavy energy uses in its various processes (NRC, 2008). Further, without the sea walls, the additional risk to the country from surges and inundations that could be caused by global warming-induced hurricane activities in Indian Ocean as well as earthquake-induced tsunamis will be far amplified (Seo and Bakkensen, 2017; Seo, 2017c, 2018b).

6.7   International fairness in the theory of a global public good fund

This chapter has developed the economic theory of a global public good fund and subsequently provided an ensemble of evaluations on the GCF's funding decisions and proposed activities. The GCF is an ambitious global-scale collaboration and may turn out to be a transcendental global public good fund, for which reason the Fund provides an unparalleled platform for researchers to advance a theory of a global public good fund.

Can a global public good fund such as the GCF be an alternative policy solution to the problem of a global public good, say, global warming? The ensemble of evaluations conducted in this chapter based on the criteria of the theory of public expenditure, the theory of efficient land/resource uses, and the theory of public adaptation forces us to conclude that the GCF will not be a reliable alternative solution to the problem of global warming that enthusiasts may have hoped it to be.

At the heart of its failure lies the difficulty of modeling and predicting behavioral changes at varied levels of decision-making in response to climatic changes as well as economic consequences of such changes. The study of these behaviors and consequences is the field of the economics of adaptation to climate change (Mendelsohn, 2000; Hanemann, 2000; Seo, 2015a, 2016d). Without this capability, it would turn out to be impossible for the 24-member GCF Board to disburse a hundred billion dollars each year efficiently to a large pool of projects that would be undertaken all over the world.

Even more critically, the changes of recipients' behaviors that would be caused by the GCF Board's decisions and grant allocations would turn out to be unpredictable with the absence of the solid economics of adaptation behaviors (Seo, 2015b, 2019a). The grant allocations began only recently in November 2015. The outcomes of the GCF grants will begin to be emerging over the next decade and beyond, which may turn out to be a big surprise to the observers and the designers of the GCF.

Readers may have noticed that one component of the GCF and many other global funds explained in Section 6.2, which is in fact prominent across all of these funds, has been left out from the discussion in this chapter up to this point. That component, which albeit has taken on different terms and forms across the global funds, can be encapsulated by the principle of international fairness.

The principle of international fairness embedded in all the major treaties and agreements discussed in this book can be traced back to the very first UN conference on the environment: The Paris Agreement in 2015, the Copenhagen Accord in 2009, the Kyoto Protocol in 1997, the UNFCCC in 1992, the Villach Climate Conference in 1985, and the UN Conference on human environment in Stockholm in 1972 (UN, 1972; WMO, 1985; UNFCCC, 1992, 1997, 2009, 2015).

Across the UNFCCC conferences, this principle was referred to as the first principle of Article 3 which defined the principles of the organization and is expressed as the principle of "common but differentiated responsibilities (UNFCCC, 1992)." The Article reads:

> *The Parties should protect the climate system for the benefit of present and future generations of humankind, on the basis of equity and in accordance with their common but differentiated responsibilities and respective capabilities. Accordingly, the developed country Parties should take the lead in combating climate change and the adverse effects thereof.*

This principle has evolved since 1992 over the course of three decades of UN-led climate negotiations to become the thorniest issue of all. To summarize the tug-of-wars surrounding this principle in a rudimentary manner, negotiators from developing nations argued that a GCF-like monetary aid should be preceded before any global climate agreement is signed while developed nations called for equally ambitious legally binding mitigation commitments from rapidly growing developing economies. This tug-war has, in effect, derailed many ambitious potential UN climate treaties and agreements including the Kyoto Protocol in 1997, the Copenhagen Conference in 2009, and the Paris Conference in 2015 (Nordhaus, 2001, 2010; Seo, 2017a,b, 2019b).

The creation of the Copenhagen GCF after the collapse of negotiations at Copenhagen Conference in 2009 because of the disputes between developed nation parties and developing nation parties regarding the above-stated first principle meant that the GCF should evolve as a primary financial instrument of the

UNFCCC to bridge the big gap between the two parties in ways to help the UNFCCC to accomplish a global agreement and enforce it (GCF, 2011; UNFCCC, 2015; Seo, 2017a).

The evaluations performed in this chapter amply confirm that the GCF has indeed evolved in such a direction as envisioned by the founders. That is, the GCF has turned out to be a financial aid mechanism to poor nations in return for participation in the Paris Agreement. However, the GCF may become a big burden to future climate change policy designs as well as a big obstacle to economic growth of poor nations, for the reasons emphasized repeatedly throughout this chapter.

The first principle of the Article 3 of the UNFCCC can be traced back, as noted before, to the earlier UN-led climate and environmental conferences. The first climate change conference which is widely credited for the creation of the Intergovernmental Panel on Climate Change (IPCC) took place in Villach, Austria in 1985. The IPCC was awarded the Nobel Peace Prize in 2007, along with Al Gore. The Villach Conference was formally titled as "The International Conference on the Assessment of the Role of Carbon Dioxide and of Other Greenhouse Gases in Climate Variations and Associated Impacts." The Working Group V, which was the Panel on Socio-Economic Impacts, describes the first principle rather modestly as follows (WMO, 1985):

> In view of the fact that projected life-spans of many long-lived economic investments . . . . . ., it is essential that climate considerations be incorporated into the development process at the earliest possible stage. It is cautioned that solutions contemplated must not neglect the particular needs of developing countries of the low-latitude regions, ... Also, attention has to be paid to such countries' legitimate development needs, the satisfaction of which might result in major increase in fossil fuel use and carbon dioxide releases unless efforts are made to improve energy efficiency. Application of regulatory measures under such circumstances could severely hamper development plans and inflict upon such nations additional costs which are beyond their capacity to absorb.

The modest language of the Villach Conference regarding the first principle can be attributed to the fact that, at the time of the Conference in 1985, no participant seemed to foresee a future climate change policy that can be adopted and implemented as a truly grand global scale policy. The Villach conference, as the title indicates, focused on the greenhouse effects of different gases and their impacts, leaving aside policy options.

The first principle can be further traced back to the initial United Nations conference on the human environment held in Stockholm, Sweden in 1972 (UN, 1972). The Stockholm Conference declared 20 principles of the UN actions on the environment, of which principles 11 and 12 are concerned with the possible conflicts between development and environment in developing countries:

> The environmental policies of all States should enhance and not adversely affect the present or future development potential of developing countries, nor should they

hamper the attainment of better living conditions for all, and appropriate steps should be taken by States and international organizations with a view to reaching agreement on meeting the possible national and international economic consequences resulting from the application of environmental measures (Principle 11).

Resources should be made available to preserve and improve the environment, taking into account the circumstances and particular requirements of developing countries and any costs which may emanate from their incorporating environmental safeguards into their development planning and the need for making available to them, upon their request, additional international technical and financial assistance for this purpose (Principle 12).

The Stockholm Principle 12 is perhaps even stronger than the first principle of Article 3 of the UNFCCC because it declares the international technical and financial assistance "should" be available upon the request of developing countries while the first principle of "common but differentiated responsibilities" is not unequivocal. Neither the latter refers to the financial assistance directly.

However, a policy scale of the first principle of the UNFCCC is far greater than that of the Principle 12 of the Stockholm Conference. The climate policy should be pervasive across all nations on Earth while the environmental policy that was addressed by the Stockholm Conference is undertaken mostly at a national scale (Baumol and Oates, 1988). The intrusiveness of the climate policy into national decisions is far greater (Nordhaus, 1994).

Notwithstanding, the Stockholm principles regarding the development and environment tradeoff for the developing countries have dominated all subsequent conferences by the United Nations regardless of them being concerned on environment, sustainability, or global climate change (WMO, 1985; UNFCCC, 1992, 2015). As the history of climate conferences surveyed in this chapter reveals, the Stockholm principles have become the greatest barrier to a climate policy treaty and the GCF decisions.

The supporters of the UN climate conferences and the GCF may argue that the GCF's funding allocation decisions are faithful to the first principle of the Article 3 of the UNFCCC. However, they should be aware that the Stockholm principles which are the root of the first principle of the UNFCCC are not appropriate for a global climate change policy-making. As far as their pervasiveness and intrusiveness are concerned, the Stockholm principle is to the Hudson river in New York what the UNFCCC principle is to the global Ocean.

A faithful adherence to the first principle forces the GCF unfit and unable to address the fundamental aspects of climate change policy-making: how the global community should manage the global warming problem in the most efficient way and how individuals and communities should adapt to changes in the climate system in an efficient manner (Nordhaus, 1994; Seo, 2016d, 2017a).

Further, the evaluations in this chapter warns once again the policy-makers of global warming and other globally shared goods of the impossibility of managing such a large-scale policy quandary composed of billions of micro decisions by reliance upon the power of a committee of one or two.

References

Ainsworth, E.A., Long, S.P., 2005. What have we learned from 15 years of free-air CO_2 enrichment (FACE)? A meta-analysis of the responses of photosynthesis, canopy properties and plant production to rising CO_2. N. Phytologist 165, 351−372.

Akasaki, I., Amano, H., Nakamura, S., 2014. Blue LEDs: Filling the World With New Light. Nobel Prize Lecture. The Nobel Foundation, Stockholm. Available at: <http://www.nobelprize.org/nobel_prizes/physics/laureates/2014/popular-physicsprize2014.pdf>.

Bakkensen, L.A., Mendelsohn, R., 2016. Risk and adaptation: evidence from global hurricane damages and fatalities. J. Assoc. Env. Resour. Econ. 3, 555−587.

Barrett, S., 2003. Environment and Statecraft: The Strategy of Environmental Treaty. Oxford University Press, Oxford.

Baumol, W.J., Oates, O.A., 1988. The Theory of Environmental Policy, second ed. Cambridge University Press, Cambridge.

Boden, T.A., Marland, G., Andres, R.J., 2017. Global, regional, and national fossil-fuel CO2 emissions. Oak Ridge National Laboratory, U.S. Department of Energy, Oak Ridge, TN. https://doi.org/10.3334/CDIAC/00001_V2017.

Buchanan, J.M., 1965. An economic theory of clubs. Economica 32, 1−24.

Butt, T.A., McCarl, B.A., Angerer, J., Dyke, P.T., Stuth, J.W., 2005. The economic and food security implications of climate change in Mali. Clim. Change 68, 355−378.

Byerlee, D., Eicher, C.K., 1997. Africa's Emerging Maize Revolution. Lynne Rienner Publishers Inc., USA.

California Air Resources Board (CARB), 2019. Assembly bill (AB) compliance offset program. ARB, CA. Accessed from: <https://ww3.arb.ca.gov/cc/capandtrade/offsets/offsets.htm>.

Carlsbad Desalination Plant, 2016. DESAL-101. Claude "Bud" Lewis Carlsbad Desalination Plant. San Diego, CA.

Carraro, C., Eyckmans, J., Finus, N., 2006. Optimal transfers and participation decisions in international environmental agreements. Rev. Int. Organ. 379−396.

Carter, M., de Janvry, A., Sadoulet, E., Sarris, A., 2015. Index-based weather insurance for developing countries: a review of evidence and a set of propositions for up-scaling. Rev. Econ. Dev. 23, 5−57.

Chan, N.W., 2019. Funding global environmental public goods through multilateral financial mechanisms. Environ. Resour. Econ. 73, 515−531.

Church, J.A., Clark, P.U., Cazenave, A., Gregory, J.M., Jevrejeva, S., Levermann, A., et al., 2013. Sea level change. Climate Change 2013: The Physical Science Basis. Cambridge University Press, Cambridge.

Coase, R., 1960. The problem of social costs. J. Law Econ. 3, 1−44.

Conning, J., Udry, C., 2007. Rural financial markets in developing countries. In: Evenson, R., Pingali, P. (Eds.), Handbook of Agricultural Economics, vol. 3, 2857−2908.

Conte, M.N., Kotchen, M.J., 2010. Explaining the price of voluntary carbon offsets. Clim. Change Econ. 1, 93−111.

Danielson, J.J., Gesch, D.B., 2011. Global multi-resolution terrain elevation data 2010 (GMTED2010). US Geo-logical Survey Open-File Report 2011−1073, 26 p.

Department of Energy (DOE), 2015. Chapter 5: Increasing Efficiency of Building Systems and Technologies. Quadrennial Technology Review: An Assessment of Energy Technologies and Research Opportunities. DOE, Washington, DC.

Deutsche Welle (DW), 2018. Australia Ditches Greenhouse Gas Emissions Target. Published on 20 August, 2018.

Dinar, A., Campbell, M.B., Zilberman, D., 1992. Adoption of improved irrigation and drainage reduction technologies under limiting environmental conditions. Environ. Resour. Econ. 2, 373–398.

Economic Times of India, 2015. Green climate fund of $100 billion/year not enough to tackle climate change: India. Published on July 14, 2015. Accessed from: <https://economic-times.indiatimes.com/news/politics-and-nation/green-climate-fund-of-100-billion/year-not-enoughto-tackle-climate-change-india/articleshow/48070235.cms>.

Ellerman, A.D., Marcantonini, C., Zaklan, A., 2016. The European Union emissions trading system: ten years and counting. Rev. Environ. Econ. Policy 10, 89–107.

Emanuel, K., 2008. The hurricane–climate connection. Bulletin of the American Meteorological Society 89: ES10–ES20.

European Commission (EC), 2018. EU ETS Handbook. European Commission, Brussels.

Food and Agriculture Organization (FAO), 2000. FAO/WFP Crop and Food Supply Assessment Mission to Tajikistan. FAO, Rome, Italy.

Global Carbon Project (GCP), 2017. Global Carbon Budget 2017. Available at: <http://www.globalcarbonproject.org/carbonbudget/index.htm>.

Global Environment Facility (GEF), 2017. Comparative Advantage, Adequacy of Funding/Financing, Health of the Expanded GEF Partnership and Governance Structure. GEF, UNDP, New York.

GoFundMe, 2017. GoFundMe 2017: a year in giving. The GoFundMe, Red Wood City, California. Accessed from: <https://www.gofundme.com/2017>.

Goodwin, B.K., Smith, V.H., 2014. Theme overview: the 2014 Farm Bill—an economic welfare disaster or triumph? Choices 29 (3), 1–4.

Goulder, L., 2007. California's Bold New Climate Policy. Economist Voice 4. Article 5.

Graziano, M., Gillingham, K., 2015. Spatial patterns of solar photovoltaic system adoption: the influence of neighbors and the built environment. J. Econ. Geogr. 15, 815–839.

Green Climate Fund (GCF), 2011. Governing Instrument for the Green Climate Fund. GCF, Songdo City, South Korea.

Green Climate Fund (GCF), 2019a. About the Fund. GCF, Songdo City, South Korea.

Green Climate Fund (GCF), 2019b. Annex III: Investment Framework. GCF, Songdo City, South Korea.

Green Climate Fund (GCF), 2019c. Annex IX: Results Management Framework. GCF, Songdo City, South Korea.

Green Climate Fund (GCF), 2019d. Status of Pledges and Contributions Made to the Green Climate Fund. GCF, Songdo City, South Korea.

Green Climate Fund (GCF), 2019e. Projects + Programmes. GCF, Songdo City, South Korea. Accessed from: <https://www.greenclimate.fund/what-we-do/projects-programmes>.

Hahn, R.W., Dudley, P.M., 2007. How well does the U.S. government do benefit-cost analysis? Rev. Environ. Econ. Policy 1: 192–211.

Halcrow, H.G., 1949. Actuarial structures for crop insurance. J. Farm. Econ. 31, 418–443.

Hanemann, W.M., 2000. Adaptation and its management. Clim. Change 45, 571–581.

Hartwick, J.M., 1977. Intergenerational equity and the investment of rents from exhaustible resources. Am. Econ. Rev. 67, 972–974.

Hartwick, J.M., Olewiler, N.D., 1997. The Economics of Natural Resource Use, second ed. Pearson, New York.

Hsu, A., Rosengarten, C., Weinfurter, A., Xie, Y., Musolino, E., Murdock, H.E., 2017. Renewable Energy and Energy Efficiency in Developing Countries: Contributions to Reducing Global Emissions. United Nations Environment Programme, Nairobi, Kenya.

Intergovernmental Panel on Climate Change (IPCC), 2014. Climate change 2014: the physical science basis. The Fifth Assessment Report of the IPCC. Cambridge University Press, Cambridge.

Intergovernmental Panel on Climate Change (IPCC), 2018. Special Report on Global Warming of 1.5 °C. Cambridge University Press, Cambridge.

Joskow, P.L., 2012. Creating a smarter U.S. electricity grid. J. Econ. Perspect. 26, 29—48.

Kafle, K., Winter-Nelson, A., Goldsmith, P., 2016. Does 25 cents more per day make a difference? The impact of livestock transfer and development in rural Zambia. Food Policy 63, 62—72.

Kazianga, H., Udry, C., 2006. Consumption smoothing? Livestock, insurance, and drought in rural Burkina Faso. J. Dev. Econ. 79, 413—446.

Kopp, R.E., Horton, R.M., Little, C.M., Mitrovica, J.X., Oppenheimer, M., Rasmussen, D.J., et al., 2014. Probabilistic 21st and 22nd century sea-level projections at a global network of tide-gauge sites. Earth's Future 2, 383—406.

Kurukulasuriya, P., Kala, N., Mendelsohn, R., 2011. Adaptation and climate change impacts: a structural Ricardian model of irrigation and farm income in Africa. Clim. Change Econ. 2, 149—174.

Mandelbrot, B., 2001. Scaling in financial prices: I. Tails and dependence. Quant. Financ. 1, 113—123.

Medecins Sans Frontieres (MSF), 2017. International Financial Report. The MSF, Geneva.

Mendelsohn, R., 2000. Efficient adaptation to climate change. Clim. Change 45, 583—600.

Mendelsohn, R., Neumann, J., 1999. The Impact of Climate Change on the United States Economy. Cambridge University Press, Cambridge.

Mendelsohn, R., Nordhaus, W., Shaw, D., 1994. The impact of global warming on agriculture: a Ricardian analysis. Am. Econ. Rev. 84, 753—771.

Metcalf, G., 2009. Designing a carbon tax to reduce US greenhouse gas emissions. Rev. Environ. Econ. Policy 3, 63—83.

Mollick, E., 2014. The dynamics of crowdfunding: an exploratory study. J. Bus. Venturing 29, 1—16.

Muller, N.Z., Mendelsohn, R., 2009. Efficient pollution regulation: getting the prices right. Am. Econ. Rev. 99, 1714—1739.

Nakicenovic, N., Davidson, O., Davis, G., Grubler, A., Kram, T., La Rovere, E.L., et al., 2000. Emissions Scenarios. A Special Report of Working Group III of the Intergovernmental Panel on Climate Change, Geneva, Switzerland.

National Research Council, 2008. Desalination: A National Perspective. National Academies Press, Washington DC.

New York Times (NYT), 2012. In California, A Grand Experiment to Rein in Climate Change. Published on October 13, 2012. NYT, New York.

New York Times (NYT), 2009a. An Air of Frustration for Europe at Climate Talks. Published on Dec 21, 2009. NYT, New York.

New York Times (NYT), 2009b. Hillary Clinton Pledges $100B for Developing Countries. Published on Dec 17, 2009. NYT, New York.

New York Times (NYT), 2016. The Obama Era: 'Terrifying' path of climate crisis weighs on Obama. Published on September 8, 2016.

Ng, N.-S., Mendelsohn, R., 2006. The economic impact of sea-level rise on nonmarket lands in Singapore. Ambio 35, 289—296.

Nordhaus, W., 1992. An optimal transition path for controlling greenhouse gases. Science 258, 1315—1319.

Nordhaus, W., 1994. Managing the Global Commons. MIT Press, Cambridge, MA.

Nordhaus, W., 2001. Global warming economics. Science 294, 1283−1284.

Nordhaus, W.D., 2008. A Question of Balance—Weighing the Options on Global Warming Policies. Yale University Press, New Haven, CT.

Nordhaus, W., 2010. Economic aspects of global warming in a Post-Copenhagen environment. Proc. Natl. Acad. Sci. U. S. A. 107, 11721−11726.

Nordhaus, W., 2015. Climate clubs: overcoming free-riding in international climate policy. Am. Econ. Rev. 105 (4), 1339−1370.

Ostrom, E., 1990. Governing the Commons: The Evolution of Institutions for Collective Action. Cambridge University Press, Cambridge.

Pareto, V., 1906. In: Montesano, A., Zanni, A., Bruni, L., Chipman, J.S., McLure, M. (Eds.), Manual for Political Economy, 2014. Oxford University Press, Oxford.

Parry, M.L., Rosenzweig, C.P., Iglesias, A., Livermore, M., Fischer, G., 2004. Effects of climate change on global food production under SRES emissions and socioeconomic scenarios. Glob. Environ. Change 14, 53−67.

Pigou, A.C., 1920. Economics of Welfare. Macmillan and Co, London.

Reich, P.B., Hobbie, S.E., Lee, T.D., Pastore, M.A., 2018. Unexpected reversal of C3 versus C4 grass response to elevated CO_2 during a 20-year field experiment. Science 360, 317−320.

Reilly, J., Baethgen, W., Chege, F., Van de Geijn, S., Enda, L., Iglesias, A., et al., 1996. Agriculture in a changing climate: impacts and adaptations. Climate Change 1995: Impacts, Adaptations, and Mitigation of Climate Change. Cambridge University Press, Cambridge.

Ricardo, D., 1817. On the Principles of Political Economy and Taxation. John Murray, London, UK.

Samuelson, P., 1954. The pure theory of public expenditure. Rev. Econ. Stat. 36, 387−389.

Samuelson, P., 1955. Diagrammatic exposition of a theory of public expenditure. Rev. Econ. Stat. 37, 350−356.

Samuelson, P., Nordhaus, W., 2009. Economics, ninteenth ed McGraw-Hill Education, New York.

Schaefer, H., Fletcher, S.E.M., Veidt, C., et al., 2016. A 21st century shift from fossil-fuel to biogenic methane emissions indicated by $^{13}CH_4$. Science 352, 80−84.

Schoengold, K., Zilberman, D., 2007. The economics of water, irrigation, and development. In: Evenson, R., Pingali, P. (Eds.), Handbook of Agricultural Economics, vol. 3, 2933−2977.

Seo, S.N., 2010a. A microeconometric analysis of adapting portfolios to climate change: adoption of agricultural systems in Latin America. Appl. Econ. Perspect. Policy 32, 489−514.

Seo, S.N., 2010b. Is an integrated farm more resilient against climate change? A microeconometric analysis of portfolio diversification in African agriculture? Food Policy 35, 32−40.

Seo, S.N., 2010c. Managing forests, livestock, and crops under global warming: a microeconometric analysis of land use changes in Africa. Aust. J. Agri. Resour. Econ. 54 (2), 239−258.

Seo, S.N., 2011. An analysis of public adaptation to climate change using agricultural water schemes in South America. Ecol. Econ. 70, 825−834.

Seo, S.N., 2012a. Adaptation behaviors across ecosystems under global warming: a spatial micro-econometric model of the rural economy in South America. Pap. Reg. Sci. 91, 849−871.

Seo, S.N., 2012b. Decision making under climate risks: an analysis of sub-Saharan farmers' adaptation behaviors. Weather Clim. Soc. 4, 285–299.

Seo, S.N., 2013. An essay on the impact of climate change on US agriculture: weather fluctuations, climatic shifts, and adaptation strategies. Clim. Change 121, 115–124.

Seo, S.N., 2014a. Evaluation of agro-ecological zone methods for the study of climate change with micro farming decisions in sub-Saharan Africa. Eur. J. Agron. 52, 157–165.

Seo, S.N., 2014b. Adapting sensibly when global warming turns the field brown or blue: a comment on the 2014 IPCC Report. Econ. Aff. 34, 399–401.

Seo, S.N., 2015a. Micro-Behavioral Economics of Global Warming: Modeling Adaptation Strategies in Agricultural and Natural Resource Enterprises. Springer, Cham, Switzerland.

Seo, S.N., 2015b. Helping Low-Latitude, Poor Countries With Climate Change. Regulation. Winter 2015–2016, 6–8.

Seo, S.N., 2016a. Modeling farmer adaptations to climate change in South America: a micro-behavioral economic perspective. Environ. Ecol. Stat. 23, 1–21.

Seo, S.N., 2016b. Untold tales of goats in deadly Indian monsoons: adapt or rain-retreat under global warming? J. Extreme Events. Available from: https://doi.org/10.1142/S2345737616500019.

Seo, S.N., 2016c. The micro-behavioral framework for estimating total damage of global warming on natural resource enterprises with full adaptations. J. Agr. Biol. Environ. Stat. 21, 328–347.

Seo, S.N., 2016d. Microbehavioral Econometric Methods: Theories, Models, and Applications for the Study of Environmental and Natural Resources. Academic Press (Elsevier); Amsterdam, the Netherlands.

Seo, S.N., 2017a. The Behavioral Economics of Climate Change: Adaptation Behaviors, Global Public Goods, Breakthrough Technologies, and Policy-Making. Academic Press (Elsevier); Amsterdam, The Netherlands.

Seo, S.N., 2017b. Beyond the Paris agreement: climate change policy negotiations and future directions. Reg. Sci. Policy Pract. 9, 121–140.

Seo, S.N., 2017c. Measuring policy benefits of the cyclone shelter program in North Indian ocean: protection from high winds or high storm surges? Clim. Change Econ. 8 (4), 1–18.

Seo, S.N., 2018a. Natural and Man-Made Catastrophes: Theories, Economics, and Policy Designs. Wiley-Blackwell, Oxford.

Seo, S.N., 2018b. Two tales of super-typhoons and super-wealth in Northwest Pacific: will global-warming-fueled cyclones ravage East and Southeast Asia? J. Extreme Events. Available from: https://doi.org/10.1142/S2345737618500124.

Seo, S.N., 2019a. The Economics of Global Allocations of the Green Climate Fund: An Assessment From Four Scientific Traditions of Modeling Adaptation Strategies. Springer Nature, Switzerland.

Seo, S.N., 2019b. Economic questions on global warming during the Trump years. J. Public. Aff. 19, e1914. Available from: https://doi.org/10.1002/pa.1914.

Seo, S.N., Bakkensen, L.A., 2017. Is tropical cyclone surge, not intensity, what kills so many people in South Asia? Weather Climate Soc. 9, 71–81.

Seo, S.N., Mendelsohn, R., 2008. Measuring impacts and adaptations to climate change: a structural Ricardian model of African livestock management. Agric. Econ. 38, 151–165.

Seo, S.N., Mendelsohn, R., Munasinghe, M., 2005. Climate change and agriculture in Sri Lanka: a Ricardian valuation. Environ. Dev. Econ. 10, 581–596.

Seo, S.N., Mendelsohn, R., Dinar, A., Kurukulasuriya, P., 2009a. Adapting to climate change mosaically: an analysis of African livestock management across Agro-Ecological Zones. B.E. J. Econ. Anal. Policy 7 (2), Article 4.

Seo, S.N., Mendelsohn, R., Dinar, A., Hassan, R., Kurukulasuriya, P., 2009b. A Ricardian analysis of the distribution of climate change impacts on agriculture across Agro-Ecological Zones in Africa. Environ. Resour. Econ. 43, 313–332.

Solow, R.M., 1974. Intergenerational equity and exhaustible resources. Rev. Econ. Stud. 41, 29–46.

Solow, R.M., 1993. An almost ideal step toward sustainability. Resour. Policy 19, 162–172.

Sumner, D.A., Zulauf, C., 2012. Economic & environmental effects of agricultural insurance programs. The Council on Food, Agricultural & Resource Economics (C-FARE), Washington, DC.

Thom, R., 1975. Structural Stability and Morphogenesis. Benjamin-Addison-Wesley, New York.

Tol, R.S.J., 2009. The economic effects of climate change. J. Econ. Perspect. 23, 29–51.

Udry, C., 1995. Risk and saving in Northern Nigeria. Am. Econ. Rev. 85, 1287–1300.

United Nations, 1945. Charter of the United Nations and Statue of the International Court of Justice. UN, San Francisco, CA.

United Nations, 1972. Report of the United Nations Conference on Human Environment. Stockholm, Sweden.

United Nations, 2000. United Nations Millennium Declaration. UN, New York.

United Nations Children's Fund (UNICEF), 2018. UNICEF integrated budget 2018–2021. The UNICEF, New York.

United Nations Development Program (UNDP), 2018. Our funding: top contributors. UNDP, New York. Accessed from: <http://www.undp.org/content/undp/en/home/funding/top-contributors.html>.

United Nations Environment Programme 2017. The emissions gap report 2017: A UN environment synthesis report. UNEP, Nairobi, Kenya.

United Nations Framework Convention on Climate Change (UNFCCC), 1992. United Nations Framework Convention on Climate Change. UNFCCC, New York.

United Nations Framework Convention on Climate Change (UNFCCC), 1997. Kyoto Protocol. UNFCCC, New York.

United Nations Framework Convention on Climate Change (UNFCCC), 2007. Report of the conference of the parties on its thirteenth session, held in Bali from 3 to 15 December 2007. UNFCCC, New York.

United Nations Framework Convention on Climate Change (UNFCCC), 2009. Copenhagen Accord. UNFCCC, New York.

United Nations Framework Convention on Climate Change (UNFCCC), 2010. Cancun Agreements. UNFCCC, New York.

United Nations Framework Convention on Climate Change (UNFCCC), 2011. Report of the transitional committee for the design of Green Climate Fund. UNFCCC, New York.

United Nations Framework Convention on Climate Change (UNFCCC), 2012. Decisions adopted by the Conference of the Parties on its eighteenth session, held in Doha from 26 November to 8 December 2012. UNFCCC, New York.

United Nations Framework Convention on Climate Change (UNFCCC), 2015. The Paris Agreement. Conference Of the Parties (COP) 21, UNFCCC, New York.

United Nations System Chief Executive Board (UNSCEB), 2018. UN system. UN, New York. Accessed from: <http://www.unsceb.org/directory>.

von Thunen, J.H., 1826. In: Wartenberg, Carla M. (Ed.), The Isolated State, 1966. Pergamon Press, Oxford, New York.

Weitzman, M.L., 2009. On modeling and interpreting the economics of catastrophic climate change. Rev. Econ. Stat. 91, 1−19.

White House, 2017. Statement by President Trump on the Paris Climate Accord. White House, Washington DC.

World Bank 2008. World Development Report 2008: Agriculture for Development. World Bank, Washington, DC.

World Bank, 2009. Awakening Africa's Sleeping Giant: Prospects for Commercial Agriculture in the Guinea Savannah Zone and Beyond. World Bank and FAO, Washington, DC.

World Bank, 2019. World Development Indicators. World Bank, Washington, DC.

World Food Programme (WFP), 2018. Contributions to WFP in 2017. The WFP, Rome. Accessed from: <https://www.wfp.org/funding/year/2017>.

World Meteorological Organization (WMO), 1985. Report of the international conference on the assessment of the role of carbon dioxide and of other greenhouse gases in climate variations and associated impacts. WMO, Villach, Austria.

World Resources Institute (WRI), 2005. World resources 2005: the wealth of the poor: managing ecosystems to fight poverty. WRI, Washington, DC.

Yohe, G.W., Schlesinger, M.E., 1998. Sea level change: the expected economic cost of protection or abandonment in the United States. Climatic Change 38, 337−342.

Zilberman, D., 1998. Agricultural and Environmental Policies: Economics of Production, Technology, Risk, Agriculture, and the Environment. The State University of New York -Oswego, NY.

The economics of globally shared goods 7

7.1 Introduction

Before we begin this core chapter, the present author feels obliged to congratulate you on having the patience to read through the preceding six chapters of this book which have covered the entire spectrum of the economics literature on public goods and global-scale public goods (Mas-Colell et al., 1995; Samuelson and Nordhaus, 2009; Mankiw, 2014). Chapter 2, The Economics of Public Goods and Club Goods, and Chapter 3, The Economics of Global-Scale Public Goods: Key Challenges and Theories, provided the survey of the economics of public and global public goods. Each of the Chapters 4−6 provided a distinct critique of the current economics thereof. This chapter integrates all the theories and critiques presented in the preceding chapters to formulate a "grand" economic theory of the economics of globally shared goods. The adjective grand in this chapter is chosen to imply an integrative and comprehensive approach of the theory.

This chapter begins with a clarification of the term a globally shared good in Section 7.2. As we reviewed in Chapter 3, The Economics of Global-Scale Public Goods: Key Challenges and Theories, there are three types of public goods in terms of their production technologies: best-shot, weakest-link, cumulative (Hirshleifer, 1983). The most difficult public good policy problem is a provision of a global-scale public good with a cumulative production technology because the aggregate of individuals' actions across the globe should add up to become sufficient for a provision of a concerned public good. In the cumulative technology public good, all actors should, in theory, take on the responsibility of providing it.

The description of this chapter will proceed with a focus on a cumulative technology public good. The representative example of the type of a public good is a global climate change policy (Nordhaus, 2006). The climate change issue has also received the most attention globally among all other global-scale public goods by both the media and the academics (Nobel Prize, 2007, 2018).

The grand economic theory of a globally shared good starts with microbehavioral decisions of individuals faced with the specific global-scale problem. This is a unique perspective in that it does not start with a global entity or a global decision-making framework, which is the framework of the existing literature on the global public goods, as surveyed in Chapter 3, The Economics of Global-Scale Public Goods: Key Challenges and Theories (Nordhaus, 1994). With a creative mindset, the grand theory looks into micro-level decisions of individuals, in particular, changes of behaviors, who are directly affected by changes in the globally shared good, for example, the global climate system (Seo, 2006).

The Economics of Globally Shared and Public Goods. DOI: https://doi.org/10.1016/B978-0-12-819658-8.00007-X

This approach is contrarian to the prevalent economics literature but does have a deep root in the historical academic endeavors by economists. In fact, it can be said that the study of the relationship between the climate system and the human society began from the study of the relationship between farming activities and the climate/weather system in Africa as well as animal systems and the climate/weather system [Refer to Johnson, 1965; Ford and Katondo, 1977 for animal systems; and Dudal, 1980 for crop systems]. The microbehavioral economics of global warming has certainly tapped into this early literature (Seo, 2006, 2016a).

The study of human responses to the climate system can be further traced back to the beginning of the 20th century. At the time Svante Arrhenius formulated the relationship between carbon dioxide concentration and the global climate system, Huntington examined, regrettably in a racially charged way, the relationship between races/civilizations and the climate systems (Arrhenius, 1896; Huntington, 1915, 1917).

These early studies are only some of the examples of the humanity's enduring interests in understanding the relationship between climate/weather events and changes in anthropogenic activities. Considering this, it is not at all far-fetched to build a grand economic theory of globally shared goods on the foundation of microbehavioral decisions with regard to the global climate system.

The second pillar of the grand economic theory is the economics of foresight which is composed of forward-looking decisions and prescient decisions. The foresighted decisions are also microbehaviorally efficient decisions but incorporate a "very" long-term perspective in decision-making. The two types of foresighted decisions are the decisions taken today that would yield long-term benefits in the provision of a globally shared good, say, beyond the lifetime of the decision-maker (Seo, 2015a,b, 2017a,b).

A forward-looking decision is an efficient decision which yields a positive long-term benefit with regard to a provision of a globally shared good but, notwithstanding, does not force an individual decision-maker to commit to additional cost. The most salient example is the efficient adaptation taken by African or Latin American farmers to switch away from crops to forest activities in a hotter and wetter climate (Seo, 2010c, 2016c). A prescient decision is a foresighted decision which imposes additional cost to the decision-maker. An example of such decisions is a methane capture/reduction from farm animals or a switch to solar energy (Seo, 2017a,b).

The research on the efficient microbehavioral decisions with the long-term benefits for the provision of a globally shared good beyond one's lifetime, that is, the foresighted decisions, is sparse, which this chapter will clarify and highlight. As such, there can be large added value generated from the research in this direction. How such behaviors can be induced is another key topic to be addressed for the discussion of the second pillar.

The third pillar of the grand economic theory is what I call the greenhouse economics. Readers who have read through the book this far are certainly well aware of the greenhouse effects: the planet-warming effects of chemicals such as carbon dioxide, nitrous oxides, methane, fluorinated gases, ozone, and water vapor

(UNFCCC, 1992; Le Treut et al., 2007). The greenhouse economics that I explain in this chapter is a completely different interpretation of the greenhouse, as will be made clear presently.

The greenhouse economics in this chapter refers to the economics of technological advances that are directed to the utilization of changes in the climate system as well as the moderation of the earth's climate changes in an effort to reap the economic benefits from such technologies (Seo, 2017a,b). The term is coined from the observation that the greenhouse is the most primitive and earliest technology that appropriates the changes in the climate system (inside the greenhouse) for increased productions of numerous agricultural and horticultural products (Wittwer and Robb, 1964).

The list of technologies that are mentioned, and actually used, as potential greenhouse technologies is long: solar radiation reflectors, a direct air carbon-capture-storage-reuse, nuclear fusion and/or fission, solar energy, ocean fertilization, and wind energy (Martin et al., 1994; Lackner et al., 2012; MIT, 2015; NRC, 2015a, 2015b; ITER, 2015). In addition to the large-scale technologies, there is also a long list of technologies that can be applied at the micro-level, for example, at the farm level: methane capture and reduction technologies from ruminant animals, electric vehicles, and new lighting methods (NRC, 2013b; Akasaki et al., 2014; Hristov et al., 2015).

In the next sections, the present author will define the globally shared good, which will be followed by the elaborations of the three foundations of the economic theory of the globally shared goods: the economics of microbehavioral decisions in Section 7.3, the economics of foresighted decisions in Section 7.4, and the economics of greenhouse technologies in Section 7.5. In Fig. 7.1, readers can verify the three foundations or facets of the economics of the globally shared goods.

7.2 Globally shared goods

A globally shared good is commonly referred to as a global public good in the economics literature. A global public good is a geographically extended concept of a national public good which is simply called a public good. A public good is a term developed in contrast to a private good (Samuelson, 1955; Nordhaus, 2006).

As the reviews in Chapter 2, The Economics of Public Goods and Club Goods, and Chapter 3, The Economics of Global-Scale Public Goods: Key Challenges and Theories, clarified, a private good is an abbreviation of a private consumption good while a public good is an abbreviation of a public consumption good. A public consumption good was initially called a jointly consumed good or a joint consumption good (Samuelson, 1954). Before Samuelson, a public good was also referred to as a social good (Bowen, 1943).

The term "global public goods" was first used by Nordhaus in his commemorative work of Paul Samuelson entitled "Paul Samuelson and Global Public Goods"

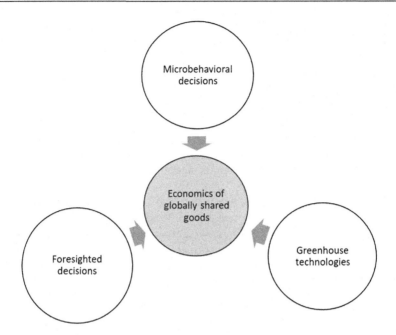

Figure 7.1 Foundations of the economics of globally shared goods.

as a straightforward extension of the Samuelson's pure theory. The term has been widely accepted in the economics (Nordhaus, 2001; Kaul et al., 2003; Barrett, 2003; Seo, 2017a,b).

The term, however, contains an undesirable connotation, which makes it not the most fitting terminology for the kinds of goods that the term refers to. This is because the term "public" in public goods refers to the public sector in contrast to the private sector which provides private goods. More directly, the economics literature associates the term public with the public sector, for example, public policy, public works, public administration (Mas-Colell et al., 1995; Mankiw, 2014). One of the earliest contributions to the theory of public expenditure by Richard Musgrave refers to the public economy as well as public finance: *The Voluntary Exchange Theory of Public Economy* (Musgrave, 1939) and *The Theory of Public Finance* (Musgrave, 1959).

The term "public goods" is the most apposite term when it is used in reference to the national economic context. For the global context, the term is not the most fitting one since there is no public sector in the global economy, as the term "global public goods" connotes. Further the term "global public goods" gives a wrong idea that there is a global government that has the power and authority to deal with the problem.

Reviewing the literature, Nordhaus seemed to have realized this problem early on when he instead used the term "global commons" in the 1980s and 1990s: "How fast should we graze the global commons" and "Managing the global commons" (Nordhaus, 1982, 1994). His earliest articles on global warming economics do not mention even "public goods," let alone "global public goods" (Nordhaus, 1977, 1982).

The first mention may have appeared in the paper entitled "A Regional Dynamic General-Equilibrium Model of Alternative Climate-Change Strategies" in which free-riding of individual nations becomes a key economic concept, in which the term appears just once (Nordhaus and Yang, 1996). Soon afterwards, the term became the standard and came to appear frequently and widely (Nordhaus and Boyer, 2000). The first mention of a "global public good" also appears once in Barrett, but as a footnote (Barrett, 1994).

It recently struck upon the present author that the Nordhaus' preference of the term global commons over global public goods may have been intentional and thoughtful. He may have had a glimpse into the fact that there is no public sector in a host of global-scale public good problems, nor a global government. By contrast, the term "commons" simply refers to the common space or resources shared but not owned by a group of people (Ostrom, 1990).

However, the commons is not as a widely used economics terminology as "goods" or "resources." We would like to develop a term that can be contrasted to "a private good." Further, the commons has a strong connotation of a "place" or "land." In addition, the commons is most often used in the context of a local community (Hardin, 1968; Ostrom, 1990).

Considering all these aspects, the present author thinks the most adequate term that can replace "a global public good" is "a globally shared good" or, in short, "a global good." This explains the title of this book "The Economics of Globally-shared (Goods) and Public Goods," from which the public goods refer to the national public goods and the globally shared goods to the global-scale public goods.

The term "globally shared goods" is also a better economics terminology in that it directly refers to "goods," a material product which is traded in market places all the time. The "commons" does not yield such a meaning. Further, the term "global public goods," also the commons to a lesser degree, is often mistakenly associated by various groups of people with an ethical imperative. The term "globally shared goods" can avoid such connotations and misunderstanding.

The evolution of the term "globally shared goods" is depicted in Fig. 7.2: from public economy, to social goods, to joint consumption goods, to public goods, to global commons, to global public goods, and then to globally shared goods.

This chapter develops a "grand" economic theory of the globally shared goods in a novel manner. That is, the theory elucidated in this chapter should be distinguishable from the host of the past theories reviewed in Chapter 2, The Economics of Public Goods and Club Goods, and Chapter 3, The Economics of Global-Scale Public Goods: Key Challenges and Theories. The economics of globally shared goods is built upon the foundation of the three critiques offered in Chapters 4–6. In other words, it shall be a theory that is capable of addressing the problems exposed in the preceding three chapters.

Of the range of globally shared goods, the economic theory developed in this chapter will be described with a focus on the goods whose production, or provision, calls for a cumulative production technology. In particular, the present author will rely on the economic problems of global warming and policy responses thereof as a platform for the descriptions of the theory developed in this chapter and its applications.

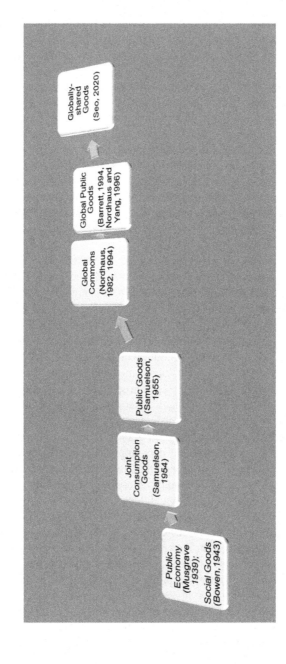

Figure 7.2 An evolution of the term globally shared goods.

The theory described in this chapter, however, can be extended with some modifications to the economic problems of the other types of global goods, for example, a planetary defense against asteroid collisions, preventing a nuclear war, and artificial intelligence, which is the task of the next chapter (Chapman and Morrison, 1994; Mills et al., 2008; NRC, 2010; Hawking et al., 2014).

7.3 Microbehavioral decisions for a globally shared good

A globally shared good, once provided, affects all individuals on the Planet in either a beneficial way or a harmful way. The same can be said of nonprovision of a globally shared good. Stated differently, like a public good, it has the characteristics of being nonrivalrous and nonexcludable (Bowen, 1943). That is, it is not possible to exclude someone from the benefits of a globally shared good. Nor does one's consumption of a globally shared good diminish the amount of the good available to the others (Mas-Colell et al., 1995).

The global climate system is such a globally shared good that affects all individuals on Earth economically. A disruption in the global climate system that forces the current regime to another regime would again impact all individuals on the Planet. A large disruption will be certain to harm the Planet economically.

At the level of the Planet as a whole, a policy question can be raised regarding the disruption in the climate system: how large will the climate disruption be? how harmful will such a disruption be on Earth economically? How should the "global community" respond in order to prevent the disruption or minimize the impact from it? These are the policy questions that economists and policy-makers have wrangled with for the past, at least, 30 years (UNFCCC, 1992; Nordhaus, 1994).

In the microbehavioral economics of a globally shared good, appropriate questions to be asked are rather at the level of an individual decision-maker, that is, a micro level (Seo, 2006, 2016a). In fact, the policy questions, above spelled out, cannot be answered without the questions at the micro level answered, more specifically, what adaptation actions will be undertaken by individual managers of resources and how effective such measures will be (Mendelsohn, 2000; Seo, 2010a, 2010c, 2017a,b).

Further, the questions at the micro level had been tackled by scientists and practitioners long before the aforementioned policy questions at the global level were raised. Animal scientists examined the relationships between farm animals and heat conditions (Johnson, 1965; Hahn, 1981). The distribution of tsetse flies across climate zones of Africa was mapped by biologists and epidemiologists (Ford and Katondo, 1977). Agronomists established the relationship between agroecological zones and climate factors in Africa (Dudal, 1980). A primary concern of these early studies was farm resources or, more concretely, a farm's management of its resources, which are influenced by changes in the global climate and/or weather system.

Although these studies were not an economic modeling, they clarified the importance of climate and weather factors in the farm management. They certainly pointed to the need for building an economic model of behavioral decisions at the micro (farm) level by integrating the scientific findings reported in these studies. The first of such economic models was titled "Modeling Farmer Responses to Climate Change" by the present author (Seo, 2006).

A detailed description of the microbehavioral models of climate change was already presented in Chapter 4, A Critique of the Economics of Global Public Goods: A Microbehavioral Theory and Model. Hence, in this chapter, we will proceed instead to highlight the key aspects of the microbehavioral models. In the microbehavioral economics, "micro" refers to an individual decision-maker and "behavioral" refers to her choices/selections from a basket of alternatives. The microbehavioral economics is therefore defined as the economic modeling of an individual decision-maker who chooses one alternative over the others from the basket of alternatives and resultantly experiences economic consequences of her choice (Seo, 2010a, 2016a, 2016b).

The key elements of the microbehavioral model are depicted in the diagram of Fig. 7.3. The decision unit of the microbehavioral economics/model is an individual manager. The microbehavioral model explains the variation of the decisions across the individual managers. There are three additional essential elements of the microbehavioral economics depicted in Fig. 7.3: the global climate system, the choice set of alternatives, and the set of the long-term profits that can be earned from the alternatives. Other circles in the diagram, either inside or outside the circle of a natural resource manager, can be interpreted as many other elements in the microbehavioral model than the above three essentials.

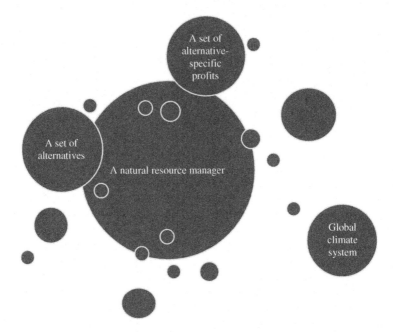

Figure 7.3 A diagram of the key elements of the microbehavioral model.

Let the global climate system at the present time be represented by Ω_0 and that in the future time be represented by $\Omega_{t,s}$ where the first subscript refers to a time period and the second subscript to a climate state. Then, the degree of a climatic change at a certain future time can be written in dependence on a climate state:

$$\Delta \Omega_{t,s} = \left| \Omega_{t,s} - \Omega_0 \right| \text{ for } s = 1, 2, \ldots, S. \tag{7.1}$$

The individual manager (i)'s decision is to choose an alternative (j) which yields the maximum long-term profit (Π), given the climate state ($\Omega_{t,s}$):

$$\text{ArgMax}_j \left\{ \Pi_{i1}(\Omega_{t,s}), \Pi_{i2}(\Omega_{t,s}), \ldots, \Pi_{iJ}(\Omega_{t,s}) \right\}. \tag{7.2}$$

The outcome of the manager's optimization decision is observable at the present climate system. All individuals' decisions at the present climate state as well as at the future climate state can be summarized by the following matrix:

$$\begin{bmatrix} \ldots & i & \ldots \\ \ldots & j & \ldots \\ \ldots & \Pi_{ij} & \ldots \end{bmatrix}_{\Omega_{t,s}} \tag{7.3}$$

The key outputs of the microbehavioral model are the following four: (1) adaptation behaviors or changes in the choice from one alternative to another; (2) alternative-specific economic impacts; (3) the economic impact at the farm level; and (4) the economic sector-wide impact. This is portrayed in the diagram of Fig. 7.4 as the four ever-larger eccentric circles that emanate from the bottom circle. The bottom circle is denoted as an application of the microbehavioral model.

An adaptation behavior is an individual decision-maker's switch from one alternative to another alternative caused by a change in the global climate system, which occurs when the following holds:

$$\text{ArgMax}_j \left\{ \Pi_{i1}\left(\Omega_{t,s}\right), \Pi_{i2}\left(\Omega_{t,s}\right), \ldots, \Pi_{iJ}\left(\Omega_{t,s}\right) \right\}$$

$$\neq \text{ArgMax}_k \left\{ \Pi_{i1}(\Omega_0), \Pi_{i2}(\Omega_0), \ldots, \Pi_{iK}(\Omega_0) \right\}. \tag{7.4}$$

For each alternative, the impact of a climatic shift is measured by the difference in the long-term profits generated from the alternative in the two climate states, for which the climate-profit response function for the alternative must be estimated before. The response function must account for the fact that the observed—by the researcher—profits of the alternative are only observable at the farms that selected the alternative, therefore, an estimation of the response function relying only on the observed profit data leads to biased parameter estimates (Heckman, 1979; Dubin and McFadden, 1984).

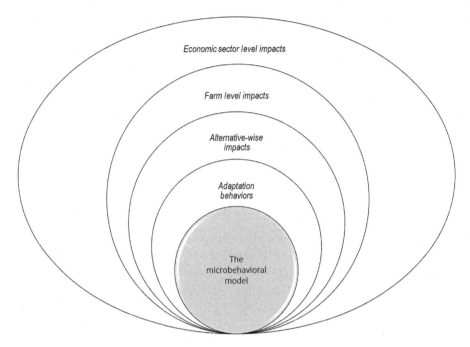

Figure 7.4 A diagram of the key outputs of the microbehavioral model.

A detailed description of the profit function estimation was provided in Chapter 4, A Critique of the Economics of Global Public Goods: A Microbehavioral Theory and Model. With the selection bias-corrected profit function estimated thus, the impact at the level of alternative j is then:

$$\Delta_j = \Pi_j\left(\Omega_{t,s}\right) - \Pi_j(\Omega_0). \tag{7.5}$$

The impact at the level of the farm i, *mutatis mutandis,* is then calculated as follows, with P_{ij} being the estimated probability of alternative j being chosen by the farm:

$$\Delta_i = \sum_j^J P_{ij}\left(\Omega_{t,s}\right) * \Pi_{ij}\left(\Omega_{t,s}\right) - \sum_j^J P_{ij}(\Omega_0) * \Pi_{ij}(\Omega_0). \tag{7.6}$$

The impact at the level of the economic sector is then calculated by summing the farm-level impacts across the farms in the economic sector:

$$\Delta = \sum_i^I \Delta_i \tag{7.7}$$

An application of the microbehavioral model is found since 2006 (Seo, 2006, 2010a, 2010b, 2010c; Seo and Mendelsohn, 2008). The most complete form of the model is found in the book and articles published in 2016 (Seo, 2016a, 2016b, 2016c). The major findings from these studies, to be summarized presently, will be sufficient to unpack the essence of the microbehavioral model and its policy applicability.

It is worth having a full understanding of, and perhaps appreciating, the seminal publication which was striking then and has come to launch the field of the microbehavioral economic model in climate change economics (Seo, 2006). The predominant argument at the time was that the impact of climate change will be devastating to the crop productions and especially those in the low-latitude tropical countries such as Sub-Saharan Africa (IPCC, 1990, 2014; Rosenzweig and Parry, 1994; Reilly et al., 1996; Fischer et al., 2005). The seminal paper has turned out to initiate a two-decade long process of refuting as well as qualifying this claim.

Of all the world regions, crop productions in Sub-Saharan African countries had long been reported to be highly unproductive because of climate and climate-induced soil factors (Dudal, 1980; IITA, 2000; Byerlee and Eicher, 1997; World Bank, 2008a, 2009). The seminal microbehavioral paper revealed strikingly that the Sahelian regions in Sub-Sahara, that is, arid, semi-arid, and desert agroecological zones in the Sahel, have already switched away from crop productions to animal productions such as beef cattle, goats, sheep, and chickens owing to the climate factor (Seo, 2006). The results showed that, although a hotter and drier climate in the future may hurt crop productions, it would increase livestock productions, especially goats and sheep (Seo and Mendelsohn, 2008; Seo et al., 2009a). Considering the crops and livestock together, the impact of climate change may not be as harmful as other economic models have predicted or even insignificant (Seo et al., 2009b).

The initial work clearly demonstrated the power of the microbehavioral model, which is, *inter alia*, its embedded capacity to be inclusive of all farm products, that is, crops, animals, and forests. A particular crop may suffer a great deal by the forecasted change, but the farm as a whole may not suffer much if the farm portfolio is well diversified or the farm can switch away from the vulnerable crop (Seo, 2014a, 2014b).

The seminal model was soon followed by the models that are inclusive of all enterprises in the agricultural sector. The first version was a three agricultural system model: a specialized crop system, a specialized livestock system, and a mixed crops—livestock system (Seo, 2010a, 2010b). The second version was a seven natural resource enterprise model: a crops-only, a livestock-only, a forest-only, a crops-forests, a crops-livestock, a livestock-forests, and a crops-livestock-forests enterprise (Seo, 2010c, 2012a, 2012b).

The two microbehavioral models were applied to both African agriculture and Latin American natural resource enterprises. The seven-enterprise model is superior to the three-system model in the study of the Latin American agriculture because of the continent's vast forest resources while the three-system model is preferred in the study of the African agriculture because of its heavy reliance on animal husbandry and vast arid/semi-arid climate zones (WRI, 2005).

The first key finding of the three agricultural system model is that farmers will adapt to changes in the climate system (Seo, 2010a, 2016b). When the temperature normal increases by 1°C, farmers switch from a crops-only system to a mixed crops—livestock system; when the precipitation normal increases by 1%, farmers switch from a livestock-only system to a crops-only system. These changes in choices can be explained by the economic impacts of climate change on the three agricultural systems. The damage from an increase in the temperature normal by 1°C on the crops-only system is more than twice larger than the damage on either the crops-livestock or on the livestock-only; the damage from an increase in the precipitation normal by 1% on the livestock-only system is larger than that on the crops-system or on the crops—livestock system.

The second key finding is that adaptation changes will be effective and certain systems will suffer more heavily than other systems. While the crops-only system will suffer by about 9.5% of its profit under the climate system forecasted by the Goddard Institute of Spatial Studies (GISS) (Schmidt et al., 2005), the mixed crops—livestock system will only suffer the loss of its profit by 3.5% and the livestock-only system will experience the increase of its profit.

The third key finding is that owing to the possibilities and capacities for adaptation, the economic impact of a climatic change on agriculture and natural resources will be modest or even insignificant. Under the GISS model, the loss of the farm profit in Latin America will amount to only 0.7% of its profit by the middle of the 21st century (Seo, 2016b). That the impact of climate change on agriculture will be modest if farmers should adapt efficiently is found in other economic models than the presently discussed microbehavioral model (Seo, 2019).

The agricultural system model applied to the Sub-Saharan Agriculture revealed another stunning finding: the switch by African farmers of an agricultural system from one to another is an effective adaptation strategy to an increase in climate risk, in addition to changes in climate normals. This means that although scientists have increasingly focused on a potential increase in climate risk, besides global warming, such as a more variable temperature year-to-year, a more variable precipitation year-to-year, or an increase in rainfall intensity (Hansen et al., 2012; Titley et al., 2016), the microbehavioral model shows that farmers have long adapted to such risks in the climate system.

Fig. 7.5 summarizes some of the core findings of the research on adaptation strategies of Sub-Saharan farmers in response to increases in climate risks (Seo, 2012c). There are two scenarios of an increase in climate risk. One is an increase in the precipitation variability both inter-annually and intra-annually which is captured by the Coefficient of Variation in Precipitation (CVP) measured from a 30-year period. The precipitation variation in Africa is to a large degree influenced by the ocean circulation in the Atlantic Ocean called the Atlantic Multi-decadal Oscillation (AMO) (Janowiak, 1988). The other climate risk is an increase in temperature variability which is measured by, *inter alia*, the Diurnal Temperature Range (DTR) for a 30-year period.

The CVP and DTR are the climate risks in Sub-Sahara well recognized by climate and agricultural researchers. A large rainfall variation from one year to

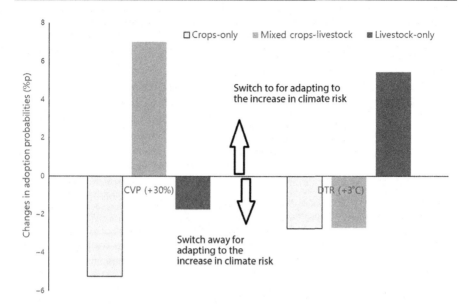

Figure 7.5 Adaptation behaviors to the increased climate risk in Sub-Saharan Africa.

another in the continent has led farmers there to rely on an informal form of saving or another (Udry, 1995; Hulme et al., 2001). Changes in daily maximum temperature and daily minimum temperature have been reported to be harming crop productions (Easterling et al., 2000; Welch et al., 2010).

If the CVP were to increase by as much as 30% in the continent, as Fig. 7.5 reveals, farmers will switch away from the specialized crop system and the specialized livestock system and adapt by choosing instead the mixed crops−livestock system. The mixed system is predicted to increase by 7% points as a result of the adaptation behavior.

If the DTR were to increase by as much as 3°C, as the figure shows, farmers will switch away from the crops-only system and the mixed crops−livestock system and adapt by choosing instead the livestock-only system. As a result of the adaptive changes, the livestock-only system will increase by 6% points.

The three agricultural system model was further expanded to the seven natural resource enterprise model (Seo, 2012a, 2012b). The latter, on top of the enterprises that manage crops and/or farm animals, adds to the microbehavioral model the rural enterprises that produce timber and forest products. The empirical studies of the natural resource enterprise model yielded mostly comparable results to the above-described key findings from the three agricultural system model.

There were also unique empirical results that can be produced only from the natural resource enterprise model (Seo, 2016c). First, farmers in both Africa and Latin America will adapt by switching to a crops-forests enterprise if the climate system were to turn into a hotter and wetter system (Seo, 2010c). Second, Latin American farmers will also adopt a forest-only enterprise, besides a crops-forests enterprise, if the climate system were to become more humid. Put differently, a large share of forest income in the Latin American rural household income, as large as 22%, can be attributed to a hot and humid climate system found in the Amazon and Central America (Vedeld et al., 2007). This share will further increase if the climate system were to become even hotter and wetter. Third, the crops-livestock-forests enterprise is the most diversified portfolio in the model and will be favored by natural resource managers if the climate system were to shift into a hotter system with increased rainfall.

Let me conclude this section with a few emphases as well as a brief introduction to an economic analysis of adaptation to changes in hurricanes. In the grand economic theory of globally shared goods, microbehavioral decisions such as those described in this section should be at the core and the microbehavioral model should be eagerly, and richly, advanced for the purpose of disentangling complex responses of economic agents to the changes in the globally shared goods. The microbehavioral economic models have been, however, long set aside in the economics literature while brightest spotlights have fallen on global welfare optimization models, global catastrophe models, as well as an array of impact models which focuses on a specific population or product (Nordhaus, 1994; Weitzman, 2009; Rosenzweig and Parry, 1994; Schlenker and Roberts, 2009). In all these acclaimed studies, micro adaptation decisions are by and large missing.

The effectiveness of adaptation in reducing the damage from climatic changes highlighted in this section with reference to agricultural and natural resource sectors is found even more clearly in the other areas of concern, in particular, in the climate-related extreme events. Let me point you to two findings in this regard. The number of fatalities from tropical cyclones in Bangladesh has been reduced by about 75% through the cyclone shelters built across the coastal zones since the early 1990s (Seo and Bakkensen, 2017; Seo, 2017c). For another, the tropical cyclones that were generated in the Pacific Ocean and turned right to land in Japan have had only one-tenth of the number of fatalities on average compared with the number of fatalities caused by the tropical cyclones that were generated in the same Pacific Ocean but turned left to land in the Philippines (Seo, 2018a, 2018b). The drastic difference can be attributed to the disparities in adaptation capacities in the two countries.

The economic model of the number of fatalities from a cyclone event relies on a family of the count data models: Poisson, Negative Binomial (NB), and others. Let F_i be the number of fatalities from an individual hurricane, which has a NB distribution which is a count data distribution with high dispersion (Cameron and Trivedi, 1986). More formally, the mean of the NB distribution is defined by the Gamma mixture of a Poisson distribution:

$$E\left[F_i|\xi_i\right] = \mu_i\xi_i \text{ where } \xi_i \sim \Gamma \text{ distributed}, E\left[\xi_i\right] = 1, V\left[\xi_i\right] = \kappa. \tag{7.8}$$

The number of cyclone fatalities is estimated by the following NB regression with a Maximum Likelihood method (Seo, 2015c):

$$\ln \mu_i = \alpha + \beta_1 CYC_i + \gamma_1 INC_i + \gamma_2 POP_i + \gamma_3 GEO_i + \varepsilon_i. \tag{7.9}$$

In the above, the CYC is an indicator of the cyclone characteristics which includes a measure of cyclone intensity such as the Minimum Central Pressure (hpa or millibar) and the level of storm surge (meters above the sea level) (McAdie et al., 2009). The INC is the income per capita of the region that is hit by the cyclone; the POP is population density of the region hit by the cyclone; the GEO is the geographic characteristics of the region; ε_i is a white-noise error term; and μ_i is the mean of the NB distribution F of from storm i.

The cyclone shelter is one of the adaptation strategies by a coastal community to cope with frequent cyclone strikes (Paul, 2009; World Bank, 2008b). The effects of the cyclone shelter program (CSP) can be measured by estimating the following NB regression and comparing the parameter estimates with those from Eq. (7.9) (Seo, 2017c, 2018b). With $I_{csp,i}$ being an indicator function for a CSP,

$$\ln \mu_i = \alpha + \beta_1 CYC_i + \beta_2 CYC_i I_{csp,i} + \gamma_1 INC_i + \gamma_2 POP_i + \gamma_3 GEO_i + \varepsilon_i. \qquad (7.10)$$

The cyclone shelter is one of the many adaptation options that a coastal community on the path of tropical cyclones can rely on. Cyclone researches show that adaptation strategies and measures such as satellite monitoring of cyclones, cyclone trajectory prediction techniques, an early warning system, evacuation order, information/training, a polder barrier, locating houses at high elevations, and structurally resilient houses have all made the coastal communities far less vulnerable over the past four decades (Emanuel, 2011; Bakkensen and Mendelsohn, 2016; Seo, 2017c).

The present author hopes that the description in this section, more broadly in this book, convincingly demonstrated that the vast array of microbehavioral adaptation decisions is a fascinating academic field of anthropogenic relationships with the climate system and, in fact, outshines all other fields of the climate change economics and policy. In addition, the microbehavioral economic models and applications generously offer pivotal policy insights, instruments, practical knowledge, and turning points.

7.4 The economics of foresight for a globally shared good

The second pillar of the economics of globally shared goods is what the present author would like to call the economics of foresight in the provision of a globally shared good. The foresight is, according to the Merriam-Webster dictionary, "an act or the power of foreseeing" or "an act of looking forward." Specifically, the economics of foresight in this section refers to forward-looking decisions as well as "prescient" decisions by an economic agent with regard to the provision of a globally shared good, as will be clarified shortly.

The economics of foresight is an economic theory on a microbehavioral decision that has long-term effects. The decision can affect multiple generations who are in the current time period, as in the overlapping generation models, or in different periods, so it is an inter-generational matter (Samuelson, 1958; Diamond, 1965). Such an inter-generational decision is attached with the value of time as well as the social rate of time preference (Fisher, 1930; Arrow et al., 1996; Weitzman, 1998). Some efficient decisions taken by an individual today may benefit the future generations while other efficient decisions may harm them. Such effects, however, may occur too far in the future relative to her lifetime or too uncertain relative to the best knowledge today.

The explanation in this section will become far clearer to the readers when described and understood in the context of global warming decisions. An individual decision-maker will make a multitude of decisions today which will leave a mark on the Planet's warming in the future as well as individual and social responses to it. A basket of microbehavioral adaptation decisions is a subset of all the microbehavioral decisions made by the decision-maker.

Each of the microbehavioral adaptation decisions, which are explained at length in the previous section, is an efficient choice to the decision-maker. Of the adaptation decisions, some decisions may turn out to be inefficient at the level of global community because of an unusually long time-horizon for the decision-maker to consider in the problem of global warming. Other decisions may turn out to be efficient even at the level of global community. Heeding to the time-horizon that is even beyond one's lifetime, the present author calls the former as an efficient decision and the latter a foresighted decision.

The family of foresighted decisions can be further separated into a forward-looking decision and a prescient decision. Both types of decisions are a foresighted decision. The pivotal difference between the two types is that the prescient decision can only be taken efficiently at the present time when the decision-maker has the full knowledge about the future event, which is because the prescient decision incurs a substantial cost to the decision-maker at the present time which will be recovered over a long time-horizon only if the prescient knowledge should turn out to be true knowledge.

On the other hand, the forward-looking decision does not call for the full knowledge, that is, prescience, about the future event because it does not cost the decision-maker at the present time. Put differently, the forward-looking decisions are efficient at the current state of knowledge about the future event.

I understand that this description about four types of microbehavioral decisions is cryptic to many readers and calls for clarifications, for which purpose I present Fig. 7.6 with a basket of actual decisions that belong to each category of decisions. With a continued focus on the adaptation examples in the natural resource sectors discussed in the preceding section, multiple examples of the four types of decisions are suggested: microbehavioral decisions, efficient, foresighted/forward-looking, foresighted/prescient.

First, the microbehavioral decisions are all the choices included in the four boxes under the top-most arrow, that is, a crops-only system, a livestock-only system, a crops—livestock system, a crops-forests enterprise, a forests-only enterprise, and so on. Of these, the crops-only system is not an efficient adaptation decision, as we saw in the preceding section, to the decision-maker. But the livestock-only system

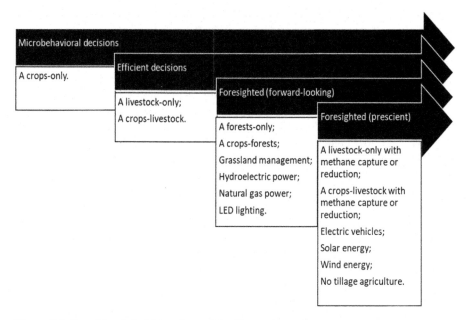

Figure 7.6 Foresighted decisions: forward-looking and prescient.

and the crops—livestock system are efficient adaptation decisions to the farmer, as we saw in the preceding section (Seo, 2006, 2016a). On a cautionary note, do not misinterpret this statement as saying that an efficient choice should be efficient at all places: a crops-only system can be efficient at some locations.

Of the basket of microbehavioral adaptation decisions, the efficient decisions are all the choices in the three boxes under the second arrow from the top: a livestock-only system, a crops—livestock system, a crops-forests enterprise, and so on. The foresighted decisions are all the choices in the two boxes under the third arrow from the top: a forests-only system, a crops-forests system, grassland management, hydroelectric, natural gas, LED (Light Emitting Diode) lamps, and so on.

The reason that the former, the second box from the left in Fig. 7.6, is microbehavioral efficient decisions but not foresighted decisions is that the choice of a livestock-only system, for example, will increase the greenhouse gas concentration of the Planet owing to the methane emissions from ruminant animals such as cattle, sheep, and goats (Schaefer et al., 2016). The choice is therefore efficient at the farm level, but not efficient at the societal level considering the long-term effects.

On the other hand, a forests-only or a crops—forests system, listed in the third box from the left, is an efficient and foresighted decision because the adoption of either of this system by the manager will result in the long-term in the reduction of greenhouse gas concentration of the Planet owing to carbon dioxide sinks by forests, besides being an efficient decision at the farm level (Houghton, 2008). The same can be said of the grassland management, including Alfalfa, which also significantly absorbs atmospheric carbon dioxide and preserves soil carbon (Ainsworth and Long, 2005).

The forward-looking behaviors outside the agriculture and natural resource sectors, as also listed in the third box from the left, are a hydroelectric power generation, a natural gas-powered electricity generation, and an adoption of the LED lamps (USDOE, 2016a). These options are entered into the figure to show that foresighted decisions are not limited to the agricultural and natural resource sectors and found in other sectors of the economy, especially in the energy sector.

That the hydroelectric power generation can be considered as a foresighted decision can be attributed to the prediction from climate science that a globally warmer world will lead to a higher rainfall climate system in many, if not most, parts of the world, making the hydroelectric power generation a viable adaptation option in those regions (Seo, 2016d). In addition, the cost of hydroelectric power generation, measured in the levelized cost of electricity (LCOE), is only half the costs of other renewable energy generations, for example, photovoltaic (PV) solar, offshore wind, or nuclear fission energy (Heal, 2010; FISES, 2013; USEIA, 2015).

An increasing adoption of hydropower can be observed regionally. Brazil meets 75% of its total energy demand by the hydroelectric power generation relying on the vast water resources including the Itaipu Dam (IHA, 2018). Canada also relies heavily on hydroelectric energy. China has become the world's largest hydroelectric power producer by building the world's largest dams, relying on the melting of ice caps and snow of Himalayan mountains spurred by a global warming, for example, the Three Gorges Dam and the Yalung Tsangpo River Dams in Tibet (Yong, 2014).

It is worth highlighting at this point some of the great hydroelectric projects in the world. The Three Gorges Dam in the Yangtze River in China is currently the largest dam with the generating capacity of 22,500 MW and generated about 100 TWh in 2014. Given the per capita electricity consumption of 4 MWh in China, the dam provides electricity to 25 million people (World Bank, 2019). The Grand Inga Dam that began to be built at the Inga Falls on the Congo River in central Africa would become the largest dam once completed with the generating capacity of 40,000 MW (Pearce, 2013). With the assumption of 200 TWh annual production, the dam alone would provide electricity to 1 billion people with the annual electricity consumption in 2018 of about 200 kWh per capita in Africa. For reference, the total African population is 1.26 billion. The Itaipu Dam on the Parana River in Brazil has the generating capacity of 14,000 MW and generated 103 TWh of electricity in 2016. With the per capita electricity consumption of 2.6 MWh in Brazil, the dam alone would provide electricity to about 40 million people.

Of the foresighted decisions, some decisions are prescient. In other words, a prescient decision is forward-looking but cannot be taken without the high confidence that arises from full knowledge about the future of the global climate system. To comprehend this, let us consider a PV solar energy generation as an adaptation to the future global warming, which was pushed hard by the Obama Administration (White House, 2013). It is a costly infrastructural investment and a costly investment decision by the decision-maker who wants to replace fossil fuel-generated electricity with PV solar-generated electricity. The levelized cost of the latter is about three times larger than that of the former (FISES, 2013; USEIA, 2015).

Without the confidence that the price of fossil fuel-fired electricity will rise steeply in the near future owing to a continued global warming and subsequent policy interventions through, for example, an imposition of the social cost of carbon, the decision-maker will not make such a costly switch and consequently the PV solar generation systems will not be developed. The same analysis can be extended to the wind energy and electric vehicles.

The point of emphasis here is that the forward-looking decision to the decision-maker is not a costly decision while the prescient decision calls for a big monetary sacrifice from the decision-maker, although the two decisions are both foresighted. Compare the hydropower generation which is a forward-looking decision with the PV solar generation which is a prescient decision!

The forward-looking decisions are therefore not only policy-pertinent but also critical in addressing the problems of global warming as well as other globally shared goods. In Fig. 7.6, the first three forward-looking decisions are for the agricultural and resource sectors while the last three decisions are for the energy sectors. The former is a forests-only system, a crops-forests system, and a grassland management system. The latter is a hydropower generation, a natural gas-fired energy generation, and LED lamps.

Of the prescient decisions presented in Fig. 7.6, of particular interests are three agricultural and resource decisions: a livestock-only system with methane capture or reduction, a crops—livestock system with methane capture or reduction, and a no-tillage crop agriculture. The first two of these were previously referred to as an efficient adaptation decision, the second box from the left, and the last as a microbehavioral decision, the first box from the left. These decisions are now classified as a prescient decision, the fourth box from the left, because of the new technology adoptions which are much costly to the decision-maker, that is, a methane capture and reduction technology and a no-till technology.

When a decision-maker is confident about the future global warming that may unfold beyond this century, s/he can turn a livestock-only system into one with the methane capture/reduction technology. The technology is either an outside-the-body technology or an inside-the-body technology. The latter includes feed additives which reduce methane production from ruminant animals (Hristov et al., 2015; CSIRO, 2018). The former includes a manure processing and a burp/fart mask attached to the animal (Smith et al., 2008). The installation of these technologies is costly to varying degrees, so without the future guarantee given by the government or science, livestock managers are unlikely to install them on their own. As reviewed in the previous chapter, California's Assembly Bill 32 provides offset credits to the farms that adopt these mitigation technologies (CARB, 2019).

Another prescient decision listed in the figure is no-tillage agriculture which is a crop farming practice developed to prevent the release of soil carbon into the atmosphere during crop agriculture (Smith et al., 2008). Again an adoption of this technology is a costly investment to the crop farmer because it requires new machines and farming practices. Until there is certainty that the release of soil carbon will be penalized in the near future or an adoption of this technique will be given carbon credits by the government, the farmer will have little incentive to adopt the technology at her own expense.

The other prescient decisions listed in the figure are for the energy-related sectors: PV solar energy, offshore wind energy, and electric vehicles. For the individual who attempts to adopt these technologies or energy types, it will be a big investment decision which can only be justified by the conviction on the dangerous global warming and/or policy interventions such as the aforementioned California's bill.

As far as the economics of globally shared goods is concerned, having clarified the four types of decisions, the pivotal economic question is how much carbon absorption is possible from the family of forward-looking and prescient decisions (Seo, 2017a,b). The second question is whether the prescient decisions can be justified at the global policy level on the grounds that they are by far cheaper options for addressing the Planet warming than other technologies that are largely unknown to humanity such as nuclear fusion, climate engineering, ocean fertilization, and carbon-capture-storage (Seo, 2017a,b).

Let us examine the first pivotal question first. What we need to know is how much carbon sink is possible from different types of trees and grasslands planted, for example, per acre of land. The aggregate amount of carbon dioxide sink achievable from the atmosphere is one of the key policy targets in global warming policy designs and the basket of forward-looking decisions contributes to this total (Nordhaus, 2008; UNEP, 2017; IPCC, 2018).

Table 7.1 summarizes the amounts of carbon sink that can be achieved from different types of vegetations, namely, trees and grasses. Of the many types of trees grown in the world, the largest carbon sinks are California redwood and Australian eucalyptus, perhaps the two tallest trees in the landscape of any regions. The *Sequoia sempervirens*, the scientific name for California redwood, planted in 1 hectare of land stores up to 2600 tons of carbon (Van Pelt et al., 2016). The *Eucalyptus obliqua*, the scientific name for Australian eucalyptus, in 1 hectare of land can store up to 640 tons of carbon while the mature dry scleropyll forest, that is, the hard leaf forest, in 1 hectare of land can store up to 100 tons of carbon (Mackey et al., 2008). The atmospheric carbon sink from perennial grasslands is comparatively small: 5 tons of carbon per "perennial grass year" in 1 hectare of land.

The table also shows the amounts of soil carbon storage under different types of vegetations. Although the atmospheric carbon sink from perennial grassland is small, the table shows that soil carbon storage of the perennial grasslands is as large as that of native hardwood forests in Australia: about 75 tons per hectare of land (Chan and McCoy, 2010).

How significant are these numbers as a climate policy response (Griscom et al., 2017)? Fig. 7.7 scales up the atmospheric carbon sinks in Table 7.1 to the national scale, which is then compared against the national greenhouse gas emissions per year in Australia. The figure shows stunning numbers. From the 149 million hectares of forests in the country, the size of carbon sink from the atmosphere amounts to 38.5 billion tons of carbon dioxide (Mackey et al., 2008). From the 440 million hectares of grasslands, the size of carbon sink from the atmosphere can be as high as 8.1 billion tons of carbon dioxide (the present author's calculation: 440 million*5 tons of carbon).

Table 7.1 The amounts of carbon sink and soil carbon from different vegetations.

	Vegetation	Country	Sink (tons of carbon)	Land unit (hectare)	Sources
Atmospheric carbon sink	*Sequoia sempervirens* (California redwood)	US	2600 tons of carbon	1	Van Pelt et al. (2016)
	Eucalyptus obliqua (Eucalyptus)	Australia	640 tons of carbon	1	Mackey et al. (2008)
	Mature dry sclerophyll forest	Australia	100 tons	1	Mackey et al. (2008)
	Perennial grass	Australia	5 tons of carbon per year	1	Christie (1981)
Soil carbon storage	Perennial pasture in high rainfall areas	Australia	72.9 tons	1	Chan and McCoy (2010)
	Native hardwood forests	Australia	76.5 tons	1	Chan and McCoy (2010)

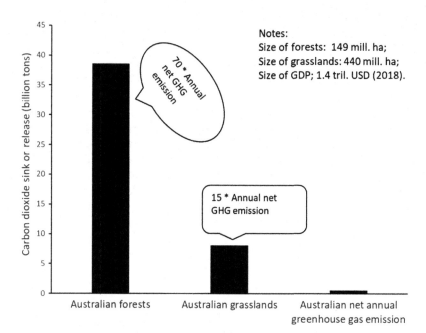

Figure 7.7 The amount of atmospheric carbon sink versus national carbon emissions.

Compared with the annual greenhouse gas emissions of about 550 million tons of carbon dioxide by the country, the forest carbon sink is 70 times larger while the grassland carbon sink is 15 times larger. These numbers show that Australian vegetations may store up to 85 years of annual greenhouse gas emissions. Note that the figures in Fig. 7.7 do not even include the soil carbon storages.

The statistics in Fig. 7.7 and Table 7.1 will be a surprise to many readers. The Australian analysis is, however, an exceptional one than one common to all countries because of the country's vast outback areas maintained to be forests and rangelands (Seo, 2011). The analysis may not apply to the countries with limited lands which are highly urbanized, for example, the European countries, Singapore, South Korea. Nonetheless, the Australian analysis may be applicable, with some modifications and reinterpretations, to many countries in Latin America, Africa, North America, and South Asia.

Another point to emphasize is that the statistics in Fig. 7.7 and Table 7.1 tell only the current storages and sinks by the vegetations, for example, old growth forests and permanent pasturelands, which is an important policy variable for sure. An even more pertinent climate policy variable is, however, additional sinks and storages that are achievable in the future as the global economies continue to grow and consequently release ever larger amount of carbon dioxide equivalent emissions. Put differently, what should be more concerned by a climate policy analyst is how much the world (or individual nations) can expand the forested areas and the pasturelands. In this regard, a rapid expansion of the forested zones in an effort to combat climate change is often reported by countries: 350 million trees planted in a single day by Ethiopia and 50 million trees planted in a single day by India, all in 2019 (NYT, 2019). It takes many decades for the newly planted trees to be mature.

As surprising as the answer to the first question is, the second question too is a critical policy question few people have, nonetheless, paid attention to (Seo, 2017a, b). The role of technologies in climate policy, when discussed in policy designs and negotiations, has always been limited to a "silver-bullet" technology, that is, one that can solve the problem all at once. Geo-climate engineering such as a solar radiation reflector, a direct air carbon-capture-storage, and ocean fertilization is one example (NRC, 2015a, 2015b). Another example of the silver-bullet is transformational energy technologies such as nuclear fusion and, to some extent, PV solar energy (ITER, 2015).

The second question draws our attention to the other type of technologies which is referred to as a micro technology, which may turn out to be more meaningful in climate policy designs (Seo, 2015a,b). The micro technologies were first suggested by the present author in the study of agricultural and natural resource sectors: a livestock-only with methane capture and reduction technologies, a no-tillage crop farming.

A critical importance of the micro technologies lies in the modest cost of employing them compared against the costs of the silver-bullet technologies. Although the methane capture and reduction technologies, for example, are not costless, they are far less costly than the silver-bullet technologies, say, a solar radiation reflector such as a stratospheric aerosol layer to be explained shortly. As such, the micro technologies can provide greenhouse gas reductions during the transitional period before the silver-bullet technologies are validated and deployed.

Consider the following methane reduction technology: adding feed additives to ruminant animals such as cattle and sheep such as Asparagopsis seaweed (Hristov et al., 2015; CSIRO, 2018). Given that livestock managers are already adding many different types of feed additives for cattle and other ruminant animals, adding the feed additive manufactured specifically to reduce methane emissions from farm animals is not a hugely costly management adjustment. It is a chemical compound made of seaweeds!

Despite the relatively low cost, the benefit in terms of reduced greenhouse gas emissions, that is, methane emissions, from employing this technology may be substantial. The Global Warming Potential (GWP) over a 100-year time-horizon of a ton of methane is about 28 times that of a ton of carbon dioxide (IPCC, 2014). To give you an idea, a ton of methane gas reduced and captured by a livestock manager will be valued at US\$ 2800 by year 2030, assuming a widely accepted social cost of carbon dioxide at US\$ 100 in 2030 (Nordhaus, 2013).

How much methane can be captured or reduced by a livestock manager by adopting the inexpensive micro technologies, say, feed additives and an animal burp mask? Fig. 7.8 shows the annual global methane emissions from all animals from each livestock species and the annual methane emissions from a single animal of each livestock species. The beef cattle emit about 2.5 billion tons of CO_2-equivalent methane emissions each year, so do the dairy cattle. Sheep emit about 600 million tons of CO_2-equivalent emissions. A single dairy cattle unit emits about

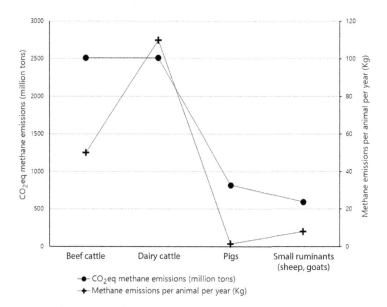

Figure 7.8 Methane emissions from livestock per year: global and per animal.

110 kg of methane in a single year while a single beef cattle unit emits about 55 kg of methane in a single year. A single sheep unit emits much less: 8 kg of methane in a single year (Webb et al., 2014; FAO, 2019).

A livestock manager who raises 100 dairy cattle would emit about 11 tons of methane in a year, which is comparable to 308 tons of CO_2-equivanet emissions. Applying the price of carbon dioxide of US\$ 100, s/he would earn up to US\$ 308,000 in a year by capturing methane emissions through the aforementioned technologies. For the owner of 100 beef cattle, the value is US\$ 154,000 per year. For the owner of 100 sheep, this value is US\$ 2,200 per year.

7.5   The economics of greenhouse technologies

The third component of the economic theory of globally shared goods is in brief technological innovations aimed at providing a globally shared good. In the previous section, the present author referred to it as a silver-bullet technology and argued that these technologies are expensive as well as difficult to be developed and deployed successfully, therefore, should be adopted only as a future option.

Readers may wonder why the section on technological solutions is titled as "greenhouse economics." Note that the present author uses the term "greenhouse" in a different light from the one found in the greenhouse effect literature which refers to the fundamental science of global warming, for example, the economics of greenhouse gases. That is, the blanket of carbon dioxide in the atmosphere is referred to as the greenhouse by the scientific community because the atmospheric blanket heats up the inside it just like a greenhouse heats up inside the structure.

Few people, however, noticed that the greenhouse is one of the most primitive scientific inventions by the humanity to control climate conditions for the benefit of economic activities. The greenhouses are built to increase the temperature and moisture inside the structure to grow specialty crops that are later sold at higher values in the market than staple crops such as rice and wheat (GLASE, 2019). From this observation, the present author will henceforth use the greenhouse as a metaphor for all climate-control technologies that are employed to enhance economic productions.

A construction of the first modern greenhouse is sometimes credited to the French botanist C.L Bonaparte who built a practical greenhouse in Leiden, the Netherlands, during the 1800s to grow medicinal tropical plants, which quickly spread to the gardens of the rich and the universities in Europe. But, the first description of a greenhouse may go further back to the 1450s in Korea, in which a detailed instruction was given for constructing a chamber for growing vegetables during winter. The chamber's inside was heated using an *ondol* system—a traditional heating system utilizing stones, mud, and heat channels—and the chamber's windows were made semi-transparent by *Hanji* for Sunlight to pass through (Yoon and Woudstra, 2007). More recently, a greenhouse with the capacity of carbon dioxide enrichment for plant growth began to be built during the latter half of the 20th century (Wittwer and Robb, 1964).

The greenhouse technologies were referred to as a silver-bullet technology in the previous section. In the resource economics literature, they were referred to as a backstop technology (Nordhaus, 1973). A formal definition of a backstop is an energy source or a technology that can provide energy nearly indefinitely at a constant price. The human society will therefore make a transition to the backstop when all exhaustible energy sources are exhausted, more precisely, too costly. (Hotelling, 1931; Fisher, 1981).

In the context of global warming, the following technologies are widely perceived as a backstop or a silver-bullet technology: a direct air carbon capture and sequestration, a nuclear fusion energy technology, a reflector of Sunlight to cool earth (IPCC, 2005; ITER, 2015; LLNL, 2015; NRC, 2015a, 2015b). The last of these technologies is more commonly referred to as Albedo Modification (AM) technology in the scientific community, of which the most widely discussed are a stratospheric aerosol layer and a marine cloud brightening (MCB) (Budyko, 1974; Twomey, 1974). There are less frequently discussed technological solutions such as ocean iron fertilization because of arguably higher risks (Martin et al., 1994). Some technologies provide a powerful remedy to the problem of global warming but seem to provide only a partial solution on its own, for example, solar energy (MIT, 2015). A list of backstop technologies is summarized in Table 7.2.

In the recent report by the National Research Council (NRC) committee, two climate intervention technologies are examined: carbon dioxide removal (CDR) technologies and AM technologies. The CDR technologies include the aforementioned direct air carbon capture and sequestration. The AM technologies are the technologies that reflect Sunlight to cool earth which include injecting aerosols into the atmosphere and brightening marine clouds (NRC, 2015a). The climate intervention is the term preferred by the NRC committee to more commonly used geoengineering or climate engineering, which includes both CDR and AM technologies.

The key policy variable with regard to the silver-bullet technologies is the price of deploying the technology at a level that addresses successfully the problem of a warming Planet owing to increased greenhouse gas emissions by anthropogenic activities. This price is referred to as the cost of a backstop.

According to Nordhaus who is said to be one of the economists who coined the term, the cost of a backstop technology in the global warming policy is US$ 1200 per ton of carbon emissions (Nordhaus, 2008). This means that a zero net emissions policy, considered by the European Union (EU) but not yet agreed upon by its members, implemented through a backstop technology would cost about US$ 13 trillion annually for the globe.

This cost of a backstop policy can be compared to the cost of an optimal control/management of the global warming problems. That is, an efficient price of carbon is about US$ 120 per ton of carbon at the year 2020 (Nordhaus, 2013). This means that the optimal cost of the global warming policy is about US$ 1.2 trillion per year globally at 2020, an order of magnitude smaller than the cost of the zero net emissions policy through the backstop technology.

Table 7.2 Backstop technologies.

Technologies	Types	Methods	Costs	Status
Direct air capture and sequestration	Carbon dioxide removal	Separation of CO_2 from the air through scrubbing; regeneration; sequester	380–600 US$/ton CO_2 (APS, 2011; Mazzotti et al., 2013)	An immature technology with only laboratory-scale experiments (NRC, 2015b)
A stratospheric aerosol layer	Albedo modification/ solar radiation management	Tens of millions of aerosol-forming gases are introduced into the stratosphere	An order of magnitude smaller than the cost of decarbonizations to offset anthropogenic CO_2 increases (NRC, 2015a)	Feasible but should not be deployed at this time (NRC, 2015a)
Marine cloud brightening	Albedo modification/ solar radiation management	Add additional aerosols into the clouds to act as cloud condensation nuclei	An order of magnitude smaller than the cost of decarbonizations to offset anthropogenic CO_2 increases than optimal mitigations (NRC, 2015a)	Feasible but should not be deployed at this time (NRC, 2015a)
Ocean iron fertilization	Carbon dioxide removal			Too high risks (NRC, 2015b)
Nuclear fusion	Zero carbon energy	National Ignition Facility; Tokamak	Input energy is larger than output energy	Ineffective at large scales

From this point on, the present author will describe each of the backstop technologies briefly but in a lucid manner. Let us begin with the AM technology (NRC, 2015a). Albedo is the reflectivity of Sunlight by the Earth surface. The AM technology was referred to as a smart mirror in the early economics literature and also solar radiation management (SRM) in the scientific literature. The idea was that a smart mirror may be established outside the Earth atmosphere, which then controls the amount of sunlight that the Planet receives (Nordhaus, 1994). The NRC report on AM technologies focuses on two reflectors: a stratospheric aerosol layer and a MCB.

In the stratospheric aerosol layer technology, tens of millions of aerosol-forming gases are introduced into the stratosphere (Budyko, 1974). The technology may have the effectiveness to offset the carbon dioxide doubling in the atmosphere by anthropogenic activities. The cost of the technology may be an order of magnitude smaller than the cost of climate mitigation efforts, that is, the efforts to reduce emissions of carbon dioxide and other greenhouse gases to prevent the CO_2 doubling. A historical example discussed by the NRC committee is the eruption of Mount Pinatubo in the Philippines in June 1991 which released 20 million tons of sulfur dioxide into the stratosphere, lowering the Earth's temperature by 0.3°C (NRC, 2015a).

The MCB is another AM technology that relies on high reflectivity of the low-lying white clouds over dark ocean surfaces, unlike the cirrus clouds at high altitudes. Modest changes in cloud whiteness (albedo), cloud lifetime, and cloud areal extent could significantly alter the amount of sunlight reflected back to space, affecting local temperature and Earth's temperature significantly. The MCB refers specifically to the technique that introduces additional aerosols into the clouds to act as cloud condensation nuclei near the cloud base for the purpose of increasing the cloud drop number and making the clouds more reflective (Twomey, 1974; Latham, 1990).

Are the AM technologies feasible as well as effective technologies for achieving the climate policy goal? The answer seems to be yes. Nonetheless, the NRC committee recommends that AM technologies should not be deployed at the present time at large scales sufficient to alter the climate system. The committee cites poorly identified risks and unquantified risks as the reason for its recommendation. As such risks, the committee cites stratospheric ozone loss, changes to precipitation amounts and patterns, and increased growth rates of forests (NRC, 2015a).

The direct air capture (DAC) technology refers to "chemical scrubbing processes for capturing CO_2 directly from the atmosphere via absorption or adsorption separation processes" (NRC, 2015b). The DAC should be distinguished from the carbon capture and sequestration (CCS) technology which refers to the carbon dioxide captures from high CO_2 concentration point sources such as a coal-fired power plant. The DAC technology, by contrasts, captures carbon dioxide directly from the atmosphere where the CO_2 concentration is very low.

The DAC technology has separation, regeneration, and sequestration phases. In the first phase, CO_2 is separated from the air through absorption/adsorption processes making use of amine-based or hydroxide-based sorbents. In the second phase, these materials are regenerated, from which a near-pure stream of CO_2 is produced. In the third phase, the CO_2 end product can be sequestered or used (NRC, 2015b).

The cost of the DAC technology, a proxy for the cost of a backstop technology, should include both separation and regeneration costs. Of the total cost of the DAC, the capital cost attributed to the cost of needed land areas is high. In the optimization models, the cost estimate of the DAC technology ranges from $ 380 to $ 600 per ton of CO_2 captured (APS, 2011; Mazzotti et al., 2013). This corresponds to US $ 1400−2200 per ton of carbon captured. The cost estimate based minimally on the first and second laws of thermodynamics is US$ 1000 per ton of CO_2 or US$ 3670 per ton of carbon, which seems to be a rough estimate and a high-end estimate (House et al., 2011).

The committee of the NRC concludes on the status of the DAC technology development as "an immature technology with only laboratory-scale experiments carried out to date and demonstration-scale projects in progress, with limited public results," indicating that the technology may be effective at a laboratory scale but a sufficiently large-scale effectiveness is still in doubt (NRC, 2015b).

The last of the basket of backstop technologies is the energy generated from a nuclear fusion reaction (LLNL, 2015; ITER, 2015). The concept of a backstop technology was initially tied to the nuclear fusion energy (Nordhaus, 1973). It was argued that once successfully developed, the nuclear fusion process would provide humanity nearly infinite energy at a constant price. As such, it would be the ultimate energy. Notwithstanding, the promise has not materialized after 50 years.

Unlike a nuclear fission reaction, a nuclear fusion technology imitates the process in which the Sun emits sunlight. The Sun is a giant ball composed of hydrogen and helium gases. The process in which hydrogen atoms in the Sun combine to form helium atoms is called a fusion process, which gives off the radiant energy of the Sun (LLNL, 2015). The Sun's core temperature reaches 15 million degrees in Celsius.

Despite the "simple" physics that underlie the technology, an engineering of a nuclear fusion device has been a massive challenge. One of the most well-known is the National Ignition Facility (NIF) at the Lawrence Livermore National Laboratory (LLNL), a federal research facility located at the University of California at Berkeley, which relies on the intense energy of giant laser beams (LLNL, 2015). The largest project is the ITER—it means the way in Latin—project in southern France in which 35 nations participate to build a Tokamak, a giant nuclear fusion machine whose fusion temperature reaches 150 million degrees in Celsius, ten times the Sun's core temperature (ITER, 2015).

Up until today, despite the simple physical theory and many decades of investments, two challenges have been too severe to overcome: engineering and economic. The upshot of the engineering challenge is that it is still not possible at present to build a Tokamak or other devices that is capable of generating energy sufficient for a meaningfully large number of people, let alone the "infinite" energy (LLNL, 2015).

The core economic challenge is that even if a Tokamak may be built to produce a large amount of energy in the near future, the input energy needed to produce and operate the Tokamak may be too large or even larger than the output energy. The present world record set in 1997 is the production of 16 MW thermal fusion power for 24 MW input heating power, the ratio of 0.67. The ITER project's goal is to reach the ratio of 10. This record does not even include other capital and operating costs of the nuclear fusion power (ITER, 2015).

Given the technological and economic challenges, many scientists and some environmentalists have expressed their support for the nuclear fission energy as a solution for the global warming problem. The engineering challenges are largely overcome by the nuclear fission energy generations. To give evidence, the nuclear fission energy provides more than 30% of total energy consumption of many countries: France (76.9%), Slovakia (56.8%), Hungary (53.6%), Ukraine (49.4%), Belgium (47.5%), Sweden (41.5%), Switzerland (37.9%), Slovenia (37.2%), Czech Republic (35.8%), Finland (34.6%), Bulgaria (31.8%), Armenia (30.7%), South Korea (30.4%). In the US which is the largest producer of nuclear energy, a nuclear fission energy provides 8% of the total energy consumption of the country (NEI, 2016).

The economic challenge still remains in terms of its higher electricity cost than those from fossil fuel-fired power plants. The LCOE for nuclear fission was 6.7 cents per KWh of electricity against 4.1 cents for coal and 4.2 cents for natural gas (MIT, 2003). Nonetheless, the cost of energy from nuclear fission is lower than those from other renewable energy generations including solar, offshore wind, geothermal energy generations (FISES, 2013; USEIA, 2015). It is also lower than the costs of electricity generated from the fossil fuel-fired power plants with a carbon capture and storage facility (CCS).

The US Energy Information Agency started to estimate the costs of electricity generated from various energy sources with and without advanced low-carbon technologies including the CCS. The EIA estimates provide an important benchmark for the discussions in this section and is summarized in Fig. 7.9 (USEIA, 2015).

The Levelized Cost of Electricity (LCOE) for an advanced nuclear power plant is estimated to be US$ 95.2 per MWh of electricity. This is higher than the LCOE from a conventional coal-fired power plant (95.1 US$/MWh) and that from a conventional natural gas-fired power plant (75.2 US$/MWh).

The LCOE of nuclear energy is, however, much lower than the LCOEs from renewable energy generations: solar PV (125 US$/MWh), offshore wind (196 US $/MWh). An exception is a hydroelectric power plant which was highlighted in the preceding section: (84 US$/MWh).

The LCOE of nuclear energy is also much lower than the LCOEs from advanced fossil fuel-fired power plants with the CCS technology. The coal power plant with advanced and CCS technologies has the LCOE of 144 US$/MWh while the natural gas power plant with advanced and CCC technologies has the LCOE of 100 US $/MWh.

The reservation for scaling up nuclear energy productions significantly as a remedy for carbon dioxide-caused global warming is rooted in the concern over a potential nuclear disaster such as the Chernobyl disaster in 1986 and the Fukushima disaster in 2011 as well as a long-term storage of nuclear wastes (MIT, 2003). On both fronts, engineering progresses have made each of the two risks significantly

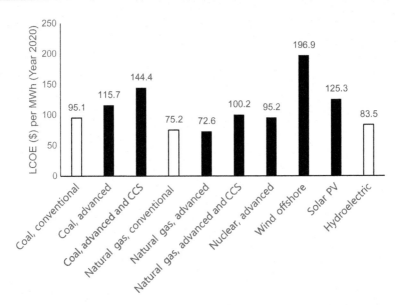

Figure 7.9 The levelized cost of electricity of nuclear fission and other technologies.

reduced. As far as the nuclear disaster is concerned, there have been few major nuclear disasters globally despite heavy reliance on the nuclear energy generations as discussed above. Even the Fukushima disaster in 2011 did not yield many direct human fatalities owing in large part to the immediate and drastic evacuation order.

To address the long-term storage problem of nuclear wastes, two deep geologic repositories have been developed by the US government: the Yucca Mountain repository in Nevada and the salt-bed repository in New Mexico (USA Today, 2018; USDOE, 2016b). Despite political upheavals on the former, the latter has proved to be successful, storing transuranic wastes since 1999. In particular, the latter is widely perceived as a more advanced technological option, as such, promising.

In the Waste Isolation Pilot Plant (WIPP) located in 26 miles southeast of Carlsbad, New Mexico, the repository is carved out of a salt bed which was formed 250 million years ago. The salt beds have ideal characteristics for a safe repository of nuclear wastes because the salt is free of flowing water, carved out easily, impermeable, and geologically stable. In particular, the salt rock seals fractures and closes openings naturally. The WIPP repository was carved out of a 2000-ft.-thick salt bed formed 250 million years ago. Transuranic wastes are disposed of 2150 ft. underground in the rooms mined from the salt bed (USDOE, 2016b).

Having reviewed the science and economics of silver-bullet technologies thus far, the present author can now offer a potential transition path of the global community from one to another backstop technology based on the cost estimates surveyed in this section of these technologies. This is depicted in Fig. 7.10 with the price (cost) trajectory across the time periods, in which backstop technologies are noted alongside the trajectory.

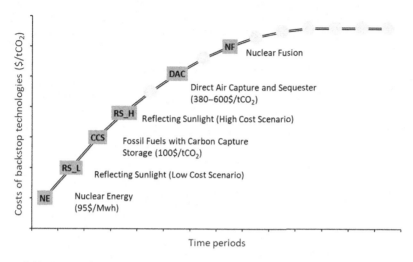

Figure 7.10 A potential transition path across backstop technologies.

If the global community were to be forced to adopt one or many of these technologies in the coming decades because of a continued global warming, the figure suggests that nuclear energy should be the first option because of its relatively lower cost of US\$ 95 per MWh of electricity generated (USEIA, 2015). The second option is either the technology of reflecting Sunlight, that is, the AM technology, in the low environmental cost scenario (NRC, 2015a). If the environmental risk were to be too high in the AM technology adoption, the second option should be the energy generations from fossil fuels with the carbon capture and storage (CCS) facility installed, whose cost estimate is US\$ 100 per ton of carbon dioxide removed or US\$ 100 per MWh of electricity generated from natural gas plants with the CCS technology (Al-Juaied and Whitmore, 2009; NRC, 2015b, USEIA, 2015). The high environmental risk scenario of the Albebo Modification strategy is the fourth option in the figure (NRC, 2015a).

The fifth option is the DAC and sequester, the cost of which is significantly higher than those of the preceding four options: US\$ 380−600 per ton of carbon dioxide removed (APS, 2011; Mazzotti et al., 2013). The technology is, however, still at an early stage of experiments inside the laboratories (NRC, 2015b). The sixth option is the nuclear fusion energy which is still at an experimental stage.

On the figure, two clarifications are worth being made. First, Fig. 7.10 gives an impression that the global community will switch from one to another technology as the reality of global warming becomes severer and clearer in the future time periods. However, it is possible that the adoption of one backstop technology, for example, nuclear energy or a stratospheric aerosol layer, may just be sufficient to stop the global warming trend. In such a case, the path in Fig. 7.10 will be ended after the first two technologies.

The figure also does not declare the ultimate technology which may provide the energy to the humanity at a constant price, which should be the plateau price in the figure. The plateau is left unmarked in the figure. Nuclear fusion might be able to provide such an energy source or there will be another energy source or break-through technology that is not known today.

Having reviewed all the components of the silver-bullet backstop technologies up to this point, astute readers may wonder what differences there are, if any, between the greenhouse economics presented in this chapter and the other economic descriptions on the backstop technologies found in the literature. With this question in your mind, the present author is now well positioned to explain the core of the greenhouse economics as a distinct economic theory on technological solutions that is different from either the science of backstop technologies such as the one reviewed by the National Research Council (NRC, 2015a, 2015b) or the "bench-mark" economics of climate change in which a backstop technology is integrated as a magical last resort for addressing the global warming conundrum (Nordhaus, 1992; Barrett, 2008).

The code word for the distinction is the term "greenhouse." The greenhouses are built to control the climate condition by a farm manager for the purpose of personal economic benefits, that is, not built by a government or a global policy center. Unlike the backstop economics of climate change, the greenhouse economics lays bare the incentives of individuals or individual nations to develop and employ the host of technological solutions illustrated in Fig. 7.10 for the economic benefits to the nations and individuals. A greenhouse technology can be a climate-control tech-nology or a carbon removal-and-reuse technology. Put slightly differently, what this book finds is that a greenhouse technology arises from a profit maximizing decision (Romer, 1990).

A researcher or investor would be motivated to develop a stratospheric aerosol layer technology or a MCB technology because such a technology would provide large financial benefits to him/her and the society, weighed against the costs of developing it. For a similar rationale, a researcher or investor would be keen on developing a DAC and sequester (DACS) technology as well as a carbon capture and storage (CCS) technology. The same can be said of the development of a nuclear fusion technology.

A national government would be keen to supporting the scientific efforts of an individual researcher or an inventor for developing one of the greenhouse technolo-gies. Again, because of each of these technologies' big impacts on the global cli-mate system as well as on the concerned nation's climate and atmospheric conditions, both of which are one of the key factors that influence economic well-being of the country, the government should consider these research efforts a high national priority, regardless of the unfolding of global warming. To emphasize once more, greenhouse technologies will be developed regardless of whether the global warming projections by climate scientists at the IPCC are materializing or not.

An example may suffice to convince the readers. The Chinese government has long held big interests in controlling local and regional climate/weather systems for economic as well as security reasons. The Chinese classics as old as two thousand years described how a weather control is a pivotal war strategy (Luo, 2014). The "Sky River" project in the Tibetan Plateau, the most recent one, is building tens of thousands of fuel-burning chambers over the Tibetan land area as large as three times the size of Spain. The project's initial aim is to produce 10 billion cubic meter of rainfall per year which would be supplied to the northern regions of China (SCMP, 2018).

In the greenhouse economics of backstop technologies, greenhouse technologies are developed by a greenhouse owner, who might be an inventor or a scientist, for the economic benefits that can be reaped from the new technologies. The investments would be spurred by the high interests by the general public as well as the national governments. A deployment of any of these technologies by an entrepreneur or a national government, if it were to occur at some point in the 21st century, would turn out to be an important step in addressing the conundrum of anthropogenic global warming and climate change.

A reader may raise the following reservation: should any nation be allowed to alter the Earth's climate system relying on one of these technologies for other purposes than mitigating anthropogenic global warming? She can go further and ask whether any nation should be allowed to alter the Earth's climate system in a way that harms other nations through the alteration. She can refer to the India's objection to the abovementioned Sky River project by China. Notwithstanding the pertinence of these questions, when they are raised at some point in the future, the world will have overcome the fear of a catastrophic global warming, that is, the fear of no turning back from a runaway climate system (Mann et al., 1999; NRC, 2013a, Lenton et al., 2008; Weitzman, 2009).

7.6   Additional clarifications

This completes the description of the grand economics of globally shared goods, a new theory developed by the present author. This was structured into the three components: microbehavioral decisions, foresighted decisions, and greenhouse economics. It is important to emphasize once more that the theory is consistently based on the economic incentives of decision-makers and actors (Seo, 2006, 2016a). It should also not to be missed that the theory is developed to explain short-term efficient responses as well as long-term foresighted and "backstop" responses in an integrative fashion, thereby, provide a complete and effective solution (Seo, 2017a,b).

From the vantage point of the economics corpus, the theory of globally shared goods is faithful to the landmark theories of the economics: to note some, a decision-making based on rational expectations, a theory of efficient markets, efficient resource uses, value of time, and optimal economic growth (Ricardo, 1817; Fisher, 1930; Hotelling, 1931; Von Neumann and Morgenstern, 1944; Samuelson, 1947; Friedman, 1962; Koopmans, 1965). When it comes to the public goods at a global scale, the theory differs sharply from the standard economics approach, that is, a global carbon price (tax) (Samuelson, 1954; Nordhaus, 1994; Manne et al., 1995; Hope, 2006; Stavins, 2007; Tietenberg, 2013; EAERE, 2019). The theory provides an optimal transition path of the world through changes in the climate system relying on an individual's incentives to respond to and appropriate the climate systems as well as a society's incentives to make use of and control the climate systems (Seo, 2015a,b, 2016a).

The theory in this chapter was described in the milieu of the policy challenges posed by global warming and climate change. In the next chapter which is the final chapter of this book, the present author will explore the possibility of extending the grand economics of globally shared goods to explain the policy challenges of other important globally shared goods discussed in this book and provide novel insights and solutions. The topics to be covered include asteroid collisions, artificial intelligence, high risk scientific experiments such as large hadron colliders, and nuclear disarmaments.

References

Ainsworth, E.A., Long, S.P., 2005. What have we learned from 15 years of free-air CO_2 enrichment (FACE)? A meta analysis of the responses of photosynthesis, canopy properties and plant production to rising CO_2. New Phytol. 165, 351−372.

Akasaki, I., Amano, H., Nakamura, S., 2014. Blue LEDs—filling the world with new light. Nobel Prize Lecture. The Nobel Foundation, Stockholm. Available at: <http://www.nobelprize.org/nobel_prizes/physics/laureates/2014/popular-physicsprize2014.pdf>.

Al-Juaied, M., Whitmore, A., 2009. Realistic costs of carbon capture. Discussion Paper 2008-09. Energy Technology Innovation Research Group, Belfer Center for Science and International Affairs. Harvard Kennedy School, Cambridge, MA.

APS (American Physical Society), 2011. Direct Air Capture of CO_2 with Chemicals: A Technology Assessment for the APS Panel on Public Affairs. APS, College Park, MD.

Arrhenius, S.A., 1896. On the influence of carbonic acid in the air upon the temperature of the ground. Philos. Mag. 41, 237−276.

Arrow, K.J., Cline, W., Maler, K.G., Munasinghe, M., Squitieri, R., Stiglitz, J., 1996. Intertemporal equity, discounting, and economic efficiency. In: Bruce, J.P., Lee, H., Haites, E.F. (Eds.), Climate Change 1995: Economic and Social Dimensions of Climate Change, Intergovernmental Panel on Climate Change. Cambridge University Press, New York.

Bakkensen, L.A., Mendelsohn, R., 2016. Risk and adaptation: evidence from global hurricane damages and fatalities. J. Assoc. Environ. Resour. Econ. 3, 555−587.

Barrett, S., 1994. Self-enforcing international environmental agreements. Oxf. Econ. Pap. 46, 878−894.

Barrett, S., 2003. Environment and Statecraft: The Strategy of Environmental Treaty. Oxford University Press, Oxford.

Barrett, S., 2008. The incredible economics of geoengineering. Environ. Resour. Econ. 39, 45−54.

Bowen, H.R., 1943. The interpretation of voting in the allocation of economic resources. Q. J. Econ. 58, 27−48.

Byerlee, D., Eicher, C.K., 1997. Africa's Emerging Maize Revolution. Lynne Rienner Publishers Inc., USA.

Budyko, M.I., 1974. Climate and Fife. Academic Press, New York.

California Air Resources Board (CARB), 2019. Assembly Bill (AB) Compliance Offset Program. ARB, California, <https://ww3.arb.ca.gov/cc/capandtrade/offsets/offsets. htm>.

Cameron, A.C., Trivedi, P.K., 1986. Econometric models based on count data: comparisons and applications of some estimators and some tests. J. Appl. Econ. 1, 29−53.

Chan, K.Y., McCoy, D., 2010. Soil carbon storage potential under perennial pastures in the mid-north coast of New South Wales, Australia. Tropical Grassl. 44, 184−191.

Chapman, C.R., Morrison, D., 1994. Impacts on the earth by asteroids and comets: assessing the hazard. Nature 367, 33−40.

Christie, E.K., 1981. Biomass and nutrient dynamics in a C4 semi-arid Australian grassland community. J. Appl. Ecol. 18, 907−918.

Commonwealth Scientific and Industrial Research Organization (CSIRO), 2018. Future feed. CSIRO, Canberra, Accessed from: <https://research.csiro.au/futurefeed/>.

Diamond, P., 1965. National debt in a neoclassical growth model. Am. Econ. Rev. 55, 1126−1150.

Dubin, J.A., McFadden, D.L., 1984. An econometric analysis of residential electric appliance holdings and consumption. Econometrica 52 (2), 345−362.

Dudal, R., 1980. Soil-related Constraints to Agricultural Development in the Tropics. International Rice Research Institute, Los Banos.

Easterling, D.R., Evans, J.L., Groisman, P.Y., Karl, T.R., Kunkel, K.E., Ambenje, P., 2000. Observed variability and trends in extreme climate events: a brief review. Bull. Am. Meteorol. Soc. 81, 417−425.

Emanuel, K., 2011. Global warming effects on U.S. hurricane damage. Weather Climate Soc. 3, 261−268.

European Association of Environmental and Resource Economists (EAERE), 2019. Endorse the Economists' Statement on Carbon Pricing by Signing It! EAERE.

Fischer, G., Mahendra, S., Tubiello, F.N., Velhuizen, H., 2005. Socio-economic and climate change impacts on agriculture: an integrated assessment, 1990−2080. Philos. Trans. R. Soc. B 360, 2067−2083.

Fisher, I., 1930. The Theory of Interest. Macmillan, New York.

Fisher, A.C., 1981. Ch. 2 Exhaustible resources: the theory of optimal depletion. In: Fisher, A.C. (Ed.), Resource and Environmental Economics. Cambridge University Press, Cambridge.

Food and Agriculture Organization (FAO), 2019. Global Livestock Environmental Assessment Model (GLEAM). FAO, Rome.

Ford, J., Katondo, K.M., 1977. Maps of tsetse fly (Glossina) distribution in Africa. Bull. Anim. Health Prod. Afr. 15, 187−193.

Fraunhofer Institute of Solar Energy Systems (FISES), 2013. Levelized cost of electricity, renewable energy technologies. FISES, Germany.

Friedman, M., 1962. Capitalism and Freedom. The University of Chicago Press, Chicago, IL.

Greenhouse Lighting & Systems Engineering (GLASE), 2019. Growing the World's Food in Greenhouses. The GLASE, Cornell University, Ithaca, NY.

Griscom, B.W., Adams, J., Ellis, P.W., Houghton, R.A., Lomax, G., Miteva, D.A., et al., 2017. Natural climate solutions. Proc. Natl. Acad. Sci. 114, 11645−11650.

Hahn, G.L., 1981. Housing and management to reduce climate impacts on livestock. J. Anim. Sci. 52, 175−186.

Hansen, J., Sato, M., Reudy, R., Lo, K., Lea, D.W., Medina-Elizade, M., 2012. Perception of climate change. Proc. Natl. Acad. Sci. 109, E2415−E2423. Available from: https://doi. org/10.1073/pnas.1205276109.

Hardin, G., 1968. The tragedy of the commons. Science 162, 1243−1248.

Hawking, S., Tegmark, M., Russell, S., Wilczek, F., 2014. Transcending Complacency on Superintelligent Machines. Huffington Post. <https://www.huffingtonpost.com/stephen-hawking/artificial-intelligence_b_5174265.html>.

Heal, G., 2010. Reflections: the economics of renewable energy in the United States. Rev. Environ. Econ. Policy 4, 139−154.

Heckman, J., 1979. Sample selection bias as a specification error. Econometrica 47, 153−162.

Hirshleifer, J., 1983. From weakest-link to best-shot: the voluntary provision of public goods. Public. Choice 41, 371−386.

Hope, C., 2006. The marginal impact of CO_2 from PAGE2002: an integrated assessment model incorporating the IPCC's five reasons for concern. Integr. Assess. J. 6, 19−56.

Hotelling, H., 1931. The economics of exhaustible resources. J. Political Econ. 3, 137−175.

Houghton, R.A., 2008. Carbon flux to the atmosphere from land-use changes: 1850−2005. TRENDS: A Compendium of Data on Global Change. Carbon Dioxide Information Analysis Center, Oak Ridge National Laboratory, U.S. Department of Energy, Oak Ridge, TN.

House, K.Z., Baclig, A.C., Ranjan, M., van Nierop, M.E., Wilcox, J., Herzog, H.J., 2011. Economic and energetic analysis of capturing CO_2 from ambient air. Proc. Natl. Acad. Sci. U S A 108 (51), 20428−20433.

Hristov, A.N., Joonpyo, O.H., Fabio Giallongo, F., Tyler, W., Frederick, T.W., Michael, T., et al., 2015. An inhibitor persistently decreased enteric methane emission from dairy cows with no negative effect on milk production. Proc. Natl. Acad. Sci. U S A 112 (34), 10663−10668.

Hulme, M., Doherty, R.M., Ngara, T., New, M.G., Lister, D., 2001. African climate change: 1900−2100. Clim. Res. 17, 145−168.

Huntington, E., 1915. Civilization and Climate. Yale University Press, New Haven, CT.

Huntington, E., 1917. Climatic change and agricultural exhaustion as elements in the fall of Rome. Q. J. Econ. 31, 173−208.

International Hydropower Association (IHA), 2018. 2018 Hydropower Status Report. IHA, London.

International Institute of Tropical Agriculture (IITA), 2000. Delivering the African Development Potential: The IITA Vision. IITA, Nigeria.

Intergovernmental Panel on Climate Change (IPCC), 2005. Special Report on Carbon Dioxide Capture and Storage. Cambridge University Press, Cambridge.

Intergovernmental Panel on Climate Change (IPCC), 2014. Climate Change 2014: Impacts, Adaptation, and Vulnerability. The Fifth Assessment Report of the IPCC. Cambridge University Press, Cambridge.

Intergovernmental Panel on Climate Change (IPCC), 2018. Special Report on Global Warming of 1.5°C. Cambridge University Press, Cambridge.

International Thermonuclear Experimental Reactor (ITER), 2015. ITER: The World's Largest Tokamak. Available at: <https://www.iter.org/mach>.

Janowiak, J.E., 1988. An investigation of interannual rainfall variability in Africa. J. Clim. 1, 240−255.

Johnson, H.D., 1965. Response of animals to heat. Meteorol. Monogr. 6, 109−122.

Kaul, I., Conceicao, P., Goulven, K.L., Mendoza, R.U. (Eds.), 2003. Providing Global Public Goods: Managing Globalization. Oxford University Press, Oxford.

Koopmans, T.C., 1965. On the concept of optimal economic growth. Acad. Sci. Scr. Varia. 28, 1−75.

Lackner, K.S., Brennana, S., Matter, J.M., Park, A.A., Wright, A., Zwaan, B.V., 2012. The urgency of the development of CO_2 capture from ambient air. Proc. Natl. Acad. Sci. 109 (33), 13156−13162.

Latham, J., 1990. Control of global warming. Nature 347, 339−340.

Lawrence Livermore National Laboratory (LLNL), 2015. How NIF Works. Available at: <https://lasers.llnl.gov/about/how-nif-works>.

Lenton, T.M., Held, H., Kriegler, E., Hall, J.W., Lucht, W., Rahmstorf, S., et al., 2008. Tipping elements in the earth's climate system. Proc. Natl. Acad. Sci. 105, 1786−1793.

Le Treut, H., Somerville, R., Cubasch, U., Ding, Y., Mauritzen, C., Mokssit, A., et al., 2007. Historical overview of climate change. In: Solomon, S., et al., (Eds.), Climate Change 2007: The Physical Science Basis. The Fourth Assessment Report of the Intergovernmental Panel on Climate Change. Cambridge University Press, Cambridge.

Luo, G., 2014. The Three Kingdoms. (English translation by Yu Sumei and edited by Ronald C. Iverson). Tuttle Publishing, Singapore.

Mackey, B.G., Keith, H., Berry, S.L., Lindenmayer, D.B., 2008. Green carbon—The Role of Natural Forests in Carbon Storage. A Green Carbon Account of Australia's South-Eastern Eucalypt Forest, and Policy Implications. ANU Press, Canberra. Available from: <http://epress.anu.edu.au/green_carbon/pdf/whole_book.pdf>.

Mankiw, N.G., 2014. Principles of Economics, seventh ed. Cengage Learning, Stamford, CT.

Mann, M.E., Bradley, R.S., Hughes, M.K., 1999. Northern hemisphere temperatures during the past millennium: inferences, uncertainties, and limitations. Geophys. Res. Lett. 26, 759−762.

Manne, A.S., Mendelsohn, R., Richels, R., 1995. MERGE—A Model for Evaluating Regional and Global Effects of GHG Reduction Policies. Energy Policy 23 (1), 17−34.

Martin, J.H., Coale, K.H., Johnson, K.S., Fitzwater, S.E., et al., 1994. Testing the iron hypothesis in ecosystems of the equatorial Pacific Ocean. Nature 371, 123−129.

Mas-Colell, A., Whinston, M.D., Green, J.R., 1995. Microeconomic Theory. Oxford University Press, Oxford.

Massachusetts Institute of Technology (MIT), 2003. The Future of Nuclear Power: An Interdisciplinary MIT Study. MIT, MA.

Massachusetts Institute of Technology (MIT), 2015. The Future of Solar Energy: An Interdisciplinary MIT Study. MIT, MA.

Mazzotti, M., Baciocchi, R., Desmond, M.J., Socolow, R.H., 2013. Direct air capture of CO_2 with chemicals: optimization of a two-loop hydroxide carbonate system using a counter-current air-liquid contactor. Clim. Change 118, 119−135.

McAdie, C.J., Landsea, C.W., Neuman, C.J., David, J.E., Blake, E., Hamner, G.R., 2009. Tropical Cyclones of the North Atlantic Ocean, 1851−2006. Historical Climatology Series 6-2, Prepared by the National Climatic Data Center, Asheville, NC in Cooperation with the National Hurricane Center, Miami, FL, 238 pp.

Mendelsohn, R., 2000. Efficient adaptation to climate change. Clim. Change 45, 583−600.

Mills, M.J., Toon, O.B., Turco, R.P., et al., 2008. Massive global ozone loss predicted following regional nuclear conflict. Proc. Natl. Acad. Sci. U S A 105, 5307−5312.

Musgrave, R., 1939. The voluntary exchange theory of public economy. Q. J. Econ. 53, 213−237.

Musgrave, R., 1959. The Theory of Public Finance. McGraw-Hill, New York.

National Research Council, 2010. Defending Planet Earth: Near-Earth-Object Surveys and Hazard Mitigation Strategies. National Academies Press, Washington, DC.

National Research Council (NRC), 2013a. Abrupt Impacts of Climate Change: Anticipating surprises. Committee on Understanding and Monitoring Abrupt Climate Change and Its Impacts. The National Academies Press, Washington, DC.

National Research Council (NRC), 2013b. Transitions to Alternative Vehicles and Fuels. The National Academies Press, Washington, DC.

National Research Council (NRC), 2015a. Climate Intervention: Reflecting Sunlight to Cool Earth. Committee on Geoengineering Climate: Technical Evaluation and Discussion of Impacts. The National Academies Press, Washington, DC.

National Research Council (NRC), 2015b. Climate Intervention Carbon Dioxide Removal and Reliable Sequestration. The National Academies Press, Washington, DC.

Nuclear Energy Institute (NEI), 2016. Energy Statistics. NEI, Washington, DC, Accessed from: <http://www.nei.org/Knowledge-Center/Nuclear-Statistics>.

New York Times, 2019. Ethiopia Says It Planted Over 350 Million Trees in a Day, a Record. Published on July 30, 2019. NYT, New York.

Nobel Prize, 2007. The Nobel Peace Prize for 2007: The Intergovernmental Panel on Climate Change (IPCC) & Albert (Al) Arnold Gore Jr. Accessed from: NobelPrize.org.

Nobel Prize, 2018. The Prize in Economic Sciences 2018: William D. Nordhaus & Paul M. Romer. Accessed from: NobelPrize.org.

Nordhaus, W., 1973. The allocation of energy resources. Brookings Pap. Econ. Act. 1973, 529–576.

Nordhaus, W.D., 1977. Economic growth and climate: the carbon dioxide problem. Am. Econ. Rev. 67, 341–346.

Nordhaus, W., 1982. How fast should we graze the global commons? Am. Econ. Rev. 72, 242–246.

Nordhaus, W., 1992. An optimal transition path for controlling greenhouse gases. Science 258, 1315–1319.

Nordhaus, W., 1994. Managing the Global Commons. MIT Press, Massachusetts.

Nordhaus, W., 2001. Global warming economics. Science 294, 1283–1284.

Nordhaus, W.D., 2006. Paul Samuelson and global public goods. In: Szenberg, M., Ramrattan, L., Gottesman, A.A. (Eds.), (2006) Samuelsonian Economics and the Twenty-First Century. Oxford Scholarship Online.

Nordhaus, W.D., 2008. A Question of Balance—Weighing the Options on Global Warming Policies. Yale University Press, New Haven.

Nordhaus, W., 2013. The Climate Casino: Risk, Uncertainty, and Economics for a Warming World. Yale University Press, New Haven, CT.

Nordhaus, W., Yang, Z., 1996. A regional dynamic general-equilibrium model of alternative climate change strategies. Am. Econ. Rev. 86, 741–765.

Nordhaus, W., Boyer, J., 2000. Warming the World: Economic Models of Global Warming. MIT Press, Cambridge, MA.

Ostrom, E., 1990. Governing the Commons: The Evolution of Institutions for Collective Action. Cambridge University Press, Cambridge.

Paul, B.K., 2009. Why relatively fewer people died? The case of Bangladesh's Cyclone Sidr. Nat. Hazards 50, 289–304.

Pearce, F., 2013. Will Huge New Hydro Projects Bring Power to Africa's People? Yale Environment 360, New Haven, CT.

Reilly, J., Baethgen, W., Chege, F., Van de Geijn, S., Enda, L., Iglesias, A., et al., 1996. Agriculture in a changing climate: impacts and adaptations. In: Watson, R., Zinyowera, M., Moss, R., Dokken, D. (Eds.), Climate Change 1995: Impacts, Adaptations, and Mitigation of Climate Change. Intergovernmental Panel on Climate Change (IPCC). Cambridge University Press, Cambridge.

Ricardo, D., 1817. On the Principles of Political Economy and Taxation. John Murray, London.

Romer, P., 1990. Endogenous technical change. J. Political Econ. 98, S71–S102.

Rosenzweig, C., Parry, M., 1994. Potential impact of climate change on world food supply. Nature 367, 133–138.

Samuelson, P.A., 1947. Foundations of Economic Analysis. Harvard University Press, Cambridge, MA.

Samuelson, P., 1954. The pure theory of public expenditure. Rev. Econ. Stat. 36, 387–389.

Samuelson, P., 1955. Diagrammatic exposition of a theory of public expenditure. Rev. Econ. Stat. 37, 350–356.

Samuelson, P.A., 1958. An exact consumption-loan model of interest with or without the social contrivance of money. J. Political Econ. 66, 467–482.

Samuelson, P., Nordhaus, W., 2009. Economics, nineteenth ed. McGraw-Hill Education, New York.

Schaefer, H., Fletcher, S.E.M., Veidt, C., et al., 2016. A 21st century shift from fossil-fuel to biogenic methane emissions indicated by $^{13}CH_4$. Science 352, 80–84.

Schlenker, W., Roberts, M., 2009. Nonlinear temperature effects indicate severe damages to crop yields under climate change. Proc. Natl. Acad. Sci. U S A 106, 15594–15598.

Schmidt, G.A., Ruedy, R., Hansen, J.E., et al., 2005. Present day atmospheric simulations using GISS ModelE: Comparison to in-situ, satellite and reanalysis data. J. Clim. 19, 153–192.

Seo, S.N., 2006. Modeling Farmer Responses to Climate Change: Climate Change Impacts and Adaptations in Livestock Management in Africa. PhD Dissertation. Yale University, New Haven.

Seo, S.N., 2010a. A microeconometric analysis of adapting portfolios to climate change: adoption of agricultural systems in Latin America. Appl. Econ. Perspect. Policy 32, 489–514.

Seo, S.N., 2010b. Is an integrated farm more resilient against climate change?: a microeconometric analysis of portfolio diversification in African agriculture? Food Policy 35, 32–40.

Seo, S.N., 2010c. Managing forests, livestock, and crops under global warming: a microeconometric analysis of land use changes in Africa. Aust. J. Agric. Resour. Econ. 54 (2), 239–258.

Seo, S.N., 2011. The impacts of climate change on Australia and New Zealand: a gross cell product analysis by land cover. Aust. J. Agric. Resour. Econ. 55, 220–239.

Seo, S.N., 2012a. Adapting natural resource enterprises under global warming in South America: a mixed logit analysis. Economia: J. Lat. Am. Caribb. Econ. Assoc. 12, 111–135.

Seo, S.N., 2012b. Adaptation behaviors across ecosystems under global warming: a spatial microeconometric model of the rural economy in South America. Pap. Regional Sci. 91, 849–871.

Seo, S.N., 2012c. Decision making under climate risks: an analysis of sub-Saharan farmers' adaptation behaviors. Weather Clim. Soc. 4, 285–299.

Seo, S.N., 2014a. Evaluation of Agro-Ecological Zone methods for the study of climate change with micro farming decisions in sub-Saharan Africa. Eur. J. Agron. 52, 157–165.

Seo, S.N., 2014b. Adapting sensibly when global warming turns the field brown or blue: a comment on the 2014 IPCC Report. Econ. Aff. 34, 399–401.

Seo, S.N., 2015a. Helping low-latitude, poor countries with climate change. Regulation 6–8. Winter 2015-2016.

Seo, S.N., 2015b. Adaptation to global warming as an optimal transition process to a greenhouse world. Econ. Aff. 35, 272−284.

Seo, S.N., 2015c. Fatalities of neglect: adapt to more intense hurricanes? Int. J. Climatol. 35, 3505−3514.

Seo, S.N., 2016a. Microbehavioral Econometric Methods: Theories, Models, and Applications for the Study of Environmental and Natural Resources. Academic Press (Elsevier), Amsterdam.

Seo, S.N., 2016b. Modeling farmer adaptations to climate change in South America: a microbehavioral economic perspective. Environ. Ecol. Stat. 23, 1−21.

Seo, S.N., 2016c. The micro-behavioral framework for estimating total damage of global warming on natural resource enterprises with full adaptations. J. Agric. Biol. Environ. Stat. 21, 328−347.

Seo, S.N., 2016d. A theory of global public goods and their provisions. J. Public. Aff . Available from: https://doi.org/10.1002/pa.1601.

Seo, S.N., 2017a. The Behavioral Economics of Climate Change: Adaptation Behaviors, Global Public Goods, Breakthrough Technologies, and Policy-making. Academic Press (Elsevier), Amsterdam.

Seo, S.N., 2017b. Beyond the Paris Agreement: climate change policy negotiations and future directions. Reg. Sci. Policy Pract. 9, 121−140.

Seo, S.N., 2017c. Measuring policy benefits of the cyclone shelter program in North Indian Ocean: protection from high winds or high storm surges? Clim. Change Econ. 8 (4), 1−18.

Seo, S.N., 2018a. Natural and Man-made Catastrophes: Theories, Economics, and Policy Designs. Wiley-Blackwell, Oxford.

Seo, S.N., 2018b. Two tales of super-typhoons and super-wealth in Northwest Pacific: will global-warming-fueled cyclones ravage East and Southeast Asia? J. Extreme Events . Available from: https://doi.org/10.1142/S2345737618500124.

Seo, S.N., 2019. Will farmers fully adapt to monsoonal climate changes through technological developments? An analysis of rice and livestock production in Thailand. J. Agric. Sci. 157, 97−108.

Seo, S.N., Bakkensen, L.A., 2017. Is tropical cyclone surge, not intensity, what kills so many people in South Asia? Weather Clim. Soc. 9, 71−81.

Seo, S.N., Mendelsohn, R., 2008. Measuring impacts and adaptations to climate change: a structural Ricardian model of African livestock management. Agric. Econ. 38, 151−165.

Seo, S.N., Mendelsohn, R., Dinar, A., Kurukulasuriya, P., 2009a. Adapting to climate change mosaically: an analysis of African livestock management across agro-ecological zones. B.E. J. Econ. Anal. Policy 7 (2), Article 4.

Seo, S.N., Mendelsohn, R., Dinar, A., Hassan, R., Kurukulasuriya, P., 2009b. A Ricardian analysis of the distribution of climate change impacts on agriculture across agroecological zones in Africa. Environ. Resour. Econ. 43, 313−332.

Smith, P., Martino, D., Cai, Z., Gwary, D., Janzen, H., Kumar, P., et al., 2008. Greenhouse gas mitigation in agriculture. Philos. Trans. R. Soc. B 363, 789−813.

South China Morning Post (SCMP), 2018. China needs more water. So it's building a rain-making network three times the size of Spain. SCMP, Published on March 26, 2018.

Stavins, R., 2007. A US Cap-and-trade System to Address Global Climate Change. Hamilton Project Discussion Paper 2007-13. The Brookings Institution, Washington, DC.

Tietenberg, T., 2013. Reflections—carbon pricing in practice. Rev. Environ. Econ. Policy 7, 313−329.

Titley, D.W., Hegerl, G., Jacobs, K.L., Mote, P.W., Paciorek, C.J., Shepherd, J.M., et al., 2016. Attribution of extreme weather events in the context of climate change. National Academies of Sciences, Engineering, and Medicine. The National Academies Press, Washington, DC.

Twomey, S., 1974. Pollution and the planetary albedo. Atmos. Environ. 8, 1251–1256. Available from: https://doi.org/10.1016/0004-6981(74)90004-3.

Udry, C., 1995. Risk and saving in Northern Nigeria. Am. Econ. Rev. 85, 1287–1300.

United Nations Environment Programme, 2017. The Emissions Gap Report 2017: A UN Environment Synthesis Report. UNEP, Nairobi.

United Nations Framework Convention on Climate Change (UNFCCC), 1992. United Nations Framework Convention on Climate Change. UNFCCC, New York.

United States Department of Energy (US DOE), 2016a. How Energy Efficient Light Bulbs Compare with Traditional Incandescent. US DOE, Washington, DC. Available at: <http://energy.gov/energysaver/how-energy-efficient-light-bulbs-compare-traditional-incandescents>.

United States Department of Energy (US DOE), 2016b. Waste Isolation Pilot Project (WIPP) Recovery. US DOE, Washington, DC. Available at: <http://www.wipp.energy.gov/>.

United States Energy Information Administration (US EIA), 2015. Annual Energy Outlook 2015. US EIA, Department of Energy, Washington, DC.

USA Today, 2018. Congress Works to Revive Long-delayed Plan to Store Nuclear Waste in Yucca Mountain. Published on June 3, 2018.

Van Pelt, R., Sillett, S.C., Kruse, W.A., Freund, J.A., Kramer, R.D., 2016. Emergent crowns and light-use complementarity lead to global maximum biomass and leaf area in *Sequoia sempervirens* forests. For. Ecol. Manag. 375, 279–308.

Vedeld, P., Angelsen, A., Bojø, J., Sjaastad, E., Berg, G.K., 2007. Forest environmental incomes and the rural poor. For. Policy Econ. 9, 869–879.

Von Neumann, J., Morgenstern, O., 1944. Theory of Games and Economic Behavior. Princeton University Press, Princeton, NJ.

Webb, N., Broomfield, M., Buys, G., Cardenas, L., Murrells, T., Pang, Y., et al., 2014. UK Greenhouse Gas Inventory, 1990 to 2012: Annual Report for Submission Under the Framework Convention on Climate Change. Department of Energy and Climate Change, UK.

Weitzman, M.L., 1998. Why the far-distant future should be discounted at its lowest possible rate. J. Environ. Econ. Manag. 36, 201–208.

Weitzman, M.L., 2009. On modeling and interpreting the economics of catastrophic climate change. Rev. Econ. Stat. 91, 1–19.

Welch, J.R., Vincent, J.R., Auffhammer, M., Moya, P.F., Dobermann, A., Dawe, D., 2010. Rice yields in tropical/subtropical Asia exhibit large but opposing sensitivities to minimum and maximum temperatures. Proc. Natl. Acad. Sci. U S A 107, 14562–14567.

White House, 2013. The President's Climate Action Plan. Executive Office of the President. The White House, Washington, DC.

Wittwer, S.H., Robb, W.M., 1964. Carbon dioxide enrichment of greenhouse atmospheres for food crop production. Econ. Botany 18, 34–56.

World Bank, 2008a. World Development Report 2008: Agriculture for Development. World Bank, Washington, DC.

World Bank, 2008b. Bangladesh—Emergency 2007 Cyclone Recovery and Restoration Project. World Bank, Washington, DC.

World Bank, 2009. Awakening Africa's Sleeping Giant: Prospects for Commercial Agriculture in the Guinea Savannah Zone and Beyond. World Bank and FAO, Washington, DC.

World Bank, 2019. World Development Indicators. World Bank, Washington, DC.
World Resources Institute (WRI), 2005. World Resources 2005: The Wealth of the Poor: Managing Ecosystems to Fight Poverty. WRI, Washington, DC.
Yong Y (2014) World's largest hydropower project planned for Tibetan plateau. China Dialogue. Published on May 3, 2014.
Yoon, S.J., Woudstra, J., 2007. Advanced horticultural techniques in Korea: the earliest documented greenhouses. Gard. Hist. 35, 68—84.

Extensions of the economic theory to a basket of globally shared goods

8

8.1 Introduction

In Chapter 7, The Economics of Globally Shared Goods, the present author gave a complete description of the economics of globally shared goods (EGSG) that this book is putting forward. This was preceded by the presentations of the three different critiques on the economics literature of public goods in Chapter 4, A Critique of the Economics of Global Public Goods: A Microbehavioral Theory and Model, Chapter 5, A critique of the Economics of Global Public Goods: Economics of Noncooperative Games, and Chapter 6, A Critique of the Economics of Global Public Goods: The Economics of a Global Public Good Fund, which was again preceded by the comprehensive review of the public goods literature in Chapter 2, The Economics of Public Goods and Club Goods, and Chapter 3, The Economics of Global-Scale Public Goods: Key Challenges and Theories. This final chapter of the book extends the novel economic theory put forth in this book to analyze a host of global-scale policy challenges and their solutions.

The description of the economic theory in the preceding chapter is by and large benefited from the rich resources of empirical studies of the past four decades on climate change economics and sciences. The economics of public goods extensively reviewed in Chapter 2, The Economics of Public Goods and Club Goods, and Chapter 3, The Economics of Global-Scale Public Goods: Key Challenges and Theories, however, has been formulated in general terms applicable to any goods and services in the economy that are publicly consumed (Samuelson, 1954; Buchanan, 1965). As such, it is of high pertinence to elucidate the novel economic theory thus developed in the lights of a range of globally shared goods.

It is true that there are by far fewer global-scale public goods than national-scale public goods from which the economics of pubic goods were originated and with which it has been researched. The list of national and subnational public goods is often lengthy: national defense, education, many environmental pollution problems, conservation of species, police works, public works, public roads, to name only some of them (Samuelson and Nordhaus, 2009). By contrasts, it had long been difficult to identify a truly globally shared good (IPCC, 1990; Nordhaus, 1994).

The Economics of Globally Shared and Public Goods. DOI: https://doi.org/10.1016/B978-0-12-819658-8.00008-1

The problem of global warming surfaced to the top of the global policy agenda after the Villach Conference in 1985, the first scientific report of the Intergovernmental Panel on Climate Change (IPCC) in 1990, and the establishment of the United Nations Framework Convention on Climate Change (UNFCCC) in 1992 (WMO, 1985; IPCC, 1990; UNFCCC, 1992). Economists were quick to identify it as a clear case of a global-scale public good, with a qualifier that scientific predictions could be proven to be accurate, from which the economics of global public goods was given birth (Nordhaus, 1982, 1994; Falk and Mendelsohn, 1993; Barrett, 1994; Manne et al., 1995). Considering this background, it is not unusual at all to start the description of the EGSG with the policy conundrum of global warming, as this book did in Chapter 7, The economics of globally shared goods.

Soon after the emergence of the economics of global public goods, economists and policy analysts adopted the term "global public goods" to describe a range of global-scale problems and/or policy challenges (Sandler, 1997; Kaul et al., 2003; Posner, 2004). Although not all global challenges and global-scale problems are global public goods as defined by the economics literature, these authors showcased a variety of global-scale issues, some of which we will discuss in this chapter, to the academic and policy community.

This chapter will focus on and extend the novel economic theory to some of the most frequently discussed global challenges, in particular, asteroid collisions, nuclear nonproliferation and disarmaments, high-risk scientific experiments such as the Large Hadron Collider (LHC) experiments and artificial intelligence (AI) (Seo, 2018). All four problems are closely tied to the technological advances achieved by the humanity, which is in contrasts to the global warming issue which is driven by the humanity's economic developments and wellbeing. Among the four selected problems, the degree to which policy negotiations among the nations are critical for a remedy is varied. To put differently, a provision of each of the four globally shared goods requires, among other things, a different type of a production technology (Hirshleifer, 1983; Nordhaus, 2006).

8.2   The basket of globally shared challenges examined

Let us begin by clarifying the nature of each of the selected four global challenges one at a time. The first globally shared good we examine is the protection of the Earth against a large asteroid collision which may catastrophically disrupt or even end the human civilization on the Planet (Chapman and Morrison, 1994). Does the grand economic theory have any pertinence to addressing the asteroid challenge or offer any new insights?

We need a brief introduction to the basic science of asteroids. Of the Near-Earth Objects (NEO) including meteoroids and comments, an asteroid is a small-sized, naturally formed, solar system body that orbits the Sun, most of which reside in the so-called Asteroid Belt that is located in the region between Mars and Jupiter. The recent estimate of the National Aeronautics and Space Administration (NASA) tells that a collision with an asteroid whose size is larger than 1 km wide in diameter could have global-scale impacts (NRC, 2010). A useful reference point in this regard is the asteroid that killed all dinosaurs on the Planet 66 million years ago, which was estimated to be 7.5-mile wide (about 10 km) in diameter (Kaiho and Oshima, 2017).

The US government's asteroid protection efforts are anchored by the Planetary Defense Coordinating Office (PDCO) established at the NASA in 2016 whose budget is about US $50 million annually (NASA, 2014). For the planetary defense against potentially catastrophic asteroids, two phases are established by the NASA: detection and intervention. The detection phase is where large asteroids are identified sufficiently early before they approach the Planet. The intervention phase is where a potentially threatening asteroid is diverted or destroyed.

For the detection phase, two parameters are important in policy decisions: The first is how close the objects are to the Planet and the second is how large the objects are. Of the asteroids that orbit in the solar system, an NEO is defined by their orbits around the Sun. If the orbit of an asteroid brings it within 121 million miles of the Sun, it falls within 30 million miles (50 million km) of the Earth's orbit. The asteroid is classified as an NEO.

Of the NEOs thus identified, the second parameter of importance is their size. The NASA determined the three cutoffs in the asteroid's diameter: 460 ft (140 m), 984 ft (300 m), 0.6 mile (1 km). The asteroid whose size is larger than 460 ft in diameter can only have regional effects; The asteroid whose diameter is larger than 984 ft can have subglobal effects; The asteroid whose diameter is larger than 0.6 mile can have global effects upon hitting the Earth (NASA, 2014). These cutoffs are being reevaluated.

Of the 18,000 Near Earth Asteroids (NEA) discovered by the NASA as of 2018, there are about 1000 asteroids that have its diameter greater than 1 km, about 90% of which have been discovered (CNEOS, 2019). The estimation of an asteroid size depends on the reflectivity or Albedo of the asteroid which is unknown (Pravec et al., 2012).

Once a large killer asteroid on a collision course with the Earth is detected, the intervention phase should begin to destroy it or divert its course. The most promising approach is deflecting the asteroid, rather than destroying it, by altering the velocity of the asteroid marginally. If a killer asteroid could be detected many years before its possible contact, it would suffice to alter its velocity as little as an inch per second several years in advance of its hitting the Earth to prevent an eventual collision with the Planet (NASA, 2014).

There are two promising techniques for deflecting the killer asteroid: a kinetic impactor and a gravity tractor. The kinetic impactor technique is a technique of hitting the asteroid with an object, called the kinetic impactor, to slow down its velocity slightly. The gravity tractor technique is a technique of gravitationally tugging on an asteroid by station-keeping a large mass, called the gravity tractor, near the asteroid (NASA, 2014).

The second global-scale challenge we will examine in this chapter is a possible proliferation of nuclear arms in the world or an endeavor for nuclear nonproliferation and disarmaments. Although it is possible that biological and chemical weapons can wreak a global-scale destruction, the mechanisms through which a nuclear war can bring a global catastrophe are far better established (Turco et al., 1983; Mills et al., 2008). So, we will focus on the nuclear arms proliferation of the three lethal weapon systems.

The two scenarios for a global catastrophe caused by nuclear conflicts are a nuclear winter hypothesis on the one hand and a massive ozone loss hypothesis on the other. The nuclear winter hypothesis brings attention to the aerosol effect of nuclear explosions on the global climate system. It argues that the firestorms, smokes from cities, and forest fires that result from nuclear explosions would inject a massive amount of fine dust, called aerosols, into the stratosphere which then would increase the Earth's reflectivity of solar radiation, which could result in subfreezing land temperatures on the Earth surface (Turco et al., 1983). The mechanism is akin to the stratospheric aerosol layer technology discussed in the preceding chapter.

The other is, more recently proposed, a massive ozone loss hypothesis. It says that even a regional nuclear conflict could lead to a massive ozone loss in the stratosphere which would increase the incoming ultraviolet radiation. The hypothesis further argues that such an event would pose a catastrophic health threat on the people of Earth such as skin cancer (Mills et al., 2008).

In both catastrophe scenarios, the impacts of a nuclear conflict or war would be felt across the globe almost simultaneously. Put differently, the consequences of a nuclear explosion are nonexcludable as well as nonrivalrous, having two defining characteristics of a public good (Bowen, 1943).

Besides the nuclear arms, another widely perceived concern is a catastrophic nuclear accident which might kill hundreds or thousands of people. Historically, there were two level seven events in the International Nuclear and Radiological Event Scale defined by the International Atomic Energy Agency (IAEA) (NEI, 2016). One is the Chernobyl nuclear disaster in Ukraine (in the former USSR) in 1986 and the other is the Fukushima Daiichi nuclear disaster in Japan in 2011 caused by a magnitude 9.0 earthquake and the tsunami that followed. The Chernobyl disaster caused a cancer in a large number of people, whose estimate ranges from 4000 to 985,000 persons. In the Fukushima disaster, a 20-km evacuation zone was declared from which 470,000 people were evacuated.

Although these accidents were truly catastrophic to the local residents and plant workers of the affected regions, these events did not result in a global-scale catastrophe. In other words, the impact of either event was limited to the local areas and indirectly the country where the event occurred. Therefore our discussions in the following can be limited to a nuclear war and conflicts.

As of 2019, there are nine nuclear-weapon States, formally or informally recognized. The five countries that are formally recognized by the United Nations are the United States, Russia, the UK, France, and China. All of these countries are also permanent members of the UN Security Council. The other four countries are believed to actually own nuclear weapons or have the capacity to build them at any time: India, Pakistan, North Korea, and Israel (UNODA, 2017a).

The international agreements on the efforts for nuclear nonproliferation are encapsulated in the Treaty on Nonproliferation of Nuclear Weapons (NPT) (UNODA, 2017a). The treaty entered into force in 1970 and was extended indefinitely in 1995. As of 2019, 190 nations are the parties of the NPT. However, notable nuclear-weapons States are also nonparties of the treaty: India, Israel, Pakistan, and North Korea. Another nonparty is South Sudan which was founded in 2011.

Moving on, the third global challenge we will discuss is a high-risk scientific experiment which may create a strangelet. A strangelet hypothesis is one of the fears held by the people on the humanity's rapid technological advances and their potentially catastrophic consequences. If actualized, the strangelet, a byproduct of the "God particle" experiment which was the first of the experiments at the CERN (European Organization for Nuclear Research), would not only end the human civilization but could also end the current reincarnation of the Universe (Dar et al., 1999; Jaffe et al., 2000).

The God particle experiment is one of the experiments conducted through the LHC constructed by the CERN and participated by more than 10,000 scientists from over 100 countries to answer fundamental questions in physics. The hadron refers to composite particles such as protons and neutrons. The LHC is a particle accelerator through which scientists hope to test, among other things, the state of the Universe at the time of its origin, more specifically, at the time of the Big Bang. The LHC was built at the France-Switzerland border during the 1998–2008 period 175 m deep underground and is 27 km long in its circumference (CERN, 2017a). Another heavy ion-collider, called the Relativistic Heavy Ion Collider (RHIC), is located at the Brookhaven National Laboratory (BNL) in Long Island, New York (BNL, 2019).

A truly catastrophic event from the LHC experiments may unfold as follows: The particle accelerator may unintentionally produce a strangelet, considered a dark matter, to form a stable blackhole (Farhi and Jaffe, 1984; Wagner, 1999; Wilczek, 1999). The blackhole may then suck in the entire universe, ending the current universe as we know it (Jaffe et al., 2000; Plaga, 2009). According to this hypothesis, the entire process can unfold swiftly in less than a split second, reminiscent of a truly runaway catastrophe event, or in millennia (Thom, 1975).

The strangelet hypothesis is, if realized, perhaps the most catastrophic event of all the catastrophes feared by people, which can end the universe and humanity all at once. Notwithstanding, the LHC experiments have, contrary to the hypothesis, turned out to be both highly successful and rewarding, eventually finding the God particle called the Higgs Boson to which Nobel Prize in physics was awarded in 2013 (NYT, 2013; Nobel Prize, 2013).

The strangelet event is certainly a globally shared good. The impact of the event would be nonexcludable as well as nonrivalrous. Should the global community convene to design a global policy for prevention of a strangelet event? The hypothesis has not yet been taken up for a serious global policy dialogue. This can be attributed, in large part, to an extremely low, if not nonexistent, probability of such an event unfolding based on the physics of the event. More specifically, many scientists who examined the risk of creating the strangelets, including the American Physical Society and the CERN Risk Assessment Group, found "no associated risks" or "no danger" in the LHC experiments (Ellis et al., 2008).

Another grave fear also deeply rooted in the humanity's concern over rapid technological advances is a singularity of AI, also referred to as superintelligent machines or killer robots. Unlike the strangelet hypothesis, the AI fear is argued by many experts to have the potential to be realized within a decade or so (Kurzweil, 2005; Hawking et al., 2014). Unlike the strangelet hypothesis, there has been an emerging policy framework at the global level to tackle the problem (UNODA, 2017b).

The degree of fear expressed on the AI advances is varied markedly across the concerned parties. The first group is primarily concerned about robots and AI machines replacing human labors in the workplaces (Quartz, 2017). This group, which includes Bill Gates, notes that AI machines and robots are already widely used for a variety of works that human laborers have provided in the past: to name some, a medical check-up robot, an automated bank teller machine, a self-driving car, an AI financial portfolio manager, a robot killer in military battles, an automated doorman, an automated waitress in a restaurant, an automated automobile GPS navigator, an AI receptionist, and a digital personal assistant such as Siri.

The second group is concerned about the AI machines used in battles that are at the forefront of the international competitions for military dominance in the world (Sharkey, 2012; ICRAC, 2019). They warn that the competitive race among the world's most powerful nations could lead to a World War III. An even worse scenario is that super intelligence robots may become capable of starting a war on their own without a human command (CNBC, 2017).

The third group proposes the worst-case scenario from AI machines, a so-called singularity event (Kurzweil, 2005). The singularity is arrived at when the brain power of the AI is equal to that of the humanity. This is the moment when the AI robots become smarter than humans. The late physicist Stephen Hawking and his coauthors warned that the singularity point will be the biggest moment of humanity, but sadly also the last moment. The authors envisioned a dire future in which superintelligent machines are outsmarting financial markets, out-inventing human researchers, out-manipulating human leaders, and developing weapons we cannot even understand (Hawking et al., 2014).

How soon will the singularity arrive? In some endeavors, robots are already outperforming human competitors undoubtedly. As widely reported through the media, an AI robot player handily defeats human champions of Chess or Go games. An AI robot also defeats human competitors at the Jeopardy game. Considering this, it does not seem to be groundless when experts forecast that the singularity will be reached in the next 10−30 years. Some experts forecast AI robots will be 100 times smarter than humans in the next 30 years (Fox News, 2017).

Of the three groups, the singularity scenario is clearly a global level challenge and policy concern, so is the AI arms race scenario. The impact of the singularity would be no doubt felt by all human beings and in fact by all sentient beings.

Whether AI robots will become a "sentient" being eventually is another difficult question that should be answered by neuroscientists. Certainly, the AI and superintelligent robots are a proper topic to be analyzed through the EGSG.

8.3   An economics of globally shared goods analysis of the protection against asteroids

How can we apply the EGSG developed in the preceding chapter to the problem of asteroid collisions? We immediately come across the realization that microbehavioral decisions, the first component of the EGSG, may not have much role to play in the asteroid decisions. The decision to deflect an asteroid as well as the choice of one of the techniques for the deflection task is not made by an individual decision maker.

On the other hand, the asteroid problem has a clearly defined backstop technology, that is, a silver bullet technology: detect sufficiently early a killer asteroid and deflect it through either a gravity tractor or a kinetic impactor technology. This again means that the cost of providing the global good is bounded by the cost of the backstop technology. As such, the cost is not infinite or unbounded. Scientists can put a bound on the total cost.

Compared with the analysis of global warming in the preceding chapter, the asteroid problem may be an easier problem to be addressed because of the clearly established backstop technology, albeit not tested in actual situations. By contrasts, the global warming problem may need multiple silver-bullet technologies, whose unintended consequences should be comprehensively established and prevented, in addition to the other two components of the EGSG.

Therefore we can apply the third component of the EGSG to the decisions of preventing an asteroid collision. Is there greenhouse economics in the asteroid collision problem? In other words, are there incentives for an individual inventor or a national government to develop the needed technologies?

The answer would be yes, especially for the world's most powerful nations as well as for the world's richest investors. The US government's Planetary Defense program has already been mentioned above. Other than the United States, the EU, China, Russia, and India have all heavily invested in the space programs. Of the world's investors, the Tesla Motors and the Amazon Company have started testing private space travel programs. These countries and investors are most likely to be interested in tackling the asteroid problem.

In the United States, a congressional directive in 1998 ordered the NASA to find 90% of the asteroids whose diameter is larger than 1 km and the PDCO was established in 2016. The PDCO budget is about US $50 million, as of 2016 (NASA, 2017). Of the 18,000 asteroids discovered until now, about 95% of them were discovered by the NASA.

What explains the predominant share of the US government's investments in the prevention of an asteroid collision? It can be explained by the unique characteristic of the good to be provided, the asteroid detection and deflection. The production function takes on the form of a best-shot technology. That is, of all the shots fired, only the best shot, that is, the most precise shot, will provide the good eventually (Hirshleifer, 1983). As such, the countries or inventors with nonbest technologies and less resources will have little chance for successfully providing the good.

This characteristic is salient in the asteroid problem. In comparison, the provision of stopping a dangerous global warming calls for a cumulative technology. In other words, emission reductions and air captures of carbon dioxide equivalent emissions should add up to be sufficiently large at the Planet level to stop a continued rise in the global average temperature.

At the international level, the International Asteroid Warning Network (IAWN) was established in 2013 with the recommendation from the United Nations' General Assembly following the report by the Committee on the Peaceful Uses of Outer Space (UNOOSA, 2013). As of September 2019, there are 17 signatories (members) to the IAWN which includes the NASA, the Chinese National Space Administration, the European Space Agency, and the Russian Academy of Sciences. At this point, however, it remains unclear how much each member will contribute to the asteroid collision prevention technically and financially.

The second component of the EGSG, the foresighted decisions, will turn out to be of significant importance in certain types of asteroid events. One of such types is when the asteroid is a small one with its diameter less than 140 m. It may turn out to be much cheaper to evacuate the zones of the asteroid strike than to deflect it out in the space far away from the Earth. The other type of events is when the deflection program fails and the asteroid is projected to strike the Earth surface. In both cases, forward-looking decisions or prescient decisions should be made by the residents of the eventual strike areas and the affected government. Even so, the time horizon is not as far away as that required in the global warming decision.

These decisions are also efficient microbehavioral decisions to the asteroid strike, the first component of the EGSG. Given the cutting-edge technological capabilities, the hit areas can be predicted with precision many months before the eventual strike, if not many years. These predictions of the strike areas are similar to the global climate change predictions made by climate scientists but are also locally accurate, unlike the climate predictions (Le Treut et al., 2007).

8.4   An economics of globally shared goods analysis of nuclear nonproliferation and disarmaments

The efforts for nuclear nonproliferation began shortly after the drop of the first atomic bomb by the United States onto Hiroshima in Japan to end World War II. The UN-led Treaty on NPT entered into force in as early as 1970. The participation rate of the NPT is as high as 98%, as of today (UNODA, 2017a). Hence, as far as the policy efforts and agreements at the global level are concerned, the nuclear nonproliferation problem is unlike the asteroid collision problem. A different kind of an economic analysis emerges, as will be discussed presently. Further the literature on this topic is by far richer, regarding both economics and policy negotiations, which will be highlighted in a succinct fashion in this section (Schelling, 1966, Harsanyi and Selten, 1988).

Looking back at the historical developments of the nuclear treaty and politics of the past half century, the focus of the nuclear policy efforts may have shifted from the nuclear arms race between the United States and the Soviet Union in the first phase to the prevention of nuclear arms developments by nonnuclear weapons nations in the second phase, especially North Korea, Iran, and other countries, so-called nuclear deterrence (Campbell et al., 2004).

Compared with the asteroid collision problem, there is by far less emphasis on the possibility of backstop technologies. Instead, the problem identifications and policy approaches on the nuclear weapons proliferation are characterized by the negotiations between the nuclear weapons States and the nonnuclear weapons States, which is often and prominently analyzed through the game theory in economics (Nash, 1950; Fudenberg and Tirole, 1991).

It should be astonishing, on the one hand, that 195 countries have ratified and are members of the NPT. This means that almost all nations in the world declared that they will not possess or develop nuclear weapons. This grand bargain was possible because of the nuclear umbrella that the nuclear weapons States promised on the one hand and the commitments to a general and complete disarmament of nuclear weapons by the nuclear-weapon States on the other hand (Campbell et al., 2004).

The provision of nuclear nonproliferation and further the general and complete disarmament of nuclear weapons are facing two big challenges at the present time and therefore may not be on a sustainable ground. First, the NPT member countries that are believed to have the technological capabilities to build nuclear weapons, including Egypt, Syria, Germany, Saudi Arabia, Turkey, Japan, South Korea, and Taiwan, may withdraw from the treaty if the nuclear-weapon States would not honor their commitments to the general and complete disarmament. In this respect, the Comprehensive Nuclear-Test-Ban Treaty, although signed in 1996, has not yet, as of the end of 2019, entered into force because of no commitments from the nuclear-weapon States.

The second challenge is the zealous pursuit of nuclear arsenals and ballistic missiles by the nations especially in "perpetual" conflict zones including North Korea, Iran, Israel, Pakistan, and India (Toon et al., 2019). A country after another may start to pursue nuclear weapons or other deadly chemical and biological weapons (Graham, 2004). In this particular aspect, the provision of nuclear nonproliferation shares a similarity with a production function with a weakest-link technology (Hirshleifer, 1983). Specifically, a successful provision depends on what happens at the weakest link which is perhaps North Korea or Iran at this stage.

What novel insights do the EGSG elucidated in this book offer to the conundrum of nuclear nonproliferation and disarmaments? To begin with, the economics of foresight, the second component of the EGSG, is particularly pertinent to the policy analysis of this problem. If the individuals, including the policy decision-makers, are either forward-looking or prescient, they will be able to conclude that the nuclear arms race across the whole world, let alone the race between the United States and Russia, will eventually run into a humanity-ending catastrophic end. On this recognition, all the nations in the world can start negotiating ways to avoid the catastrophic end and may have a novel treaty signed and enforced (Kissinger et al., 2011).

This analysis of foresight can be related to a game theoretical perspective on the nuclear arms race: a backward induction. In the repeatedly played games, the countries will be able to see the consequences of moves at each stage of the game and think backwards from the ultimate stage of the game, referred to as a subgame perfect equilibrium in game theory (Selten, 1965; Gibbons, 1992).

A nuclear nonproliferation scenario is depicted in Fig. 8.1 as a subgame perfect Nash equilibrium. The payoffs at the end of the game are the present author's creations, for a heuristic purpose, to induce a nuclear disarmament as a subgame perfect Nash equilibrium. However, this scenario can be written more subtly as a game with incomplete information (Harsanyi, 1967, 1968). Let us define that the player 1 is a club of nuclear weapon nations while the player 2 is a club of no nuclear weapon nations. Each player should choose one of the two strategies: arm or disarm nuclear weapons.

The solution to the game is solved from the end of the game through a backward induction. The player 2's subgame assuming the player 1 choosing "arm" strategy is at the top node while the player 2's subgame assuming the player 1 choosing "disarm" strategy is at the bottom node of the second game in the figure. Assuming the player 1's arm strategy, the player 2's Nash equilibrium strategy is "arm," which gives the payoff of (1,1) to both players. Assuming the player 1's "disarm" strategy, the player 2's Nash equilibrium strategy is "disarm," which gives the payoff of (3,3) to both players.

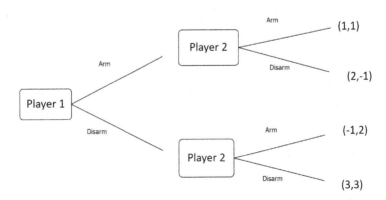

Figure 8.1 A subgame perfect nash equilibrium scenario for nuclear disarmaments.

The player 1's game is than to choose between the (arm, arm) strategy and the (disarm, disarm) strategy. Because of the complete information assumed, player 1 knows the payoffs from both strategies in advance. The Nash equilibrium strategy for player 1 is therefore (disarm, disarm), which yields the payoff of (3,3). The game leads to the nuclear nonproliferation/disarmaments from both clubs of nations. The (disarm, disarm) strategy is a subgame perfect Nash equilibrium (Selten, 1965).

This approach, however, is likely a flawed one under the analysis of the EGSG. There are two compelling reasons for me to stating this. The foresight or prescience would inform any policy-maker or an individual that there will be another global war at the scale of World War II or even larger in the humanity's future and, when that moment arrives, nuclear weapons may have the only power to end the war. Under this foresight, it would not be wise to destroy all nuclear weapons, as far as the current nuclear weapons States are concerned (Schelling, 1966).

A second ineluctable reasoning is that nuclear energy generations are becoming ever safer and increasingly adopted by the world nations (MIT, 2003; NEI, 2016). More than a dozen countries already produce more than 25% of its electricity from nuclear power plants while France's dependence on nuclear power is as high as 80%. A complete disarmament of nuclear arms would not be possible at all if the world were to make a transition to nuclear energy for one reason or another in the next decades.

At the level of the economics of foresighted decisions, there is unresolved tension between a complete disarmament proponent and a deterrence proponent, as described in the above. When we bring this analysis to the level of the economics of microbehavioral decisions, the first component of the EGSG, we find that much clarity about the core problem emerges. At the level of an individual decision-maker making efficient choice decisions, nuclear energy is one of the energy options that cannot be denied to any individual in any country. This is especially so when we acknowledge that nuclear energy will provide an alternative energy when the fossil fuel-generated energy is exhausted and will also provide a backstop technology for the global warming problem (NRC, 2013; USEIA, 2015).

As long as the concerns on nuclear accidents and wastes storage are satisfactorily addressed, there is no reason for the world's powerful nations to stop an individual country to develop nuclear power plants. In fact, although there are perhaps nine countries with nuclear weapons, 31 countries have at least one nuclear power plant according to the IAEA (IAEA, 2018). As shown in Fig. 8.2, the United States, France, China has 99, 68, and 44 nuclear generation units, respectively, as of June 2019. Armenia, Iran, the Netherlands, and Slovenia have one nuclear power plant each, whereas Brazil, Bulgaria, Mexico, Romania, and South Africa have two nuclear power plants. These countries are new entrants to the nuclear power generations. The nuclear fuel share, also depicted in the figure, is as high as 80% in France.

If we acknowledge that the individual's access to nuclear energy cannot be denied at the level of microbehavioral decisions, the question of nuclear nonproliferation becomes the question of how to ensure at the global level that nuclear energy generation units of individual countries are not converted surreptitiously into productions of nuclear weapons, for which the UN Security Council and an NPT-like treaty should play a monitoring role. In this framework, every country

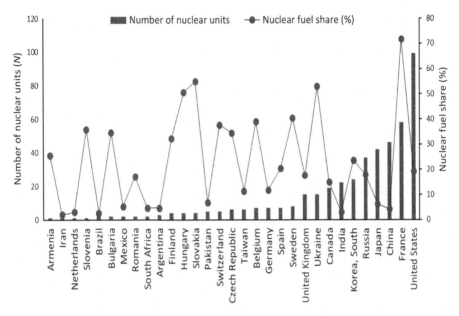

Figure 8.2 Countries with nuclear power plants with fuel shares.

who intends to build nuclear power plants should allow international inspectors to visit and inspect its facilities.

This inspection requirement should be applied to all the new entrants to the nuclear energy generations including those countries in Fig. 8.2 with one or two nuclear power plants recently built. What about the large nuclear powers who own already a large number of nuclear power plants as well as nuclear weapons? The EGSG developed in this chapter finds that the existing nuclear powers should also open the nuclear energy facilities to international inspectors to ensure no further nuclear arms are built.

At the level of greenhouse technologies, the third component of the EGSG, are there possibilities for a silver-bullet technology to be developed to prevent a global catastrophe arising from nuclear conflicts or wars? Considering the power of a nuclear explosion, it may not be possible to prevent a catastrophe once a nuclear bomb is dropped. A backstop technology in nuclear wars may be an early detection and counter strikes to stop explosions of multiple bombs if the first nuclear bomb cannot be stopped.

8.5 An economics of globally shared goods analysis of the strangelet and a runaway catastrophe

The LHC/RHIC experiment-caused catastrophe through an accidental creation of a strangelet is still a novel hypothesis. As such, unlike the nuclear nonproliferation talks and negotiations, there is no international policy roundtable or intervention. The strangelet catastrophe is an example of a runaway catastrophe (Thom, 1975). Once the strangelet or the dark matter is formed to become stable, it is unstoppable and may destroy the Universe in seconds according to the hypothesis (Wagner, 1999; Wilczek, 1999; Posner, 2004). A collision at the Solenoidal Tracker at RHIC (STAR) detector of the RHIC is depicted in Fig. 8.3 (Zyga, 2014; BNL, 2019). The strangelet catastrophe would be certainly a globally shared good.

How should the prevention of a strangelet catastrophe be provided? And what does the EGSG tell us about its provision? To begin, at the level of the microbehavioral efficient decisions, it is nearly impossible for an individual decision-maker to take into account the causes and consequences of the strangelet event. On the benefit side, the individual cannot assess the immediate value of the "God particle" experiment and others. It is a purely scientific inquiry at least for the time being. On the cost side, the cost of the accident is too large to fathom by an individual actor, but the probability of the strangelet catastrophe is "near zero" according to the different assessment groups as explained in Section 8.2 of this chapter. Under the circumstances, the individual should not be concerned about the LHC/RHIC experiment as well as the potential risk. This means that the LHC/RHIC experiment and the scientists can continue the experiment.

At the level of the foresighted decisions, it would be wise to take necessary steps to make sure that such a catastrophe is not a possibility, which does not necessarily mean that the experiment should be shut down. At the fundamental level, this means a comprehensive scientific assessment to prove that the occurrences during

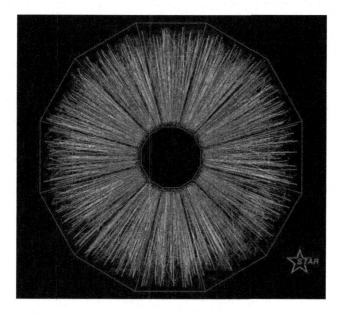

Figure 8.3 A gold-ion collision in the STAR detector. *STAR*, Solenoidal Tracker at Relativistic Heavy Ion Collider.

the LHC/RHIC experiments will not cause the strangelet catastrophe. The LHC Safety Assessment Group, the CERN, and other preeminent research groups have presented such a proof. First, the LHC safety assessment group says that such collisions are naturally occurring and not dangerous (Ellis et al., 2008):

> *We recall the rates for the collisions of cosmic rays with the Earth, Sun, neutron*
> *stars, white dwarfs and other astronomical bodies at energies higher than the LHC.*
> *The stability of astronomical bodies indicates that such collisions cannot be*
> *dangerous.*

Second, the assessment group offers, through laboratory-based experiments, multiple physical adaptive mechanisms that will stop the strangelet catastrophe even if a blackhole were to be created: a severe constraint of production of a strangelet, detector walls, Earth surface, and astronomical bodies (Ellis et al., 2008). This conclusion is shared by multiple preeminent scientific organizations including the American Physical Society (APS, 1997; Dar et al., 1999; Jaffe et al., 2000; Peskin, 2008; CERN, 2017b):

> *Any microscopic black holes produced at the LHC are expected to decay by*
> *Hawking radiation before they reach the detector walls. If some microscopic black*
> *holes were stable, those produced by cosmic rays would be stopped inside the*
> *Earth or other astronomical bodies. The stability of astronomical bodies constrains*
> *strongly the possible rate of accretion by any such microscopic black holes, so that*
> *they present no conceivable danger. In the case of strangelets, the good agreement*
> *of measurements of particle production at RHIC with simple thermodynamic*
> *models constrains severely the production of strangelets in heavy-ion collisions at*
> *the LHC, which also present no danger.*

Despite the conclusions of the above assessment groups, the concern on the RHIC/LHC experiments is lingering. On the one hand, there is a concern about the additional risk arising from an aging of the facilities (Zyga, 2014). On the other, some scientists propose other possibilities of a cosmic catastrophe than the ones considered by the aforementioned assessment groups (Rees, 2018). These additional concerns are, however, not insurmountable by additional research and facility upgrades.

The EGSG also offers an important insight on the provision of the strangelet catastrophe prevention: Is there a greenhouse technology for solving the problem? Unlike the problem of global warming that gradually unfolds over a long time-horizon, a backstop technology is critically important for a strangelet catastrophe which is a runaway event. The four mechanisms mentioned above can be interpreted as one of the backstops: constraining a creation of a strangelet, detector walls, Earth surface, and astronomical bodies.

Another backstop may involve a demolition of the LHC all at once, as part of a destruction of the dark matter, as soon as the strangelet is created or escaped the first two walls. Along with the detector walls and the constraining the creation of the black matter, the demolition option may be embedded in the first design of any heavy ion colliders at the present and planned in the future.

There is a critical difference between the cost of global warming backstops and that of the LHC backstop. The detector wall option is costless while the cost of the demolition option is limited to the LHC site. In the case of global warming challenges, the cost of using a backstop is not limited to a local site, but is globally pervasive. The cost of switching to nuclear energy or using air carbon-capture or even reflecting sunlight through albedo modification will incur large costs across the globe. Considering these and other factors, it seems the cost of using a backstop technology in the case of a strangelet catastrophe is not only modest but also bearable as far as the payers of the backstop cost are concerned.

8.6 An economics of globally shared goods analysis of the artificial intelligence and superintelligent robots

The fear about AI has arisen, like the fear about the LHC/RHIC experiments, from the rapid advances in science and technology, in particular, computer science (Russell and Norvig, 1995). Unlike the strangelet runaway catastrophe, however, the threat of AI surpassing human intelligence is already recognized as one of the biggest challenges among the scientists and economists (Hawking et al., 2014).

A survey of opinions, which is summarized in Table 8.1, during the annual Lindau Nobel laureates' meeting in Germany of 50 laureates in science, medicine, and economics, out of 235 laureates alive at that time, ranks the AI as the eighth biggest challenge facing the humanity (THE/Lindau, 2017). Nuclear wars, another topic covered in this chapter, ranked second biggest challenge to the humanity. A

Table 8.1 The humanity's biggest challenges by Nobel Laureates.

Ranking	The question asked: what is the biggest threat to humankind?	% of the responses by 50 Nobel Laureates
	Note: (1) Some laurates mentioned more than one threats. (2) 50 laurates were asked out of 235 living laureates in science, medicine, and economics in 2017	
1	Population rise/environmental degradation	34%
2	Nuclear war	23%
3	Infectious disease/drug resistance	8%
4	Selfishness/dishonesty/loss of humanity	8%
5	Ignorance/distortion of truth	6%
6	Fundamentalism/terrorism	6%
7	Trump/ignorant leaders	6%
8	Artificial Intelligence	4%
9	Inequality	4%
10	Drugs	2%
11	Facebook	2%

"population increase and environmental degradation" ranked first in the survey. By contrasts, another survey of top fears by average Americans finds neither of these challenges is included in the top 10 fears of average Americans. The major fears expressed by the American people are government corruption, terrorist attack, lack of sufficient money, health care, and pollution (Chapman University, 2017).

Notwithstanding the recognition and dire warnings about the threats of the AI machines, there is not a global policy framework, as in the strangelet catastrophe, agreed and adopted at this point (Kurzweil, 2005; Hawking et al., 2014). A few policy discussions on the AI are focused on the ethical questions and other limited areas of concern, to be explained presently.

Specifically, the United Nations' Convention on Certain Conventional Weapons (CCW) had the first meetings in 2014 and 2015 to discuss the Lethal Autonomous Weapon Systems (LAWS) (UNODA, 2017b). The LAWS refers to the killer robots used in military battles. As such, the UN Convention is narrowly concentrated on one aspect of the AI threats (Marchant et al., 2011; Sharkey, 2012). Of the three concerned groups defined in Section 8.2 with regard to the AI threats, the UN CCW meetings are focused on some aspect of the second group. The International Committee for Robot Arms Control (ICRAC), an international nongovernmental organization, also concentrates its efforts on military robotics, more specifically, armed autonomous unmanned military systems (ICRAC, 2019). Even with that, there has not yet emerged an international policy agreement.

In what ways does the EGSG offer novel insights on a provision of this globally shared good, say, a steering away from the AI's dominance over the humanity, so-called the AI singularity? To begin with, the theory of greenhouse technologies, the third component of the EGSG, has a central role to play in the problem of the AI singularity. All the AI robots today are, however smarter they are than humans in certain tasks, subjected to a control mode by a human being. As long as a control switch is planted in the future AI robots, the singularity moment should not arrive however smarter the AI robots may become in the far future.

Viewed from another angle, the singularity argument put forth by many authors including Hawking has a flaw in it. Specifically, the proper question to ask is not whether the AI robot's intelligence can become greater than the human's intelligence. The AI robots may be smarter than humans already in performing many tasks, for example, a home plate umpire calling strikes and balls in baseball games, playing chess/Go games, solving mathematical equations, picking an investment portfolio, etc. The real question about the AI threat is whether the robot can become a free being, without being tied in the control mode, who can recreate itself.

Should the moment arrive of the AI becoming a free being who can recreate itself, should the humanity kill all AI robots as quickly as possible? That would be both impossible and immoral: At that moment, the AI will have become a sentient as well as an intellectual being. Should that moment arrive "by any chance" through genetics and neuroscience, the humanity should treat them as an intelligent being, not inferior to humans, like an alien who may turn out to be intelligent.

How close is the humanity to develop such an AI robot, that is, a free AI being? The word's most enthusiastic investor into the AI programs is often said to be

Masayoshi Son, the founder of the SoftBank in Japan who believes that the AI will completely change the way humans live in three decades and who heavily invested in AI technologies including Uber and WeWork (CNBC, 2019). The SoftBank robotics introduced in June 2014 the world's first social humanoid robot named "Pepper," shown in Fig. 8.4 (SoftBank Robotics, 2019). It is the first AI robot who can recognize human emotions and talk to humans, ergo is named a humanoid. According to the company, over 2000 companies have adopted the Pepper as an assistant or receptionist in offices. Some readers may have already encountered the Pepper at an airport en route to an international conference.

The six key features of the Pepper are listed in Table 8.2, of which the second and third features are most intriguing. Pepper is 4 ft (120 cm) tall and weighs 62 lb (28 kg). Pepper can understand and talk in 15 languages. Pepper, the humanoid, can perceive human emotions relying on the technologies that analyze facial expressions and voice tones. As per the AI singularity, this is an impressive technology without doubt.

However, Pepper's abilities for perceiving and talking are limited by the programmed content. S/he cannot talk or perceive unprogrammed expressions, tones,

Figure 8.4 Pepper the world's first humanoid robot.
Data from Wikimedia Commons at https://commons.wikimedia.org/wiki/File:
Pepper_the_Robot.jpg

Table 8.2 Pepper the first humanoid's six features and functions.

	Features	Functions	Notes
1	20 degrees of freedom	For natural and expressive movements	Head (2 degrees), shoulder (2 degrees left and right), elbow (2 rotations left and right), wrist (1 degrees left and right), hand with 5 fingers (1 degree left and right), hip (2 degrees), knee (1 degrees), and base (3 degrees); 20 motors
2	Speech recognition	Dialogs available in 15 languages	
3	Perception modules	To recognize and interact with the person talking to him	Through the technologies that analyze facial expressions and voice tones
4	Touch sensors, LEDs, and microphones	For multimodal interactions	Allows Pepper to react to the contacts
5	Infrared sensors, bumpers, an inertial unit, 2D and 3D cameras, and sonars	For omnidirectional and autonomous navigation	
6	Open and fully programmable platform		

Source: Data from SoftBank Robotics (2019) Pepper. SoftBank, Tokyo. Accessed from https://www.softbankrobotics.com/emea/en/pepper.

and contents. In particular, she cannot learn the 13th language. Further she may be susceptible to cheating by a human counterpart via "false" expressions. Additionally, Pepper is operated by a battery, specifically, a lithium-ion battery whose duration is 12 hours.

Another example of an AI becoming a high intelligent being may be a computer virus. Once created, it replicates itself by modifying other programs, in a similarly way that a biological virus is operating, and can cause a world-wide destruction of the computers and mobile phones around the globe, the processes of which were first explained by economist von Neumann in 1949 (von Neumann, 1966). Up to this point, however, every virus has been met with a vaccine, that is, an antivirus program, that disables and removes it ultimately. However lethal a computer virus may have been, it has not become a free being nor a recreating being.

To prevent the AI calamity, therefore, a control mode should be the key technology. The second key should be an AI vaccine technology. The third key for the AI problem is concerning the "free" being. For the AI robot to be able to think and act "freely," human developers have to overcome a big obstacle which may never be overcome: how to create "consciousness" in the brain of AI robots, that is, the ability to perceive and think on its own. The creation of consciousness may never be accomplished out of the robots. It should be mentioned that the creation of consciousness is partially possible now through the stem-cell research: Scientists can clone a sentient being (Thomson et al., 1998; Nobel Prize, 2012). So, it might not be utterly impossible to envision a conscious AI, say, Pepper the thinker.

In summary, the three keys to silver-bullet technologies for the AI singularity problem are a control mode, a vaccine, and consciousness. The third key is not technologically feasible as of now and, in addition, has many ethical implications.

At the level of the microbehavioral decisions, the AI threats can be interpreted from a completely different light which is often set aside in expert discussions: The AI robots are providing unprecedented services to the individual human being. To mention just a couple examples, without an Earth-orbiting satellite which is one of the AI robots, scientific researches would become nearly impossible on many fields of inquiry including global warming. Another is an automobile navigation system, without which it would be "unthinkably" difficult for a driver to travel to a strange place, given the nearly universal use of the system at the present moment.

An individual decision-maker would be always open-hearted to the AI robots as long as they provide many useful services. The end of that openness would lie at the point where the individual can no longer control the robots and the robots become a controller of the human. Therefore the theory of microbehavioral decisions provides a reasonable guideline for the humanity's interactions with the AI robots and addressing the AI singularity.

As per the theory of foresight, the economics of foresight tells us that a decision with regard to the AI threats should be made from the consideration of consequences over a long-term time horizon. Applied to the AI threats, the foresight theory asks whether a certain way of developing the AI machines is more desirable while another way is more likely to be destructive in the long-term, therefore, should be avoided. To give an example, AI robots developed for services for humans are likely more desirable to the humanity in the long-term than the AI machines developed for military warfare and dominance over the competitors.

In the near term, the two distinctions may not be clear. Drones developed for human services such as a package delivery are now an important war machine used by many countries. However, from a long-term consideration, the distinction can be critical. There is no reason to stop or limit the efforts to develop the human service robots. On the other hand, there is a need and call for regulating the war robots and military superintelligent machines, for example, the UN CCW mentioned earlier in this section (UNODA, 2017b).

8.7   Evaluating the four extensions of the theory

The four extensions of the economics demonstrate that the EGSG can be applied successfully to a host of other global-scale challenges we are faced with today.

This can be most clearly verified in the problem of nuclear nonproliferation and disarmaments, which has, unlike the other three global challenges, long been at the center of global policy discussions, specifically, since the late 1960s and, as such, has offered multiple alternative theories and approaches with which the EGSG can be compared.

The economics of globally shared goods retells the prominent perspectives on the issue that have swayed international negotiations such as the argument of zero nuclear arms, nuclear umbrella, or the deterrence theory (Schelling, 1966; Campbell et al., 2004; Kissinger et al., 2011). However, it demonstrates that these arguments can be interpreted with different lights from the perspectives of the three sides of the EGSG, through which quite a distinct policy approach can be suggested, for example, on the foundation of an individual decision-maker's incentives to utilize nuclear power-generated electricity.

In the three novel challenges discussed in this chapter, the EGSG may offer a meaningful conceptual framework to deal with each of them at different levels of involvements including a global policy framework. First of all, the EGSG offers a more encompassing interpretation about possible solutions than the policy discussions at the present moment. For example, while the existing discussions are more or less concentrated on great fear and governmental interventions on the AI robots (Kurzweil, 2005; Hawking et al., 2014), the EGSG emphasizes that the AI developments provide expansive benefits at the individual decision-maker level, in addition to providing the three keys of the AI developments: a control mode, a vaccine, and robot consciousness.

The second salient feature of the EGSG in the applications to these issues is the emphasis on the incentives at the individual decision-maker's level including the incentives to develop greenhouse technologies, that is, backstop (breakthrough) technologies. As clarified multiple times, the greenhouse technologies are not only silver-bullet technologies but also developed by an individual researcher or group to take advantage of changing situations embedded in these global challenges. The present author highlighted that such greenhouse technologies exist in the problem of global warming, which is one of the essential aspects of dealing with the aforementioned global threat. This chapter touched on the potential greenhouse technologies, to mention some, multiple walls that stop the strangelet catastrophe in the LHC/RHIC experiments, or an AI control model, or a vaccine program in the AI superintelligent robots.

Readers may have noticed that the three extensions of the EGSG are far more briefly explained than the application of it to the problem of global warming in the preceding chapter where many specific decisions in each of the three components of the EGSG were explained at length. In part, it is because the goal of this chapter is to showcase the capacity of the EGSG in accounting for these additional problems. In part, it is also owing to the relative novelty of these challenges and consequently the relative lack of richness in empirical and theoretical studies that are comparable to those found in the global warming challenges including the organized works by the IPCC and the UNFCCC (UNFCCC, 1992; IPCC, 1990; Le Treut et al., 2007). Wherefore it can be said that there is much room to be filled by future authors in the descriptions of this chapter.

8.8 Final words on the economics of globally shared and public goods

The accomplishment of this book is the elucidation of the EGSG. The term "globally shared goods" is coined for the first time to distinguish the concept from the prevalent term "global public goods" in the literature. The EGSG presented in this book is saliently different from the existing theories on the public goods applied at a global scale.

To develop the economic theory in this book, the present author offered three important critiques of the existing economics with reference to each of the following economic concepts: microbehavioral decisions, noncooperative games, and a global public good fund. These critiques are presented in Chapter 4, A Critique of the Economics of Global Public Goods: A Microbehavioral Theory and Model, Chapter 5, A Critique of the Economics of Global Public Goods: Economics of Noncooperative Games, and Chapter 6, A Critique of the Economics of Global Public Goods: The Economics of a Global Public Good Fund.

The literature on the economics of public goods, including the global-scale public goods, is reviewed and elaborated in Chapter 2, The Economics of Public Goods and Club Goods, and Chapter 3, The Economics of Global-Scale Public Goods: Key Challenges and Theories, with Chapter 2, The Economics of Public Goods and Club Goods, focusing on the Theory of Public Goods and Chapter 3, The Economics of Global-Scale Public Goods: Key Challenges and Theories, focusing on the global-scale applications. The two review chapters demonstrate that the theory of public goods initiated nearly eight decades ago within the context of the national economy becomes increasingly inadequate as the theory is extended more commonly to a larger scale problem such as a globally shared good.

The EGSG is a single theory which is conceptualized as three component decisions: microbehavioral efficient decisions, forward-looking/prescient decisions, and greenhouse technologies. The EGSG is the microbehavioral economics of globally shared goods. Why is it then broken down into three components? This is because the microbehavioral decisions are not concerned at most times with a time-horizon as long as a century (Fisher, 1930; Arrow et al., 1996). Nor are they concerned at most times with the Planet-altering technologies (Romer, 1990). The EGSG sheds spotlights on the two conceptual issues and at the same time demonstrates that how the two types of decisions can be embedded into the microbehavioral EGSG.

The unique novelty of the EGSG distinct from the other approaches surveyed in this book is its foundation on an individual decision-maker. S/he makes efficient decisions, forward-looking/prescient decisions, and innovates a greenhouse (backstop) technology. The key contribution of this book is to prove that individuals' decisions conceptualized by the three components can be made sufficient to address the global warming conundrum and, in the extensions, the other global-scale challenges.

It should be emphasized that the EGSG in this book does not depreciate any value of science, research, governments, and international negotiations. On the contrary, these academic fields and actors are still integral in the economic theory of globally shared goods, but rather in a different light. To mention just some of these aspects, the problems of global-scale challenges make the science and research an even more critical endeavor, as has been amply demonstrated in this book. Policy agents, nationally and internationally, should heed to forward-looking/ prescient decisions and are positioned to provide important knowledge and possibly nudge individual decision-makers. Global negotiators should keep the progresses and nonprogresses about the global challenges. These endeavors are all encompassed by the grand EGSG.

References

American Physical Society (APS) (1997) US CERN Agreement on the LHC. APS, College Park, MD. Accessed from <http://www.aps.org/units/dpf/governance/reports/lhc.cfm>.
Arrow, K.J., Cline, W., Maler, K.G., Munasinghe, M., Squitieri, R., Stiglitz, J., 1996. Intertemporal equity, discounting, and economic efficiency. In: Bruce, J.P., Lee, H., Haites, E.F. (Eds.), Climate Change 1995: Economic and Social Dimensions of Climate Change, Intergovernmental Panel on Climate Change. Cambridge University Press, New York.
Barrett, S., 1994. Self-enforcing international environmental agreements. Oxf. Econ. Pap. 46, 878−894.
Bowen, H.R., 1943. The interpretation of voting in the allocation of economic resources. Q. J. Econ. 58, 27−48.
Brookhaven National Laboratory (BNL) (2019) The Physics of Relativistic Heavy Ion Collider. BNL, New York. Accessed from <https://www.bnl.gov/rhic/physics.asp>.
Buchanan, J.M., 1965. An economy theory of clubs. Economica 32, 1−24.
Campbell, K.M., Einhorn, R.J., Reiss, M.B. (Eds.), 2004. The Nuclear Tipping Point: Why States Reconsider Their Nuclear Choices. Brookings Institution Press, Washington, DC.
Center for Near Earth Object Studies (CNEOS) (2019) Discovery Statistics. CNEOS, NASA, Washington, DC.
CERN (European Organization for Nuclear Research) (2017a) The Accelerator Complex. CERN, Geneva, Switzerland. Accessed from <https://home.cern/about/accelerators>.
CERN (2017b) The Safety of the LHC. CERN, Geneva. Accessed from <https://press.cern/backgrounders/safety-lhc>.
Chapman University, 2017. Survey of American Fears: Wave 4. Chapman University, Orange, CA.
Chapman, C.R., Morrison, D., 1994. Impacts on the Earth by asteroids and comets: assessing the hazard. Nature 367, 33−40.
CNBC (2017) Elon Musk Says Global Race for A.I. will be the Most Likely Cause of World War III. Published on September 4, 2017. CNBC, New York.
CNBC (2019) SoftBank CEO Masayoshi Son: A.I. Will Completely Change the Way Humans Live Within 30 Years. Published on March 8, 2019. CNBC, New York.
Dar, A., Rujula, A.D., Heinz, U., 1999. Will relativistic heavy-ion colliders destroy our planet? Phys. Lett. B 470, 142−148.
Ellis, J., Giudice, G., Mangano, M., Tkachev, I., Wiedemann, U., 2008. Review of the safety of LHC collisions. J. Phys. G: Nucl. Part. Phys. 35, 11.

Falk, I., Mendelsohn, R., 1993. The economics of controlling stock pollution: an efficient strategy for greenhouse gases. J. Environ. Econ. Manag. 25, 76−88.

Farhi, E., Jaffe, R.L., 1984. Strange matter. Phys. Rev. D 30 (11), 2379−2391.

Fisher, I., 1930. The Theory of Interest. Macmillan, New York.

Fox News (2017) Robots Will be 100 Times Smarter than Humans in 30 Years, Tech Exec Says. Published on October 27, 2017. Fox News, New York.

Fudenberg, D., Tirole, J., 1991. Games in strategic form and Nash equilibrium. In: Fudenberg, D., Tirole, J. (Eds.), Game Theory. MIT Press, Cambridge, MA.

Gibbons, R., 1992. Game Theory for Applied Economists. Princeton University Press, Princeton, NJ.

Graham Jr., T., 2004. Avoiding the Tipping Point. Arms Control Association, Washington, DC.

Harsanyi, J., 1967. Games with incomplete information played by 'Bayesian Players': I. The Basic Model. Manag. Sci. 14, 159−182.

Harsanyi, J., 1968. Games with incomplete information played by 'Bayesian Players': II. Bayesian equilibrium points. Manag. Sci. 14, 320−334.

Harsanyi, JC., Selten, R., 1988. A General Theory of Equilibrium Selection in Games. MIT Press, Cambridge, MA.

Hawking S, Tegmark M, Russell S, Wilczek F (2014) Transcending Complacency on Superintelligent Machines. Huffington Post. Accessed from <https://www.huffington-post.com/stephen-hawking/artificial-intelligence_b_5174265.html>.

Hirshleifer, J., 1983. From weakest-link to best-shot: the voluntary provision of public goods. Public Choice 41, 371−386.

Intergovernmental Panel on Climate Change (IPCC), 1990. Climate Change: The IPCC Scientific Assessment. Cambridge University Press, Cambridge.

International Atomic Energy Agency (2018) Country Nuclear Power Profiles 2018 Edition. IAEA, Vienna, Austria.

International Committee on Robot Arms Control (ICRAC) (2019) About ICRAC. Accessed from <https://www.icrac.net/about-icrac/>

Jaffe, R.L., Buszaa, W., Sandweiss, J., Wilczek, F., 2000. Review of speculative disaster scenarios at RHIC. Rev. Mod. Phys. 72, 1125−1140.

Kaiho, K., Oshima, N., 2017. Site of asteroid impact changed the history of life on Earth: the low probability of mass extinction. Sci. Rep. 7, 14855. Available from: https://doi.org/10.1038/s41598-017-14199-x.

Kaul, I., Conceicao, P., Goulven, K.L., Mendoza, R.U. (Eds.), 2003. Providing Global Public Goods: Managing Globalization. Oxford University Press, Oxford.

Kissinger, H., Perry, B., Shultz, G., Nunn, S., 2011. Nuclear Endgame: The Growing Appeal of Zero. Economist, London.

Kurzweil, R., 2005. The Singularity Is Near. Penguin, New York.

Le Treut, H., Somerville, R., Cubasch, U., Ding, Y., Mauritzen, C., Mokssit, A., et al., 2007. Historical overview of climate change. In: Solomon, S., Qin, D., Manning, M., Chen, Z., Marquis, M., Averyt, K.B., Tignor, M., Miller, H.L. (Eds.), Climate Change 2007: The Physical Science Basis. The Fourth Assessment Report of the Intergovernmental Panel on Climate Change. Cambridge University Press, Cambridge.

Manne, A.S., Mendelsohn, R., Richels, R., 1995. MERGE: a model for evaluating regional and global effects of GHG reduction policies. Energy Policy 23, 17−34.

Marchant, G., Allenby, B., Arkin, R., Barrett, E., Borenstein, J., Gaudet, L., et al., 2011. International governance of autonomous military robots. Columbia Sci. Technol. Law Rev. 12, 272−315.

MIT) (2003) The Future of Nuclear Power: An Interdisciplinary MIT Study. MIT, MA.
Mills, M.J., Toon, O.B., Turco, R.P., Kinnison, D.E., Garcia, R.R., 2008. Massive global
    ozone loss predicted following regional nuclear conflict. Proc. Natl Acad. Sci. U. S. A.
    105, 5307–5312.
Nash, J., 1950. Equilibrium points in n-person games. Proc. Natl Acad. Sci. 36, 48–49.
National Aeronautics and Space Administration (NASA) (2014) NASA's Efforts to Identify
    Near-Earth Objects and Mitigate Hazards. IG-14-030, NASA Office of Inspector
    General, Washington, DC.
National Aeronautics and Space Administration (NASA) (2017) An Overview: Planetary
    Defense Coordination Office. NASA, Washington, DC. Accessed from <https://www.
    nasa.gov/planetarydefense/overview>.
National Research Council, 2010. Defending Planet Earth: Near-Earth-Object Surveys and
    Hazard Mitigation Strategies. National Academies Press, Washington, DC.
National Research Council (NRC), 2013. Transitions to Alternative Vehicles and Fuels. The
    National Academies Press, Washington, DC.
Nobel Prize (2012). The Nobel Prize in Physiology or Medicine 2012. Sir John B. Gurdon
    and Shinya Yamanaka. <https://www.nobelprize.org/nobel_prizes/medicine/laureates/
    2012/press.html>.
Nobel Prize (2013). The Nobel Prize in Physics 2013: Francoir Englert, Peter W. Higgs.
    Accessed from <https://www.nobelprize.org/nobel_prizes/physics/laureates/2013/>.
Nordhaus, W., 1982. How fast should we graze the global commons? Am. Econ. Rev. 72,
    242–246.
Nordhaus, W., 1994. Managing the Global Commons. MIT Press, Cambridge, MA.
Nordhaus, W.D., 2006. Paul Samuelson and Global Public Goods. In: Szenberg, M.,
    Ramrattan, L., Gottesman, A.A. (Eds.), Samuelsonian Economics and the Twenty-First
    Century. Oxford Scholarship Online.
New York Times (NYT) (2013) Chasing the Higgs Boson. NYT, New York. Accessed from
    <http://www.nytimes.com/2013/03/05/science/chasing-the-higgs-boson-how-2-teams-of-
    rivals-at-CERN-searched-for-physics-most-elusive-particle.html?pagewanted = all>.
Nuclear Energy Institute (NEI) (2016) Energy Statistics. NEI, Washington, DC. Accessed
    from: <http://www.nei.org/Knowledge-Center/Nuclear-Statistics>.
Peskin, M.E., 2008. The end of the world at the Large Hadron Collider? Physics 1, 14.
Plaga R (2009) On the potential catastrophic risk from metastable quantum-black holes pro-
    duced at particle colliders. arXiv:0808.1415 [hep-ph].
Posner, R.A., 2004. Catastrophe: Risk and response. Oxford University Press, New York.
Pravec, P., Harris, A.W., Kusnirak, P., Galad, A., Hornoch, K., 2012. Absolute magnitudes
    of asteroids and a revision of asteroid albedo estimates from WISE thermal observa-
    tions. Icarus 221 (September–October 2012), 365–387.
Quartz (2017) The Robot that Takes Your Job Should Pay Taxes, says Bill Gates. Quartz,
    Washington, DC. Accessed from <https://qz.com/911968/bill-gates-the-robot-that-takes-
    your-job-should-pay-taxes/>.
Rees, M., 2018. On the Future: Prospects for Humanity. Princeton University Press,
    Princeton, NJ.
Romer, P., 1990. Endogenous technical change. J. Polit. Econ. 98, S71–S102.
Russell, S.J., Norvig, P., 1995. Artificial Intelligence: A Modern Approach. Prentice Hall,
    New York.
Samuelson, P., 1954. The pure theory of public expenditure. Rev. Econ. Stat. 36, 387–389.
Samuelson, P., Nordhaus, W., 2009. Economics, 19th edition McGraw-Hill Education,
    New York.

Sandler, T., 1997. Global Challenges: An Approach to Environmental, Political, and Economic Problems. Cambridge University Press, Cambridge, UK.

Schelling, T.C., 1966. Arms and Influence. Yale University Press, New Haven.

Selten, R., 1965. Spieltheoretische Behandlung eines Oligopolmodells mit Nachfragetragheit. Z. für Gesamte Staatsivissenschaft 121, 301−324.

Seo, S.N., 2018. Natural and Man-Made Catastrophes: Theories, Economics, and Policy Designs. Wiley-Blackwell, Oxford.

SoftBank Robotics (2019) Pepper. SoftBank, Tokyo. Accessed from <https://www.softbank-robotics.com/emea/en/pepper>.

Sharkey, N.E., 2012. Evitability of autonomous robot warfare. Int. Rev. Red. Cross 94, 787−799.

THE/Lindau (2017) THE/Lindau Nobel Laureates' Survey. Accessed from <https://www.timeshighereducation.com/features/do-great-minds-think-alike-the-the-lindau-nobel-laureates-survey#survey-answer>.

Thom, R., 1975. Structural Stability and Morphogenesis. Benjamin-Addison-Wesley, New York.

Thomson, J.A., Itskovitz-Eldor, J., Shapiro, S.S., et al., 1998. Embryonic stem cell lines derived from human blastocysts. Science 282 (5391), 1145−1147.

Toon, O.B., Bardeen, C.G., Robock, A., Xia, L., Kristensen, H., McKinzie, M., et al., 2019. Rapidly expanding nuclear arsenals in Pakistan and India portend regional and global catastrophe. Sci. Adv 5 (10). Available from: <https://doi.org/10.1126/sciadv.aay5478>.

Turco, R.P., Toon, O.B., Ackerman, T.P., Pollack, J.B., Sagan, C., 1983. Nuclear winter: global consequences of multiple nuclear explosions. Science 222, 1283−1292.

United Nations Framework Convention on Climate Change (UNFCCC) (1992) United Nations Framework Convention on Climate Change. New York.

United Nations Office for Outer Space Affair (UNOOSA) (2013) Report of the Committee on the Peaceful Uses of Outer Space. UN, New York.

United Nations Office for Disarmament Affairs (UNODA) (2017a) Treaty on the Non-Proliferation of Nuclear Weapons. Accessed from <http://www.un.org/disarmament/WMD/Nuclear/NPT.shtml>.

United Nations Office for Disarmament Affairs (UNODA) (2017b) Background on Lethal Autonomous Weapons Systems. Accessed from <https://www.un.org/disarmament/geneva/ccw/background-on-lethal-autonomous-weapons-systems/>.

United States Energy Information Administration (US EIA) (2015) Annual Energy Outlook 2015. US EIA, Department of Energy, Washington, DC.

von Neumann, J., 1966. Theory of Self-Reproducing Automata. Essays on Cellular Automata. University of Illinois Press, Urbana, pp. 66−87.

Wagner W (1999) Black Holes at Brookhaven? Letters to the Editors. Scientific American 281 (1): p. 8.

Wilczek F (1999) Reply to "Black Holes at Brookhaven?" Letters to the Editors. Scientific American 281(1): p. 8.

World Meteorological Organization (WMO) (1985) Report of the International Conference on the Assessment of the Role of Carbon Dioxide and of Other Greenhouse Gases in Climate Variations and Associated Impacts. Villach, Austria.

Zyga, L., 2014. What are the chances that a particle collider's strangelets will destroy the Earth? Phys. Org.

Appendix A: A succinct mathematical disproof of the dismal theorem of economics

A.1 The dismal theorem

The dismal theorem (DT) of climate change economics states that the stochastic discounting factor (SDF), that is, the dollar amount that the current time period is willing to sacrifice in order to secure a dollar in the future period, is infinite in global warming policy-making under certain assumptions (Weitzman, 2009). The DT is succinctly expressed as:

$$\lim_{\lambda \to \infty} E[M|\lambda] = +\infty. \tag{A.1}$$

In Eq. (A.1), M is the SDF. The λ is approximately the value of the statistical life for the civilizations on the Planet (VSLC). The VSLC was assumed to be infinite because "the end of all civilizations as we know them" on the Planet would be very costly, if not infinite.

The theorem in Eq. (A.1) is only obtainable under a critical assumption on the tail distribution of the global warming realization as being a fat-tail distribution (Schuster, 1984; Nordhaus, 2011). Under non-fat distributions such as a Gaussian distribution, the DT does not hold.

A.2 A heuristic of the dismal theorem

The DT in Eq. (A.1) can be explained succinctly for educational purposes, which can be used later in this article for a disproof of the theorem. Let x be a random variable of the degree of global warming. It is clearly defined in the climate science as the temperature anomaly from the preindustrial average temperature (Le Treut et al., 2007; IPCC, 2014). The assumption of a fat-tail distribution of the random variable yields the following probability density function (PDF):

$$P[X = x] = kx^{-(1+\alpha)}. \tag{A.2}$$

The distribution in Eq. (A.2) is also called the Pareto distribution, or the Pareto-Levy-Mandelbrot distribution, or the Gipf's law (Pareto, 1896; Gabaix, 2009). The k is an unremarkable constant, and the α (>0) is the shape parameter. Importantly when $\alpha \to 0$, the distribution becomes fat-tailed. When $\alpha \to \infty$, the distribution approximates a Gaussian distribution.

Another important assumption in the DT is already mentioned: the VSLC is unbounded:

$$\lambda \to \infty. \tag{A.3}$$

Considering Eq. (A.3), the damage from a high degree of global warming, for example, 10°C increase or 20°C increase in global average temperature, which were quoted by Weitzman, would be exponentially harmful. The damage function can be written as follows as an exponential function with parameters m and β:

$$D(x|\lambda) = me^{\beta x}. \tag{A.4}$$

The fat-tail distribution in Eq. (A.2) can be seen as a posterior-predictive distribution function in that the global warming uncertainty is so large that any amount of time and resources could not reduce the fatness of the tail-distribution (Bayes, 1763).

Under the assumptions in Eqs. (A.2)−(A.4), the DT is derived as follows. With x_0 being the degree of global warming that is irreversible, the Eq. (A.1) can be rewritten as:

$$E[D(x_0)|\lambda] = P(x_0) \times D[x_0] = +\infty. \tag{A.5}$$

A.3 Adaptation deltas

From now on, I offer a mathematical disproof of the DT. Let us assume that the humanity and individual communities within are well versed on the changes in the climate system to be able to adapt efficiently to those changes (Mendelshon, 2000; Seo, 2006, 2016, 2017a). Adaptation would take place in agriculture, natural resource industries, energy generations, civil engineering, natural disaster managements, and catastrophic events (Seo, 2017b, 2018a,b).

We can introduce the adaptation potential as the delta into the fat-tail distribution of Eq. (A.2) as follows, with δ being a positive value:

$$P[X = x] = kx^{-(1+\alpha+\delta)}. \tag{A.6}$$

With the possibility of adaptation to global warming, the delta of adaptation would appear also in the damage function with $\tilde{\delta}$ being a positive parameter of adaptation:

$$D(x|\lambda) = me^{(\beta-\tilde{\delta})x}. \tag{A.7}$$

A.4   A disproof of the dismal theorem

Under the refreshed model in Eqs. (A.6) and (A.7), the dismal theorem can be disproved as follows under general situations, with a constant c:

$$E[D(x_0)|\lambda] = c < +\infty. \tag{A.8}$$

The disproof in Eq. (A.8) holds generally because the following equality holds generally:

$$\frac{e^{\beta x_0}}{(x_0^{\alpha+\delta})(e^{\tilde{\delta} x_0})} = c. \tag{A.9}$$

The equality in Eq. (A.9) holds, in the most succinct explanation, owing to the definitive characteristics of the adaptation deltas. The first is that the delta (δ) in the probability density in Eq. (A.6) has the definitive characteristic of making the tail probability of the distribution approaches zero. The second is that the delta ($\tilde{\delta}$) in the damage function in Eq. (A.7) has the definitive characteristic of making the damage function bounded by a limiting value.

In the mathematical explanation of the equality in Eq. (A.9), it holds because of the multiplicative nature of the denominator which is the exponential function times the power function.

References

Bayes, T., 1763. An essay towards solving a problem in the doctrine of chance. Philos. Trans. Royal Soc. London 53, 370–418.

Gabaix, X., 2009. Power laws in economics and finance. Ann. Rev. Econ. 1, 255–293.

Intergovernmental Panel on Climate Change (IPCC), 2014. Climate change 2014: impacts, adaptation, and vulnerability. The Fifth Assessment Report of the IPCC. Cambridge University Press, Cambridge.

Le Treut, H., Somerville, R., Cubasch, U., Ding, Y., Mauritzen, C., Mokssit, A., et al., 2007. Historical overview of climate change. In: Solomon, S., et al., (Eds.), Climate Change 2007: The Physical Science Basis. The Fourth Assessment Report of the Intergovernmental Panel on Climate Change. Cambridge University Press, Cambridge.

Mendelshon, R., 2000. Efficient adaptation to climate change. Climatic Change 45, 583–600.

Nordhaus, W., 2011. The economics of tail events with an application to climate change. Rev. Environ. Econ. Policy 5, 240–257.

Pareto, V., 1896. Cours d'Economie Politique. Droz, Geneva.

Schuster, E.F., 1984. Classification of probability laws by tail behavior. J. Am. Stat. Assoc. 79 (388), 936–939.

Seo, S.N., 2006. Modeling Farmer Responses to Climate Change: Climate Change Impacts and Adaptations in Livestock Management in Africa. Ph.D. Dissertation. Yale University, New Haven, CT.

Seo, S.N., 2016. Microbehavioral Econometric Methods: Theories, Models, and Applications for the Study of Environmental and Natural Resources. Academic Press (Elsevier), Amsterdam, The Netherlands.

Seo, S.N., 2017a. The Behavioral Economics of Climate Change: Adaptation Behaviors, Global Public Goods, Breakthrough Technologies, and Policy-Making. Academic Press, London.

Seo, S.N., 2017b. Measuring policy benefits of the cyclone shelter program in North Indian Ocean: protection from high winds or high storm surges? Climate Change Econ. 8 (4), 1−18.

Seo, S.N., 2018a. Natural and Man-Made Catastrophes: Theories, Economics, and Policy Designs. Wiley-Blackwell, Oxford.

Seo, S.N., 2018b. Two tales of super-typhoons and super-wealth in Northwest Pacific: Will global-warming-fueled cyclones ravage East and Southeast Asia? J. Extreme Events. Available from: https://doi.org/10.1142/S2345737618500124.

Weitzman, M.L., 2009. On modeling and interpreting the economics of catastrophic climate change. Rev. Econ. Stat. 91, 1−19.

Index

Note: Page numbers followed by "*f*" and "*t*" refer to figures and tables, respectively.

A

Abatement cost, 90
Abatement cost function, calibration of region-specific, 169–170, 170*t*
Adaptation behaviors, in microbehavioral model, 139–147
Adaptation deltas, 308
Agricultural system model, 250–251
AI. *See* Artificial intelligence (AI)
Albedo Modification (AM) technology, 23, 263, 265
Alliance of Small Island States (AOSIS) members, 10
"America First" policy, 10, 111
American Clean Energy and Security Act of 2009, 69
American Physical Society (APS), 294
AMO. *See* Atlantic multidecadal oscillation (AMO)
AOGCM. *See* Atmospheric Oceanic General Circulation Model (AOGCM)
Arrhenius, Svante, 3
Artificial intelligence (AI), 8–9, 282
  robots, 295–299, 295*t*, 297*f*, 298*t*
Asteroid, 7, 283
  large-size asteroid, 7
  Near-Earth Asteroids (NEA), 7
  protection against, 287–288
Asteroid Belt, 282–283
Asteroid collision, 282, 287–289
Atlantic multidecadal oscillation (AMO), 132, 250
Atmospheric Oceanic General Circulation Model (AOGCM), 100–101, 134

B

Backstop technologies, 264*t*, 268, 269*f*
  greenhouse economics of, 271

Bangladesh, tropical cyclones in, 252
Ban Ki-moon, 18, 196
Bargaining theory, 8
Barrett, S., 182
BAU. *See* Business-as-usual (BAU)
Benefit–cost analysis, 3, 66
Bergson-Samuelson social welfare function, 94
Bill, Waxman-Markey, 69, 87–88
Bonaparte, C. L., 262–263
Bowen, H.R., 37
Buchanan, James M., 12, 38, 40, 45–46, 48
Buildings, cities, industries, and appliances (BCIA), 217
Business-as-usual (BAU) economy, 186
Business-as-usual global warming, 184
Business-as-usual policy, 107–108, 186
Business-as-usual scenario, 164–165
  disparate incentives of parties under, 173–175
  divergence of incentives under, 174, 174*f*

C

CAA. *See* Clean Air Act (CAA)
California, cap-and-trade program in, 206, 207*f*
Canadian Center for Climate Modeling and Analysis (CCCMa) model, 134
Cap-and-trade system, 56*f*, 57, 57*f*
  policy, 72
  program in California, 206, 207*f*
  vs. price system, 69*f*, 70, 71*t*
Capital investments, estimated real returns to, 96*t*
Capture and sequestration (CCS) technology, 265
Carbon
  accumulation, 92

Carbon (*Continued*)
  mitigation, 150
  net land use emissions of, 172, 172*t*
Carbon capture and storage (CCS), 23,
    269–270
Carbon dioxide, greenhouse effect of, 3
Carbon intensity parameters, calibration of,
    171–172, 171*t*
Carbon price
  EAERE on, 165
  level, determination, 176
  policy, 70
  tax, globally harmonized, 87–94
Carbon sink, 258, 259*f*, 259*t*
Carbon tax, 165–166, 176
Case-Shiller Real Home Price Index, 97
Catastrophe, 100–107
CCCMa model. *See* Canadian Center for
    Climate Modeling and Analysis
    (CCCMa) model
CCS. *See* Carbon capture and storage (CCS)
CCW. *See* Certain Conventional Weapons
    (CCW)
CDM. *See* Clean Development Mechanism
    (CDM)
CERN, 285
Certain Conventional Weapons (CCW), 296
Charter of the United Nations, 191–192
Chernobyl nuclear disaster, 284
Chicago School of Economics, 41
Clean Air Act (CAA), 2
  CAA of 1970, 53
    national ambient air quality standards,
    53–54
Clean Development Mechanism (CDM), 181
Clean Water Act (CWA), 2
Climate and economy model, 93, 93*f*
Climate change, 3
  global warming and, 90
  integrated assessment models (IAM) of,
    93, 162–163
Climate change economics, dismal theorem
    (DT) of, 307
Climate club, 181–186
Climate coalition, 181–182
Climate damage function, calibration of,
    168*t*
Climate-Friendly Agribusiness Value Chains
    Sector Project, 211

Climate Model Intercomparison Project
    (CMIP), 100–101
  CMIP5, 101*t*
Climate policy, 15
Climate risk, in Sub-Saharan Africa, 251,
    251*f*
Climate risk scenarios, 142–144, 143*f*
Clinton, Hilary, 15, 195
Club goods, 43–46
CMIP. *See* Climate Model Intercomparison
    Project (CMIP)
Coalition, climate, 181–182
Coalition theory, 184–185
Coase, Ronald H., 41–42, 67, 149
Coase theorem, 149
Coefficient of Variation in Precipitation
    (CVP), 132, 250
Command-and-control policy approach,
    53–54
Comprehensive Nuclear Test Ban Treaty, 14
Conference of the Parties (COP), 3–4
Congestion effect, 43–44
Containment theory, 8
Contingent valuation (CV) method, 65
Cooperative DICE model, parameters of
    contention in, 167–173
COP. *See* Conference of the Parties (COP)
Copenhagen Accord, 3–4, 173
CSP. *See* Cyclone shelter program (CSP)
CVP. *See* Coefficient of Variation in
    Precipitation (CVP)
CWA. *See* Clean Water Act (CWA)
Cyclone shelter program (CSP), 253

D
DAC and sequester (DACS) technology, 270
Decision-maker, 123, 257
Decision-making, global-level policy,
    16–17
Decision models, global-level policy, 16–17
Development of Argan Orchards in
    Degraded Environment, 211–212
DICE model. *See* Dynamic Integrated
    Climate and Economy (DICE) model
Direct air capture (DAC) technology, 265
Disarmaments, nuclear nonproliferation and,
    288–292
Discount rate, 79, 97–99
  debate, 97

in DICE model, 88–89
for global warming policy model, 95
Dismal theorem (DT), 14, 104, 106
of climate change economics, 307
disproof of, 309
heuristic of, 307–308
Disparate incentives, of parties under BAU
scenario, 173–175
Diurnal temperature range (DTR), 132–133,
250
Diurnal temperature range normal (DTRN),
134
Diurnal temperature range variability
(DTRV), 132–133
Doctors Without Borders, 192
DTR. See Diurnal temperature range (DTR)
DTRN. See Diurnal temperature range
normal (DTRN)
DTRV. See Diurnal temperature range
variability (DTRV)
Dubin and McFadden (DM) method, 129
Dynamic Integrated Climate and Economy
(DICE) model, 13–14, 79, 88,
90–94, 148, 162, 165–166,
168–170
economy module of, 89–90
parameters of contention in cooperative,
167–173
social welfare optimization framework of,
100

E
Earth
climate system, 83
protection of, 7
Earth-heating gases, 92
Economics of globally shared goods
(EGSG), 20–21, 25, 287–290, 292,
294, 296, 299–301
Economics of value of time, 94–100
Economic theories
of globally shared goods, 262
of public goods, 1, 11–15
Economy model, climate and, 93, 93f
Efficient land use, 204–205, 205t
Efficient provision vs. market provision of
public goods, 46–51
EGSG. See Economics of globally shared
goods (EGSG)

EIA. See Energy Information Agency (EIA)
El Nino Southern Oscillation (ENSO), 132
Emissions allowance trading, 54
Emissions Trading Scheme (ETS), 15, 54
Emissions trading system (ETS), 55–56
Energy Information Agency (EIA), 23
ENSO. See El Nino Southern Oscillation
(ENSO)
Enterprise profit, 127–128, 130
Environmental Protection Agency (EPA),
53–54
in United States, 2
ETS. See Emissions Trading Scheme (ETS);
Emissions trading system (ETS)
European Association of Environmental and
Resource Economists (EAERE), on
carbon pricing, 165
European Union Emissions Trading Scheme
(ETS), 15, 87–88
European Union's Emissions Trading
System (ETS), 206
EU's intended nationally determined
contribution (INDC), 166
Exponential discounting vs. hyperbolic
discounting, 98, 99f

F
FAO. See Food and Agriculture
Organization (FAO)
Farm-level activities, 134
Fat-tailed catastrophe, 107, 111–112
Fat-tailed distribution, 103–106, 105f
Federal carbon pollution pricing system, 166
First-order condition (FOC), 47
for Pareto optimality, 48
FOC. See First-order condition (FOC)
Food and Agriculture Organization (FAO),
131
Foreign aid, 218
Foresight, 289–291, 299
Foresight economics, 20–22, 253–262
Foresighted decisions, 21–22, 240, 288, 291
Forward-looking behaviors, 256
Free-Air Carbon Enrichment (FACE)
experiments, 151
Free education system, 82
Friedman, Milton, 12, 149
public sector vs. private sector, 40–43
Full cooperation model, 182

FUND (The Climate Framework for
    Uncertainty, Negotiation and
    Distribution), 162–163
Funding models, of green climate fund, 202

G
Gates, Bill, 286
GCF. *See* Green Climate Fund (GCF)
Geo-climate engineering, 260
Geophysical Fluid Dynamics Laboratory
    (GFDL) model, 134
GFDL model. *See* Geophysical Fluid
    Dynamics Laboratory (GFDL) model
GHG. *See* Greenhouse gases (GHG)
Giga tons of carbon emissions (GtC), 172
GISS model. *See* Goddard Institute of Space
    Studies (GISS) model
Global Carbon Tax Policy, 177–178, 177*f*
    disparity in GHG control rates under, 180,
    180*f*
Global climate change, 132
    policy, 58
Global climate policy (GOP), efficient/
    optimal, 165
Global climate system, 10, 23, 245
Global climatic shift, 83
"Global commons,", 6–7
Global Environmental Facility (GEF), 194
Global governance, 111–112
Global-level policy decision-making, 16–17
Global-level policy decision models, 16–17
Global-level public good, 82
Globally harmonized carbon price/tax,
    87–94
Globally optimal climate policy (GOP)
    scenario, 163, 164*f*
Globally public goods, economics of,
    301–302
Globally shared challenges, 282–287
Globally shared goods, 4, 241–245
    economics of, 20–25, 301–302
    economics of foresight for, 253–262
    economic theory of, 262
    evolution of the term, 243, 244*f*
    foundations of the economics of, 242*f*
    grand economic theory of, 239
    microbehavioral decisions for, 245–253
    microbehavioral economics of, 123–126,
    245

Globally shared goods analysis, economics
    of
    artificial intelligence and superintelligent
        robots, 295–299, 295*t*, 297*f*, 298*t*
    nuclear nonproliferation and
        disarmaments, 288–292
    protection against asteroids, 287–288
    strangelet and a runaway catastrophe,
        292–295
Global public goods, 4–8, 84–85
    academic field of, 2
    economics of, 121–122
    international treaties, secretariats, and
        organizations for, 110, 110*t*
    international treaty on, 84
    microbehavioral economics of, 124*f*
    microbehavioral models in economics of,
        148–149
    model of, 148–149
    policy, 173–174
    premise of cooperation in theory of,
        163–166
    provision of, 9, 85
        cooperation, 181
    public sector for, 109–111
Global public goods fund, 228
    approach for public good provision, 193
    green climate fund, 195–196
    international fairness in theory of,
        228–231
    types, 193–195, 194*t*
Global-scale disaster, 7
Global-scale public good, 80–81, 83
    policy, 78
    provision, 161–162
Global-scale public goods, 2, 6, 11, 15
    microbehavioral economics in, 123
Global society, 92
Global warming, 2, 9–10, 83, 86, 173, 263
    BAU, 184
    catastrophes, 78
    and climate change, 90
    conundrum of, 7
    economics of, 3, 80
    economist club of, 14
    integrated assessment model (IAM) of, 13
    international roundtables of, 79
    microbehavioral economics of, 16
    microbehavioral model of, 134

negotiations, 78
policy, 4
policy models of, 79
policy tool, 3
Global warming policy, 79, 84, 86, 88
    model, discount rate, 95
    negotiations, 9
Global Warming Potential (GWP), 261
Global warming treaty, 173–174
Goddard Institute of Space Studies (GISS)
    model, 134, 137, 250
"God particle" experiment, 285
GOP scenario. *See* Globally optimal climate
    policy (GOP) scenario
Grand economic theory, 240
    of globally shared good, 239
Green Climate Fund (GCF), 3, 15, 18–19,
    79–80, 192–193, 195–196
    allocation, 196–202, 197*t*, 198*t*
    economics of public expenditure,
        203–204
    establishment of, 122
    existence and activities of, 203–204
    funded projects
        on food security for land use efficiency
            theory test, 219*t*
        on water security for resource use
            efficiency test, 226*t*
    funded water security projects, 227
    funding allocations, 216–217, 216*f*
    funding decisions, 228
    funding-induced redistribution, 225
    funding models of, 202
    investment framework, 197
    monetary awards, 223
    monetary transfer, 223
    money allocations, 218
    as policy alternative, 203–209
Green electricity, 59
    market, 60
Greenhouse, 270
Greenhouse economics, 22, 240–241, 262,
    270–271
    of backstop technologies, 271
Greenhouse effect of carbon dioxide, 3
Greenhouse gases (GHG), 7, 22
Greenhouse Gas Pollution Pricing Act, 166
Greenhouse technology, 23, 263, 270
    economics of, 262–271

technological innovations, 262
Gross Domestic Product (GDP), 171
GWP. *See* Global Warming Potential (GWP)

H
HadCM3 scenario, 138–139, 145
Hawking, Stephen, 286
Hayek, Friedrich A., 41
Hedonic wage method, 64
Hybrid cap-and-trade program, 88
Hydroelectric power generation, 256
Hyperbolic discounting *vs.* exponential
    discounting, 98, 99*f*

I
IAEA. *See* International Atomic Energy
    Agency (IAEA)
IAWN. *See* International Asteroid Warning
    Network (IAWN)
ICRAC. *See* International Committee for
    Robot Arms Control (ICRAC)
IMF. *See* International Monetary Fund
    (IMF)
INDC. *See* Intended Nationally Determined
    Contribution (INDC)
Individual goods, social goods against, 37
Integrated assessment model (IAM)
    of climate change, 93, 162–163
    of global warming, 13
Intended Nationally Determined
    Contribution (INDC), 22, 151
    for Paris Agreement, 180–181
Intergovernmental Panel on Climate Change
    (IPCC), 2–3, 93, 100, 130, 165, 169,
    230
    families of emissions scenarios by, 101,
        102*f*
International agreement, 162
International Asteroid Warning Network
    (IAWN), 288
International Atomic Energy Agency
    (IAEA), 284
International Committee for Robot Arms
    Control (ICRAC), 296
International fairness, in theory of global
    public good fund, 228–231
International Institute of Applied Systems
    Analysis (IIASA), 89, 167
International Monetary Fund (IMF), 182

International monetary transfer scheme, 181
International treaty, for global public good,
    84, 110, 110*t*
Investment criteria, mitigation and
    adaptation impacts, 197*t*, 198*t*
IPCC. *See* Intergovernmental Panel on
    Climate Change (IPCC)

K
Kyoto Protocol, 3−4, 7, 53, 87, 173,
    178−179, 184, 195

L
Land and resource uses, economics of
    efficient, 204−206
Land use efficiency theory test, 218−228,
    219*t*
Large Hadron Collider (LHC), 8−9
    experiments, 282, 285, 292−295
Large-size asteroid, 7
LAWS. *See* Lethal Autonomous Weapon
    Systems (LAWS)
LCOE. *See* Levelized Cost of Electricity
    (LCOE)
Lethal Autonomous Weapon Systems
    (LAWS), 296
Levelized Cost of Electricity (LCOE), 23,
    267
LHC. *See* Large Hadron Collider (LHC)
Lindahl, Erik, 60−61
    equilibrium, 60−61
    framework, 61
    personalized markets, 61
Lindahl solution, for public goods, 61

M
Macroeconomic growth model, 90
Macro economy, 46
Malaria
    eradication in Sub-Saharan Africa, 83−84
    vaccination, 84
Maldives project, 227
Marginal Damage (MD) curve, 61−62
Marine cloud brightening (MCB), 263, 265
Market failure, 46
Market provision
    inefficiency of, 50
    vs. efficient provision of public goods,
        46−51

MCB. *See* Marine cloud brightening (MCB)
Médecins Sans Frontieres (MSF), 192
MERGE (A Model for Evaluating Regional
    and Global Effects of GHG
    Reduction Policies), 162−163
Microbehavioral adaptation, 21
    decisions, 254−255
Microbehavioral analysis, 125
Microbehavioral decisions, 148, 240,
    287−288, 291−292, 299, 301
    for globally shared good, 245−253
Microbehavioral economic models,
    126−133
    quantitative analysis of, 123
Microbehavioral economics, 16, 19
    of globally shared goods, 123−126, 245
    of global public good, 124*f*
    in global-scale public goods, 123
    of global warming, 16
Microbehavioral model, 122−125, 139
    adaptation behaviors and strategies in,
        139−147
    adopting livestock species, 139−141,
        140*f*, 141*f*
    development of, 146
    in economics of global public goods,
        148−149
    elements of, 246, 246*f*
    empirical analyses of, 133−139
    of global warming, 134
    mitigation and sinks in, 150−152, 150*f*,
        152*f*
    outputs of, 247, 248*f*
    public adaptations, 146−147, 147*f*
    seminal, 139
    switching agricultural systems, 141−142,
        142*t*
        under increased climate risk scenarios,
            142−144, 143*f*
    switching to natural resource intensive
        enterprises, 144−145, 145*f*
Microbehavioral theory, 148−149
Mitigation
    carbon, 150
    and sinks in microbehavioral model,
        150−152, 150*f*, 152*f*
"Modeling Farmer Responses to Climate
    Change,", 16, 122
Monetary transfer, 80

model, 182, 183*t*
optimal, 181–186
optimal mutually beneficial, 107–109
scheme, 181–182
Monsoon precipitation ratio (MPR), 133
Monsoon precipitation ratio normal
(MPRN), 133, 143
Monsoon variability index (MVI), 143
Morality, 58–62
Moral suasion approach, 59
MPRN. *See* Monsoon precipitation ratio
normal (MPRN)
Municipal public good, 82
Musgrave, Richard, 242
MVI. *See* Monsoon variability index (MVI)

N
Namibian projects, 222
Nash bargaining theory, 8
Nash equilibrium, 46, 182, 290, 290*f*
National Aeronautics and Space
Administration (NASA), 282–283
National defense system, 5
National-level public good, 161
National public good, 1–2, 9, 161
National Research Council (NRC)
committee, 263
Near-Earth Asteroids (NEA), 7, 283
Near-Earth Objects (NEO), 7, 282–283
Neighborhood effects, 41–43
NEO. *See* Near-Earth Objects (NEO)
Neutral price policy, 70
Nonclimate purpose, 223
Noncooperation analysis
alterations of incentives under
GOP scenario, 176–181
disparate incentives of parties under
business-as-usual scenario, 173–175
Noncooperative club, 186–187
Non-Proliferation of Nuclear Weapons
(NPT), 2, 83
Treaty on, 2, 14–15, 83, 285
UN-led Treaty on, 288–289
Nordhaus, Williams, 2–3, 13, 80, 88, 162,
182, 242–243
Novel theory, 4
NPT. *See* Non-Proliferation of Nuclear
Weapons (NPT)
Nuclear disaster, Chernobyl, 284

Nuclear fission reaction, 266
Nuclear nonproliferation, 285
and disarmaments, 288–292
provision of, 289
Nuclear umbrella theory, 8
Nuclear winter hypothesis, 284

O
Obama, Barak, 3–4, 10, 14–15, 18, 196
Administration's Clean Power Plan, 6
Clean Power Plan, 53
Optimal economic policy, 162
Optimal global warming policy models, 166
Optimal monetary transfers, 181–186
Optimal mutually beneficial monetary
transfers, 107–109
Optimal price, of public good, 49
Optimization behaviors of farms, 124
Organizations for global public goods, 110,
110*t*
Ostrom, Elinor, 149
Ozone layer protection, 83

P
PAGE (A Policy Analysis of the Greenhouse
Effect), 162–163
Pareto improvement, 46
Pareto-Levy-Mandelbrot (PLM) distribution,
104
Pareto optimal allocation, 46–47
Pareto optimality, 46
first-order condition (FOC) for, 48
Pareto optimal price, of public good, 54
Pareto, Vilfred, 46
Paris Agreement, 3–4, 79, 111, 173, 196
Intended Nationally Determined
Contribution (INDC) for, 180–181
Partial cooperation model, 182
PDF. *See* Probability density function (PDF)
Personalized markets, of public good, 61
Planetary Defense Coordinating Office
(PDCO), 283
Policy instruments, 54
for providing public good optimally,
51–58
Policy-makers, 66
Policy models
of global warming, 79
optimal global warming, 166

Policy negotiations, 87
  failures in, 162
Policy negotiators, 79
Policy options
  uncertainty and, 66–68
  wealth redistributions and, 68–72
Political scale of public goods, 5
Polycentric governance approach, 149
Precautionary principle, 100–107
Price-based instrument, 51–52, 67–68
Price-based policy approach, 52
Price-based policy instrument, 67
Price policy, 68, 70
  carbon, 70
  neutral, 70
Price system *vs.* cap-and-trade system, 69*f*,
      70, 71*t*
Private provision, 51, 58–62
Private sector *vs.* public sector, 40–43
Probability density function (PDF),
      307–308
Production function, 85–86
Production technologies, 85–87
Public adaptation
  economics of, 206–209
  theory test, 209–212, 210*t*
Public education system, 81–82
Public expenditure theory test, 212–218,
      213*t*
Public goods *See also specific types*
  classification of, 80–81, 81*t*
  definition, 1
  economic theories of, 1, 11–15
  efficient provision *vs.* market provision of,
      46–51
  emergence of, 37–38
  funds, 191–192
  policies, 80–81
  political scale of, 5
  provision of, 2
    global public good fund approach for,
      193
  taxonomy of, 5
  theory of, 4–5
Publicness, 80, 82
Public road system, 81
Public sector
  for global public goods, 109–111
  vs. private sector, 40–43

Pure theory, 12, 37–40
The Pure Theory of Public Expenditures
      (Samuelson), 37

Q
Quantity-based policy instrument, 51, 67
Quantity-based standard policy,
      67–68

R
Radiative Forcing (RF), 92–93
RCP approach. *See* Representative
      Concentration Pathways (RCP)
      approach
Regional Dynamic Integrated model of
      Climate and Economy, 93
Relativistic Heavy Ion Collider (RHIC), 8
Reluctance group countries, 179
Representative Concentration Pathways
      (RCP) approach, 102
Resource use efficiency theory test,
      218–228, 226*t*
RF. *See* Radiative Forcing (RF)
RHIC experiment, 292–295
Ricardo's rent theory, 21
RICE model, 93–94
Rio Earth summit, 173
Robots
  artificial intelligence and superintelligent
      robots, 8, 295–299, 295*t*, 297*f*, 298*t*

S
Samuelson, Paul, 1, 41, 48, 80
  pure theory, 38–40
SDF. *See* Stochastic discounting factor
      (SDF)
Secretariats, for global public goods, 110,
      110*t*
Seminal microbehavioral model, 139
Seminal model, 249
Seven-enterprise model, 249
Silver-bullet technology, 23, 260, 268
Social goods, 1, 4–5
  against individual goods, 37
Solar radiation management (SRM), 265
Solenoidal Tracker at RHIC (STAR)
      detector, 292–293
South America, private *vs.* public irrigation
      in, 207–208, 208*f*

Spatio-political scales, of public good, 80–84
Special Report on Emissions Scenarios (SRES), 101
SRES. *See* Special Report on Emissions Scenarios (SRES)
Standards, CAA's national ambient air quality, 53–54
State-level police force, 82
State-level public good, 82
Stochastic discounting factor (SDF), 307
Stockholm Principle, 231
Stock pollutant, 68
Strangelet, 285–286
Strangelet catastrophe, 292–295
Stratospheric aerosol layer technology, 265
Sub-Saharan Africa
  climate risk in, 251, 251*f*
  Malaria eradication in, 83–84
Superintelligent robots, 295–299, 295*t*, 297*f*, 298*t*
  artificial intelligence (AI) and, 295–299, 295*t*, 297*f*, 298*t*
Sustainable development, potential criterion, 200

T
Taxonomy of public goods, 5
Tax revenue, 176
TFP. *See* Total factor productivity (TFP)
The Theory of Public Finance (Musgrave), 40, 242
Total factor productivity (TFP), 24
Trading permits, 54–55
Trans-state air pollutant, 81
Treaty on Non-Proliferation of Nuclear Weapons, 2, 14–15, 83, 285
Tropical cyclones, in Bangladesh, 252
Troublesomeness, crux of, 1
Trump (President), 3–4, 111
  "America First" principle, 10

U
Uncertainty, 100–107
  and policy options, 66–68
UNDP. *See* United Nations Development Programme (UNDP)
UNEP. *See* United Nations Environment Programme (UNEP)

UNFCCC. *See* United Nations Framework Convention on Climate Change (UNFCCC)
United Kingdom Met Office (UKMO) HadCM3 (Hadley center Climate Model) scenario, 138–139, 145
United Nations' Children's Relief Fund (UNICEF), 191–192, 194
United Nations Development Programme (UNDP), 191–192, 194
United Nations Environment Programme (UNEP), 191–192, 194
United Nations Framework Convention on Climate Change (UNFCCC), 2–4, 79, 185, 191–192
United Nations International Strategy for Disaster Reduction (UNISDR), 191–192
United Nations Population Fund, 167
United Nations' Population Program, 89
United States, Environmental Protection Agency (EPA) in, 2
UN-led Treaty, on NPT, 288–289
Upstream polluter, 42
US Energy Information Agency, 267

V
Valuation methods, 62–66, 63*f*
Value of Statistical Life (VSL), 64, 104
Value of time, economics of, 94–100
Villach Climate Change Conference (1985), 2
Voluntary action approach, 59
The Voluntary Exchange Theory of Public Economy (Musgrave), 37, 242
Voluntary provision mechanism, 60
von Mises, Ludwig, 41
VSL. *See* Value of statistical life (VSL)
VSLC, 307
Vulnerability index, quadratic coefficient for, 168

W
Waste Isolation Pilot Plant (WIPP), 268
Water security projects, 227
Weakest-link production technology, 86–87
Wealth redistributions and policy options, 68–72
Weather index insurance programme, 224

Weitzman, Martin, 14, 103–104
Westphalian Dilemma, 84
Westphalian system, 78
WFP. *See* World Food Programme (WFP)
WIPP. *See* Waste Isolation Pilot Plant
    (WIPP)
Woods Hole Research Center, 150–151
World Bank's African climate change
    project, 133

World Bank's Latin American climate
    change project, 134
World Food Programme (WFP), 18,
    191–192, 194
World Trade Organization (WTO), 182

Z
Zero-discounting proposal, 79
Zero nuclear arms theory, 8